JOHN WOOLMAN
QUAKER

to apprehend
The point of intersection of the timeless
With time, is an occupation for the saint.

T. S. ELIOT

JOHN WOOLMAN
· QUAKER ·

By
JANET WHITNEY

author of
"ELIZABETH FRY" "JENNIFER"

With five plates in half-tone
and
chapter decorations by
GEORGE GILLETT WHITNEY

GEORGE G. HARRAP & CO. LTD.
LONDON   TORONTO   BOMBAY   SYDNEY

To my son
WILLIAM GILLETT WHITNEY

First published 1943
by GEORGE G. HARRAP & CO., LTD.
182 High Holborn, London, W.C.1

BOOK
PRODUCTION
WAR ECONOMY
STANDARD

THIS BOOK IS PRODUCED IN
COMPLETE CONFORMITY WITH THE
AUTHORIZED ECONOMY STANDARDS

Composed in Aldine Bembo type and printed by
William Clowes and Sons, Ltd., London and Beccles

Made in Great Britain

AUTHOR'S NOTE

In 1871, just after the close of the Franco-Prussian War, the poet Whittier published a new edition of John Woolman's Journal, with an introduction and some notes. This edition, unlike the many much-edited earlier ones, clung close to the text of the folio manuscript, and has become the most popular version of Woolman's Journal, reprinted many times by various publishers.

In 1922, just after the close of the first great World War, another edition of John Woolman's Journal was published by the late Amelia Mott Gummere, chiefly following the folio text, but including some variations from the other two Journal manuscripts in brackets or footnotes. All of Woolman's essays were also included, printed under one cover for the first time, and a long Biographical Introduction and full notes and appendices added. The value of such a collection is permanent, though new facts and some new manuscripts have come to light since 1922.

The present volume, which has entailed several years of research, is not a new edition of the Journal but an attempt to present John Woolman himself in the setting of his times. A man's writings arise out of his life. All quotations not otherwise specified are taken from the earliest incomplete manuscript of the Journal, seldom quoted from elsewhere, and here rendered entire.

My warm thanks are due to the following for exceptional kindness :
In the use of libraries :
John Nickalls and Muriel Hicks, Friends' House, London.
Audubon Davis, Library Company of Philadelphia.
Katharine H. Miller, Pennsylvania Historical Society.
Virginia Walker, Swarthmore College Library.
Katharine Ricks, Guilford College, North Carolina.
Bertha E. King, Homewood Meeting Records, Baltimore, Maryland.
Eleanor Starr, Park Avenue Meeting Records, Baltimore, Maryland.

In the loan of private documents or pictures :
Walter Rhoads White, Philadelphia.
Bertram F. Crosfield, London.
Mrs Edward Wanton Smith, Philadelphia.

J. Frederick Braithwaite, London.
Rachel B. Braithwaite, Banbury.
William Worsdell, York.
John Cadbury, Philadelphia.
Richard Mauleverer Abbott, Philadelphia.
John Woolman Wharton, Harvard University.

In rendering access to Woolman relics at York :
K. E. T. and Marion Wilkinson.
John Kay.
Arnold S. Rowntree.

Special gratitude is due to George de Cou, unrivalled expert on the geography and history of Burlington County, New Jersey, for his generous co-operation in helping me to track down elusive clues, and to my cousin Alfred Braithwaite for his goodness in dealing with special points arising on the proofs of the English edition.

JANET WHITNEY

CONTENTS

ILLUSTRATIONS

I

BACKGROUND

THE valley of the Delaware had been preparing for countless ages to be the nurse and cradle of a great race ; to surpass in importance perhaps its notable rivals, the Euphrates, the Tiber, and the Nile, whose streams have become one with the stream of history itself. The Red Men, native to the soil, were not equal to their opportunity. A man contented with a mess of pottage is bound to lose his birthright, and the heritage was seized by eager, active, enterprising men from far across the sea, who took the land and water, not by war, but by the indomitable right of the power to use them.

How marvellous were the vast, silent forests to the newcomers. The great trees, mighty in girth, grew down to the water's edge. When Major Fenwicke came up the river "with some others" and "built a pretty Town and call'd it Salam" he moored his sailing-ship the first night by a rope around a gigantic trunk, where it strained at the leash like a wild gull far from its native ocean, captive in the dim forest aisles. A strange sight for the Indian hunter to glimpse between the trees.

The Indian loved the silence, and preserved it. His arrow was as quiet as a bird's flight ; his canoe slipped down the waterways like a leaf ; his footfall, treading with animal care in the underbrush, made no sound.

When he travelled in parties he arranged the company in single file, and even among a garrulous people that is not an order which encourages conversation. The Indians were not garrulous, and their women—in this race, as in others, the more inclined to light-hearted chatter—had to save their breath to carry the burdens that the men might be free to hunt and fight.

But the white men, stepping on to the river-shore with a tread that crackled on the twigs, had no awe of the forest wilderness. They treated Nature not like her servants or respectful children, but like careless masters. Their shouts awoke the echoes, they whistled and sang as they built their camp fire, and both game and Indian were presently deafened for a half-mile round by the shattering explosion of a musket. But above all and most conquering, a new note stirred the air's vibrations in those solitudes—the sound of casual human laughter.

The grave Spaniard, the sober Dutch, and the gallant French all struggled for the domination of this vast virgin continent, and all left their mark. But the prize fell whole at length, north and south and east and west, to the nation whose excess of energy found vent in common laughter, fed by a pedestrian humour which exceeded melancholy resolve or plodding patience or bitter wit as a means of making life livable under duress—the English humour, less cleverness than vitality, which found fun in commonplace labours and took the fright out of danger by making it ludicrous.

None the less they were serious men with serious purpose who founded Salem, and so were those others who a few years after came in a ship from London and another from Hull and "sail'd thither with more People who went higher up into the Country and built there a Town and called it Burlington, which is now the chiefest Town in that Countrey though Salam is the ancientest."

A few miles below Burlington a broad stream, called by the Indians the Rancocas,[1] flows into the Delaware on the left bank. In 1678 a shipload of well-to-do settlers arrived, most of whom were Quakers who took up land previously purchased along the shores of the Rancocas.

[1] There is an Indian deed of 1749 "For land on South River [Delaware] from Rankikes Kil northward to a Kil on south end of an island called Tinnekonek." The white men wrote the Indian names down by ear. "Rancoquess Kyl" was another effort, in 1655. See George de Cou's pamphlet, *Historical Sketches of Rancocas and Neighbourhood*, p. 1. The form Ancocas was another corruption.

One of these Quakers was a young man of twenty-three from Glou-
cestershire, England, whose name was John Woolman. His grandson
and namesake became the famous journalist.

The colony of West New Jersey had been purchased from the Duke
of York by a loosely combined group of gentlemen, farmers, and merchants, organized and inspired by the famous Quaker courtier, William
Penn. The liberal and far-seeing genius of Penn was manifested both
in the constitution of the colony and in the system of distribution of
land.

Here was the great Delaware, a river such as the white settlers had
never seen, even as high as Burlington running nearly a mile wide, and
plenty more of it unexploited beyond that. Dwellers by the Thames
and the Severn, the Trent and the Usk and the Ouse, the Derwent and
the Clyde, were intoxicated by the sheer size of this mighty flow. The
Dutch patroons had been allowed to take up sixteen miles of the river
banks, either all in one strip or eight miles on either bank, and as much
land back therefrom as the situation of the occupiers would permit.
Why stint oneself in the midst of unlimited plenty ?

But William Penn foresaw a thickly populated country. He foresaw
the troubles of farms in the hinterland with an enemy or an exploiting
neighbour or a competitor between them and the vital water. And in
the colony of West New Jersey it was laid down from the first that for
every forty perches of frontage upon a stream or river, one hundred
acres of land must be taken up, and no man must own land on both
banks. This caused the West Jersey plantations to be long and narrow,
and ensured a maximum of fair play in the uses of the river. This one
point went far towards the contentment and success of the colony at a
period when the rivers provided not only irrigation but the means of
travel.

John Woolman's frontage upon the Rancocas was about two hundred
and fifty yards, and extended north two miles. He left to his descendants two hundred acres of the virgin soil.

In many old records of Gabriel Thomas and of Robert Proud can be
read the exhilaration of the Englishman when set down in the flower of
his manhood upon the richly yielding land. The unbreathed air of the
wilderness was so stimulating and sweet ; above all the unstinted sunshine lifted the heart. These colonists had been sturdily bred in the more
northern climate and under the prevailing grey skies of England ; they

were almost over stimulated by the daily acceleration—the mental and physical speeding up—of the ultra-violet rays, the dazzling sky of cloudless blue. They performed prodigies. The forests rang, first with the dull blows of their axes, then with the music of their saws and the sharp rhythms of their hammers. The ships that brought them were well stocked. It is a continual marvel in retrospect how much those little ships could carry. The houses that rose in the cleared land along the Delaware were many of them built of brick, and every brick for those first houses was brought across the wide Atlantic—ballast in the deep keel of the top-heavy ships.

And the inhabitants of the houses were English people, who felt the needs and established the ways to which they were accustomed. They did not have to go through a prolonged, rough stage of semi-Indian living, with the one-roomed log hut, the clothing of skins, the food dependent upon the skill of the hunter, such as was experienced before them by the settlers in New England and after them by the pioneers to the great West.

The good ship the *Shield* came up the Delaware with the wind in her sails on a day in December, and moored to a tree beside the little new settlement of Burlington, founded the year before by those who came on the *Kent*. The *Kent*, however, had not sailed so far up the river.[1] Her passengers had disembarked at New Castle, across the river from Salem, and those who had purchased land higher up had made their way thither by the old Indian trail or by canoe. But theirs was summer travel. They landed in the middle of August.[2] But the passengers on the *Shield* had to contend with winter travel conditions, and the faithful ship pushed on between the curving forest banks until the sight of a cluster of houses on Burlington Island proclaimed the farthest outpost of the new colony. When they woke up in the morning, eager to set foot on land after two months at sea, they found the ship locked fast in solid ice. It was incredible to the Englishmen, accustomed to the thin

---

[1] The White MS. says (i, 28) that the *Kent* anchored near Salem to disembark some passengers, but "Others passed on to Burlington, New Jersey, in the vessel." The White MS. does not quote a contemporary record or give other authority for its statement. Samuel Smith's *History of New Jersey* says the *Kent* did not proceed beyond Salem.

[2] "16 of the 6th month O. S. 1677" (Smith, p. 93). In the Old Style calendar March was the first month. The calendar changed in England and the colonies in 1752.

and treacherous ice of an English winter, that this great river, nearly a mile wide where they stood, and still affected there by ocean tides, could have frozen thick enough to walk on in a single night. But so it was. So the welcoming people from the shore proved it by casual demonstration. And John Woolman and his old father, William Woolman, came ashore on the ice, with Daniel Taws, ship's master, and John Borton, and many more. The ground beneath their feet was like iron, the leafless trees stretched huge bare branches to the sky, but behind the delicate upper twigs the sky was blue beyond compare, and over frozen land and river fell the magic of the brilliant winter sunshine.

It is a puzzle why colonists to such a new, unbroken country did not take pains to time their arrival for a milder season. The voyage across took about two and a half months. Unlike the earliest comers to Virginia or to New England or New Amsterdam, the settlers of New Jersey did not embark on a voyage of unknown length. Start late in September—a very nice time to start—and you could count on arriving some time in December (if you did not go to the bottom first, or get caught by pirates). And December is not such a nice time to arrive. Why not start in June and arrive in September? It was perhaps partly due to the casualness of an unscheduled age. The ship had no definite departure date, it set sail at the first convenient wind and tide after all the passengers and their goods had tediously arrived and been stowed. And perhaps it was partly owing to the harvest, those passengers who were farmers needing to get the harvest in and sold to add to their resources before sailing.

However, arriving in December, whether they had foreseen the hardships before them or not, there they were, and nothing for it but to dig themselves in for the winter. They followed the example of the warm-blooded furry animals, snug in their burrows, and with instruction from the Indians made wigwam huts against the sides of banks or in the shelter of sloping ground where a roof and front of turf and logs could be added. Firewood only waited gathering ; food was to be had for the hunting or purchased from the natives—"we have very good stomachs to our victuals ; here is plenty of provision in the country ; plenty of fish and fowl and good venison very plentiful and much better than ours in England for it eats not so dry but is full of gravy like fat young beef."[1]

[1] White MS., p. 29.

And the simple red men, fascinated by the godlike and courteous new-comers, were proud to show the hospitality of their forests, to give hints on how to weather the winter, and how and what to plant in the spring.

With the final thaw the hundred or more new settlers dispersed to their holdings and set to work at once to clear their land, plant some crops, and get themselves proper houses built against the next winter.

Young John Woolman, like all the rest, had bought his land entirely on paper. He and his father had put all they possessed into the purchase and the requisite supplies and the passage money. If they had been deceived their plight was sore. But they were not deceived.

The province of New Jersey had been 'given' by the Duke of York in 1664 to Lord Berkeley and Sir George Carteret in reward for their defence of the Channel Island Jersey on behalf of Charles II.

The Duke himself had been given by his royal brother the huge, loosely defined area known formerly as New Amsterdam when held by the Dutch, and it had been an easy, and surely legitimate, piece of gene-rosity to cut off a slice of the map of this territory to reward two honest and deserving adherents.

It was not nearly so large a piece of the New World as was given seventeen years later by King Charles to William Penn, but it had, what Pennsylvania had not, a sizable bit of sea coast, and it lay richly between two mighty rivers, the Hudson and the Delaware.

The two new proprietors first acted as partners, and drew up a docu-ment to attract settlers to their jointly owned province. Their idea was the quite simple one that had guided the earlier founders of Virginia—namely, that of making money. The method was to be the collection of quit-rents, and a solid, thrifty type of permanent settler was a *sine qua non* if the colony was to pay. But it required a very strong motive to drive that type of man away from his native country. England was sparsely populated ; there was more than room for all. Chances of success were excellent for enterprising men, among familiar and beloved surroundings. The mere offer of land beyond the sea (site unseen) was not enough to tempt them, even at moderate annual quit-rent comparing very favourably with rents in England. The worldly wise Lords found the requisite driving motive for settlers of the type they wanted in the fact of religious persecution. Themselves complete conformists, they cynically offered religious liberty in their far-off unknown colony. What did conscience formulas matter there ? It was like sending people to the moon ; only the quit-rents would not be any fairy gold, but good solid exchange, whether in furs or sterling.

The ruse was successful. Settlers at once began going to the new colony—here a ship, and there a ship. Elizabeth was founded, and New Ark—the latter by settlers already in America, discontented with the lack of religious toleration in New England. But a few hundred people, slowly increasing, could not exploit the riches of the region fast enough. The quit-rents did not come up to expectation. And in 1674 Berkeley offered his half of the area for sale for the astonishing sum of one thousand pounds sterling, the biggest bargain in land ever offered by a white man to white men. The offer was snapped up by the Quakers, themselves passionate believers in religious liberty on a broader scale than any of their co-religionists. Here was their chance to make a community on their own lines, with no oaths of fealty, no compulsory church, no tithe land given to parishes for the support of any "hireling ministry."

The actual purchaser of Lord Berkeley's share was John Fenwicke, who had been a major in Oliver Cromwell's army before he became a Quaker. Fenwicke was agent and trustee for another Quaker, Edward Byllynge, and he made the purchase with Byllynge's money, reserving a good piece of land for himself as commission on the transaction. But Byllynge made loud objections to the whole business, and William Penn, trusted by both parties, was called in to arbitrate. Since Byllynge presently found himself bankrupt, he further placed his New Jersey property in trust for the benefit of his creditors, and appointed William Penn his trustee, which gave Penn a major control.

Penn's first care was to find out exactly what Fenwicke had purchased, since Berkeley and Carteret had never divided the province. What constituted Lord Berkeley's half? None of the people concerned had ever seen the country. They now got together over maps, inaccurate and curious, drew lines here and there, and agreed upon a boundary line which could not exist in nature. However, in all good faith a line was drawn on paper from Little Egg Harbour, about the middle of New Jersey's sea coast, right up to the northernmost bend of the Delaware in latitude 41° 40′, and Carteret took the lion's share to the east of the line, containing the settlements of Elizabeth and New Ark, while the undeveloped country west of the line was allotted to the Quaker trustees.

William Penn then helped in the organization of a company of one hundred and fifty shareholders, twelve partners, and twelve members of a board of control, drew up a charter of government called the Concessions and Agreements,[1] and divided West Jersey on the map into one hundred equal parts, of which Fenwicke was allotted ten. This part was the first settled, and was known as Fenwicke's Tenth. Christopher White purchased a thousand acres in this section, and was one of those who sailed with Fenwicke in the *Kent* and founded Salem.

Four years later Sir George Carteret died, and William Penn and eleven other Quakers bought the whole of East New Jersey from his widow, thus uniting the two into one province under one form of government. But since William Penn acquired a larger and richer province as his own private grant from the Crown in that very same year, he ceased to take an active part in the affairs of New Jersey.

He had left the Concessions and Agreements, however, as a permanent monument to his own statesmanship and as the foundation of democracy in America. And it was the assurance given by this charter that caused such an acceleration in the colonization of West Jersey that in the first four years of its application shipload after shipload of settlers, Quakers and others, had gone there well equipped for permanent settlement, to the number of three thousand.

Thanks to these Concessions the government of New Jersey was more liberal than any in the world up to the American Declaration of Independence one hundred years later. It provided that the settlers should elect their representatives annually by ballot to an assembly which was to be a legislature with full power to make, alter, or repeal laws; that every male adult should be eligible to vote or to hold office (no religious restriction was made, as in Pennsylvania's Frame of Government later, where these rights were limited to professing Christians). Trial by jury was to be unrestricted and untrammelled. Complete freedom of conscience was established, including absolute religious toleration.

No one realized better than Penn that this charter was a landmark in democratic government.

---

[1] The full title was the Concessions and Agreements of the Proprietors, Freeholders, and Inhabitants of the Province of West New Jersey in America, contained in forty-four chapters, dated March 3, 1676. All purchasers of land were required to put their signature to the Concessions and Agreements before leaving England. See White MS. (p. 25), and *Grants and Concessions of New Jersey* (Leaming and Spicer), pp. 382, 409.

In the public letter which was distributed in England and the colonies along with the Concessions, Penn wrote as with the yet unborn spirit of Abraham Lincoln, "In the fear of the Lord and in true sense of his Divine Will we try here to lay foundations for after ages to understand their liberty as Christians and as men, that they may not be brought into bondage but by their own consent ; for we put the power in the people."

II

FATHER AND GRANDFATHER

THE pioneer John Woolman was a man who was rather difficult to get on with. The decided character which brought all the early settlers out of an environment in which they were at loggerheads to try to carve a new one to their own pattern did not make for easy and supple dispositions. But Woolman's record seems to show a more than common absence of the necessary oil of amenity which makes for happy human association. It is probable that he was not quarrelsome but only immovably stubborn, too certain of being in the right and too determined to carry his will. As a young man of twenty-three the joy and zest of adventure might have sweetened him ; but there was something which clouded his prospect. Whether it was an unhappy love affair, or a dead bride left behind him, or whether his aged father and companion insisted too long and unwisely on parental authority and caused a daily friction, the pioneer Woolman was not a gentle or an easy man. He was upright, energetic, respected. He cleared his plantation, built a substantial brick house, was one of the responsible Quakers who signed documents to the London Yearly Meeting, was a representative here and on that committee there, and handed down a thriving estate to his heirs. But his old father refused to end his days with him, and spent the last four years of his life in the house of his neighbour, George Elkinton. And it is on record that the care of him in his last illness and the expense of his burial were all borne by George Elkinton and his wife, showing plainly a final and complete estrangement.

William Woolman before he died gave to the Elkintons seventy-five acres of the hundred and fifty which he had obtained by arbitration as his share of his and his son's joint estate at the time of their great and final split.

Seventy-five acres of good freehold land would seem sufficient payment for four years' board, lodging, and nursing, and a simple Quaker funeral, but Elkinton's friends were willing for it to go on record that William Woolman had been right in being "fully sensible that the gift was far from being a full satisfaction for what the said William had received from the said George Elkinton," and John Woolman never disputed it. John Wills, as a well-informed neighbour, made a legal deposition of the facts in 1742, and estimated that the seventy-five acres was worth about six or seven pounds, an interesting sidelight upon the value of both land and money.

One of the few other records extant of the first John Woolman concerns a dispute over fences between himself and his nearest neighbour, Joshua Humphries, who laid a complaint against Woolman for "damage by Cretuers on his Corn." It took six months of arbitration to obtain a peaceful settlement.

These stories, told in the bald, unbiased phrase of legal documents, do not shadow forth a man of amiable temper. Yet his relations with his own household were affectionate and just. There he did not meet with the opposition which irritated him. Perhaps it was fortunate that his wife, Elizabeth Borton, was eight years his junior. "So grows she to him, so sways she level in her husband's heart." She had been a girl of sixteen when she landed at Burlington with her family, perhaps coming on the same ship as the Woolmans, and the Woolmans, without woman attachments, had helped the Bortons settle into the new life. The Borton land was also on the Rancocas Creek, and young Elizabeth had probably promised John to become his wife very early in their acquaintance. A marriageable girl was soon snapped up. It was five years, however, before they could marry, and this may have been one of the times when old father Woolman succeeded in putting a spoke in his son's wheel. Be that as it may, they were married at last,[1] and when after thirty-four years together they died in the same month, they left one son

[1] Appendix I.

to carry on the name, and five daughters. "My well-beloved Wife," said John Woolman the elder, in unusual warmth of phrase.

The son, Samuel Woolman, inherited the plantation and the substantial brick house on the shores of the Rancocas. That must have been a sizable house. Samuel had brought a bride home to it, Elizabeth Burr, four years before his parents' demise. The old couple saw three little grandchildren, all girls, added to the family ; and three unmarried daughters were still at home. An apprentice named Satterthwaite lived with them. Besides these eleven people, there also had to be room for the looms, for John and Samuel were weavers.

One of the young aunts[1] was married two years after her parents' death, in the spring of the same year which saw the birth of Samuel Woolman's fourth child and first son. Nine years later the two youngest aunts finally left the old home to live in Philadelphia, squeezed out by the pressure of Samuel's growing family. When that family had completed its steady enlargement it numbered thirteen children, six daughters and seven sons, a sturdy stock, all living to maturity, all marrying but two.[2] Mrs Woolman lived to the ripe age of seventy-eight, outliving by one year the most famous of her sons.

[1] Her name was Mary, and she married William Hunt, who took her not long after to settle in North Carolina.
[2] Appendix II.

III

CHILDHOOD AND SCHOOL

THAT most famous son opened his eyes in this world on October 19, 1720, on a houseful of women : his strong young mother, twenty-five years old, his three sisters, Elizabeth, Sarah, and Patience—the youngest a toddler of two—and his two young aunts, Hannah and Hester.

Three times in former years Mrs Woolman's helpers had cried out to her as she lay in the exhaustion and triumph of completed birth, "It's a girl !" And the third time the baby was significantly named Patience. But now it was a boy at last, a son to carry on the name, and with filial honour, and also in silent witness to the excellent terms on which he had stood with his outwardly difficult father, Samuel Woolman named the boy John.

Before John Woolman was aware of his exalted position in being the only boy of the family, and for long hours of the day the only male creature in the house, his brief uniqueness was over. Two brothers followed him, Asher and Abner, and the excellent balance of the family was established. From then on boy or girl was equally looked for, either contributed in pleasant variety to the tide of life that flowed in the Woolman house as constant and abundant as the rippling Rancocas than ran before the door.

When John was born his eldest sister Elizabeth was five. When you are the youngest of a family five is very young, but when you are the eldest of four children it appears by comparison mature. Elizabeth had long forgotten baby ways. She could knit not only a sturdy muffler but a woollen stocking complete, and turn the heel. She could wash up the wooden mugs and trenchers, card wool, and spin flax, and sew a pretty neat hem. The presence of three active grown-up women in the house prevented anyone from being overworked, but every one was busy according to ability, all had their allotted tasks in the household economy.

With the coming of the new baby a new feeling awoke in Elizabeth's little heart, a tender, protective, maternal feeling, and she entered eagerly into the sweetness of caring for this live doll. It cried and laughed, waved its hands and feet, soon manifested recognition of her and need of her. Deep chords were touched, and a mutual bond was forged between the little mother and her tiny charge that remained for both of them one of the strongest in life.

The real mother, Mrs Samuel Woolman, had another baby to tend before John was two. It was Elizabeth who guided his childish steps, who showed him first the wonders of stream and forest, who comforted his hurts and told him all the stories that she knew.

Mrs Samuel Woolman was not an intellectual woman. Books went for little in her busy life. But her vigorous native intelligence admired the education of her husband and his sisters, and she shared his ambitions that her children should be educated as well as possible. Their usefulness in farm and home was not allowed to interfere. They were all sent to school at an early age.

A mile walk through woods and hayfields along the bank of the Rancocas, with the morning sun at their backs stretching their long shadows before them on the dewy or the frosty ground, brought them to the little schoolhouse. It stood in archaic simplicity, twenty feet square, in a bower of flowering magnolias beside an Indian spring. There the sons and daughters of the planters from the ages of four to fourteen gathered to learn the rudiments, and with them also gathered a few of the sons of the Indians. Their forefathers had owned the spring from time immemorial, they graciously shared its pure and sparkling water with the palefaces, but in return they expected to share whatever benefits accrued to the palefaces upon that spot. If it was thought good by the tender-skinned but clever newcomers that their children should study the horn-book, and learn to make queer scratches in the sand, perhaps it would also benefit the more intelligent among the hardy children of the redskins. So there they sat together upon the beautifully finished hand-made benches, beneath the fine hand-hewn rafters, and set their feet upon the broad hand-sawn and fitted floorboards ; and brought in water from the spring in the thirsty summertime in a plain leathern pitcher, and poured it ice-cold into a wooden mug. The flies and the bees and butterflies passed freely in and out through open door and casement into the dim, cool interior, and the "musketto-fly" came in his season and drove his poisoned stiletto into the tender skin behind ears and inside sweaty little wrists, while the scents of pine and honeysuckle sweetened the printed word. And after school, turning their backs to the west, the Woolman and Wills and White and Borton and Elkinton children sauntered homeward, playing by the way ; hours of timeless and unnoticed happiness, stored with such honey for the future that when, at thirty-five, John Woolman took up a practised pen and proceeded to write himself a Journal his first sentence is the full statement of a happy man. "I have often felt a desire to leave some brief hints in writing concerning my Experience of the Goodness of God," which began on the ways to and from school before he was seven years old.

When winter closed upon the valley of the Delaware, and the sudden ice congealed the surface flow of streams and rivers, and snow drifted in the forest paths, the day's experience was sharpened by the pain of cold. Jefferson himself speaks of his boyhood dread of the bitter wintertime, and John Adams for his part wished that he could sleep like a dormouse from autumn to spring. In the family circle round the one great hearth, carding wool or mending harness at the end of the long day, the little John Woolman could hardly keep his eyes open. Again and again his hands would slacken, the pleasant darkness of the eyelids fall between him and the roaring brightness of the cedar logs. But when he climbed up the chilling stairs to the unheated bedroom he was shocked into a shivering wakefulness. The heavy hand-spun linen sheets lay like snow itself upon the warm limbs. But in a large family there was little solitary sleeping. Bed space was too scarce. Sister lay snuggled with sister and brother with brother, and warmed each other, like rabbits in a burrow, in the deep feather beds. Early rising, considered virtuous in itself until the end of the nineteenth century, was a simple necessity on the Woolman plantation, when the utmost busyness of every hand from dawn to dark could just keep the household going. Not only stock to feed and cows to milk and endless wood to chop and all the care of the land with simple implements for menfolk, and not only the cooking and cleaning and sewing and mending and knitting which are enough even on the twentieth-century farm to substantiate the proverb that women's work is never done, but also the soap- and candle-making, the spinning of linen and wool, the dyeing of yarn.

John Ball's democracy of the Garden of Eden was firmly established in every colony of the New World. "When Adam delved and Eve span, Who was then the gentleman?" It is true that as the necessary specialization of civilization set in, not every Adam delved. But it remained true for far longer that every Eve span ; with rich and poor, lawyer's lady and labourer's wife, the spinning-wheel hummed, and the daily task was patiently and lovingly performed. It was the cure of ennui in long, bookless hours. It combined a happy monotony with a visible accomplishment. And to take a 'bottom drawer' full of household linen spun and sewn by herself to her husband's home was the pride of every bride. So spinning might be said to be a pillar of American democracy, and America's great and simple organization, after the Revolution, to be a homespun affair.

The aim of the planters, however, was not to make each plantation completely self-supporting, but to move towards differentiation and specialization, as in the home country. Sawmills and flour-mills were early established ; professional shoemakers went round from house to house, staying long enough at each to equip each member of the household with shoes by mending and making ; carpenters and furniture-makers brought their skill to add to the rougher efforts of the householder ; brick kilns produced bricks of native clay, regulated by law and inspected as to uniformity of quality and size ; and weaving itself was not for the most part done by the woman in the home, but by professional weavers, trained masters of their craft.

Old John Woolman bequeathed "unto my Son Samuel Woolman all my looms and all other of my tools of all sorts belonging to the Weaver's trade." His friend and contemporary, Christopher White, who had taken up a broad thousand acres of land at the beginning, was a master fuller, and established a fulling and dyeing mill.

One reason for the rapid prosperity of the Quaker colonies was the fact that the majority of the men of substance who came over to them were master craftsmen, not, like the Virginians, aristocrats unpractised in anything but land and horses, or, like the first men on the Hudson and Delaware, merely traders wishing to buy furs cheap and sell them dear. The New Jersey planters used their farms as a direct source of food and places in which to breed sheep and cows for their meat, wool, and leather, but they expected their craft to be their chief source of money revenue. Many of them wished to grow rich, but none expected to grow rich at farming. The mill, the dye vat, the loom, the smithy, formed the foundation of many a sound fortune, while the plantation provided immediate necessities and made a frame for the kind of ample, stable, honourable life the colonists wished to live.

To possess land and to bequeath land had always been the chief mark of honour in the old country, and it gratified a deep need in them when they came to the new. Seldom has any society felt more secure than the New Jersey colonists in the eighteenth century. The present was full of interest and energy, and the future full of promise. Only four persons suffered legal execution in a hundred and fifty years.

It is natural that the first adventure of the soul that John Woolman could remember was a vision of Paradise.

> I was born in ye year 1720 and before I was seven years old I was Sensible of his Love and often found a care upon me how I should please him. I was through the care of my Parents taught to read near as Soon as I was Capable of it, And it was even then of use to me. I remember as I went from School one Seventh day of the week, my Company playing by the way, I went forward out of sight and sat down and read the 22nd chap of Revelations. He Shewed me a River Clear as Chrystal etc. In reading of it my mind was made to Seek after and long for that pure Habitation which I then believed God had prepared for his Servants. The place where I Sat and the Sweetness that filled my mind remains fresh in my memory as tho the time since was much Shorter.

The passage which little John Woolman read that day to the ripple of the Rancocas and the sound of summer breezes in the trees, and which filled his mind with sweetness and with longing, is as follows :

> And he shewed me a pure river of water of life, clear as crystal, proceeding out of the throne of God and of the Lamb. In the midst of the street of it, and on either side of the river, was there the tree of life, which bare twelve manner of fruits, and yielded her fruit every month : and the leaves of the tree were for the healing of the nations.

And there shall be no more curse : but the throne of God and of the Lamb shall be in it ; and his servants shall serve him : And they shall see his face : and his name shall be in their foreheads.   And there shall be no night there ; and they need no candle, neither light of the sun ; for the Lord God giveth them light : and they shall reign for ever and ever.

IV

HOME AND MEETING

JUST as children in ancient Persia pondered on fairy-tales of jewelled trees in subterranean countries, and as children in ancient Greece heard legends of the Garden of the Hesperides, so the little American John Woolman dreamed of the gardens of Paradise, and with an even greater nostalgia, because he took the description as literal fact, the very habitation "which I then believed God had prepared for his Servants."

Throughout the world in the early eighteenth century there was prevalent a conviction of the immortality of the soul. Even as late as 1790 the French Revolution, uprooting orthodox religion because the Church had that in charge, still demanded national belief in a Supreme Being and in the life after death. This faith works differently in different people. It drove the poet Cowper mad. It preyed on the mind of King Philip V of Spain so that he wore his confessors out with frequent confession day and night. When John Woolman was four years old the far-away Spanish King abdicated the throne in order to give his whole time to preparation for heaven, though since his successor promptly died of smallpox he was persuaded to resume his kingship. When Woolman was two Frederick William I, King of Prussia, father of Frederick the Great, took time off from his energetic creation of the Prussian military system—then new to Europe—to write a memorandum for his son in case of his death : "Since my twentieth year, I have put my whole trust in God ; I have continually besought Him mercifully to hear me, and

He has always heard my prayer." He exhorted Prince Frederick, when he should become king, not to tolerate such unchristian and subversive activities as plays, operas, and masked balls. But above all not to reduce the standing army and its huge revenue, or there would fall upon him "the curse which God laid upon Pharaoh." Frederick the Great did not share his father's religious views, but he paid heed to the advice about the army, and between them both the army of the small kingdom of Prussia became equal in artillery and fighting strength, and superior in discipline, to those of the Great Powers of France, Russia, Austria, or England. The religious faith of its creator was compatible with extraordinary measures of press-gang, arbitrary conscription, and the big stick. Suffering here was rather salutary, and the saved would enjoy heaven all the more.

That same year, 1722, John Wesley was an undergraduate at Oxford, and was introducing his fellow-students to a new fervour of religion and a methodical life of scheduled prayer, Bible reading, study, and good works, which got him and his friends the nickname of "methodists." So it did not mark young John Woolman as a peculiar child that he should run ahead of his crowd of playmates and find a lonely spot among the trees in order to read a few verses out of the Bible that had aroused his curiosity and imagination. There were few of his contemporaries who did not regard the Book of Revelation as authentic news about conditions in heaven. But where many were allured by the palaces of the measured glittering City, with its golden streets and twelve gates, every gate a jewel, the boy Woolman fastened on the description that is pure poetry, the orchard-garden of heaven. Second-generation American, son of the rich open spaces, the unwalled forests, and unexplored hinterland of a continent, he had never seen a walled city nor ever hoped to see one ; yet it was in a walled city that he was to die.

Morning and evening the long board was taken out and placed upon the trestles and spread with the white homespun cloth and the wooden and pewter table service. John Woolman from boyhood upward never saw that board not well furnished with children. By the time he was four there were six of them ; when he was nine there were eight. Mr and Mrs Samuel Woolman, at the head and foot, looked round serenely at the crowded benches and saw the double row of rosy faces increase and never diminish. When the savoury roast or stew, the big crocks of hot vegetables, the home-made bread and butter and home-brewed ale or cider, the jam, honeycomb, and pie were all placed upon the board together, healthy appetites, stimulated by nose and eyes, were held in pause to remember that man does not live by bread alone. The peaceful silence of the Quaker grace descended. Then, at the father's signal, chatter broke eagerly out, wooden platters were loaded with wholesome food, and the meal went cheerily forward.

On Sunday and on Thursday they went to meeting—"first days and week days meeting." The meeting-house was "30 foot long from oute to oute and 22 foot wide from oute to oute and 12 foot in hight on ye wall,"[1] built on the Wills plantation from the native logs.

The children went by the same path they took to school, the road beside the stream, marked out from time immemorial as an Indian trail. They passed the schoolhouse on their way. The grown-ups rode on horseback and took the children pillion behind them, except Mrs Woolman, who carried the baby in her arms. Right up to the time when John Woolman left home at the age of twenty there was always a baby in the family. Sometimes the ox-wagon would be used, and they would all be carried in that. No one rebelled, even in thought. Going to meeting was an outing and a social occasion, as well as a sacred necessity. Other families, behind or before them, took the same road, and all met at last at the same destination, tethered their horses under the shed, and went in the simple door.

Silence spread around the meeting-house, broken only by the song of birds, the chatter of squirrels and insects, or the stamp of a restless horse. Meeting 'began' when the first persons entered the meeting-house, and the deep silence was the chief part of the ritual. Although to the Quakers no one place was more holy than another, and they never had their meeting-houses dedicated or sanctified, nor their burying-places consecrated, they had yet chosen for the site of their first meeting-house in this neighbourhood a place hallowed to the Indians for long past as a burying-ground.

It seemed to the simple Quakers that a burying-ground already established in a central spot was a suitable place to use for their own dead. God was everywhere and the Father of all. So while the meeting for the first twenty-five years was held in private houses—the homes, in turn, of three leading settlers, of whom the pioneer John Woolman

[1] Records of Burlington Monthly Meeting, 4th of 11th mo., 1702.

was one—the body of the first to die, Mary Kendal, was laid to rest by her husband and friends in 1687 in the Indian burying-ground, on land held by Dr Daniel Wills ; and there Mary Wills, the wife of Dr Daniel, was placed in 1691 ; and there was laid the body of William Woolman, and of his host and friend, George Elkinton, in 1713, and of Mary, his wife ; and there laid John Woolman's grandfather and grandmother, John Woolman, the pioneer, and Elizabeth, his wife ; and many more. The Indian dead, sitting upright in their barrows with their pottery and dried corn and bows and arrows beside them for use in the Happy Hunting-grounds, mingled their dust with that of the Quakers who lay reposeful and empty-handed, trusting God for provision in the future life as in the past. And as their dust was with the passage of time indistinguishable in the earth, and equally mingled in the life of the quiet grass, so no monuments above ground distinguished the one from the other. Gabriel, if he came with his trumpet, could not read the list of names elsewhere than in the Lamb's book of life. It was against Quaker custom in those early days to have so much as a headstone. The meeting minute-books and individual family records alone furnished the information. So when the Quakers on the Rancocas were ready to build a meeting-house its site was a foregone conclusion. Convenience and habit dictated that it should stand beside the burying-ground.

To little John Woolman the meeting-house was as familiar as his own home. He could not remember any time when he did not go there, for he had been taken before memory became conscious. There was no symbol inside, no cross or altar, to mark the house as a temple, but yet it was solemn in there, it was different. When one entered the dim interior from the outside brightness one felt a hush. On one side of the centre aisle sat the women, on the other the men ; and the same division was maintained on the two raised facing benches, where the elders and ministers sat. Behind the elders' bench, to the south-east, was a small window made of four panes of bull's-eye glass, and in the south-west wall, on the women's side, was a large fireplace. In winter, when the door was shut, most of the light in the meeting-house came from the leaping fire that roared bravely in the brick chimney, and in extreme weather the women and children whose seats were farthest from it would move closer and gather near the warmth with decorous informality. In summer most of the light came from the open door, and the child whose wandering attention sought for something to fasten upon, seeing in front of him only the grave, shut faces of the elders and the blank, greenish shimmer of the bull's-eye window, not allowed to gaze behind him into the interesting out-of-doors, would rejoice in a waving leaf shadow in the oblong of sunlight that graced the well-smoothed floor.

At times another shadow silently appeared, the black silhouette of a man half-naked with a single feather upright in his hair. The Indian peered in to see the white man's doings, and never needed telling it was worship. Only the movement of his shadow told his entrance to take his place among the silent forms and share their inward salutation to the Great Spirit in a language which he too could understand.

It was a heavy responsibility to break that hush by speech. Although there were some who rushed readily into the vocal ministry, an opportunity open to all, a sensitive spirit trembled and forbore. Yet the ministry, by sermon or by prayer, was a necessary part of the perfect meeting, and meetings held for long periods in a silence that was never broken were found to become weak and dead. For this reason a definite 'call to the ministry' was favoured by Friends, and after a few spontaneous 'appearings in the ministry' of one whose words seemed to feed the spiritual life of the rest, encouragement was given by making a minute recording "the recognition of their gift." This recording minute of the Monthly Meeting, the local executive of the church, was all that it meant to be a minister among the Quakers. It did not in any sense appoint a minister to preach, much less pay him for doing so ; and it did not release those not recorded as ministers from the duty of obeying a rare call to speak in meeting when the Divine impulse was felt. The Spirit of God knew no distinction of persons in this service, neither of age nor of sex, of wealth nor of poverty. Recorded ministers sat on the facing benches with the elders, simply because to one more likely to speak than others it was an advantage to be slightly raised and to face the company.

To go to meeting and to return, in all weathers, to perform at home the minimum of necessary household tasks in feeding and watering stock, milking the cow, preparing and clearing the meals, provided enough activity even for restless childhood, so that sitting still thereafter was pleasant. The rebellion against meeting or against Sunday quiet that was secretly in the hearts of their contemporaries, the well-to-do

Quaker children in England, whose energies, never taxed to the full, found outlet in fidgeting, was not shared by the young Quakers in the colonies.

"We being A large Family of Children," wrote Woolman in his Journal, "it was customary with my parents after meeting on first days to put us to read In the Holy Scriptures or Some good Books, one after Another the rest Seting without much Conversation ; This I think was of Some use."

V

SUN WORM, ROBIN, AND RUDENESS

THE meeting spread the background of eternity against their daily life in just as simple and inescapable a way as the sky by night and by day spread the background of infinity. But only the soul gifted with the curious sensitiveness of genius is fully aware of these great and simple sensations. Every saint and every poet has many followers, because the saint and the poet explain and make clear to the ordinary man a crowd of thoughts and feelings which he only half knew. Thousands of shepherds watched the sky for weather to one who could sing, "The heavens declare the glory of God and the firmament showeth His handiwork."

John Woolman at nine years old, a healthy and active boy in a large family, with little time for dreaming or solitude, was yet never far from the borders of the heavenly country which so closely impinged upon this one, where the tree of life bore fruit perhaps resembling peaches, and the dark Rancocas, sparkling in the sunshine, was an earthly shadow of the river of crystal. It was not sentimental: it was merely delightful, it gave a great width to childish reverie. So when John Woolman was nine he had a queer dream, so meaningless apparently, like some of those dreams in the Bible, and yet so peculiarly his own, that he always remembered it.

I had A dream about the ninth year of my age as follows. I saw the moon rise near the West and run on a regular course Eastward So

Swift that in About A quarter of an hour She reached our meridian At which time there descended from her A small Cloud which on A direct line came to Earth on a Pleasant green About twenty yards from the doore of My Father's house in which I Stood And Imediately turned into A beautiful tree.   The moon run on with Equal Swiftness And Soon Set in the East, At which time the Sun Arose at the place of his comon rising in the Sumer, And Shining with full Radiance In a Serene air It appeared as pleasant A morning as Ever I saw.   All this time I Stood Still in the doore in an awfull frame of mind ; And as heat increased by the rising Sun, it wrought So powerfully on the blooming tree that the leaves and Branches thereof began to wither, and before noon it appeared dry and Dead then there appeared a Being Small of Size full of Strength and Resolution moving swift from the North Southward call'd a Sun worm. tho I was A child this dream was instructive to me.[1]

No interpretation of this dream has been offered.   One might say that the boy John Woolman was himself a Being small of size, full of strength and resolution, but though he did in time to come move southward, his progress was by no means swift, and the definition of the words "sun worm" remains mysterious.   No wonder, however, that it fascinated him.   Developing as he did into a man of singularly logical and clear intellect, these visions of blooming trees with leaves outlined in light perhaps afforded him the emotional release which in another environment he might have found in music or in art.   Puritanism at its most repressive era owed much for the richness of its mental life to the fact that the Scriptures were Oriental.

The two other incidents of childhood which John Woolman in retrospect considered worthy of remark were both such as any normal country boy might experience and remember.

Another thing remarkable while I was a little boy was that going to A neighbours house on the way I saw A robbin Seting on her nest and as I came near She went of, but having young ones flew backward and forward, and with many cries Shewed her concern for them, I threw Stones at her till one Striking her She fell Down dead, however pleased with the Exploit I was Shortly Seized with horrer and Remorse, as having kill'd An Innocent Creature while She was carefull for her young ; I considered they must now perish for want of their dam to feed them ; After some painfull thoughts I climbed up the tree, took her young ones And kill'd 'em, as Judging that better than for 'em

---

[1] Original first manuscript of Journal, Swarthmore College.

to pine Away miserably ; I went on my Errand, but for Some hours could think of little else but my Cruel conduct toward the poor old bird which thoughts were very Afflicting.

"I mention this," added the mature Journalist, apologizing for having included this unwontedly intimate story,

to Show how God the parent of All Creatures hath placed that in the human mind which doth Instruct and incite to Exercise Goodness towards All his creatures. This being Singly Attended to people grow compassionate And Sympathising, But being frequently and Totally rejected the heart Shuts its Self up in a Contrary Disposition.

The other incident was owing to that familiar development of obstreperous boyhood known as 'feeling his oats,' and gives a light also upon the discipline exercised in the Woolman family.

The eighteenth century was an era of violent domestic punishment. "Spare the rod and spoil the child" was a popular motto. Woolman's contemporary, Samuel Johnson, when asked how he had learned so much Latin, replied, "My master whipt me very well. Without that, Sir, I should have done nothing." Prince Frederick of Prussia, soon to be Frederick the Great, whose character was to affect the affairs of the American colonies, was seldom an hour in the presence of his father without being struck and reviled. The mother of John Wesley, eventempered and just, brought up what her husband casually described as "a numerous offspring, eighteen or nineteen children,"[1] by a judicious use of corporal punishment. And in the Quaker city of Philadelphia the schoolmasters flogged their pupils at their pleasure, even compelling the girls to remove their stays in preparation for the punishment.

But no such methods were in use in the Woolman home.

Another thing I Remember I believe About the twelfth year of my age, My Father being Abroad, my Mother reproved me for Some misdeed to which reproof I made an undutifull reply.

The next first day as I was with my Father returning from Meeting, He told me he understood I had behaved Amiss to my Mother and advised me to do better. I knew mySelf Greatly to blame, and in Shame and confusion remained Silent. Being thus awakened to A Sense of my wickedness I was troubled And Geting home I retired Alone And prayed to the Almighty to forgive me. And I do not remember that I ever Afterward Spoke unhandsomely to Either of my Parents afterwards, however foolish in other things.

[1] John Kirk, *The Mother of the Wesleys* (Jarrold and Sons, 1876), p. 134.

These incidents show the uninhibited development of a sensitive character in an environment congenial to its growth. No childish bitterness of grief or resentment entered into the blood of the future man. Confidence and peace, fair dealing, rebuke without anger, complaint without rancour, mutual respect and affection, united husband and wife and parent and child. It was a household of archaic charm. There was no show and no stint. But what security made tranquil the growing lives!

John Woolman is almost as impersonal as Shakespeare in reference to his family life ; but a memory of his father and mother echoes through many a sentence on the responsibility of parents to their children.

"Their stability and firmness, through a Divine blessing, is at times like dew on the tender plants round about them, and the weightiness of their spirits secretly works on the minds of others."[1] And to the settlers of North Carolina, who were opening a new frontier in 1757, his advice is an indirect commentary upon the value of his heritage.

And now, dear friends and brethren, as you are improving a wilderness, and may be numbered amongst the first planters in one part of a province, I beseech you, in the love of Jesus Christ, wisely to consider the force of your examples, and think how much your successors may be thereby affected. It is a help in a country, yea, and a great favour and blessing, when customs first settled are agreeable to sound wisdom ; but when they are otherwise the effect of them is grievous ; and children feel themselves encompassed with difficulties prepared for them by their predecessors.

[1] Epistle to North Carolina Yearly Meetings, Whittier edition of the Journal, p. 99.

VI

ADOLESCENCE; THE ART OF MIRTH

ADOLESCENCE changed John Woolman as it changes every one. At the age of sixteen people found him an attractive youth, livelier-witted than most, with an irrepressible fund of high spirits and overflowing friendliness, which as he emerged from the home circle commanded for him a wide variety of friends. He had had "Schooling pretty well for A planter," and fine houses in Burlington and in Philadelphia were open to him, which contained good libraries. He borrowed and read a store of literature, and that love of words and their apt and right use engendered in him by the early study of the Bible and by the Sunday-afternoon family-circle readings at home burned in him in a new and creative form. Like all young men from Shakespeare downward who discover the art of words he loved to play on speech, to pun, to use words as blown-glass baubles to glitter in sunlight ; and for such tricks one must have an audience. "Having attained the age of sixteen years I began to love company. . . . Advancing in age the number of my acquaintance Increased." Wit and laughter were iridescent about him as about the young Francis of Assisi five hundred years before.

"I felt Sharp and cuting Reproofs at times," writes Woolman "but did not get low Enough to Cry for help, for I loved Folly to that Degree that I had no resolution to Leave it."

37

Not that it ever lay on his conscience that he had been guilty to such an extent "as to Comit things Scandalous." His sins were not of the hot order of Saint Augustine's. But "to Exceed in the Art of foolish Jesting And to promote Mirth were my Chiefest Study."

What scope did Woolman have for the practice of the art of mirth ? The narrow shape of the Rancocas farms made for sociability, and Woolman's mother was a Burr, a family noted for its hospitality. Cousins, uncles, aunts, and neighbours kept the house always a-buzz, and farm festivals of corn-husking, apple-paring, slaughtering, and the like combined neighbourliness with utility as the seasons went round. But when Woolman says he began to love company he is obviously meaning something else than this sort of company, familiar from his childhood. He is meaning the tasting of different circles, the young man's experiment with life.

Long accustomed to the use of a horse, with which as a boy he had carried corn to the grist-mill on the Wills plantation and webs of his father's weaving to the fulling and dyeing mill at the Whites', he would now, work done, ride the seven miles west to Burlington and join a party where a life cultivated and simply elegant as that in the great world was in full swing. The house of the Honourable Richard Smith, member of the New Jersey Legislature, contained four sons and a daughter—Samuel, John, Elizabeth, William Lovett, and Richard—who gathered round them the cream of the neighbourhood. Elizabeth was a grave girl, four years John Woolman's junior, compelled by her mother's death to put on the dignity of a woman before her time, and often detached from the company of the young ones by the requirements of acting as hostess to her father's friends. But Samuel Smith was John Woolman's exact age, born in the same year, and John Smith was only two years younger and closely shared his tastes and interests.

The two young men could range freely together outdoors and in ; at a tea-party, at a river jaunt, at a strawberry feast on the Governor's lawn, at a quiet tête-à-tête along the Burlington wharf to see the Honourable Richard Smith's ships come in and unload from the West Indies, and to appraise the cargo, and talk with the keen good sense of rising youngsters about trade and its prospects and pitfalls ; and all three could share quiet hours with books in the Smith library, discussing thoughts expressed and ways of expressing them, appraising literary

style with the same acumen as West India cargo.   In years to come all
three of them wrote and published books.   Samuel Smith's *History
of New Jersey* was acclaimed in his own lifetime as a most important
work ;   and in his lordly way, as Secretary of the King's Council and
Treasurer of the Province, he picked up James Parker, official "King's
Printer," and moved him bodily, bag, baggage, and press, clear across
the province from Woodbridge, Middlesex County, to Burlington until
the work was done.   John Woolman's books were brief, and modestly
produced ;   aroused no public stir ;   and his greatest, his Journal, not
published until after his death, was long neglected.   But now the scales
have slowly but inexorably settled the other way, and while only the
research scholar finds a rare and dilapidated volume of Smith's *History*
mouldering on a neglected shelf in reference libraries, the Journal of
John Woolman is a living classic.

A longer horseback ride in the opposite direction brought Woolman
to Haddonfield, to the wealthy and spacious home of Elizabeth Haddon
Estaugh and her scholarly husband, John Estaugh.   The wide acres of
the Haddonfield plantation had been purchased, on paper, by Elizabeth's
father, John Haddon, but he had been prevented from coming to take
it up, and his only daughter, then nineteen years old, had sailed alone to
the New World in 1701, attended by a chaperon and servants, and done
some colonizing on her own account in her father's name.   The expectation had been that her father would shortly follow her, but it was not
ordered so.   John Haddon died in England.   Meanwhile, a young man,
John Estaugh, had come over to Pennsylvania and New Jersey on a
Quaker religious concern in 1700, and he came in due course to Haddonfield, where the orphan heiress was efficiently struggling to establish
her ample estate.   Romance bloomed unexpectedly between them.
But John Estaugh had little to offer except good looks, a cultivated mind,
and a deeply religious character.   The lady's wealth stood between
them.   She perceived it, and with the free boldness that had characterized
all her actions and made her a successful pioneer in a wilderness she
gallantly and gravely offered him her hand.   Young Estaugh, with
equal grace and sincerity, reserved his answer, and continued his journey
without engagement.   But he came back again to claim her, and his
wife left testimony after his death in 1742 that "few if any in a married
state ever lived in sweeter harmony than we did."

When John Woolman and Samuel and John Smith and others of their group rode to Haddonfield John's favourite sister, Elizabeth, was often of the party. In spite of difference of years, a warm and lively friendship existed between her and Elizabeth Estaugh. At Haddonfield also there was a library, and a host who loved books, as well as a gracious "open house" which drew a constant variety of guests.

Or did John Woolman wish to "make an Excursion to the pretty City of Philadelphia, 20 miles from hence—a fine Turnpike Road," as Governor Belcher said, there was a society as rich and easy, in its decorous way, as any in the colonies, and many of its most distinguished members were his friends. John Smith, his Burlington intimate, would take him to the house of James Logan, where he was courting one of the daughters, Hannah, in a leisurely and diffident manner which did not become articulate until 1743 or culminate in an engagement until 1748. The Logans, the Pembertons, the Benezets, the Farringtons, the Franklins, were all ports of call. All unconsciously helped to develop Woolman's natural gentleness into a social grace which his subsequent denial of some of the forms of etiquette could not diminish—it had by that time become much deeper than manners, and had developed into that finest breeding only found among the earth's noblemen. But it is good for a young man to mingle with the world, and fortunate if his lot is cast during his formative years among the best society of his neighbourhood.

In the first half of the eighteenth century the best society in Pennsylvania and New Jersey was Quaker society. The Quakers commanded trade, had a majority in both Assemblies, and set their disapproval upon the theatre, dancing, and card-playing in a decided manner which gave a tone to the amusements of the time. Before the Revolutionary War the non-Quaker elements in Philadelphia had succeeded in establishing a more modish life, centring upon the elaborate Assembly Balls, with their low-hung chandeliers, blazing with hundreds of candles which endangered the ladies' high-dressed hair. Yet even then such wealth and elegance was possessed by the Quakers that General Howe chose for his headquarters a Quaker home, James Logan's splendid house of Stenton ; and commandeered for his use a Quaker lady's chaise and horses, as being the finest in the city.

In Woolman's youth the two greatest families of Philadelphia were the Logans and the Pembertons. Mrs James Logan and Mrs Israel Pemberton were sisters, daughters of Charles Reade, and natives of

Burlington. They were acquaintances of Woolman's parents at home and had belonged to the same Monthly Meeting. Israel Pemberton, junior, was five years older than John Woolman, and James Pemberton was three years younger. Hannah Logan was exactly the same age as Woolman.

James Logan, who had first come to Pennsylvania as secretary to William Penn, was Chief Justice of Pennsylvania and President of the Council. Ill-health, caused at first by a broken hip which left him permanently lame, kept him at Stenton, his country home at Germantown, after 1732, so that house had become a centre of affairs of State. The most noticeable of these to a visitor were the Indian consultations. The Indian deputations were as large as they were picturesque, sometimes three or four hundred appearing at one time to add weight to their appeal by numbers. The Logans, father and son, had always been good friends to the Indians, following the policy of their patron, William Penn, and James Logan had arrangements made for entertaining these large deputations in his grounds, with an Indian gesture of hospitality appreciated by the hospitable red men. The idea of the inn—the place where you paid for board and lodging—always cut sharply across the aristocratic open-handedness of these lordly sons of nature, and their native culture possessed no equivalent to it. An Indian chief at the Treaty with the Six Nations made in Philadelphia said :

> Brethren, we called at our friend James Logan's on our way to this city, and to our grief found him hid in the bushes. . . . We pressed him to leave his retirement and prevailed with him to assist once more on our account at your council. He is a wise man and a fast friend to the·Indians, and we desire when his soul goes to God you may choose in his room just such another person of the same prudence and ability in counselling, and of the same tender disposition and affection for the Indians.

James Logan's relations with the Indians were the more to his credit as he had built his fortune on the trade with Indians for furs. Quick as they were to detect deceit, and implacable to avenge it, they were satisfied that neither in trade nor in politics had Logan ever been guilty of double-dealing, and their trust in him was unshakable.

On visits to Stenton, therefore, John Woolman became aware of the Indians, not as hunters, playmates, or neighbours, in which capacities they were familiar, but in their political aspect, injured, anxious, sometimes warlike, potentially dangerous ; and he became aware of their wrongs.

As soon as one turned one's back, however, upon that wild and alien encampment on the lawns, screened from the house by trees, and entered the well-built brick mansion, one might have been in the surburban mansion of a London merchant prince. Nothing here bespoke the raw or the new. A great double staircase soared up from the entrance hall, on either side opened lofty rooms panelled with fine woodwork, and the arched niches over the wide mantels contained rare pieces of china and silver set out for display.

The furniture, no longer of the severe utilitarian pioneer simplicity that Woolman had grown up with, showed curved legs and backs, claws and splay feet ; an imported carpet spread its magnificence in more than one room, and chandeliers and lustres multiplied at night in dazzling degree the simple light of candles. Woolman saw the contrast of the squalid camp and the stately house without fully realizing it, as the artist in every medium draws later from his memory impressions he had not known he had recorded. But the spell of James Logan's youngest daughter, Hannah (named after William Penn's second wife), fell upon more young men than John Smith, and it was she who drew the young people about her. A casual caller from Virginia, William Black, one day attending a weighty commission to her father, left a full description of his visit, typical of an eighteenth-century afternoon in colonial urban society. And one can read in it not only the influence of youth and wealth and a sheltered life but also the delicate austerity, even in frivolity, of the Quaker touch.

At last the Tea Table was Set, and one of his Daughters [Hannah] presented herself in Order to fill out the Fashionable Warm Water : I was really very much Surprized at the Appearance of so Charming a Woman in a place where the seeming moroseness and Goutified Father's Appearance Promised no such Beauty, tho' it must be allow'd the Man seem'd to have some Remains of a handsome enough Person. . . . But to return to the Lady, I declare I burnt my Lips more than once, being quite thoughtless of the warmness of my Tea, entirely lost in Contemplating her Beauties. She was tall and Slender, but Exactly well Shap'd, Features Perfect, and Complection tho' a little the whitest, yet her Countenance had something in it extremely Sweet. Her Eyes Express'd a very great Softness, denoting a Compos'd Temper and Serenity of Mind, Her Manner was Grave and Reserv'd and to be short she had a Sort of Majesty in her Person and Agreeableness in her Behaviour which at once Surprized and Charmed the Beholders.

After the Tea Table was remov'd we were going to take leave, but it appear'd we must first view his Library, which was Customary with him to any Persons of Account. He had really a very fine Collection of Books, both Ancient and Modern. He seem'd to Regrate that none of his Sons knew not how to use them, and that he design'd them as a Legacy to the City when he died.[1]

The library was in fact the finest collection of books in Philadelphia, and took up half of the front of the house in the second story. When Benjamin Franklin—Woolman being twelve years old at the time—began his project of the first lending library in the world, and obtained sufficient subscribers to send to London for books, he and his friends appointed a committee to wait upon James Logan to ask for his kind suggestions as to the first list of books to order, since he was "the best judge of books in this part." And the list he furnished them was exactly fulfilled.

If James Logan had educated his daughters to the use of his library instead of his sons he might have had better luck. During a courtship lasting more than eight years the charms of Hannah's conversation never palled upon her lover, and (we have his word for it) almost equalled those of her person. But Logan's theories of the education of women were rather those of John Milton than of his own great religious leader, George Fox. In one of his letters he remarks that his daughter,

> besides her needle, has been learning French, and this last week has been Very busy in the dairy at the plantation, in which she delights as well as spinning ; but is this moment at the table with me (being first-day afternoon and her mother abroad) reading the 34th Psalm in Hebrew, the letters of which she learned very perfectly in less than two hour's time, an experiment I made of her capacity only for my diversion, though I never design to give her that or any other learned language, unless the French be accounted such.[2]

Although Monthly Meetings would minute protests against the use of "hooped skirts and other extravagances," there was no distinctive Quaker dress at this period. John Woolman went well and inconspicuously tailored in cloth of his father's weaving, knee breeches, buckled shoes, cocked hat, stock, and handkerchief. His friend, John Smith, would wear for every day a "fustin" jacket, and for best a suit of "hair Camblet."[3] William Penn's advice had been "Choose thy clothes

---

[1] *Hannah Logan's Courtship*, edited by Albert Cook Myers (Ferris and Leach, Philadelphia, 1904), pp. 6, 7.
[2] *Ibid.*, p. 8.   [3] *Ibid.*, p. 35.

by thine own eye, not another's. Plain and simple, not fantastical nor unshapely." For country wear, leather or buckskin breeches were popular, and for city wear wigs or perukes were in favour. A healthy countryman, sweating in the ox-drawn hay wagon or at the plough's tail, of necessity wore his own hair, tied back tightly at the neck ; and conversely leather breeches, resistant to thorns and weather, were too cumbersome for the indoor life of store and counting-house. But with such differences, the group of young men dressed similarly, and to describe the clothes of one is as good as to describe another's. Woolman has left on record his dislike of being in any way singular or conspicuous, and though at the time when he confessed to this he had decided none the less to *be* singular, the words are sufficient evidence of his previous conformity to the current fashions.

There is no clear description extant of the physical appearance of John Woolman.[1] "He was about my height," says one friend. Which reminds one of Orlando's ambiguous description of Rosalind, "just as high as my heart." But his attractiveness is spoken for by his popularity. He found it the hardest thing in the world to shake his friends when his mental growth needed solitude. They still continually sought him out. And to the end of his life he felt the danger of his easy tendency to friendship. "I had at times been sensible that a superficial friendship had been dangerous to me."

At the Pemberton house Woolman was again in the current of affairs, one might say in the full tide of them. The Pembertons were by no means 'hid in the bushes,' their house being at the south-west corner of Front and Market Streets.[2] All the bustle of the city was at their doors, and all the stir and ardour of political dispute was to be found within their doors. They were a large family, and both Israel Pemberton, the father, and Israel Pemberton, junior, were in their turn members of the Pennsylvania Assembly. Israel junior was a young man of hot, outspoken temperament, and was constantly the centre of fierce controversy. He was the leader of the great row in the Assembly in 1740 between the citizens and the Proprietary Party, when he enunciated for the first time in the colonies the old principle of English Parliamentary liberty, "no taxation without representation," in resistance to what seemed to be an

[1] See Appendix XIII.
[2] They did not occupy their beautiful house, Clarke Hall, at Third and Chestnut until 1745.

attempt at tyranny on the part of the Proprietors. John Adams fell foul of him in later years, and quite unjustly called him "that Quaker Jesuit" —perhaps because it seemed impossible that so belligerent a gentleman could sincerely be a religious pacifist when it came to bearing arms. His common nickname was "The King of the Quakers," and it was his wife's chaise that was used by General Howe. His younger brother James was nearer Woolman's age, and was the close companion of John Smith and his friends. His mild, steady disposition helped to keep the atmosphere of the home free from the quarrels which his brother's positiveness and heat might have engendered, besides acting as a protection to the diffident youngest brother, John, and the Pembertons stood together through thick and thin. But James, too young to be yet so much engaged in business or public affairs as Israel, was the sharer of the gay jaunts got up by the younger crowd.

In winter, farm work more or less at a standstill, John Woolman could the more easily be one of the group who would ride "to Scuylkill. Had a small spell of Skeeting but not quite agreeable, the Ice being Rough." Or would join John Smith and Jemmy Pemberton in a quiet evening : "Read in the Evening in *Don Quixote* . . . in Chambers's Dictionary . . . in Desideratus . . . in Sir Thomas More's *Utopia* . . . in *Paradise Lost.* . . ." Or again with Jemmy Pemberton and several other friends would spend the day with John Smith at his plantation, and "found an Agreeable place to Slide on the Creek. We went and Returned in Slays. All safe and pleased." Or advantageously mixing grave and gay, "was at Meeting. Spent the afternoon Skeeting on Skuylkill with several Agreeable Acquaintances."[1]

Such vivid details of pastimes and diversions are to be found in plenty in the journals and letters of John Woolman's known friends. But if Woolman ever kept a journal of such day-to-day doings he destroyed it utterly. Looking back from the age of thirty-five, he condemns sweepingly, without detail, the lightness of his youth.

"Vanity was Added to Vanity."[2] "Serious reflections were uneasy to me, and youthful vanities and diversions were my greatest pleasure."[3] "My heart was replenished with mirth and wantonness, while pleasing scenes of vanity were presented to my imagination. . . . I was often

[1] MS. diary of John Smith.   [2] MS. No. 1.
[3] Journal, Whittier ed., p. 44.

sad and longed to be deliver'd from those vanities ; then again my heart
was strongly inclin'd to them, and there was in me a sore conflict." "In
a while I resolved totally to leave off some of my vanities, but there
was a secret reserve in my heart of the more refined part of them."[1] "I
found in me a plant Strong & Extensive which brought fourth wild
Grapes."[2]

"Things scandalous" in the common modern sense, implying errors
of bodily intemperance, were almost unknown among the Quakers.
And especially in communities so small, hard-working, and intimately
known to each other. Ten years later Governor Belcher reported of
the towns of New Jersey, "I have not seen one that has in it 200 dwelling-
houses, & after weighing all things I have pitct upon this City[3] (as call'd,
tho' but a Village of 170 houses) for the place of my Residence." Scandal
in the colonies was scandal indeed, and any Friend guilty of things
scandalous in the mildest degree would be promptly "read out of Meeting." Although New England's scarlet letter was unknown in New
Jersey, any woman who bore a child out of wedlock was compelled to
stand at the whipping-post on market-day with a placard stating her
offence hung round her neck, and if her partner was known he was
forced to stand there with her. If either of the pair had an injured
husband or wife a public whipping "well laid on" was added to the
shame of exposure. Drunkenness was punished by the stocks ; and it
is unlikely that anyone frequently visiting Philadelphia could grow to
maturity without seeing some thief or other whipped at the cart's tail
through the streets of the city.

So the major forms of wantonness as practised, for instance, by Prince
Hal or by the young Saint Francis are out of court. Yet Woolman's
behaviour met with remonstrance from his parents. "My Dear Parents
Several Times in A private way admonished me, and their admonition
entered into my heart & had a good effect for a season. But still I was
not low enough ; for when the Tempter came he conquered me."

There does not seem good reason to suppose that apart from a greater
simplicity of life due to country habits and less wealth, the parents of
Woolman should have been stricter in their standards than the parents
of the Logans, Smiths, and Pembertons.

Yet no hint of self-reproach or of family remonstrance enters into the

---

[1] Journal, Whittier ed., p. 46.
[2] MS. No. 1.　　　　　　　　　　[3] *I.e.*, Burlington.

records made by these young people of theirlight-hearted doings. In the later pages of their journals their grave and responsible maturity looked back unashamed at their young days, and they were aware of no sharp cleavage dividing their life in two. Middle-aged seriousness and weight in the counsels of the Church and of the State ripened naturally from the green wood of their sapling beginning. And they did not destroy their early journals. They valued them, rather, as a depository of memory, and sometimes turned past pages with a touch of wistfulness.

Are we to conclude that Woolman's "wild grapes" were essentially worse and different?

A light pierces Woolman's reserve by a comparison with some other journals written by contemporaries who were not among his friends in youth, but three of whom became the friends of his later life. These journals, like his own, were only started in middle age, and speak retrospectively of their early years. Samuel Neale, of Dublin, Samuel Fothergill, of England, Rebecca Jones, of Philadelphia, John Wesley, and George Whitefield all alike speak with regret of "wild" or "wanton" behaviour and of a period of distress and struggle ending in a marked change. The wildness, the remorse, the struggle, and the change all took place, in each case, between the ages of thirteen and twenty-two. Sixteen to eighteen generally seem to be the crucial years.

By standards such as these vanity and folly take on a different aspect, and are perhaps less to be considered as any kind of loose behaviour than as the attitude of levity which gives little weight to the passing hour. The very words "pastime," "diversion," carried their own self-criticism. The passing of time was all too swift; one feared anything that would divert from one's purpose in life. And what was one's purpose in life? No less than close obedience to a Divine Director. The hours ran through one's fingers, Skeeting and Slaying, idling on the Governor's lawn, laughing and jesting, taking trips in wherry-boats to taverns— parties of young men and maidens—not doing anything particularly wrong, but not doing anything particular at all. This was to dissipate life; and life might be taken from one at any moment. Smallpox, dysentery, lung disease, "lingering putrid fever," lay constantly in wait. And what would it mean to go before the Judge of All the Earth with nothing to show but empty hours and mundane tasks?

Elizabeth Drinker, who was by no means a strait-laced Friend, and allowed herself in her private journal a great deal of latitude in thought and reading—including the usually forbidden romances ("although I would not encourage my children doing much of that business")—records her concern at such doings. "Molly (and seven other young people) were all at Gray's Ferry this afternoon, so Molly informs me ; which I by no means approve of. Friends' children going in companies to public houses is quite out of character."[1] And even to spend the evening at the respectable home of a Friend did not save them from all blame, since numbers might make for riotousness. "They spent the evening at Edwd Shoemaker's with near thirty young people ; 'tis not the way I could wish my children to conclude the year—in parties—but we can't put old heads on young shoulders !"[2]

But there is that word "wantonness," and we are dealing with an exact artist, a master in words. For this reason one gives full weight to Woolman's every statement, even when it expresses an extreme remorse for which he does not choose to give a detailed cause.

"While I Meditate on the Gulf toward which I travelled," says Woolman,

> And Call to mind my youthful disobedience, For these thins I weep mine Eye runeth Down with water . . . my way grew more Dificult the comfort I had Sometimes found in reading the Holy Scriptures and Contemplating the Divine Goodness was now removed from me. . . . Serious reflections were uneasie to me, And I Seemed happyest when I thought least About true Virtue. Runing in this road I found many like my Self, And we were united in that which is reverse to true Friendship.
>
> In this Swift race it pleased God to visit me with sore Sickness that I doubted of recovery.
>
> Then did darkness horror And Amazement with full Strength Sieze me, even when my pain And Distress of body was verry great I thought it had been better for me never to have had A being than to See the day I now saw. Thus I lay in a piteous Condition And with bitter Lamentations bewailed my misery.[3]

The view that sickness was a direct act of God upon the person, sent as a kind of threat or warning, was prevalent, and gave a peculiar terror to mortal ill. The approach of death was awful under such circumstances, and the words "ruin" and "destruction" were no metaphors.

---

[1] *Journal of Elizabeth Drinker*, May 5, 1795.
[2] *Ibid.*, December 31, 1795.
[3] MS. No. 1.

Many a young man feverishly endeavoured to compound with offended Deity at such a moment with promise of amendment in return for an extension of time. And when their sickness took a turn for the better and they got well they felt under an obligation; a "covenant" had been made, a treaty subscribed to, the terms of which were well known.

So John Woolman, stricken with the prospect of death in the midst of his gay and careless life, records ;

I was Strongly Engaged in mind that if he was pleased to restore my health I might serve him faithfully.

After my Recovery this Exercise remained with me A considerable time, And I had hopes of Standing ; But by Degrees giving way to Youthfull Vanities they gained Strength And geting with wanton young people, I let go my hold of God's covenant. He had Spoken peace to me in A time of Bitterness, Yet I now most ungratefully turned Again to folley.

VII

THE WINTER EVENING

SUCH friends of John Woolman's as are known by name—Smiths, Logans, Pembertons, Whites, Haineses, and the rest—could not possibly be described, by the severest afterthought, as "wanton young people." There are others who loom in this phrase more faintly and quite anonymously behind the veil of the Journalist's reserve. Hardly any names of friends or relations or everyday companions appear in Woolman's narrative ;[1] he will seldom even mention a book by name. His account is stripped, objective, even when most self-confessing. He is not, like Gibbon, telling the story of his life for his own amusement. He would gladly retreat, as a person, behind the universal aspects of his experience ; and he equally respects the reserve and the privacy of others. But if we would press to pass from the general to the particular, a delicate indication can be found here and there buried in the phrases about vanity and wanton company that Woolman's chief temptation was that commonest of all to lively adolescence, one which a warm and mirth-loving temperament is particularly subject to, and which is in fact "a plant strong and extensive," apt to bear wild grapes. That is, the temptation provided by the company of provocative girlhood. Mirth can be promoted by teasing and play as well as by witty speech. At corn-husking bees the rare red ear was well honoured by kissing the girl who husked it ; ring-a-rosy and the rough, tumbling game of hunt-the-

---

[1] Except those associated with his religious visits. These he names with care, as if 'making a minute' of their companionship or hospitality, to do them public honour.

slipper were at least as exciting as the forbidden dance ; the country lasses, working hard and long, were often irrepressible in their brief hours of freedom, wild as young colts, innocent but ready for much dalliance. What youth that has tasted the charms of such sport finds it easy to break off ? Even though common sense may recognize, and elders warn, that it is a playing with fire, how almost impossible to break the strong spell cast by some girls—or perhaps, harder still to break, that cast by one girl in particular. It was something powerful indeed with which Woolman wrestled, and which drew him back again and again into a snare to avoid which his education and his better judgment and his religious feeling all struggled in vain.

Once having spent part of a day most wantonly, Going to Bed at night, In A window near my bed lay A Bible. I opened it, And I first Cast my Eye on the Text "we lie down in our shame and our confusion covereth us." This I knew to be my Condition, And meeting with it so unexpectedly I was Affected with it and went to bed under remorse of conscience which I shortly cast off again.

Thus time passed on . . . and looking over my past life the prospect was moving. At times I turned to folly and then again sorrow and confusion took hold of me. . . .

My Dear Parents Several Times in A private way admonished me, and their admonition entered into my heart and had a good effect for a season. But . . . when the Tempter came he conquered me.

And now I Come to A winter Evening which to me is Memoriable. I had spent Some time in reading A pious Author with which I was Affected ; I walked alone. And feeling the Spirit of Supplycation upon me, I prayed to the Lord for his help that I might be preserved from these Vanities which So Ensnared And Afflicted my mind : I found help in my distress and through faith Mountains were removed. . . . But not keeping in that Strength that Gives Victory I lost Ground, the Sence of which Entred Deep ; I sought Desarts And lonely places, And there with tears Did Confess my Sins to God, And humbly craved help of him. . . . I was lead to look carefully at the means by which I was drawn from his Testimony ; And I learned that if I would live in the Life which the faithfull Servants of God lived in I must not go into Company in my own will, but All the Cravings of Sence Must be Governed by A Superiour principle. . . . I found it My true Interest to serve God in Faithfulness, and *being Young and believing A single life Best for me At Present, I was Strengthened to keep from Such Company which had often been A snare to me.*

The word 'hell,' it is worthy of remark, does not figure in Woolman's confessions. The Wesleyan movement, which made hell one of its principal persuading points, was now well under way, in all its astonishing power. George Whitefield was in Philadelphia in '39 and again in '40, stirring up the people. Huge crowds assembled to hear his fascinating sermons, being told, as John Smith drily wrote to James Pemberton,[1]

> of a Dreadful Burning Tophet, An Eternal Hell, Scorching, Blazing fiery Brimstone ready to overtake them, Sure Damnation, Certain Destruction and unavoidable Desolation where they must forever Dwell with Devills, fallen Angels, Damned Spirits, fiery furies, forever Burning, Tormenting, and never, never to be released.

Enough, indeed, to frighten children into fits and cause them "Dismally to Shreik and Cry out," while parents and grown people "made hideous noises and violent Distortions of the Body."

But the explosive force of this movement passed the Quakers by. They had only just recovered themselves from being an extravagant and persecuted sect, and they were enjoying the sensation of being respected and prosperous. Their attitude towards Whitefield was benevolent but cool, though none of them met John Wesley's own magnetism and sincerity unmoved.

But John Woolman, if he felt in his sensitive tendrils the ripples of this stir, was moved by different motives. Not fear of hell and brimstone haunted his secret thoughts, but a sense of loss and longing. He needed to break out from dark and tangled places of the soul into the clear and sunlit air to which he had been accustomed. He wanted to cut loose from "Vanities," because they ensnared and afflicted his mind. He hungered to resume his vivid consciousness of the Divine Goodness. And the gulf towards which he travelled was that of indifference and callousness, of a coarsening of fibre which would make him increasingly insensitive to the exquisite delicacy of the movements of the Spirit. Saint Augustine before him had said, "Thou hast made us for Thyself and our hearts are restless until they find rest in Thee"; and the poet Wordsworth after him would say,

> . . . trailing clouds of glory do we come
> From God, who is our home.

To those who have once breathed that air of Paradise, to sink into a foggier and more mundane atmosphere is exile.

Woolman could not explain himself to those whom he so suddenly abandoned. He did not think them "wicked," he had no desire to

---

[1] Pemberton Papers, viii, 47.

criticize them. But whoever they were—or she was—he broke loose from their powerful fascination, and even with bleeding wounds he struggled up once more into what had been his native air. "My former Acquaintance was left to Judge of me as they would for I lived in private and these things were Sealed up in my own breast."

Such an effort could not be made without pain, and the suffering of that cleavage is reticently expressed in such phrases as "I lived under the Cross," "Now tho I had been Strengthened to bear the Cross In many Instances, I still Saw my Self in great Danger, having many weaknesses Attending me, And great temptations to wrestle with." Yet the result was a gradual, profound change which brought an extraordinary happiness. "While I Silently ponder on that Change which I found in me," says Woolman—as a creature with the experience of wings might look back at the final splitting of the chrysalis—"I find no language Equal to it, nor Any means to convey to another A Clear Idea of it. . . . This will be understood by those who have trod the Same path."[1] Then, after the most lyrical passage in his Journal on real beauty and true harmony, he adds, "Yet all these together do not fully shew forth that Inward life, to such as have not felt it. But this white Stone and new name is known rightly to Such only who have it."

[1] *Cf.* Whittier ed., p. 48.

VIII

LAST YEARS AT HOME

"ALL this time," says Woolman, "I lived with my Father and Wrought on the plantation," and dismisses in the phrase the outward pattern of events which none the less coloured his memories and shaped the course of his life. He adds that during the latter part of his time at home he "lived retired." This means that during the last year at least he withdrew from his own personal social activities, and confined himself to those necessitated by the family movements. But these alone would prevent anything like solitary living. The books with which he improved himself in winter evenings had to be studied by the common fireside, and in order to obtain the quiet to meditate upon them which every student needs, he had to fling on his warm outdoor things and walk outside in the biting air, the exquisite peace of the moonlit frost. Then as the season softened, with book in his pocket after the heavy labour of the farm day he would avoid the group of his brothers and enter the "Desarts And lonely places" of the cathedral woods, or walk along the banks of the dark and silent stream. But it was not easy to get away, and there were many times when he could not. Besides visiting to and fro with relatives—chief of whom was Grandfather Henry Burr, whose wealthy home and large estate was an easy ride, and Uncle John Burr, Surveyor-General of the Province at Mount Holly—there were the habits of the Quaker community. The Society of Friends was exactly what its name implied, and it conducted its affairs by group action. The Woolmans went every month to Burlington for the Monthly Meeting, an executive unit comprising several individual meetings ; and every quarter they rode alternately to Burlington or to Chesterfield for the Quarterly Meeting, which comprised several Monthly Meetings. Twice a year the whole of Quakerdom in the valley of the Delaware gathered for the Half-year and the Yearly Meeting, alternately held in Burlington and Philadelphia. Although representatives were appointed in form to each of these meetings, the practice merely ensured that people from each neighbourhood comprised should be present. All Friends, whether appointed as representatives or not, had an equal right to stand up and "speak to business." The Quaker theory of the Meeting for Worship held good also for their Meetings for Business, that is, the direct control and leading of the Divine Spirit, working through the sensitive spirits of chosen men and women.

The word 'democracy' was not yet popular, but the practice among the Quakers preceded the theory, and owing to the genius of Fox, who had left them an organization both close-knit and free, they presented a perfect working model of democratic government. So all were expected to come to all of the meetings, and the amount of mutual hospitality practised by the main centres, Burlington, Chesterfield, and Philadelphia, was very great, and the level of mutual acquaintance among the Quakers was high.

John Woolman took his sister Elizabeth pillion behind him on many such a trip, Asher taking Sarah, and Abner taking Patience, and when their journey's end was Philadelphia they baited at the famous inn of Thomas Moore, on the Burlington Road, and then went on down to cross the Delaware at Cooper's Ferry.[1] Moore, himself a Quaker, was the father of numerous sons, and a canny dealer in real estate, so the settlement served by his tavern, originally called Chestertown, came to be called Moorestown. Large families bent on travel made quite a demand on horses, and a young man who had no sister to take in to Monthly, Quarterly, or Yearly Meeting could make himself and his horse useful by taking in some one else's sister. Certainly pillion riding lent itself to courtship ; and in families too well provided with brothers and horses some mutual exchange of partners was often arranged for the return trip. Twilight or moonlight of a spring or summer evening, the horse walking softly through the forest paths, and the scent of sweet

---

[1] Now Camden.

fern and locust on the breeze, a young man, with his partner's hands upon his belt, had no cause to envy the world's people in their ballrooms.

John Woolman at seventeen and eighteen toyed with such sweets. And with whom did Elizabeth ride home, she who later also condemned her wanton and airy youth ? As for Asher and Abner, nothing loth, they found themselves often exchanged with by Robert Elton and young Joseph Moore. Woolman was in his seventeenth year when his first sister was married—Sarah, to Robert Elton ; and he was in his eighteenth year when Patience married Joseph Moore. A wedding is an exciting event in a family, especially a daughter's wedding, with previous months of preparation of clothes and linen, and weeks of preparing food for the gathering of guests. The eldest son and brother had a lively share in both. Mrs Woolman supervised her daughter Sarah's wedding in April and had another baby herself before Christmas. Little Abraham had to hurry up to be born in order to establish his proper dignity as an uncle and be older than his niece, for Elizabeth Elton was born in the spring, and the proud grandmother, forty-two years old, cherished her nursing child at her breast between her tasks of assistance at her daughter's labour. It is likely that John Woolman, the eldest son, was her escort on this occasion, and the one who, nearest in age to the young husband, gave him sympathetic and brotherly company during the long hours of waiting.

Baby Elizabeth succeeded in being older than her Uncle Eber, born a year later, and her proud place as first grandchild always gave her a special favour in her grandmother's heart. She was the only grandchild mentioned more than once in Mrs. Woolman's will—she was mentioned three times—and received a generous legacy of furniture and goods. But at present she could only blink at the benign shapes around her, and squirm engagingly in the arms of her Uncle John Woolman, who was well accustomed to the expert and tender handling of the very young.

Along with the vital family rhythm of courtship, marriage, and childbirth ran farm talk of care of beasts in winter, of mending fences and tools, and household talk of flour that was not keeping well, of wool that must be carded, of wheat that all who were able to ride must at once carry to the mill ; and of interesting accidents and disasters that always add an uneasy spice to the flavour of human life. The winter of '39 to '40 was rich not only in the birth of little Eber, and the "memoriable" evening of John Woolman, but in dangers by fire and flood. There was a fire at Burlington Meeting-house and an accident at Burlington ferry. John Smith was an excellent raconteur, and he had seen the one and had an eyewitness's account of the other. So the conversation of the inhabitants of Burlington County, at market, at meeting, on pillion ride, and at quilting-bee, and round the table in the Woolman household, carries clearly across two hundred years. The weekly newspaper was scantily subscribed to, and tales passed round by word of mouth were discussed and told again and again, enriched by comment and question, and—like tales now told to children—only the more interesting for repetition. "The fire? Ah, yes," says John Smith eagerly (and his hearers later carefully repeated, and contradicted each other, and added drama to the dialogue).

That Night of February fourth, thro' the carelessness (as was Supposed) of Ann White (that us'd to mind It) the fire In the Upper Chamber of the little Meeting house kindled and (as is Suppos'd) Some of it fell off the hearth on to the floor and So Set it afire ; But it Was not Discovered till about 11 o'clock the Next Day when (thro' Mercy) by the help of the Engine & many People Most part of the Roof of the Great house was Saved And the Lower floor of the timbers of the Upper, In the little one, were Also Saved, but the Roof of the little House & the S.W. Side of the Roof & the Lanthorn of the Great House were All Burnt. As the Engine was playing In the Great House Some Timbers of the terret fell and hurt Several people. Samuel Brown had his collar-bone broke.[1]

Burlington, starting out to be the centre of American colonial Quakerism, had built a hexagonal meeting-house in 1683, "a Six Square building of Forty Feet Square from Out to Out,"[2] with a maximum of floor space for its size, in which the Yearly Meeting of the whole valley of the Delaware could be accommodated, and still was in alternate years. But though this building was delightfully cool in summer, in winter it was difficult to heat, and the Quakers, whose first meetings had been held in private houses, were accustomed to be warm. They had no tradition of the chilly stone church which caused the New England Puritans to shiver and freeze in unheated meeting-houses, warming up in a different, unconsecrated building between services. So in 1696 Burlington Monthly Meeting decided on the building of a Winter House, "A Brick

[1] John Smith's MS. Memorandum Book.
[2] Burlington Monthly Meeting Records, Ye 5th of ye 12 mo., 1682.

House of Brick & half Thick . . . & ye Wall to be of Equal Height
with ye old Meeting house & the Roof to be covered with Cedar &
Joyn on the other Roof, the Breadth to be Equall with one of the Squares
of ye Old House & length 30 foot."[1]

The Woolmans, coming into the February Quarterly Meeting, found
the warm house black and gutted, and with the other Friends had to
cram into temporary quarters in a private house, probably Richard
Smith's mansion.

Then in the spring freshets, with the Delaware in flood and rough
to cross,

the ferry-boat going over to Bristol [from Burlington] with five
passengers & as many horses Sunk about the middle of the River,
four of the passengers were Saved by taking hold of the horses who
Swimming dragged them Ashore And Two or Three Persons went
off in a Canoe And took up the Other just as he was Sinking Nothing
to be Seen Above Water but the End of his Whip So that he was
Speechless but After some Applications he recovered. . . . He was
brother to Joseph White's wife who had gone over before and these
were going to Accompany her home.[2]

But difficulties of travel never discouraged anyone. Not only was
there an unusual mobility within the local Quaker community, but it
extended across the sea. Visitors from the London Yearly Meeting,
the parent body in England, came in a steady stream to visit their brothers
in the colonies ; and return visits were steadily paid by the colonists
to the meetings in the home country. These visits were not organized
by any central body or head. The concern to "travel in the ministry"
arose spontaneously in the individual heart, was long considered and
weighed in all its bearings, and was at last submitted to the local Monthly
Meeting. A committee of two or three "weighty Friends" was then
appointed to consider it. The committee would talk privately with the
concerned Friend, and report favourably or unfavourably to the next
gathering of Monthly Meeting. If the verdict was favourable a Travelling Minute or Certificate was furnished, recommending the visitor to
the "Christian care" of the Friends among whom he should come, and
guaranteeing that he was "in good standing" with his local meeting.
Most of such visitors travelled at their own expense, but the cost was kept

---

[1] Burlington Monthly Meeting Records, Third mo. 4th, 1696.
[2] MS. letter of John Smith, 2nd mo. 8, 1740, Memorandum Book.

to a minimum by local hospitality. And travelling funds were always available for Friends whose finances were unequal to the strain. It would be unreasonable to suppose that the compelling word of God could come only to the well-to-do.

When John Woolman was sixteen "John Fothergill (from Old England) Visited friends In these American Parts. It being the third time he had been here, on that account. He was An Antient Man, tall and Well Shap'd, Very Zealous against Sin and Iniquity. . . . He had a Very Loud Voice."[1]

But the loud voice rolled in vain over the keen and critical ear of young Woolman. It was his friend, John Smith, who was impressed. When Woolman was eighteen another Friend from Old England came, one John Hunt, who had uncommon qualities. "He was a Young man of Low Stature," says John Smith, "Somewhat Slow of Speech (In his testimony) Yet Safe and very Correct."[2] Young Smith and others came over to Ancocas Meeting[3] to hear him, and John Woolman also, with them, heard him at the Youth's Meeting at Burlington, at the Monthly Meeting there, and at the Half-year's Meeting and Yearly Meeting at Philadelphia, at which meeting young Smith considered that John Hunt "was Extraordinarily Opened to Speak of the things of God."[4] But the Englishman was too safe and correct for John Woolman. At any rate, he made no visible mark.

These strangers and others were sometimes entertained at the Woolman homestead, and brought with them something of the manners and point of view and news of the Europe of which they were a part. It was interesting to see them and be with them, and their mere accent was a curiosity. But if, in more 'worldly 'talk around the table, they passed from accounts of Quaker affairs or adventures in travel by land and sea to talk of the political situation in Europe as their newspapers reflected it, and mentioned the conduct of affairs in England, or the rumours of a possible fresh war with Spain, they spoke of things which were not remote from the lives of their American hearers in this far-distant place. Part of the danger of trading ships now was the risk of being held up on the high seas by Spanish men-o'-war and searched for contraband, and stories were spreading of English sailors being hauled off English ships

[1] MS. of John Smith's diary, 1736.
[2] Ibid., 1738.
[3] MS. of John Smith's Memorandum Book, 1738, 11th mo.
[4] Ibid., 1738.

and thrown, loaded with chains, into Spanish prisons. The visitors commented, with regret, that feeling in England was running high. It would not take much to set the spark. And presently the explosion came. In February 1739 John Smith noted in his diary, "This Month We had account from Old England that there War against Spain was Declared the 23rd of the Eighth Month" (October). And in April there was a public ceremony in Burlington of which all the outlying settlers received notice, and since it was held on a market-day most able-bodied people attended it. "Last Seventh day War against Spain was declared here in due form together with our Governor's Proclamation for Encouraging Volunteers to go in the Intended Expedition against some of the Spanish West Indies." In November Admiral Vernon, with colonial help, took Porto Bello.

No one seemed to inquire closely as to the real cause of the war.

When Israel Pemberton wrote to England to complain about some of the Governor's measures the Englishman, Richard Partridge, who acted as agent in London for the Pembertons and several other important Quaker merchants, wrote back, "The expedition against the Spanish West Indies you may know is a very popular Measure and therefore everything that would contribute to its advancement is greatly relished."[1]

If the English public had known the truth the war would not have been so popular. If Pemberton had known it he could have made great play with it. But those who knew what lay beneath the surface were interested parties. The bottom of the trouble was the slave-trade.

By the Peace of Utrecht, which had closed the wars that had troubled the colonies seven years before Woolman was born, England had been yielded by France the privilege of the *asiento*, which France had recently won from Spain. This word of ill omen, *asiento*, denoted the right of the monopoly of trade in African slaves with all the Spanish colonies in the West Indies. To quote the wording of the agreement,

Her Britannic Majesty [Queen Anne] did offer and undertake by persons whom she shall appoint, to bring into the West Indies of America belonging to his Catholic majesty, the King of Spain, in the space of thirty years, one hundred and forty four thousand negroes, at the rate of four thousand eight hundred in each of the said thirty years, paying, on four thousand of them, a duty of thirty-three and a third dollars[2] a head.

[1] Letter, II mo. 7th, 1740. Pemberton Papers.
[2] Spanish dollars.

The holders of the *asiento* might introduce as many more as they pleased above this minimum at the lower rate of duty of 16⅔ dollars a head. The term "West Indies" was understood to cover all the Spanish-American colonies along the Gulf of Mexico, the Atlantic, and the Pacific. As England already had the monopoly of trading in all kinds of merchandise with her own colonies, and Negroes by English law were merchandise, the possession of the *asiento* made England the exclusive slave-trader in the New World. Philip of Spain hastened to share by investment in the profits of the British South Sea Company, formed to exercise the monopoly which he no longer owned, and he was able to purchase one quarter of the common stock. This made him the largest slave-merchant in the world, and enabled him to turn contentedly back to his religious exercises, indifferent to the *asiento*.

But the English in England did not buy or use slaves. Indeed, the idea of slavery was so repugnant to the normal Englishman in his own land that a theory was prevalent that any slave who touched the soil of England became automatically free, and a special legal opinion had to be obtained (1729) that this theory did not apply to Negroes who should happen to visit England with their masters. The English slaver, therefore, was never under close observation by the British public. He sailed from home with a cargo of cheap trinkets, textiles, or out-of-date rifles as purchase money to use with native slave-catchers on the African coast, and spent a long time far from home plying to and fro between Africa and the West Indies. When he reappeared in English waters, to replenish his crew and refresh himself with his gains, he had not a slave on board. This is why the trade attracted so little public notice, and even the "widows and orphans" and other numerous investors in South Sea Company stock were unaware of the hideous sources of their income. All they ever saw was an empty ship.

But was it really empty, or only empty of slaves? That is what the Spaniards wanted to know. The *asiento* gave the English the right to trade with the Spanish colonies in slaves alone. All other traffic in merchandise and raw materials, going and coming, was the monopoly of Spain. And it did not take the Spanish colonists long to perceive that the English were using the *asiento* to cloak extensive smuggling. A considerable part of the population of Jamaica, for instance, lived on the profits of the contraband trade with Spanish ports.

The cheated Spaniards, almost ruined by the double loss, first of the *asiento* and then of their proper commerce, demanded the right to search the British ships. Since the English Government remained deaf to protest, Spanish men-o'-war sailed out to conduct forced search, and, catching smugglers red-handed, were not able to behave with patience and good sense, but sometimes took rude and resisting Englishmen prisoner and carried them off to Spain. One Captain Jenkins came back from such an enforced visit and told the British Parliament that the wicked Spaniards had cut off his ears. "I commended my soul to God and my cause to my country!" In an instant England was in a flame. The Inquisition became the devil of the piece, the matter took on a religious aspect, Jenkins was made a martyr, the South Sea Company whipped up the war, and the Prime Minister, desiring common sense and peace, was forced to declare war. At once the commerce of England and Spain was stopped, the *asiento* was suspended, and so was the smuggling. The South Sea Company intended the actual capture of the Spanish colonies, like the greedy dog who had substance and grasped at shadow also. For Spain was weak. Two centuries of the Inquisition had made the people low-spirited, and the population was thinned. Moreover, Spain had expelled three million Jews, and her total census was less than seven million souls. The Spanish navy had not nearly enough ships to meet the British navy on the sea.

It looked like a brief and simple business. But here France stepped in. The financiers who were surreptitiously directing the war party in England had bargained on Louis XV not paying attention to anything so far afield, and on Fleury, his Prime Minister, desiring peace. And they were not mistaken in their general premises. But Fleury none the less lent to Spain fifty of the French ships of the line. England's angry remonstrance met with a reasonable and placating plea. "It is our object not to make war on England but to induce it to consent to a peace. France, though it has no treaty with Spain, cannot consent that the Spanish colonies should fall into English hands"; and Fleury reiterated that France herself did not wish to "seize or annoy" one British ship, or "to take one foot of land possessed by England in any part of the world."

Governor Thomas, of Pennsylvania, inquiring not into any rights and wrongs, nor into anybody's good intentions, glanced at recent past experience in Queen Anne's War, and looked to his northern frontier.

So the helpless and tormented slaves of the middle passage revenged themselves upon their masters.

It was yet only a little cloud ; an excuse for adventure, to those who were not Quakers, and especially an excuse for the civilized piracy of privateering. A few privateers were prepared and launched at Burlington—not at the Smiths' wharf—taken to Philadelphia, and fitted for sea ; burden perhaps two hundred and thirty tons, to carry eighteen carriage and twenty-four swivel guns, with one hundred and fifty men, all gentleman sailors, putting in their share of the expense and proportionately sharing the spoil.

Meanwhile Thomas, no Quaker but a good prophet of trouble, raised eight companies of one hundred men each for expected trouble on the frontier with the French, and, being unable to get a grant of funds for military purposes from a Quaker-dominated assembly, paid for them by private subscription.

Woolman left no commentary on these daily matters, small or great. But his acute awareness of the passing scene is reflected in the meat that he got out of it. Like Thoreau when he took to the woods, he noted not so much circumstances as their causes and effects. It was the underlying stuff and texture of life itself which absorbed his thoughts. At the age of a young man in the graduating class at college he put himself to school in the very philosophy of living. Whitefield that year, fresh from England, called ten thousand people at a time in the squares of Philadelphia to confute "the false Doctrine" of "Justification by Works" while at the same time skilfully collecting "one Hundred & Ten Pounds Sterling for my poor Orphans,"[1] and the Commissary, chief representative of the Church of England, denying Whitefield a pulpit, preached savagely upon the contrary doctrine of the efficacy of Works, but took up meagre collections. The Smiths were stirred and interested by the controversy. Woolman listened and in solitude evolved his own theory of religion.

I . . . was early Convinced in my mind that true Relegion Consisted in An inward life wherein the heart does reverence God the Creator And learns to Exercise Equal Justice and Goodness not only towards All men but Also towards All God's Creatures. That as the mind was moved on An inward principle to love God as an invisible Incomprehensible being, on the Same principle it was moved to love

---

[1] The orphanage in Georgia.

him in All his outward Manifestations In the Visible Creation ; that as By his breath the flame of life was kindled in all Animal and Sensitive creatures, to say that we love God as unseen and at the same time to Exercise Cruelty toward the least creature moving by his life, or by life derived from him, was a contradiction in it Self.

This is Woolman's sufficient comment on the distant wars that were reaching out towards the colonies, and on injustices that he began to observe in the social order around him, and on the roughness towards the brute creation often taken for granted in a farming and hunting community.   And as for the religious arguments which began to arouse all their Old World prejudice and heat, he displays his close examination of them and his conclusion concerning them in a brief and single sentence.   "I found no narrowness respecting any Sects as believing Sinseer and uprighthearted people in Every Society who truly loved God were Accepted of him."

But besides these large thoughts and, as he says, "openings of truth," his mind was also engaged by practical thoughts concerning his own future.   However much he might for a time feel it necessary to live retired, he had nothing of the monastic temperament.   An uneasy ambition stirred within him, and an increasing restlessness to leave home, to stand on his own feet, and make his own life.   In these thoughts his sister Elizabeth was his confidante.

The winter of 1740–41 was extraordinarily severe.   The Delaware "was frozen over the 15th December, on the 16th John Hall came over on it & So it has Continued passable" until the middle of March, for "yesterday a man Came over alone on it."   An ox was roasted whole on the ice opposite Philadelphia, and market was regularly held there all winter, midway between the shores.

"Poor country people," wrote John Smith to his cousin Jemmy Pemberton,[1]

are almost Continually Complaining for want of Hay, Corn, meat etc. and abundance of their horses, Cattle, hogs & Sheep die for want. One Man hath Lost 5 or 6 Cattle above 20 sheep & near 40 hogs Many are forced to give them Wheat to keep them alive, & it is well for them that Can get it for themselves to Eat for it and almost Everything Else but frost & Snow is very Scarce up in the Country.

[1] John Smith's MS. Memorandum Book.

And a month later, on April 14, he noted in his diary¹ that "the Trees are but very little put out and there is Scarce Grass Enough to keep Creatures alive" and "it is Supposed the Peach Trees are mostly Killed with the nipping frosts."

Although there is no hint in John Woolman's memories that the Woolman household ever suffered want, the rigour of this winter was no doubt one of the influences which clinched the decision that had long been forming within him to take up some other career than farming. "I had for Some time found my mind less given to husbandry than heretofore, having often in View Some other way of living."² His serious illness had left its mark. The hard labour to which he had been bred fatigued him, and "though I was middling healthy," he explains,

yet my nature was not fitted to endure so much as many others.

"And being now upward of Twenty years old A man in much business Shopkeeping and Baking Asked me if I would hire with him to keep Books and tend Shop. I told my Father of the offer And after Some days deliberation it was agreed for me to Go.³

It is typical of the sort of thing that Woolman does not mention that this, his first and only employer, never gets a name. He is always "the man" or "my master." How long they had been acquainted, where they met, what gave "the man" the idea that Samuel Woolman's eldest son was looking for a job, are not on record. If Samuel Woolman had intended to breed his son to trade he would have bound him apprentice to some reputable shopkeeper—perhaps in Philadelphia or Burlington—where he would have served for seven years at least, learning the business, most of the time without pay. But thirteen to twenty were the apprentice years, and they were now past. John Woolman had served his apprenticeship on the farm. Yet now he proposed to turn to trade, and had an employer ready to take him. The immediate opportunity was undeniable ; and farming was hard hit by the bad winter, and Samuel Woolman had many sons.

So with goodwill, candid discussion, final approval, and businesslike clearness on all points, John Woolman left home for his new career. And though he did not leave home far, he left completely. From the

---

¹ John Smith's MS. diary, 2nd mo. 14th, 1741 (O. S.).
² Whittier ed., p. 158.   Also MS. No. 1.
³ MS. No. 1.

beginning to the end of his life his decisions, never impulsive, were always clear-cut.

The man who Employed me furnished a Shop in Mountholly About five miles from my Father's house And Six from his own. There I lived by my Self And tended his Shop. . . . And as I had now left My Father's house outwardly, I found My Heavenly Father to be mercifull to me more than I Can Express.

IX

MOUNT HOLLY

PADDLING upstream from John Woolman's old home, one came at once to the Forks, where two streams of equal size, from widely separated sources, ran winding down to join in the Rancocas. The Indians called these the North Branch and the South Branch of the Rancocas, and on the narrowed point of land where they came together the Turtle Clan of the Lenape had established a village, long, long ago. John Woolman as a boy at play and work on his father's plantation could see the Indians plainly, moving about their quiet business. Steering one's canoe to the left of the Indian village and following up the winding waterway on the North Branch, never seeing more than a few yards ahead between the deepening banks, turning and turning with a never-failing surprise into fresh pictures on the leafy stream, one came at length to the wharf of the Mount Holly settlement. The mysterious ocean pulse, felt twice a day up the Delaware as far as Burlington, spread sideways up the creeks, in spite of all the curves of the soft soil. And this inland village of Mount Holly stood at the very head of tide-water. Twice a day, conveyed by the very power of the ocean itself, its blunt, small scows, bateaux, and flats took produce from the farms and forest, downstream to Philadelphia on the ebb ; and twice a day the faithful ocean carried them back upstream on the flood, laden with merchandise.

Navigation of these sturdy little boats on the creek was quite a trick, since round any corner one might encounter a batch of timber afloat.

Gaskill's dam, even, which made a dead end for boats at Mount Holly, had a raft gate in it for letting through lumber from higher up the stream.

As early as 1693 an Act had been passed by the West Jersey Assembly dividing each county of New Jersey into townships. John Woolman had been born in the scattered settlement of Rancocas in Northampton Township, and he had now moved into a clustered settlement in the same township. Mount Holly was already beginning to call itself a town. If Burlington could be a city with but one hundred and seventy houses, surely Mount Holly could be a town with almost a hundred. Even the great city of Philadelphia, eighteen miles off, was of such dimensions that Benjamin Franklin, when Woolman was three years old, could slip past it by night on a boat in the black dark and never notice it was there, and have to come back and look for it by daylight.

Mount Holly had first attracted settlers because of the little hill, which made an easy landmark, rising up suddenly and conspicuously from the plain among the curls of the Rancocas, and visible for miles in all directions, one of the highest points of land in all South Jersey. But a piece of luck had befallen it. A Quaker settler named Edward Gaskill had come and built a dam, dug a mill-race, and started a sawmill there in the year of Woolman's birth, the first sawmill in the neighbourhood. And once Gaskill had got his power and saw the planters coming to his mill to get their timber cut into logs or into planks for building, his enterprise perceived another need, and another use for his water-power, and with four partners he established a grist-mill. This was the regular pattern of the growth of all the Delaware Valley towns—first the sawmill, then the grist-mill. It was an advantage to settlers to live within close reach of such conveniences. And in that same year Mount Holly added another. A young man by the name of Josiah White—grandson of Christopher, the pioneer—came from Salem with brains and capital and, seeing a thriving community and well-harnessed water-power, bought the land called Gaskill's Neck, a hundred acres between the mill-race and the creek, arranged to dig a raceway connected with Gaskill's mill-race, and built a fulling mill which remained in active operation for a hundred years.

These advantages were much, but there was one more, so remarkable that in perspective it seems surprising that Mount Holly did not fulfil the promise it then had of becoming a hive of modern industry. The small hill on the south side of the creek, about a mile from the holly mound to the north, was found to contain iron, and Woolman's uncle, John Burr, with two partners, established the ironworks in the same year of Josiah White's arrival, the year in which Woolman was ten.

John Woolman and his brothers and sister came sometimes and stared at the great water-wheel that turned the mill, revolving in even rhythm, driven by "a start-wheel under an eight-foot head of water in the pond of water raised by the dam." And did they manage, any of them, to escape from home—under pretext perhaps of visiting Uncle Burr's new building in the making—and see the great witch trial which excited the countryside in the bright fall weather ?

The *Pennsylvania Gazette* of the week October 15–22, 1730, carried a racy article about it from its Burlington correspondent. "Saturday last at Mount Holly, about 8 Miles from this Place, near 300 People were gathered together to see an Experiment or two tried on some Persons accused of Witchcraft." One man and one woman were charged specifically with

> making their Neighbors Sheep dance in an uncommon Manner and with causing Hogs to speak & sing Psalms etc to the great Terror & Amazement of the King's good & peaceable Subjects in this Province & the Accusers being very positive that if the Accused were weighed in Scales against a Bible, the Bible would prove too heavy for them ; or if they were bound & put into the River they would swim.

The accused persons had the common sense to volunteer to undergo the trials if the most violent of their accusers would do so with them, and the challenge being accepted made a great day for Mount Holly. Interested spectators came to see it not only from the surrounding countryside but even from Burlington itself.

"The Parties being met & the People got together," a "Committee of Men & a Committee of Women" were appointed to search the witches "to see if they had anything of Weight about them, particularly Pins." A large pair of scales had been fixed on a gallows erected for that purpose opposite the Justice's House so that his wife and other ladies might see everything conveniently. Then "a huge great Bible belonging to the Justice of the Peace being provided . . . a grave tall man came out of the house bearing the Bible," and

> the Wizard was put first in the Scale & over him was read a Chapter out of the Books of Moses, & then the Bible was put in the other

Scale (which being kept down before) was immediately let go ;
but to the great surprise of the Spectators, Flesh & Bones came down
plump . . . their Lumps of Mortality severally were too heavy for
Moses & all the Prophets & Apostles.

Next, for the trial by water, they were taken in procession to the
mill-pond, stripped (the women allowed their shifts), bound hand and
foot,

> and severally placed in the Water lengthways from the side of a
> Barge or Flat . . . a rope about the Middle of each which was held
> by some in the Flat. The Accused Man being thin & spare with
> some difficulty began to sink at last, but the rest every one of them
> swam very light upon the Water. The Woman Accuser . . .
> declared that she believed the Accused had bewitched her to make
> her so light. . . . The accused Man, being surprised at his own
> Swimming, was not so confident of his Innocence as before but said,
> If I am a Witch it is more than I know.

The indeterminate result was universally satisfactory (except to the
Woman Accuser), and the day's entertainment proved the end of witch-
hunting in those parts. Bear-hunting was more to their taste ; and in
Woolman's twelfth year the *Gazette* reported that :

> there has lately been killed near Mount Holly, in the Jersies, the
> largest Bear that has been known in these Parts ; his Forehead measured
> two Spans wide, his Leg just above the Foot as big as could be grasped
> with both Hands after the Skin was off, & tho' exceeding lean he
> weigh'd upwards of 300 weight. There has been another of the same
> gigantic size seen about the same place.

To move into this stirring community was a tremendous change after
the farm. The first path through the woods to the mills had become a
beaten track, then a road, and was soon to become Mill Street, the main
street of a town which could also boast of Pine Street, White Street,
the Philadelphia Road, Springfield Road, Wood Lane, and Race Street.
The lanes and roads, which began to multiply for human convenience,
leading directly from place to place, crossed the wayward creek by
necessary bridges so many times that some practical citizens made an
abortive effort to rechristen their village "Bridgetown," but the name
refused to stick, in spite of charters and official documents ; the holly
hill to the north, all of one hundred and eighty-five feet above tide level,
was still noticed by the stranger long before the bridges, and Mount
Holly the town began and ended.

To open up a shop in such a promising settlement was not a bad business opportunity for a young man. And shopkeeping was by no means looked down upon. Three years after Woolman began to tend shop in Mount Holly, John Smith began his career in a similar way. "I opened a dry Good Store at Philadelphia of 10th mo : 1743. Took Lodgings at Coz Wm Callender's."[1] It was an opportunity which could rapidly lead to wealth if a man had the right gifts for it, as John Smith demonstrated and Woolman learned.

John Woolman's employer's shop was one of the best business sites in the town.[2] It was in Mill Street, close to the Three Tuns Tavern, and a few yards from the wide central market-place where stood the stocks and whipping-post, and where the Market-house was building. Come out of his door and turn to the left, cross one of the bridges, and there were Josiah White's house and fulling mill, familiar to Woolman from childhood. Or go on a little farther, cross a bridge over the mill-race, and presently another one across the creek, and you were at the foot of Ironside Hill, by Uncle Burr's ironworks, with the clang of the smithies, the glow of the smelting furnaces, and all the grime and sweat of honest labour in the metal which, after long use of wooden ploughs and wooden harrows, was at last coming into its own.

The Black Horse Tavern stood on the corner of the market-place, with its gable end towards the street, and a sign of King George in a scarlet uniform on a black horse. (It began as George I, went on as George II, finished up as George III, and when that gentleman fell into disrepute—beyond our story's limit—was transmogrified into George Washington.) The Cross Keys Tavern, oldest and most dignified of all, there in place for travellers in the Burlington Road before there was a market-place or a market or a town, was a few yards back from the upstart Black Horse. But three inns were none too many for entertainment and sociability of an evening, or for the transaction of business on market-day, or for the refreshment and housing of passing travellers. Though perhaps they were too many for sobriety and good order.

Rum was the favourite drink, and was thought of as a cheering and warming beverage—in moderation. Woolman saw no harm in it. His friends the Smiths were the great importers of it in those parts ; and he stocked it in his shop for those who wished to buy it for home

---

[1] John Smith's diary (MS.).
[2] *I.e.*, assuming, as is most probable, that it was the one Woolman later purchased.

consumption. This information we obtain from Woolman himself, and it refers to the time when he was master of his own shop.[1]

What Woolman sold for his master during the few years of his clerk-ship is never exactly described. But since he refers to "the man" in one place as a baker[2] and in another as a tailor,[3] it is reasonable to suppose that the shop retailed foodstuffs and general groceries and also materials for clothes in the way of homespun cloth, buttons, thread, and hats. But it was not the kind of general country store where everything could be bought, from nails to garden seeds. Life in Mount Holly was already too specialized for that; and a number of other shops competed for attention in Mill Street. Harness-maker, wheelwright, chair manu-facturer, shoemaker, tailor.

The planters' wives and daughters riding into market—Woolman's mother and sisters among them—with a big pannier either side the saddle in which to carry back their goods, had choice of places to buy, could pick and choose; and could lay orders to have special goods brought up from Philadelphia by the regular pack-horse caravan or by water.

The question is irresistible why, if Woolman was going into business, he did not start with some of the obvious openings available to him that might have led to immediate advancement and perhaps final partnership. With his Uncle Burr, for instance, in the major business of the neigh-bourhood, the prosperous ironworks? Or with his friend, Josiah White, in the dyeing and fulling business? Or with the Smiths, in their enter-prises at Burlington and Philadelphia? Why pick up with this unrelated man, not even named, in general merchandise connected with baking and tailoring, and offering only such a future as one could make for oneself from scratch? At the age of twenty, quite green to the ways of business, Woolman had not yet formulated the theories which might have made him an awkward partner in later years to capitalistic friends and relatives. But whatever the reason for his choice, Woolman achieved from the first what perhaps he knew he most wanted—complete inde-pendence. Unbiased by bonds of kinship or friendship, he was free to find out for himself what the process of buying and selling for profit involved; and for the first few difficult months of initiation he was even left alone to find it out.

The amount of responsibility placed upon a new employee itself

<hr>

[1] Whittier ed., p. 206.   [2] Ibid., p. 49.   [3] Ibid., p. 57.

throws light upon what were some of Woolman's qualifications for the job. The "man" was not looking for an ordinary clerk, still less for an apprentice. He needed an assistant who would be able to take complete charge of his new shop at Mount Holly until he himself was ready to move there with his family. The assistant must be an able accountant, his honesty must be above reproach, and he must combine pleasing manners with a capacity to keep himself out of mischief, even when left entirely on his own, next door to a tavern. John Woolman had learned accounts from his father and his father's sister. Aunt Hannah had been treasurer of the Burlington Women's Monthly Meeting before she went away to live in Philadelphia. And his manners spoke for themselves. The position appealed to Woolman, perhaps partly because of the very element of complete responsibility and trust—and he held it to the end of its term, gaining what he most cared to have from that particular man and his family—their respect.

It was an exposed situation for a young man, widely known for his sociable characteristics and gaiety of temper, whose sobriety was comparatively new. A shopkeeper is accessible to all the world. He cannot withdraw, lock a door, deny his company. Anyone may come and lean upon his counter and take up his time. And Woolman's first difficulties were with his old companions. The friends whom he had quitted without telling them why did not know that he had condemned his association with them as reverse to true friendship. They missed him, and wanted him back. Woolman's company, by all kinds of people, was always found "savory."

"Shortly after my Settlement here," says Woolman,

I was visited by Several Young People of My former Acquaintance who knew not but Vanities would be as agreeable to me now as Ever ; At these times I looked to the Lord for help, for I felt my Self verry weak. After A While my former Acquaintance gave over Expecting me as one of their Company.

The details of their efforts and their repulse remain dim, but the relationship suggests, in fainter colours, that between Prince Hal and his forsworn companions. And if they were hurt, and some of them hurt uncommonly —as their repeated attempts to win him back seem to suggest—he hurt himself as much, and turned passionately to the love of God "to draw me from many pollutions And to be A constant Succor to me through A Sea of Conflicts with which none on Earth were fully Acquainted.

"By Day I was much Among people. . . . But in the Evening I was mostly Alone."

There were many to call in and pass the time of day with the new-comer—relatives, friends, and strangers ; there was merchandise to arrange, there were books to organize ; market twice a week, Wednes-days and Saturdays, with a large influx of visitors. It was interesting and absorbing, and Woolman found himself responding to the sturdy ebb and flow of the human life around him.

But the nights were lonely. The thirteenth child, little Eber, had just been born when Woolman left his home ; little Abraham was three, and Rachel five ; Jonah was seven, and Esther ten. The house bubbled and boiled with children. Uriah at twelve, and Hannah fourteen, though still at school, aspired to share in the responsibilities of the older ones, and regarded the brothers and sisters below them as very, very young ; while Asher and Abner considered themselves already men. There they all were, so well and intimately known to him each one, carrying on their lives without him. And when the business of the day was over, and the shutters closed, when the shadows drew in from the forest, and early sleep folded down upon the hamlet, John Woolman sat long by his book, snuffing and resnuffing the candle, trying to feel the sweetness of the silence and not its vacancy. ". . . The Spirit of Supplycation was often upon me And I Called upon the name of the Lord, the Everlasting God."

X

GHOSTS AND INNKEEPERS

Woolman's first companions in the empty house were a bunch of roughnecks, and it was in connexion with them that he experienced for the first and last time the sensation of physical fear.

In a few months after I had been here my Master bought Several Scotch men Servants from on board A Vessel And brought them to Mount Holly to Sell, having Sold Several the rest were left with me one of which was taken Sick and died.

The latter part of his Sickness being Delirious he used to Curse and Swear most Sorrowfully.

After he was buried I was left to Sleep alone the Next night in the Same Chamber where he died.

I perceived In me A timerous disposition I knew however I had not Injured the man, but had taken Care of him in his Sickness According to my Capacity, And I was not free on that Account to ask any one to Sleep with me.

Woolman's master was acting as middleman between sea captains and employers, and making his profit off the transaction just as off a bale of molasses purchased at the wharves of Philadelphia and retailed in the Mount Holly market. The bound or indentured servant was an emigrant who sold his time and labour for four years in return for passage.[1]

[1] Appendix III.

75

If he ran away before his time was up he could be apprehended and whipped at the public whipping-post. The newspapers were always full of advertisements for runaway servants.

Two years before John Woolman moved to Mount Holly his Uncle Burr had advertised in the *Pennsylvania Gazette* : [1]

> RUN AWAY on the 12th inst from Mount Holly Iron Works in Burlington County, a Servant Man named Cornelius Kelly, about 21 Years of Age, tall & slim, thin face, short brown Hair. . . . Had on when he went away a Felt Hat, a new brownish colored Coat much too big for him. . . .

But no Quaker in good standing would deliver his servant to the whipping-post ; and Woolman was not stirred to protest about the bound servant's lot as such. He discerned it as a part of a larger whole, a disagreeable fruit of a root which he had not yet dug down to. His relations with the rough Scots were those of a kind young master to servants temporarily under his care. Yet the ruffian, dead, had terrors.

To the Indians, the forest was peopled with spirits. And solitary living, among unbroken nature, promoted a sense of uncanny Presence, often—after a criminal death—filled with horrid threat.

All children knew the large black walnut in Burlington called the Pirate's Tree, beneath which the terrible Blackbeard had buried a hoard of treasure, and set a ghost to guard it. When the Woolmans and their companions were gathered into Burlington by their elders for Monthly Meeting or on market-day, and were released for an hour to play together, they would approach this spot with a delicious terror. Ruffling the golden leaves in autumn, they would imagine the gold beneath the ground, and that its grisly guardian stirred in his sleep and lifted, perhaps, a wary head at their disturbance. Protected by company and the sunshine, they hallooed at him, and fled helter-skelter, as if blown away themselves with the whirling leaves. And even grown-up people avoided the spot after twilight had deepened the tree's shadow. All knew the tale of the night—three years before John Woolman was born—when Blackbeard stood in the circle with his men above a fresh-dug pit and called for and obtained a volunteer and shot him neatly through the head with a "magic bullet" that left no mark, and sunk him down upright in the pit with his feet on the treasure chest to stand sentinel until Blackbeard came again or until Doomsday.

[1] August 17–24, 1738.

Doomsday it would have to be, since Blackbeard not long after met with his deserts and was killed in battle on board his vessel. His ferocious madman's head, with his long black beard tended like a woman's hair, combed and beribboned, was set up on the bows to grin its last defiance at the breaking waves, while the King's flag replaced the black flag of the pirates at the masthead, and Cape Fear in North Carolina, the winter settlement and stronghold of the pirates, ceased to deserve its name.

In Burlington the restless sentinel on many a stormy midnight walked in Wood Street, followed at the heels by a Black Dog, the well-known "familiar demon" of the spirits of the lost.

So Woolman endured a terror common to many, under circumstances peculiarly calculated to provoke it. But he disdained the weakness of seeking any aid but that of God alone, while the wind sighed under the door, and hollow blasphemies seemed to echo down the chimney.

Meanwhile Woolman found the daily conduct of business not irksome but fascinating. He rapidly learned the ropes. And his friendly charm—which, with his best efforts to make friends more cautiously, he could not suppress—attracted customers for his master as well as new and worthier friends for himself. If anyone had suspected that he had one dark ghost-ridden night written down that he had perceived a "timerousness," they would have experienced a fellow-feeling. There was nothing timid about the easy-moving young man, grave, punctilious, but at home with life, as his flashes of gaiety, his spontaneous warmth, bore witness. There was nothing stiff, nothing repressed. That passion for the service of God that had taken possession of his inward life had nothing formalistic, creedal, ritual, ascetic, self-conscious about it. On the contrary, it was a source from which, he noted in his Journal, "springs a lively operative desire for the good of others."

He did not find, like Saint Francis, that he had to build a church. He had to build a business, and to become an integral part of a town. This is the religious spirit translated direct into the American vernacular. A salesman, a merchant, a book-keeper, a real-estate conveyancer, an amateur lawyer, a citizen, he buys and sells, he loses and makes profit ; so how can he come clear with the clarity of those who of old forsook the ways of normal living in order to demonstrate the religious life ? If he can do so he is putting something quite new into the world.

John Woolman was a layman to the bone. He had never any desire or call to be a missionary, like Brainerd or Whitefield, or a semi-professional preacher, like some "publick Friends." He liked being in the world and of the world. From the beginning of his business life he planned to save money against some day getting married. He valued financial independence, and had no quarrel with the profit which brought it. And he so much enjoyed the company of his fellows that even, he said, "if I go to a religious meeting it puts me on thinking whether I go in sincerity . . . or partly from a sensible delight which my animal spirits feel in the company of other people."[1]

But he had that peculiarity of genius, the disconcerting faculty of seeing things fresh. He might have fallen from Mars, so clear and unbiased was the eye that he turned on the community, and so surprising —to the community—the conclusions that he drew. Use and wont, the basis of common law, the sacred fetish of the conservative Anglo-Saxon, had no weight with him. He weighed everything in private scales geared somehow to the universal measure of truth and right.

But he was young and humble-minded, and might easily make mistakes. He reined in his action. He waited for orders, confident, if he could be still enough to hear it, that he would receive the direction of an inward Guide.

The seasons made their full march, and Woolman, like Joseph in the house of Potiphar, paid close attention to the outward affairs of his master, and they prospered. The employer and his family had now moved to Mount Holly, and Woolman had become a boarder in their home, always a little aloof, never quite intimate, "respected in his master's family."

But he was not only an employee, he was a citizen. Ever since he had sloughed off the shell of his adolescence he had felt himself irrevocably joined with other people in the mutual effort to live well.

When he saw something amiss he was unable to free himself of responsibility about it. He could not say to himself that it was not his business. If not his, whose ? Why, everybody's. But "everybody" was the sum of individual persons ; and what person can I set to work but myself ? Or who can I make volunteer for obedience but me ?

The first thing that struck him unpleasantly about the town life was the rowdiness of the taverns ; above all, at Christmas-time. The season celebrated by the non-Quaker community as the anniversary of the founder of the Christian religion was a season, in Mount Holly, of wild orgy. Respectable fathers of families reeled out into the snow, dead drunk, devoid of dignity or sense ; young men, shouting and gibbering beside themselves, roared obscenities under the stars, and the Indians from the forest came in, on their snow-shoes, envious and scornful, to see the white men ruined by their own strong liquor, and to try to cadge some for themselves.

The Quakers, like the New England Puritans, did not observe Christmas ; but they did not escape altogether the getting drunk. It was hard for some to resist the conviviality of an inn where they had gone, perhaps, merely to transact business. And it was a sad and humiliating sight—one to give gooseflesh to a sensitive observer—to see a respectable Friend, his wife and sons present, with greying hairs concealed under his wig, rise at the close of meeting on Firstday and, advancing with heavy, unwilling feet to the front of the meeting-house, turn to face the silent rows of his neighbours and relations, and read aloud the required paper of condemnation.

"Friends," muttered the gruff, faltering voice, "I am made by the Convictions of God & the guilt of my own conscience to Confess my wicked act of Drunkeness before God & this Meeting, It being an act detestable In The Sight of God & all good men. Therefore I have given great occasion to The enimies To speak of The way of Truth by my not Taking heed To walk accordingly as The same Blessed Truth directs." That was all that was needed, but more sometimes came, and there was a wistfulness in its appeal. "Friends I have something more Lyes upon me (if I may be worthy) to advise all people but especially friends not To goe to a publick place of meeting without a necessity of honest & Lawfull business require them Least having none such business That great enemy of mans Soul The Devil finds Them Some to doe for him as I by Sad experience can tell."

The Monthly Meetings in New Jersey, Pennsylvania, North Carolina, Baltimore, had frequently to minute the discipline of Friends who erred in this regard.

But this painful procedure did not seem to John Woolman to go to the root of the matter. He had not lived so near a tavern all this time for nothing, and it occurred to him that the trouble could be better prevented by being dealt with nearer the source, at the tavern itself.

This was a civic duty, but who would undertake it ? Nobody seemed to feel that it lay under his own particular jurisdiction. What, for instance, ought to be done, and how ? The tavern-keepers, if they were not Quakers, could not be reached by Quaker discipline. And they were breaking no 'law.'

So John Woolman took up his task of full citizenship in a democracy.

At one house in particular there was uncommon Reveling . . . people both from the Country and Dwellers in the Town . . . Spent their time in drinking and vain Sports tending to deprave & corrupt one another. . . . That it looked like A duty laid upon me to go And Speak to the master of that house About it. I considered I was young, And that Several Elderly friends in town had oppertunity to See these things, And tho I feign would have been Excused yet could not feel my mind clear. My Exercise was heavey And I looked at the Duty of A watchman as the Almighty opened it to Ezekiel . . . .

Then after Some deliberation I went to the Said publick house, And Seeing the man of the house Amongst other people I told him I wanted to Speak with him, so we went ASide And there In the Fear of the Lord I Expressed to him the matter that lay Upon me ; which he appeared to take kindly And Shewed Afterward more reSpect to me than Aforetime.

In A few years after he died middle aged And I often thought that had I neglected my duty in that case, it would have Given me Great remorse. And I was Humbly thankfull to my Gracious Father that by his Aid I had Discharged what he lay'd upon me.

This was Woolman's first adventure in public-spirited action, and his way of recording it shows that he regarded himself as a man under training. His task was to learn the practice of the will of God, as a soldier has to learn to drill, or a well-mettled horse to obey both spur and bridle. He obeyed what he believed to be that Will, and he had precedent for the belief and the obedience. Ezekiel, for instance ; and, nearer at hand, George Fox and William Penn, Mary Fisher, the Boston martyrs, and probably Mr Whitefield and Mr Wesley, and the Catholic mystics of Port Royal.

But the method of obeying was peculiarly Woolman's own, and displays even in this very first public effort the strongly individual pattern of his behaviour. He possessed what the religious fervour of the prophet—especially when indulging in criticism—so seldom does possess, and that is tact. The records of the early Quakers show their zest in denunciation. They were tremendous people for public admonition. King or Cromwell, judge on the bench or misbehaving neighbour, they would "deal with them faithfully" and never spare their feelings. Almost any one of them that we can think of would have marched into that tavern and with blazing eye and arresting finger have made a grand scene on a splendidly Old Testament scale. Such a performance requires a certain self-intoxication, and this filled the performer with impervious rectitude. He never thought how uncomfortable it would be for the object of rebuke. Indeed, like the schoolmaster who flogged a pupil, to create a salutary discomfort was part of his business.

But John Woolman's greatest concern, next to his desire to see a wrong thing righted, was to preserve the feelings of the tavern-keeper from hurt. And this sheds a very strong light upon Woolman's inner self. Only a proud spirit knows the smart of wounded pride ; and only the man to whom self-respect is as necessary as the breath of life knows how not to hurt the self-respect of others. Woolman, a stripling of twenty-one, approaching a man twice his age with a remonstrance in the cause of public welfare and decorum which in any other mouth would have sounded like a reprimand, succeeded in conducting the affair with delicacy and diplomacy. How did he manage it ? Not only did it go off well at the time, but it left no aftermath of embarrassment or ill-feeling. The tavern-keeper liked him the better for it, not the worse.

Part of his success was due to the grace of manner which he had acquired "in the world" ; ease, both possessed and conveyed, is the best gift of a trained behaviour ; but beneath that outward grace he carried a sensitiveness to the other's point of view and a humility as to himself which disarmed anger and prevented pique. He assumed the other man's good will and good intention. Do we not all want to do right ? "I feel addressed and probed," said Thoreau, "even to the remote parts of my being when one nobly shows, even in trivial things, an implicit faith in me. . . . A threat or a curse may be forgotten, but this mild trust translates me."[1]

When the tavern-keeper returned to his customers in the pleasant main room of the inn, where a fire six feet wide roared up the great chimney and illuminated the sanded floor, the dark low rafters, the high-backed settles, and provoked gleaming reflections from wooden mugs and pewter tankards, his outlook upon it all was not the same.

[1] *Familiar Letters of Thoreau*, Walden ed., p. 56.

F

He felt more of the dignity of the host and less of the irresponsibility of the tradesman. He glanced at the trapper who was adjusting his deerskin coat snugly for return to his cold business in the frozen woods, and at the smith who was draining a leisurely tankard of hot cider to brace him for the long hours at the forge, and at the basket-maker from a few doors down whose trade was slack and who was making an excuse to warm his chilblained fingers at a good fire ; and he saw them not as customers to whom he must sell the utmost, but as fellow townsmen and neighbours, whose welfare was partly in his keeping when they came into his house. He was flattered at the thought of his influence in the community. And he looked back at the recent conversation with a feeling near to pleasure. Seldom had he been treated with such respect, and the real worth of his character so recognized.

The interview remained private between the two men. And the change that took place in the regulation of that tavern seemed as fortuitous as a change in the weather. No one traced it to the influence of their newest citizen.

XI

THE BILL OF SALE

AND now a crisis stole up unperceived which marked John Woolman's life for ever.

One of the qualifications which made Woolman valuable to his employer was the ability to perform legal business. Samuel Woolman had formed the practice, and trained his eldest son in it, of drawing up wills, conveying property, acting as trustee, and other jobs undertaken usually by an attorney. Lawyers were scarce, and business had to be done. Samuel Woolman had a number of clients, and John Woolman later increased this form of practice to such an extent that it seems as if he could easily have adopted the legal profession. A few years articled to the Honourable Richard Smith or another full-fledged lawyer would have been sufficient, and would have been a more natural transition from his accustomed activities and a more obvious use of his talents than the vocation which he finally chose. But it was in connexion with his amateur law business that the Unseen Forces in which he believed aroused his attention on the matter which later generations were to regard as his true lifework.

In Mount Holly a number of families owned Negro slaves, as did the Smiths, in Burlington, the Pembertons, Logans, Drinkers, and many other of Woolman's acquaintance, as well as his Grandfather Henry Burr. Their black African faces were familiar in the streets as they went about the tasks and errands, well fed and cleanly kept, neither as

harshly treated nor as hard-worked in many instances as the redemptioners, in whom a close-fisted employer had no property interest.

The man who employed Woolman kept a Negro slave in the house,
and her service was taken as a matter of course by every one, Woolman
included. She was an inconspicuous part of the household machinery,
and if he noticed her now and then at her tasks she was doing on the
whole no other things than those which he had been used to seeing his
mother and sister do. Yet Woolman had regarded her entirely as a human
being, and had not been roused to concern about her situation only
because she was feeling none herself. But when suddenly, one bright
morning, this human being was brought without warning into the shop
as a dehumanized object of merchandise—her purchaser there waiting to
take her away—she having no more to say about it than if she were a
horse or a cat or a bale of goods—that was something else. It was a
horribly illuminating shock.

The crisis was on Woolman before he was aware of it. His employer's
request to make out a bill of sale was honestly casual. Woolman had
only an instinct, an inward recoil, not a point of view to present. He
sat mending his pen, frowning, flushed, disturbed, weighing his duty to
his employer against the sudden conviction of wrong. No one present
but himself felt anything disturbing. The seller, the buyer, the apathetic
slave—none saw the transaction as hideous, abnormal. They patiently
waited while the clever young man, whose ability to draw up and
execute a bill of sale was necessary to the business, took pains in mending
his pen. The buyer was a Quaker in good standing, and Woolman
never acted on impulse. So he tells in detail and with regret :

Within a year after my coming to Mountholly my Master having
A Negro Sold her And told me to write A bill of Sale. the thoughts
of writing an Instrument of Slavery for one of my fellow cretures
Gave me trouble, and I was Distressed in my mind About it. At
length I considered that I was hired by the year, it was my Master bid
me do it, And that it was an Elderly man, A member of our Society,
who bought her, So I wrote the bill of Sale. But at the Executing of
it I was depressed in my mind and Said before my Master And the
friend that I believed Slave-keeping to be a practise Inconsistant with
the Christian Religion ; Saying So Abated my unesiness ; yet as
often as I reflected Seriously upon it, I thought I Should have been
clearer if leaving all Consequences, I had Craved to be Excused from
it, as a thing against my Conscience ; for Such it was.

Woolman now had a point of view and was ready to act on it. He was not to be caught out the same way twice. As far as his personal relations with slavery were concerned, he had made up his mind.

Some time after A young man of our Society Spoke to me to write an Instriment of Slavery, he having lately taken A negro into his house. . . . I told him I was not Easie to write it, for tho many people kept Slaves in our Society as well as others, & Seemed Easie in it, I however Could not Se it to be right And craved to be Excused from it. I Spoke to him in Goodwill, And he told me that keeping Slaves was not clearly Agreeable to his mind, but that the Slave was a Gift to his wife from Some of her friends, and So we parted.

And that, for the time being, was all the consequence of the affair.
It is characteristic of the concreteness of mind which made Woolman a good man of business that it was always encounter with a fact which stimulated him to a theory of conduct. He did not begin with an abstraction and work out a theory ready-made to fit all cases. He put the fact under the clear lens of his attention, and his movement was unhurried. Before he took another step he made sure of his ground. It was five years before Woolman had fully crystallized his opinion about slavery ; and more than ten years before he gave public expression to it and began the definite and vigorous attack on the whole slave system which only ended with his death. But his deliberateness was self-justifying. Before he came out to do battle he had perfected his technique, and he had seen the evil in its full size. He wasted no time in cutting off the heads of the hydra. He went straight for its heart. Meanwhile he did not go out of his way to meet problems that were not presented to him. He had his hands full dealing with those that met him where he was. And the first and most urgent of these was in connexion with his own career, his choice of occupation for life.
Woolman's talent for business was now evident, his charm had added to itself unmistakable strength and steadiness, and many tempting offers began to be made to him. What they were exactly can only be surmised by what we know were available ; but whatever they were—the legal profession, the iron manufactory, the importing business, and trading in a big way—John Woolman looked them over, grave and detached, and finally refused them all. But not without weighing them. He measured to the full the opportunities they offered. Wealth and influence were within their gift. And he looked with disconcerting

clarity at his wealthy friends to discern the effects of riches and worldly importance on a life. His private comments, confided only to his Journal, would have startled those important men, and before he died he carried his thoughts farther, and said them all, and gave the prosperous a nasty jar. But at present, like his first comment on slavery, he applied them only to his own life. Clear your own land first, was John Woolman's simple but unusual rule. "I saw," said John Woolman, "that where the heart was Set on Greatness Success in business did not Satisfie the Craving but that with an Increase of wealth, the desire of wealth Increased."

Woolman's objection to wealth in his early manhood was based on two things—the distraction of mind which it necessarily entailed, and the encroachment on time. Like Thoreau he might have said, "I love a broad margin to my life." He saw those who had become rich— Smiths, Logans, Pembertons, Drinkers, Uncle Burr—enslaved by their riches, keeping long hours, bound by a multiplicity of engagements, involved in problems of bills, debts, foundering ships, far-flung investments, bad and good seasons on their large land estates, difficulties of justice to an unmanageable number of employees—and he rejected that kind of living for himself. "I had Several offers of buisness" (a word which, like many of us, he could not spell) "that looked profitable, but there appeared too Great A Share of Cumber to Attend it." And he made a decision, not from a bleak asceticism but as the choice of that which was most happy, "that a way of Life pretty free from much cumber Appeared the most Agreeable, tho the Income was Small."

This moderate tone is very different from the dramatic, poetic embracing of Poverty by Saint Francis of Assisi. Not riches on the one hand, no. But not poverty and indigence, or dependence, on the other. A moderate sufficiency, earned in such a manner as to ensure a measure of both liberty and leisure—this was Woolman's idea. Nor did he for a moment consider the simplification of life ensured by celibacy. He was already healed enough to foresee a second spring, and his mental vision sometimes strayed over a liberal array of Quaker girls, considering the possible qualities of each as a life partner. "I was thoughtfull what way I Should take for A living In case I Should Settle." The practice of a craft appeared to him at length to be the answer. His own father and grandfather had practised the weaver's craft. But the looms at home were still in use by Samuel Woolman, and new equipment for himself would be very costly. Also, where could it be housed? He would have to rent a place. And he was not ready to leave his employer and the enjoyable enterprise of being a merchant. He wanted to feel his way into a new occupation, and not to burn his boats. A craft, sufficiently profitable and in constant demand, though not in itself very attractive to Woolman, was ready to his hand.

My Master tho now A Shop-keeper was by trade A Taylor And kept A Servant man who worked at it in his house ; My business in the Shop growing Slack, it came in my mind to learn the Taylor's trade, thinking by this, and A little Shopkeeping, A plain man might live without the load of Great buisness And have opportunity for retirement and inward Recollection.

I mentioned it to my Employer And we Soon Agreed on terms, And at All leisure times I worked with his man.

I believed the hand of providence pointed out this buisness and was taught to be content with it tho it was reverse to the creaturely will (though I felt at times a disposition that would have sought for something greater[1]). I Saw the happyness of humility and laboured for it, And in this labour I was often in Supplycation to the Most High And in Some of these private Exercises my mind was so Environed with Heavenly Light and Consolation that it made things Easie which had been otherways.

Although John Woolman knew well how to keep his own secrets and those of others, he was not of a secretive temper. His nature was open and flowing, and these decisions were arrived at not in the dark cellar of silent brooding, but in the sun and air of friendly discussion. Among friends and neighbours in Mount Holly to whom he had become warmly attached were Peter and Esther Andrews and Josiah White, the men older than himself but strongly akin to him in thought. His friends at Burlington and Haddonfield were as accessible to him as before. But his closest and most constant confidants were his father, Samuel Woolman, and his sister Elizabeth. Seldom have a father and son lived in a warmer, steadier, more sympathetic friendship than John Woolman and his father.

As for Elizabeth, she who always stood closer to John Woolman than his mother, how much she knew of her brother's past troubles and of his present complete solution of them no one can tell. But when John Woolman left home Elizabeth left too. Not, like sisters Sarah and Patience, led away by a bridegroom in the triumphant marriage procession, but acting on her own initiative, independent in a quite modern

---

[1] Version in the folio manuscript used for the Whittier edition, p. 57.

way, cutting loose from the bonds of home for a career. The place of mother's right hand was left to be filled by young Hannah, fourteen years old. Did Mrs Woolman readily relinquish so valuable a housekeeper, nurse, second hostess, in the large, busy, hospitable family group ? She was won to consent, however, and Elizabeth took herself, her abilities, her administrative power, her wisdom, and her well-skilled needle to Haddonfield, where she established herself in a house of her own and prepared to earn her living as a tailor. The secret history of Elizabeth, well known to her brother, is even more jealously guarded by him than his own. Did she take with her a broken heart ? Did the suitor who carried off Sarah come first for her ? Or had she set her fancy in some other, higher, more romantic place, among the group of her own and her brother's friends ? At all events she took refuge close beside her long-admired friend, Elizabeth Estaugh, and made for herself a busy and gracious life after her own pattern, refusing the irksome subordination of an adult daughter at home. The little touch of secret pride peeps out in her correct designation of her vocation ; not a seamstress, who will go to people's houses to sew and mend by the day, but a "Taylores," who, as good as any man, will cut and design clothes in her own house.

The elegance and peace of that house, and Elizabeth's description of the quiet of hours spent with thoughts released by the silent rhythm of the needle, or her evident pleasure in those other, active hours designing purposeful, well-fitting clothes for friends and neighbours, were probably what first led John Woolman's thoughts to the craft of tailoring. Sitting at tea with Elizabeth, with her "Square Walnut Table, her nest of Drawers, her Lesser Looking glass, her Tea Table, Tea Kittle, and Tea pot," all her China Ware and Silver Spoons (which, as well as her "Bed, Bedstead and all ye furniture to them belonging, and her Cloath Saddle and the bridle thereto belonging," she left itemized in her will to her sister Hannah), John Woolman might visualize the sort of well-bred simplicity, removed as far from the rough or the crude as from the luxurious, which his own married home might present in time to come.

So John Woolman, who was naturally not a handicraftsman but an intellectual, became a tailor, and did not regret it because it promoted his intention "so to pass my time that nothing might hinder me from the most steady attention to the voice of the true shepherd."

XII

THE TAILOR

As soon as Woolman was proficient enough in tailoring to take an order his first patron was his friend, Elizabeth Estaugh, and with her name and order Woolman started an Account Book of his private earnings apart from his master's business. The first entry, "To work Done for Eliz. Estaugh 2 Days ½ Cash 00.03.09," is dated "ye 8 mo [October] 1743." The last entry, "To Work Done for Thos. Redman 1 da. 00.01.00," is dated "6 mo. [August] 2nd 1746." Since there is plenty of room left in this small Account Book—so that Woolman turned it round the other way and used the back end for accounts of his executorships—there must be some reason for its abrupt finish at that date. And the reason was not that Woolman left off being a tailor ; quite the contrary. So this almost certainly marks the date at which Woolman severed relations with his employer and started off on his own. He then needed to keep more than a spare-time record, and began the Ledger for both income and outgo[1] which furnishes a rough chart of his life almost up to the end.

The Small Account Book has sometimes been called the Apprentice Account Book, but Woolman was never apprenticed to tailoring in the ordinary sense. Had he been so he would have been indentured as a learner for at least three years, more likely seven, full time, without pay ; whereas on the contrary he used only his spare time to learn the

[1] Both Account Books are preserved by the Historical Society of Pennsylvania.

89

craft, and was in a position to earn money by it in less than two years. It was evidently a very free-and-easy arrangement on all sides. Woolman's master was theoretically in control of all of his working time. But there were many hours, on many days, when even a prosperous shop was idle. Torrential rain swept down upon the hamlet, churning the unpaved roads into mud and leaving beautiful but inconvenient puddles to discourage traffic and reflect the sky. Summer heat filled potential shoppers with drowsy indolence, and caused the housewife to look out from her shady house with distaste at the outer glare and the buzzing, biting flies. Snow blocked the streets, or again, over clear roads with ruts made hard as metal by the frost, the icy north wind nipped the unwilling rider and kept the pedestrian indoors until driven abroad by necessary errands that could not be postponed. Or there were other days, calm and mild, when the temporary supply of all demand in the self-helpful community made business slack. At such times, with the shop door closed against the various hostility of the weather or open to the indifferent day, as long as the books were made up and the merchandise in order and all things swept and neat, Woolman's master could not see that he gained anything by keeping the young man standing idle at the counter while the tall, corner clock ticked heavily away the hours. Since young Woolman had the enterprise to take up the idea of learning tailoring, why not let him, at such times, slip through into the little lean-to at the side, where the tailor, who was also in the master's employ, industriously plied his trade ? Woolman paid a fee to learn ; and a man deft with his hands and of quick intelligence could be useful to the master craftsman even while learning. Sewing on buttons, turning in hems, and basting can be learned in one lesson, and may save the superior a lot of time. It worked out well for all parties. But on market-day or other times when business in the shop was brisk Woolman remained with the merchandise, and perhaps for days together hardly visited the tailor at all.

The agreement was supple, unbound by red tape or legal documents ; and when, in the fall of 1743, Woolman was in a position to earn money by tailoring there was no difficulty about his doing so. The double problem of what time he had a right to use for work paid for outside his shop wages, and that presented by his entering apparently into competition with his master's tailor, was so easily settled that not a ripple appears. "To making a Stomacher for Eliz. Matlack—

£ oo. S. o2. d o6," notes Woolman serenely. "To makeing Calaminck gown for Achsah Matlack 3ˢ. 6ᵈ." Not until he has practised on at least ten other people does he get an order from his sisters. "To makeing a Short Cloak for Sarah Elton 2ˢ . . . To makeing a poplin gown for Sarah Elton . 3ˢ.6ᵈ . . . . To makeing a pair of Stays for Hannah Woolman 18ˢ."

Young Hannah must have been particularly exigent, or her stays must have been very fancy, to drive her strictly just brother into pricing them so high. They are the highest-priced article in the whole Small Account Book, and only John Craig's "Pair of Trousers 16ˢ", a whole year later, comes anywhere near them. Achsah Siddons only had to pay three shillings for her "Pair of Stays" in 1745.

Woolman did not charge for his work entirely by time. Payment 'by the hour' had not been thought of, and a 'day' varied in length, though it is safe to say that it would not have recognized itself in a limit of eight hours. The average charge Woolman makes for "a day's work" is one shilling ; but "To work done for Samuel Woolman 5 days" is charged eight shillings, and in the same half-year he only makes Elizabeth Estaugh pay one shilling for "2 days work." Again, did it take him a whole day to make "a short Clock" for his baby niece, Ann Elton, Junior, in the late summer of '44 ? But it turned out to be a shilling's worth of work ; while "making a Little bonit for Amey Gill" —surely harder than a cloak ?—was so amusing that he only charged her parents tenpence. "Quilting a Petecoat for Eliz. Estaugh" was quite a job, but far less trouble than Hannah's stays. It cost eight shillings ; sixpence more than Thos. Robson had to pay for his "Great Coat." But time and skill alone were charged for. Materials were provided by the customer.

Perhaps the question of materials holds the clue to the employer's complaisance. It was good for trade to have customers come into the shop, wishing to be tailored by the attractive young man, John Woolman, and after due discussion with him to purchase at the counter the necessary yards of poplin, fustin, "Flaning (for a wais coat or a Jackit), leather (for Britches, or to Plait for a Bridle), oznabriggs (for Jackit and Britches), or Hollan," with buttons, thread, and accessories.

In the other end of the little book Woolman notes the fees received concurrently for odd bits of legal business. "To my Time & Expense at proving Will, etc. 4:6." For "Clerkship at Ye Appraisement, 6 sh."

And with expenses entirely covered by his job in the shop, which included board and lodging, he steadily laid by a modest hoard at the rate of upward of twenty pounds a year.

The best investment for savings by an enterprising young man along the Delaware was to join with others in the purchase or stocking of a ship for trade to the West Indies. This was the way taken by John Smith.

> In the 10th mo. 1744 (December) I Joined with Israel Pemberton, John Reynell & Israel Pemberton Junr in purchasing a small schooner which we made a Brig^t of & Called her the *Dolphin*. Loaded her ourselves, Appointed John Peal m^r & she sailed for Barbadoes the 13th 11 mo.

John Smith had had the advantage of going to see Barbados for himself on one of his father's ships in December 1741, when entering on his twentieth year. He saw nothing disagreeable there (though some other visitors had) and came back filled with enthusiasm for the beauties of the island, its climate, and its abundance of natural riches. He was at Mount Holly Meeting to attend a wedding in May, and it is likely that his suggestions and offers were among those which were tempting to John Woolman.

But in two anecdotes which John Smith had to tell the shadow of war fell lightly across the young men. One was in relation to the mysterious disaster which had happened just as young Smith and his Coz were bowling merrily down the Delaware on the outward voyage. They were told of it by a "Pilott boat." Captain Redman's great new ship had, through some fault of ballast or build, turned turtle just outside Philadelphia and sunk in the Delaware, with distinguished guests and all hands. She had one hundred and fifty pipes of wine on board and "mounted 24 guns." The other incident had occurred just as they anchored at Barbados—"the man of war boat Came on board & prest 2 of our men."

Woolman, money-making aside, would have no part in any commerce that had to be defended by force of arms or that ran the risk of delivering free and peaceable seamen into the compelled service of the British fleet. Yet those men-o'-war were there in defence of American commerce.

How clear could any Quaker business man keep himself from indirect involvement in the war? This was another train of thought roused in

Woolman to be studied while he became mechanically proficient at tailoring, as Spinoza worked out his philosophy while grinding his lenses.

John Smith was lively, enterprising, orthodox, and not closely logical. But Woolman was logical. And so was the great James Logan, whose daughter Smith was courting.

In September 1741 Logan let loose a broadside[1] on the members of the Yearly Meeting then convened in Philadelphia. The prominent members of the Yearly Meeting were identical in many cases with the prominent members of the Assemblies of Pennsylvania and New Jersey, men who had the weight of the government in both provinces. The immediate occasion of Logan's protest was the controversy over the raising of troops. Governor Thomas, in difficulty with the filling of his quota, had had the bright idea of offering to any discontented redemptioners a chance to throw over their bond with their employers and work out their time in the army. Many redemptioners had rushed to the colours, and masters were left suddenly without men. Crops were ruined, manufactories at a standstill. It was an illegal action, but the outraged employers could not get redress. The power of the Crown was behind the Governor, and protests to England were unavailing. Thomas had also stated his case there, and the Crown sympathized with his difficulty, and wanted troops. The Quaker-dominated Assembly of Pennsylvania had thereupon—unable to get back the escaped servants —revenged itself upon the Governor. And Logan protests "that the Governor, for his 'false Step' last Year in Encouraging our Servants to inlist, has been abridged by the Assembly of the usual allowance of salary, for a year and a half." Yet Logan says that "Friends now make, on a moderate Computation, not above one Third of the Inhabitants," and urges that those who are out-and-out pacifists should withdraw from politics and not stand for re-election to the forthcoming Assembly.

"In the last French War," he argues,

Pensilvania was but an inconsiderable Colony ; but now, by its extended Commerce, it has acquired a very great Reputation ; and particularly that Philadelphia has the name of a rich City, is known to have no manner of Fortification, and is, as has been said, a tempting Bait by water from the Sea ; & by Land, the whole Country lies

[1] Included in the Pemberton Papers, vol. 3. The word "broadside" is used here in a double sense, since it was in fact a printed one-page leaflet technically called a broadside.

exposed to the French, with whom a War is daily expected. . . .
That our own Indians unhappily retiring Westward, have open'd a
ready Road & Communication between this Province & Canada . . .
& the French have many large Nations of Indians in Alliance with
them to facilitate their Conquests . . . our numerous back Inhabitants,
as well as others, ought to be obliged to furnish themselves with
Arms, & to be disciplined as in other Colonies for their own proper
Defence.

Any orthodox Quaker knew the answer to this, and was well prepared
to stand forth with very lofty religious language and put James Logan
in the wrong. But Logan, himself a Quaker, had learned their rhetoric
by heart, and with pitiless logic forestalled them and turned their flank
in an unexpected manner. There are Quakers, says he, who deny even
the lawfulness of self-defence ("though I ever condemned offensive
War") as being

> contrary to the peaceable Doctrine of Jesus . . . yet without
> Regard to others of Christ's Precepts, full as express, against laying up
> Treasure in this World, and not caring for to-morrow, they are as
> intent as any others whatever in amassing Riches, the great Bait and
> Temptation to our Enemies to come and plunder the Place.

John Woolman was at that Yearly Meeting, received and read the
pamphlet, heard the answering speeches (many of them, to his mind,
long and windy), and later saw the Quakers campaign for re-election
to the Assembly on a peace platform and win the election by a sound
majority in spite of counter-campaigning by Logan, Thomas, and
Benjamin Franklin. Woolman was on the side of the peace party ;
yet he recognized that Logan had used an argument difficult to answer.
And it came just at a time when, after his first few months at Mount
Holly, he was beginning to feel the fascination of business. Logan
would have been astonished, and more than a little disconcerted, to know
what seed he had sown in a sensitive mind that was even more logical
than his own.

Its first evidence was merely Woolman's decision not to enter into
partnership with seagoing commerce. But it led him further to conclude that the pursuit of wealth in any direction was closely bound up
with the roots of war. In the ripeness of his maturity he went further
and decided that it was the very cause of war itself. Logan argued,
Therefore accept war. Woolman reasoned, Therefore reject wealth.

But at present he kept his revolutionary thoughts to himself, regarding them as primarily a guide for his own life.

There were other thoughts which struggled for expression, thoughts which belonged to that heavenly sweetness and light which filled him with such unconquerable happiness. These thoughts must sometimes break forth in speech, as the kindred dammed-up emotion of the poet must break forth in verse. And there were Sundays or weekdays when in the cumulative corporate spiritual exercise of Mount Holly Meeting John Woolman rose up trembling and broke the silence with words that came, he felt, only too easily. Many an hour of shame he passed in solitary walks, or in discussion with his friends Peter Andrews and Josiah White about his tendency to readiness of speech. Was a Quaker meeting the time for fluent sentences and polished phrases, when the soul should be standing in stark sincerity before God? How often as a youth he had silently condemned the egotism and verbosity which would trample underfoot and break in pieces the precious crystalline silence of a Quaker meeting.

Devoid of timidity or false shame, with a natural ease in human intercourse, John Woolman did not have the difficulty some had in bringing themselves to expose their hidden thoughts to the criticism of others, to make themselves uncomfortably conspicuous among their fellows. It was an inward warmth which drove him to his feet, especially for people of his own age, who might be struggling as he had struggled.

From one month to Another this love And tenderness Increased and I found it too Strong And forcible to be much longer Confined to my own breast . . . till one day feeling the word of the Lord in my heart I Stood up & Said some words in A Meeting but Not keeping close to the true Opener I said more than he directed me to Say. I was Soon Sensible of my Error And Afflicted in mind Some weeks. . . .

Let no one think this feeling exaggerated. Woolman, like Blake, like Thoreau, like. Saint Francis, was able to experience the rarest and highest emotion, that of awe. And he had trespassed on a holy place. If the truth is tampered with even a little it is no longer the truth. But to an active and healthy nature the way to rectify a failure is to try again and do better.

. . . After this my mind being Calm And Quiet and feeling the Spring of Divine Love opened and A concern to Speak I Said A few words in A Meeting in which I found peace. This I believe was about Six or Seven weeks from the first time. And as I was thus humbled And Disciplined under the Cross my understanding became more Strengthened To know the language of the pure Spirit which moves upon the Intellectual deep, And to wait in Silence Sometimes many weeks together, Untill I felt that rise which prepares the creature to Stand like A trumpet through which the Lord Speaks to his people.

The language of the Quaker ministry is not that of personal confession. So remote from the message, so utterly an 'instrument,' did some Quaker ministers feel that they believed themselves unrefreshed by the divine word which they passed on to others, as in our day a telegraph operator gets no good from the most eloquent telegrams which he delivers. "Alas," said Samuel Fothergill, when visiting the colonies in 1756, "I feel like a tube ; some liquid crystal stream runs through me to others, but I doubt little remains."[1] But Woolman never approached this excess of impersonality. It was upon his own intellectual deep that the Spirit moved, it was his own personal gift of words that was used and disciplined by the Divine. And this sense, awful and sweet, of personal contact, of intimate control, was a source of consolation even in the miserable abasement of consciousness of error. He was corrected, he learned ; and though it was by the warmest impulse, the impulse of love to his friends, that God moved him to speak, he controlled a too ready tongue and a too eager nature, he waited to be certain of command, and even in the midst of speaking he watched for the subtle direction of the Unseen Guide.

All Faithfull people are not Called to the publick Ministry : But whoever are called to it Are called to Minister of that which they have tasted and handled Spiritually. The outward modes of Worship are Various, But wherever men are true Ministers of Jesus Christ it is from the opperation of his Spirit upon their hearts, first purifying them And then giving them A feeling Sence of the Conditions of the people.

This truth was Early fixed on my mind, and I was taught carefully to watch the opening least while I was Standing to Speak my own will Should get uppermost Uttering words from worldly wisdom And So Depart from the true channel of the Gospel Ministry."

Woolman was not speaking the language of his time when he admitted the intellect to any place in inspired speech, and the phrase was edited

[1] *Memoirs of Samuel Fothergill*, by George Crosfield (Collins Bros., New York, 1844), p. 251.

out of his printed Journal. But he recognized the contrary danger of using his mind to the exclusion of the deeper impulse familiar—under different names—to every creative soul : that mysterious force which can use technical excellence, but which no technical excellence can capture. The Inward Light, the Holy Spirit, under whose sway—guiding his tools of speech, pen, chisel, brush—the creature becomes a trumpet through which the Lord speaks to his people.

Nothing is more moving to a Quaker meeting than the sense that a speaker is all the time closely conscious of the Presence of the unseen, and is speaking by its power. John Woolman's theory and practice of the ministry not only affected his meeting, but had a strong influence on his less articulate friends, Josiah White and Peter Andrews. White was fifteen years Woolman's senior, and Andrews twelve, both men of reading and cultivation, but backward hitherto in taking up their useful share in the meeting. Both perhaps had a shyness and a fear of the criticism of their neighbours which stood in the way. Under the sunny and heart-opening companionship of their new neighbour they broke through their inhibiting crust ; and they and John Woolman were recommended as ministers by the Burlington Monthly Meeting on the same day in August 1743.

The minute, recorded by the Quarterly Meeting of Ministers and Elders at Burlington, simply reads, "The Monthly Meeting of Burlington have recommended our friends, Peter Andrews, John Woolman, and Josiah White . . . as Friends whom they have unity with, to be members of this meeting."[1]

---

[1] *I.e.*, Members of the Meeting of Ministers and Elders. This was all that made Andrews, Woolman, and White rank hereafter as "recorded Ministers."

G

XIII

FIRST JOURNEYS [1] AND WAR SHADOWS

ALL this time Woolman had not been farther from home than Philadelphia, now grown to be one mile long and half a mile wide, the central and chief city of the American colonies. But soon after his 'recording' an older Friend with a concern to travel in the ministry invited him to go along as his companion. It was very usual for Quakers to travel in pairs, one having the burden of concern, the other being merely minuted as "accompanying" and bearing most of the responsibility for the physical arrangements of the journey. And since the Society of Friends depended for its continued existence upon spontaneous impulses of this kind, it was most important that the older generation should train the younger in the practice. Very soon after young men or women showed a vocation for the invisible priesthood their gift was recognized by recording them as members of the select Meeting of Ministers and Elders, and the next older Friends who had a concern to travel would have their eye upon them as possible disciples in the old Eastern sense of the word—both helpers and learners.

"My Esteemed friend Abraham Farrington being About to make A visit to Woodbridge and thereaway Asked me to bear him Company And after A Conference with Some friends I agreed to Go." Abraham

[1] Appendix XI.

Farrington was a man of fifty-two, a powerful influence among the Quakers in those parts. In another version of his Journal Woolman calls him "my ancient friend,"[1] but this evidently means my friend of long standing. Woolman had known Farrington ever since he himself was five years old, and had often seen him sitting on the facing benches or heard him speak in Chesterfield Meeting and Burlington. Farrington had now moved from Chesterfield to Burlington, from Burlington to Mount Holly, and had recently used the younger man as his assistant in various business of real estate, wills, and trusteeships.

We Set of 5th day, 9 mo, 1743—had An Evening Meeting at A Tavern in Brunswick, the Room was full and the people quiet. Thence to Amboy And had An Evening Meeting in the Courthouse to which came many people, Among whom were Several of the Assembly (they then Sitting there). . . . Thence we went on, had twelve other Meetings Several of which were made up cheifly of the presbyterians. My Dear friend was frequently Strengthened to hold forth the word of life Amongst the peaple on my part I was prety often Silent through the Meeting, And when I Spoke it was with much care that I might Speak only what truth Required. My mind was often tender and I learned Some profitable lessons ; we were out About two weeks.

Woolman does not often favour us with an exact date, but now that there is one, discrepancies occur by comparison with the carefully dated private Account Book. The Journal suggests that it was *after* this journey, not before, that Woolman considered tailoring as a trade and began to learn it.[2] But the dates in the Account Book prove this to be inaccurate. On the contrary he had completed, and been paid for, nine tailoring jobs before the blank between November 4 and November 18 marks the fortnight's holiday he took for the journey.

This is merely another instance of the way in which Woolman uses the material of his life with artistic freedom, and is more concerned with truth than facts. *Why* he chose tailoring is important to his story, and he explains it clearly ; *when* is unimportant, within a year or two, as he glances backward.

Perth Amboy was a seaport, and there came ships of the African Company, unloading slaves fresh from their native parts, and selling them, chained and untamed, in the open market. They were all much

---

[1] Whittier ed., p. 55.   [2] See Whittier ed., pp. 55-57.

of an age, young, but not small children.   No man over twenty-two, no woman over nineteen ;   many more men than women.

"A parcel of likely Men and Women Slaves with some Boys & Girls of different Ages," ran the advertisements.   Or "A parcel of Choice likely Young Slaves."   Sometimes their particular breed was boasted of, as a hardy Shetland pony or a wire-haired terrier might be.

It is generally allowed that the Gambia Slaves are much more robust and tractable than any other slaves from the Coast of Guinea, and more Capable of undergoing the Severity of the Winter Seasons in the North-American Colonies which occasions their being Vastly more esteemed and coveted in this Province & those to the Northward than any other Slaves whatsoever.

But a slave-market was also to be seen at Cooper's Ferry, when the crowded slave ships, smelling bad to windward, came up the river from the sea.   Each sight and scent of evil sank into John Woolman's mind to become part of the deposit which was slowly crystallizing into the hard diamond of resistance.

The slaves, sold off, were taken to homes, were bathed and clothed and fed, were trained as gardeners, coachmen, grooms, house servants. In the spring they were given rhubarb or sulphur-and-molasses ;   in winter an occasional dose of cordial.   They were cared for in sickness and old age.   They need never go hungry.   Were they so badly off ? Their relationship with their owners was close and personal.   It some-times became filled with a doglike devotion on the one side, protective affection on the other.   An old slave coachman belonging to Richard Smith, at Burlington, could not long survive his master's death, but died of a broken heart.

Woolman saw it all, and noted it silently.   He also saw such things as Elizabeth Drinker noted casually in her journal : "Henry has sold Scipio to George Emlen, and we have given him our little Peter Savage. I hope he will be a good boy, but he is little worth at present."

The same mistress, on first obtaining little Peter at the age of seven, had "washed him this afternoon in a tub of warm soapsuds, his head with larkspur and rum, and changed his apparel."   And another time notes with something of a sigh, "I have much to do for the little black boys ;   these small folk ought to be of service when they grow bigger, for they are very troublesome when young to those who have their good at heart."

John Woolman's grandfather, Henry Burr, dying the year before, had employed his law-practised grandson to write his will and had left free in it his Negro slave, Maria, along with some goods to help her settle comfortably in her new life. And Maria, happily free to choose an employer, or to work out by the day—not handed over to anybody of her late master's choice, like a pet dog—had joyfully hired herself to young Miss Elizabeth Woolman, and gone to live at Haddonfield. So the pattern of Elizabeth's life became even more gracious and leisured, like a well-designed garment, austerely cut, yet easy in the sleeves. She could do more for her friends, she could live unhurried days, and, unlike her ever-active mother, she could sometimes spend an hour in quiet musing, feeling through to that eternal golden world beyond the veil of time. Such moments were sometimes set off by a book, sometimes by talk with a friend—who lingered, perhaps, after a fitting, to pour out timid hidden thoughts to one who so clearly had time to listen. And sometimes it was by the sweetness of the outdoors, as with her brother John. When John Woolman paid his frequent visits to his favourite sister, riding over after work, or on a Firstday, he found that her company drew him nearer to that unsullied atmosphere he loved ; and his brother Abner often came with him. The feeling of impermanence casts a sort of rainbow iridescence about the independent home of an attractive young woman.

The visiting brothers were right in dimly feeling that those years were short, in almost hearing the footsteps of impending change. But it was death and not a bridegroom that was riding through the woods towards Elizabeth to gather the mellowed fruit of her thirty-one years.

In 1743 Elizabeth was only twenty-eight, and when death visited her thoughts it was chiefly in relation to the spreading war which was demanding more and more urgent attention in the Quaker colonies.

The safety of ocean-borne commerce had been destroyed in the kind of free-for-all that was now taking place on the high seas. Pirates from the North African coast swarmed out to replace the fifteen hundred pirates that had been put down on the American coast by the British fleet in Woolman's childhood. The fleet was now busy on its own fight, and could no longer police the seas ; and Elias Bland, of London, wrote to James Pemberton :

There is advice of the Algerian rovers having taken two Spanish Privateers and carr'd them into Algiers. Several English Ships are

taken off the Bar of Oporto. There is several Ships that came out with
the Fleet under Convoy of the *Lyon* Man of War that are not yet
arriv'd, it is fear'd are lost.

Business in the colonies was directly affected, and Woolman recorded
that his master was "doing less at trading than heretofore."

Also the imminence of trouble on land grew closer, and the non-
Quaker inhabitants of Pennsylvania became more and more restive, as
Logan had foreseen.   In the middle of the summer they went behind the
Assembly and sent over to England a direct appeal to the Crown ; and
the secret, unorthodox petition was secretly answered direct to the
Governor, in a way very subversive of the democratic self-governing
habits of the two Quaker colonies.   Partridge, the faithful agent, alert
to everything that affected his patrons, got hold of a copy and sent it at
once to James Pemberton.

Instruction issued at Whitehall in reply to a petition received by
the King from divers Merchants & other Inhabitants of the Province
setting forth that the said Province is without fortification destitute of
arms and ammunitions and the people under no Obligations to Military
Duty & praying that His Majesty wd order for their safety what shall
be thought meet & convenient.

Thomas was instructed to present detailed suggestions to the Regency
and Council.   And here was all the set-up for direct rule of a British
colony by the home government through the person of the Governor,
reducing the elected Assembly to impotence.

But, thanks to Pemberton's early notice of this, it was nipped in the
bud.   The Assembly controlled all the machinery for funds, and the
Governor perceived that he could not go too far.   When in October
'44 there was a question asked in the House of Commons as to whether
Pennsylvania and New Jersey could not be coerced into rendering aid
in the war, the legal opinion was put on record that "a colonial assembly
cannot be compelled to do more towards their own defence than they
shall see fit, unless by the force of an Act of Parliament which alone can
prescribe rules of conduct for them."

Meanwhile Partridge kept his patrons closely informed as to the
progress of the war in Europe.

" Yesterday," he wrote on June 24, 1743,

an Express arrived from Germany with ye news of a Victory
obtained by ye British Forces etc under our King against great part

of ye French Army under their Gen[l]. Noailles w[h] is the first Stroke begun between ye two Nations but yet as these Armys are Auxiliarys it is not certain yet whether or no we shall have a General War with France. Time must manifest it."[1]

And a month later.

It is now conjectured that the Allied Army will endeavour to recover Lorrain from the French for the Queen of Hungary as a Compensation to her for the loss of Siletia which she ceded to the King of Prussia upon ye peace[2] made between them. It's not known yet whether we shall have a French War or not.

The victory was the battle of Dettingen, the last in which an English King personally took arms. "The Duke of Cumberland was wounded but like to do well again," reported the faithful Partridge. "The King received no hurt. . . . Further measures probably will be to Drive the ffrench out of Germany & then endeavour to take Lorain from them for the said Queen by way of compensation." And late in August he has news very pertinent to his patrons in the colonies. "I hear orders are sent over from hence to ye Sev[l] Gov[s] of our Plantations to be upon their Guard to prevent any Invasion from a Foreign Enemy from whence I am apt to think the Ministry are apprehensive of a French War." And another letter the next day, "There is much talk of a French War & our King [George II] is abroad on Matters of great moment. . . . Goods are Risen which is another Discouragement which can't be Help'd, & am sure from what have Observ'd we shall go to Market as Cheap as any."[3]

At the same time Latham Clarke wrote to James and Israel Pemberton from Jamestown, Virginia :

There has but A small Number of our Vessels arriv'd from the West Indies the last of which who was from Jamecia informs us that all our Vessels from that Island under Convoy of some Men of War sail'd from thence six Days before him and gives us to fear that they have met with some ill fortune. We have certain Accounts that 6 of our Vessels have been taken by the Spaniards viz 2 Briggs, 2 Sloops & A Schooner [sic], since last Winter and a seventh lost by Reason of A Spanish Privateer on the Coast of Guinea The Master of which being a

---

[1] Pemberton Papers.
[2] The Treaty of Berlin, 1743, a separate peace made between the cynical Frederick and Maria Theresa, Queen of Austria-Hungary.
[3] Pemberton Papers, 1743.

Timerous Blockhead discrying the Enemy at three Leags distance was so affrighted that he with all his Men left her & she was plundred by the Negroes the Spaniards Never coming up with her the Vessel belonged to Capt Whipple who made the Master of her pay dear for his folly.

Yet, against this background of unrest business boomed in Philadelphia and Burlington. It was precisely now that John Smith opened his "dry Good Store at Philadelphia" and began to prepare himself to support James Logan's daughter in the style to which she had been accustomed ; a prospect which might drive a young man's ambition as far as it liked. Mount Holly might find trade slack, but raised prices and higher profits caused by demand exceeding supply were a stimulus to more adventurous merchants.

Meanwhile Governor Thomas, continuing in his efforts at defence, summoned the Indians of the Six Nations to a conference at Lancaster, Pennsylvania, together with commissioners from Maryland and Virginia. It was explained to the Indians that the two sets of white men in their borders, the French and the English, were again at war, and their support was claimed for their old friends, the English, against all attack by the other party. Four hundred pounds and a belt of wampum changed hands, a fresh treaty was ratified, and the dignified head chief, Canassatego, spoke with the extraordinary elegance of language which marked all the major statements of the Indians of any tribe, though none had any written tongue, and all had behind them thousands of bookless years. "The covenant chain between us & Pennsylvania," said Canassatego,

is an ancient one & has never contracted rust. We shall have all your country under our eye. . . . The Six Nations have a great authority over the praying Indians, who stand in the very gates of the French ; to show our further care, we have engaged these very Indians & other allies of the French ; they have agreed with us that they will not join against you.

The praying Indians were the Algonquins, over whom the French Jesuit missionaries had obtained a remarkable hold. The Catholic use of shrine, symbol, and ritual had, in the long run, an appeal to the Indian through the senses which no other practice of Christian worship could maintain. The element of personal influence was also strong. These highly cultivated, well-trained, subtle men, directing all their time and all their gifts to the service of God in the mastery of primitive people, often bringing elements of beauty and order into savage life, healing the sick, training young braves as acolytes and servers, laid an almost hypnotic spell on the Indian heart. John Brainerd, the Presbyterian missionary to the Indians in New Jersey, was never so loved. The Quakers pursued no missionary endeavours. So the French, who benefited politically by the activity of the priests, said with much satisfaction that the English held the savage by self-interest and trade, while the Frenchman held him by religion.

" Our own Indians," alluded to by James Logan as having retired westward and thereby left the way open between Pennsylvania and Canada, were the Delawares, the Lenape, those peaceable and agricultural Indians with whom William Penn had made his original famous treaty. They had withdrawn just because they were peaceable, before the encroachments of the white men and of the Iroquois. This latter warlike race, grouped in the powerful confederation of the Six Nations, had ordered the Lenape off with scorn some years before at a Council in Philadelphia, in the large Quaker Meeting-house.[1] "We don't give you the liberty to think about it. You are Women ; take the advice of a Wise Man & remove immediately." And they moved, not all at once, but gradually, melting away in little bands through the woods, moving from their ancestral haunts among the innumerable winding streams in the valley of the Delaware, to the unfamiliar reaches of the Ohio. And there they gathered and brooded revengeful return.

The French and English colonists cared as little as the Indians themselves whether Maria Theresa sat upon the throne of Austria-Hungary or owned Silesia (the French had some opinions about Lorraine). The war that was thus gradually moving into position in America was never called the War of the Austrian Succession ; it was called simply King George's War, to distinguish it from Queen Anne's War before. Both wars had a common cause in the colonies, though a different fighting point. And the cause was simply, where was the boundary to lie between the British colonies and the French ? Or could one of them obtain complete mastery over the other ?

France wanted the boundary to be the Alleghenies, and above all she wanted possession of the whole valley of the Ohio. Nothing could have

---

[1] Some histories have reported this as the Fourth and Arch Street Meeting-house, but that was not built until 1804. The one alluded to here was probably the Old Bank Meeting-house, the largest of several extant. It was in Front Street above Arch.

drawn the English colonies more quickly into an emotional accord. When France struck the first blow, and took the New England fishing village of Canseau by surprise, burned the fort and the fishing-boats, and carried eighty men off to captivity in Louisburg, the news throbbed along the nerve of suddenly united states.

New England settled that little business herself, with the aid of some British men-o'-war, but when the idea began to go about that there would be no safety on the northern frontier as long as the French held Canada it was recognized as the common danger and the common task of all. And Governor Hamilton, of New Jersey, convened the New Jersey Assembly in 1746 to "raise equip and support" five hundred men to aid in the conquest of Canada. A bounty of six pounds a head proved adequate, the enterprise was popular, and six hundred and sixty men were got in two months by voluntary enlistment. Five companies were formed, and marched away to the Canadian border, where they and the other companies from other colonies stayed for a long while inactive for want of generalship.

George Washington was a boy of fourteen, a loyal young subject of the King, growing up peacefully in Virginia. Perhaps he and John Woolman passed each other one rare June day with a word or two of greeting as one rode by on his horse, the other wandered in the woods "sometimes spending the best part of a day admiring the trees and richness of the land."[1] For on the twelfth of May, 1746, John Woolman saddled his horse and with his friend, Isaac Andrews, rode away from Mount Holly on a three months' visit to the South, to, as he says in his Journal, "the Back Settlements of pennsylvania & Virginia . . . and also to Maryland, Virginea and North Carolina."

Woolman is kind enough to give us the exact date both of departure and of return, "Set of the 12da. 3mo. 1746 [May] . . . reached home ye 16th. 6mo [August] 1746, Having Been out three months and four Days And traveled by Estimation 1500 miles."[2] And as usual when he tries to date his reminiscences, he is wrong. The little Account Book says that on August 2 he did a day's work, priced at one shilling, for Thomas Redman. Both can't be true. If the Journal is correct, on August 2 he was a fortnight's journey from home on the western shore of Maryland.

[1] Washington's diary in Sparks's *Washington*, II, p. 416.
[2] MS. Journal.

The Account Book, which was a day-to-day record made at the time, is no doubt right, and Woolman probably arrived back on August 1, while one can preserve an open mind as to the date of his departure (May 1 would be a likely choice[1]). It does not matter now, except for the light it casts on character. Meticulous exactitude was not one of Woolman's traits.

Woolman is on safer ground when he uses his favourite phrase, "about this time."

The reason then why, about this time, he was suddenly so foot-loose was that his employer's wife died and the employer retired from business, so John Woolman was without a job.

Woolman intended to buy the business,[2] but the "man" took some time to settle up his affairs, and Woolman, never in a hurry, was less so at this time than ever. He had long meant to go on some extended travels, and here was the opportunity. His friend, Isaac Andrews, who lived at Haddonfield, had an equal and similar concern for the Southern journey, and each obtained a minute from his own Monthly Meeting to travel together, "he from Haddonfield and I from Burlington."

[1] So as not to cut the time away by two weeks.
[2] Or to buy a business—but the circumstantial evidence is very suggestive.

XIV

FIRST SOUTHERN JOURNEY (I)

It was one of the gifts of the Church to mankind in the Middle Ages that restlessness of heart could be expressed and relieved by going on a pilgrimage. Thwarted love, domestic pressure, remorse, or mere spring fever, then longen folk to go on pilgrimage, and dignity and merit were given to their lust to travel. The Society of Friends offered to its members something very similar. Young men all over New Jersey were shaking off the bonds of routine that spring and going off to war. Some of this pervading stir entered the hearts of John Woolman and his friend, on the human side, and it was with a lively pleasure that they turned their horses' heads towards Cooper's Ferry and rode away through the verdant woods.

The Andrewses, whom Woolman liked so much, were a colourful family. Their grandfather was cousin of that Sir Edmund Andros (or Andrews) who had been a major in Rupert's Horse and had been rewarded with first the governorship of New York (where he got embroiled with the Jerseys), then the governorship of New England (where he set the Indians by the ears, upset Connecticut, and finally provoked the far from patient men of Boston to open rebellion), and finally the governorship of Virginia (where he fell foul of the hard-hitting Dr Blair). Each time he was recalled home and awaited trial, but was never tried. The storm died down, and Andros was quietly slipped into a different governorship. After the third and last recall, however, the home government, unconvinced that Andros was not the stuff for a governor, but at least convinced that he was not the stuff for the New World, appointed him to the mild office of Governor of the Channel Island of Jersey, in which post he died.

The grandmother of Peter and Isaac Andrews was the Mary Wright who, as a young girl, had accompanied Margaret Brewster to Boston in the days of the Quaker persecution, and had endured the outrage and agony of being whipped at the cart's tail. Her daughter, also called Mary, had died very rich, left her three nephews between them (Mordecai, Peter, and Isaac) eleven hundred acres of land in New Jersey, and bequeathed to other relatives and friends some very un-Quakerly jewellery, and "to Mrs Moore, of Moore Hall, my parrotts Jacob and Africa."[1] Isaac, younger than Peter, was a man of John Woolman's own age. Their travelling minutes were equal in weight, and it is clear that before their three months of close association were over they had had some differences of opinion which tested their good humour and friendship. The eldest son of a family seldom escapes a touch of the habit of domination, even quite unconscious and unwished for, and John Woolman had had little opportunity of opposition from his equals. His mental superiority to his companion made it inevitable that he should assume leadership, naturally, without noticing it. But Isaac Andrews had all the sturdy independence of the Quaker, and was unwilling to acknowledge any other man's Inward Light as being clearer than his own—not, at any rate, John Woolman's, who had no advantage of years. It is an acid test of a man's real desire to learn humility if he can give in graciously under such circumstances, and John Woolman passed the test with honours. "I may say," he says, in one of those sentences of his which half veil and half reveal, "that through the assistance of the Holy Spirit which mortifies selfish desires, my companion and I travelled in harmony and parted in the nearness of true brotherly love." In all his many journeys with many companions this is the only mention of mortifying selfish desires or having a struggle to do it.

At first the young men's journey lay through a green rolling country unfamiliar in itself but containing a familiar type of life, the comfortable Quaker farms and settlements of Chester County, Pennsylvania, and the fertile German lands round Lancaster. But then the travellers forded the shallow, blue, swift-running Susquehanna, with its many islands smiling

[1] *The Friend*, Philadelphia, XXI, 268.

in the sun, and came at once into the unfamiliar rawness of the frontier. "A new Settlement Called the Red Lands the oldest of which was within ten years. It is the poorer Sort of people," noted Woolman, "that commonly begin to Improve remote desarts. With a Small Stock they have houses to build, lands to clear and fence, Corn to raise, Cloaths to provide, And Children to Educate."

Here, instead of good feather beds, they lay on earth floors, where fleas tormented them, and the evil smells of unclean and crowded habitation offended their nostrils. "Friends who visit Such," said Woolman, "may well Sympathize with them in their hardships in the wilderness." And there is a half-scornful side glance at companion Isaac when he emphatically adds that it is unbecoming "to Express uneasiness At coarse Entertainment when in Good will they give us their Best." It was all part of the adventure of pilgrimage. But Woolman never belittled discomfort or believed that it was in itself salutary. Here in the Red Lands he saw poverty at close quarters, and it influenced him to protest its existence. He never, like Saint Francis, welcomed lice as "little pearls" or thought that neglect of cleanliness and other basic refinements of physical living promoted the spiritual life.

Yet when the travellers passed onward to the rich plantations of the old settled South Woolman found there worse pitfalls for the soul. "Our exercise in general was more painful in these old settlements than it had been amongst the back inhabitants." The journey itself was full of charm, and a young man's delight in travel sometimes breaks through the lines. After leaving Shanando and setting off with a guide through the entangled forest, where flowering vines hung from the trees and the bayberry bush and the myrtle replaced the cranberry and sumach, Woolman records :

> the first night we with our pilot lodged in the woods, our Horses feeding by us, he being poorly provided with a Horse for travelling, we being young And having good horses, were free the Next day to part with him and did so. Once In a while we met with A house and Enquired, And for our money took Such refreshment as the people had, And in two days besides the first afternoon We reached to our friend John Cheadles.

And now, though they moved within the Quaker commonwealth (in Quaker parlance they were within the precincts of Virginia Yearly Meeting), they might have crossed an ocean to a foreign country. The whole aspect of life was different. When they came to their first destination in old settled Virginia it was not Cheadlestown after the master, nor any nostalgic place name carried over from the old country —a Chester, a Nottingham, a Bristol. It was just "John Cheadles's house." And so in all their journey they never came to any gathering of houses in Virginia large enough to be a settlement or a village, much less a town. Thirteen years later, when Jefferson went away from his home plantation to enter William and Mary College, at Williamsburg, at the age of seventeen, he had never before seen so much as a settlement of a dozen houses grouped together. In Williamsburg, the seat of government, he was impressed by a town of two hundred houses, mostly wooden and poorly built, with the streets between them still left in their native earth. Yet the population of Virginia was equal to that of the whole of Pennsylvania and New Jersey put together, with half New York State added.[1]

When John Woolman and Isaac Andrews rode out of the woods into Cheadles's plantation the setting sun upon their right hand shone over a vast green expanse, not of rolling pasture nor of corn and wheat, but of "the bewitching Vegetable, Tobacco."

Many Negroes were at work between the rows, the men in red cotton drawers and battered broad hats, the women in faded dresses with white kerchiefs turban-wise round their wool. A white overseer leaned against a tree in the shade, responsible all day long for preventing idleness, but now getting ready to blow the whistle at sunset. The cheerfulness of the close of day was on them all, fatigue forgotten in anticipation of immediate relaxation, and John Woolman, sensitively observing, could see no outward sign of unhappiness. Rather the contrary. The black faces that ran with sweat were cheerful, and if a hand might go to an aching back as the welcome whistle shrilled out the owner grinned a greeting when her husband and pickaninny joined her. But the bare legs and feet that presently scuffled along in the dusty road were thin and stricken with sores. There were no fat ones among them.

Later John Woolman, attending personally to the comfort of his horse in the stable, saw the double row of Negro cabins behind the house. They looked neat and respectable. Many had vines—morning-glory or

---

[1] Chalmers' *American Colonies* (II, 7) gives a table of population in 1715 estimating Virginia at 95,000, Pennsylvania 45,800, New Jersey 22,000, New York 31,000; Negroes in all cases included (but not Indians).

whatnot—growing over them, veiling the gasping planks with gay beauty. The slaves were grinding corn and busying themselves preparing their evening meal ; at first sight it was a scene of cheerful bustle. The soft Negro voices chattered and called, the tiny children who had been left behind all day in the care of an old granny were rejoicing in reunion with their own mothers ; was it not an idyllic life, after all, a wholesome rhythm of work and rest with a pleasant place to live and nothing to worry about ?

Woolman had himself worked long days in the fields on his father's plantation. He said to his host, "Do these people have to grind their own corn after they come in before they can get anything to eat ?" Well, said the master, the thing was, if you gave them any extra corn they ate it up. Give them corn for a week, and let it all be ground up at once—a sensible and time-saving plan—and it would all be gone by— well, say Tuesday. They could only get along with an exact daily ration. And naturally they had to grind their own. At the meeting next day a number of planters and their families gathered, but there were no Negroes present. Woolman wanted to know afterwards if the slaves ever came to meeting, and if not did they hold a meeting of their own, or what was done for their religious enlightenment ? Nothing at all ? Were they then, in fact, left to live like animals ? Then how did this affect their whole moral sense ? What standards had they of duty, honesty, right, and wrong ? And what about their marriages ? If they never went to any sort of church who married them, and when, and how ?

The well-meaning hosts, delighted to have visitors, and fascinated by John Woolman—so easy a talker, so open and friendly, and so well-informed as to the stirring affairs of the outer world—found they had been entertaining in this graceful young man an armed thief who robbed them of their complacency. Yet his manners were such that they bore it. And in the host's heart there was left a memory of a conversation that had searched his soul. For it was always conversation, always give and take, always two talking, never a monologue. Woolman was an inquirer, wishing to learn about the slave system, anxious to have the owner state his case, listening earnestly to all that was said ; but always bringing the subject into the light of what seemed to the planters an impractical idealism. Yet, since most of Woolman's hosts on this journey were Quakers, they could not deny the validity of his standards.

He left them uneasy, and after he was gone they thought of many better answers that they might have made and wished for his return to hear the much better case that they could make out now.

For in these lonely plantations conversation was at a premium.   Almost any discussion of anything was welcome.   Day after day passed monotonously with no mails, no newspapers, no one at all from outside riding through the forest trails into the wide green tobacco fields.   At stated time the expected ship came up the river to the planter's private wharf, and days of energy and excitement followed while goods from London, Liverpool, Glasgow, the West Indies, were unloaded, and bales of picked and dried tobacco took their place to be carried overseas.   At this time came batches of mail, and books, and out-of-date newspapers, as well as tools and furniture and clothes.   Apart from horseshoes and the coarsest kind of weaving and carpentry, the Virginian manufactured nothing. It paid him better to send his slave-grown tobacco abroad and barter it for all that he desired.   The very ships that carried the tobacco were built and owned by the energetic, seafaring men of Boston, Nantucket, and Rhode Island.   There was no room in Virginia for a middle class, no room for free labour, no chance, over two-thirds of the country, for any form of vital creative energy.

Perhaps Woolman's acute perception of this was one of the things which made difficulties between him and his travelling companion. For every luxury and every comfort in the planters' houses was the direct profit of the slave.   Once you looked in that direction you could see nothing else.   The slave grew the tobacco, and the tobacco was exchanged direct for the carved table, the woven carpet, the glass and silver, the lady's gown, the book of poems or sermons—and the ever-present rum.

Wherever they went in these richer settlements of the South the fact of widespread slavery and of a leisured class living on slave labour was "as a Dark Gloominess hanging over the Land."

John Woolman was not a man who could observe evil in a pained and discreet silence.   Nor could he take the existence of evil for granted.

"Two things were remarkable to me in this Journey," said Woolman :

first in regard to my Entertainment when I Eat Drunk And Lodged free cost with people that lived in Ease on the toil of their Slaves I felt uneasie and as my mind was inward I found from place to place this uneasiness to return upon me through the whole Visit. Where the

H

Masters bore A Considerable Share of the Burden And living on
moderate Expenses made their Servants labour moderately And live
pretty well I felt Some Easier But where they lived in A costly way,
aquited labour And laid the whole on their Slaves my Exercise was
Sore. Secondly this trade of Importing them from Guinea being So
much Encouraged among them ; And the white people living so
much without labour. The Nature of this trade to Guinea And the
tendency of it in these Southern Colinies was frequently the Subject
of my Serios thoughts. And I Saw So many vices And coruptions
Spreading in A great measure Occasioned by this trade and way of
life. . . . And tho now many do willingly run into It yet in future
the consequences will be Grevious to posterity. I Express it as it
appeared to me not once nor twice but as a matter fixed in my mind.

It is worth noticing that in this first impact upon him of the Southern
slave system, moving in among it and seeing it close, Woolman's first
impression was not one of physical cruelty. The two things that were
remarkable to him on this journey had little to do with the suffering of
the blacks. Contrast Whitefield's impression, covering the same country
eight years before. Whitefield wrote a letter to the inhabitants of
Maryland, Virginia, and North and South Carolina all about the "miseries
of the poor negroes."

As I lately passed through your provinces . . . I have viewed your
plantations cleared and cultivated, many spacious houses built, and the
owners of them faring sumptuously every day, my blood has frequently
almost run cold within me to consider how many of your slaves had
neither convenient food to eat nor proper raiment to put on, notwithstanding most of the comforts you enjoy were solely owing to their
indefatigable labours. . . . Not to mention what numbers have been
given up to the inhuman usage of taskmasters who by their unrelent-
ing scourges have plowed their backs and made long furrows and at
length brought them even unto death.[1]

Many a planter, converted, as the phrase is, by Whitefield's fervour
and receiving this letter, if he found his conscience touched could easily
rectify such conditions as these. The rule could go forth at once—
more food, less beating. Whitefield did not probe uncomfortably deep.
When it came to the principle of slavery itself he hedged.

Whether it be lawful for Christians to buy slaves, and thereby
encourage the nations from whom they are bought to be at perpetual

[1] Goodell, *Slavery and Anti-Slavery*, p. 15.

war with each other I shall not take upon me to determine. Sure I am it is sinful when they have bought them to use them as bad as though they were brutes, nay worse ; and whatever particular exceptions there may be (as I would charitably hope there are some) I fear the generality of you who own negroes are liable to such a charge.[1]

Woolman, on the contrary, noticed first the harm done to the white population. In his first glimpse of the tobacco fields he had not been aware of the miseries of the Negroes so much as the unhappiness of the overseer. Work on the better plantations was not over-arduous. Whitefield did not look at farm work with the eye of a farmer. Woolman did, and was less ready to speak of indefatigable labours. But in all those labouring hands there was but one will. The white man, hour by hour, soaked out by the sun, bored, exhausted, had to supply all the driving-power, all the motive, for every man and woman in the fields. The labourers had no ambition, no initiative, no interest in the work. Like inefficient mechanisms, each was geared by one desire—to do as little as possible. The overseer's task of Sisyphus was to coax, to praise, to scold, to persuade, hour by hour and day by day ; to set his purpose behind their inertia and ineptitude and somehow get the necessary minimum of work accomplished. It was not surprising that, like the schoolmaster, he often took the short cut of blows. And once that route was taken, with unlimited power and no one to interfere, it could lead sharp downhill to the foulest excesses.

But these excesses were not universal, and Woolman on this journey mentions none. The easy-going planters of Virginia and Maryland did not expect or require a maximum efficiency from their slaves, and many of them inspired activity by doing some work on their plantations themselves, at least in the way of personal oversight. This was better, said Woolman, but it was simply a poor system, detrimental to the estates, the economy of the South, and the whole white population ; bad for everybody. And as for Christian treatment, is there any Christian way to treat a slave except to set him free ? The disturbed planters accused him of an unfair view, of neglecting to consider their interests. He replied, "Whoever rightly advocates the Cause of some, thereby

---

[1] Whitefield himself, after writing this, felt compelled to use slaves in the cultivation of the flax fields at his Orphanage, Savannah, Georgia. His patroness, the Countess of Huntingdon, heard of it and remonstrated. Whitefield then reduced the number of slaves to fifty, which at his death he left to the Countess in his will, presumably so that she might have the fun of setting them free.

promotes the Good of all." They pled the inevitable ruin of themselves and their children if they should venture to fight the competition of slave-run estates with free wage labour. Woolman answered, "Our Duty and Interest are inseparably united." They tried to daunt him with their worldly wisdom, and reproached him with youth and inexperience, coming there and trying to change a system of whose ramifications he was crassly ignorant ; and Woolman had none of the thunders of hell for them.

He did not, like Whitefield, roar upon them an eternal future and presently have them foaming at the mouth and howling with terror. He met them with a sweetness which was something new to them in man-to-man relationships. "My inclination is to persuade and entreat and simply give hints of my way of thinking." But having disarmed them by his gentleness, how swift and shrewd he could pierce. "If we do not consider these things aright, but through a stupid indolence conceive views of interest separate from the general good of the great Brotherhood . . . what then shall we do when God riseth up ? . . . To our great Master we stand or fall."

Their ear was caught by a new phrase—a dangerous phrase. What did he mean by "the great Brotherhood" ? Woolman explained. Sitting on the horse block, or strolling up and down the shady avenue, or seated by candlelight after the evening meal, nuts and wine upon the polished board, and the large wax candles sweating in the heat, Woolman slowly and modestly evolved his thought to the bewitched planter, who could only complain that it was too lofty for the present time, for current use.

"When we remember," said Woolman,

that all nations are of one blood, that in this world we are but sojourners, that we are subject to the like afflictions and infirmities of body, the like disorders and frailties in mind, the like temptations, the same death, and the same judgment, and that the All wise Being is Judge and Lord over us all, it seems to raise an idea of a general brotherhood. But when we forget these things and look chiefly at our outward circumstances in this and some ages past, constantly retaining in our minds the distinction betwixt us and them, our breasts being apt to be filled with fond notions of superiority, there is danger of erring in our conduct toward them.

We allow them to be of the same species with ourselves, the odds is, we are in a higher station and enjoy greater favours than they. To consider mankind otherwise than brethren, to think favours are peculiar to one nation and exclude others, plainly supposes a darkness in the understanding. For, as God's Love is universal, so where the mind is sufficiently influenced by it, it begets a Likeness of itself, and the heart is enlarged towards all men.

When self-love presides in our minds, our opinions are bias'd in our own favour. In this condition, being concerned with a people so situated that they had no voice to plead their own cause, there's danger of using ourselves to an undisturbed partiality till, by long custom, the mind becomes reconciled with it, and the judgment itself infected.

To humbly apply to God for wisdom that we may thereby be enabled to see things as they are and ought to be, is very needful. Hereby high thoughts will be laid aside, and all men treated as becometh the sons of one Father, agreeable to the doctrine of Christ Jesus.

He moved them, yes. But he went on his way and left them, and the worries of every day flooded back and claimed their attention, and they lost again—only too willingly—that large perspective. Indeed, they had plenty of troubles on their hands. The very day that John Woolman left home on his journey south the *Pennsylvania Gazette* had carried :

an account of ships taken by the Enemy belonging to Virginia and Maryland—

The *Dragon* from Virginia to London.
Two ships from Virginia to Liverpool.
The *Duke of Argyle* from Virginia to Bristol.
The *Greenly* from Virginia to Scotland, taken by the *Sultana* Privateer of St Maloes.
A ship from Maryland, taken by a French privateer—

seventeen ships listed in all.

Tobacco was not only the export crop but the money currency, and heavy losses such as these were widely felt, and were depressing in effect.

Yet the tremendous increase in the number of Negro slaves was seen by Virginia's best thinkers to be dangerous. Twenty years before Woolman's visit there had been ten white men in Virginia to every Negro. When Woolman went there were as many Negroes in the province as whites ; while in South Carolina, sparsely settled as yet, there were fifteen black men for every white.

There were some in the Virginia legislature itself who would have agreed with Woolman that "in future the consequence will be grievous to posterity."

A lot of water had flowed down the James river since that hot, moist day in August 1620 when a Dutch man-o'-war, curiously nosing up to the new settlement, had made a handsome profit, offering to exhausted English gentry a batch of twenty Negro slaves for sale.

XV

FIRST SOUTHERN JOURNEY (II)

WHEN John Woolman, with Isaac Andrews, went up the James river to "a new settlement" he came into an atmosphere that was like home. His immediate objective there was to visit people whose relatives he already knew, New Jersey Quakers who had moved south from Salem and Nottingham, landless sons of large families who wanted an opportunity to obtain grants of fertile and free land and better themselves and their descendants. The careful Quaker records show a steady seeping in of Pennsylvania, New Jersey, and New England folk to the rich empty regions of south-west Virginia and North Carolina all through the eighteenth century. But many of the new settlers were also Presbyterians recently come from Scotland and Ireland, the former escaping from the aftermath of the rebellion of Bonnie Prince Charlie, and the latter escaping from the intolerable disabilities pressed upon Presbyterians in northern Ireland by the always intolerant Church of England —schools, marriages, and professional careers disallowed.

Some of the Scots-Irish, particularly, had joined Friends. It was difficult to organize a Presbyterian church without a qualified paid minister. These new Quakers were thankful to be visited by Woolman and Andrews and to be drawn into the deeper places of their not yet fully familiar way of worship. And others not Quakers were eager for visitors in their lonely places, and gladly took a holiday from ordinary tasks to gather for the silent fellowship of a Quaker meeting, and the words of cheer and light which the travellers might bring. These people had small estates, few or no slaves, and were labouring with their hands, far enough from the old settlements to begin a new type of Virginian life without incurring contempt or social ostracism. "As the soil is natural and friendly to grass, they will, for many years to come, raise great quantities of neat cattle."[1]

The journey thence into North Carolina was rough going. Other travellers about the same time report the crossing of swollen rivers in canoes, swimming the horses, and the howling of the wolves about them when camping for the night in the woods. But even in parts of New Jersey wolves were still running free, and a bounty was offered for their skins. There were unusually close links between North Carolina and the New Jersey-Pennsylvania provinces. William Penn had been a friend of the philosopher Locke, they had discussed together many times the exact pattern of the perfect state, and when Penn drew up the constitutions of New Jersey and of Pennsylvania some of Locke's ideas entered in, whereas when Locke drew up the constitution for Carolina he incorporated some of William Penn's. The constitution for Carolina contained, notably, a clause of complete religious toleration. But the absentee proprietors who owned the province conceived of the Church of England as the bulwark of religion and order, and were only less active than Virginia in enforcing its support. In early Virginia a Quaker had been fined twenty pounds in cash for every month of absence from church, and two hundred pounds of tobacco for every time he attended a Friends' meeting ; while the host who entertained a travelling Quaker in his home could be fined five thousand pounds of tobacco, half the fines in each case to be paid to the informer. Yet these penalties, in spite of the informer-profit clause, had been too difficult to enforce for long in such scattered communities. Quakers had been attracted to Carolina, and had become powerful there. The Governor who had first pulled the colony out of its perpetual troubles with the Indians (nothing to do, here, with the French—just plain personal quarrel, mutual treachery, kidnapping, and massacre) was a Quaker, John Archdale. And when the Lords Proprietors of a later day instituted the religious persecution of the Test Act it was a Quaker, John Porter, who headed the opposition and was strong enough to depose one governor and set up another. When Woolman was eight years old King George II

---

[1] MacSporran, "America Dissected," appendix to Updike's *History of the Church in Narragansett.*

had purchased the whole turbulent province—at the request of Parliament and with money provided—and it had been made into two crown colonies, North and South Carolina. South Carolina formed an aristocratic society centred in Charleston, while absentee landlords and unsupervised overseers on the large estates made the lot of the Negroes particularly hard. Woolman did not go down into South Carolina. In North Carolina the greater simplicity of life made Bancroft call it " the paradise of the Quakers." And Archdale's report of it had been, "The country produces plentifully all things necessary for the life of man with as little labour as any I have known ; it wants only industrious people, fearing God."

Even here, however, slavery was the serpent in the paradise. And the evil was two-edged, in that the small plantation worked by a few slaves was not productive enough to give the best of the Virginian culture—the books, the sending sons home to England for an education, and some of the other advantages that go with wealth. Woolman did not find the spiritual condition of the smaller landholders of North Carolina any better just because they were less well-to-do. True, one could find five Quaker meeting-houses within a compass of thirty miles, and six or seven hundred people would gather from far and near to hear a stranger. But the Friends' meetings themselves were in a peculiar state. Quakerism cannot long survive in acquiescence to a widespread social evil. Time after time the regular records in the carefully kept Minute Books of Monthly and Quarterly Meetings—faithful indexes of the Church's life—consist of a single line, "No Business offered to this Meeting that requir'd Entry."

But at the Quarterly Meeting at Herring Creek, Virginia, attended by Isaac Andrews and John Woolman on this journey, "on 6th of ye 6th month [August] 1746," they were in for a piece of business that did require entry. That was the final submission of the disorderly Friends at Elk Ridge, reported a year before, and struggled with ever since.

This Meeting[1] being informed by a member thereof who had lately Visited Elkridge Meeting that . . . Seventeen Persons thereto belonging or attending . . . had at Evening the 21st day of ye 4 Mo. Last fell into a Strange Disposition of Minde, all praying or preaching at once or So many of them that it could not be Distinguished what was Said by any one of them, and Continued all night and for Several

[1] MS. minutes of Herring Creek, Virginia, in care of Homewood Meeting, Baltimore.

Days . . . & the friendly and Neighbourly advices alRead given by
Several friends not accepted whereupon this Meeting

referred to the Apostle's advice that things be done decently and in
order, and desired the Elk Ridge Friends "to repent of their Errors &
keep out thereof for the time to come & make necessary acknowledgment
thereof in our Quarterly Meeting . . . & be Delivered from all the
Deluding Imaginations or powers of Darkness & Self-conceitedness."

Elk Ridge refused appearance or answer for three Quarterly Meetings
running, but at this one in August 1746 report was at last made that they
had submitted and "asked to be taken under the care of Friends." A final
paper of acknowledgment was delivered and read at the next Quarterly
Meeting. The Elk Ridge people seem (after categorically admitting
everything) to have relapsed into complete silence in their meetings.

John Woolman does not mention anything of this queer but destructive
trouble. There would be no evidence that he knew about it, even, but
for the old Minute Book, which after the Elk Ridge discussion has one
more minute to add :

> Isaac Andrews produced to this meeting a Certificate from the
> Monthly Meeting of friends at Haddonfield in the County of Glocester
> in New Jersey And John Woolman also produced A Certificate from
> the monthly meeting of friends at Burlington wch Certificate was Read
> in and to the Satisfaction of this Meeting and Certificates for them to
> their S^d Monthly Meetings are Sign'd by and in this Meeting.
> No more business offering this meeting concludes.

This is a concrete glimpse of a part of what lies behind John Woolman's
edged understatement that "In our journeying to & fro we found some
honest-hearted Friends who appeared to be concerned for the cause of
truth among a backsliding people."

The chief sign of life among the slave-owning Quakers of Virginia
and Maryland was their hearty resistance to two impositions which they
readily recognized as being against their vital doctrine and tradition.
One of these was the levy made in both these provinces for the support
of the Church of England, and the other was the levy made in Virginia
for the militia. On both these counts Friends grimly endured distraint
of goods.

> Taken from Thos. Pleasants for fines & prests demands one feather
> bed (valued at £5). Taken from ditto on ye acct aforesaid, 1 lb Tobaco

720—£6. Taken in Goochland for prests demands 2 young negroes for 460 lb. Tob° £3.16.8. A Hors for abt 80 lb Tob° worth £3, a gun for 20 lb Tob° worth £1.15

are typical entries of distraint for "melisha fines & Church" or "prest's demands." They were carefully itemized by a Meeting for the Sufferings of Friends appointed by the Virginia Yearly Meeting. In the first of these exactions, the church levy, the Quakers, with their dogged capacity to suffer, were the spearpoint of colonial resistance, the front line of a majority group. It was one of the errors of the home government to try to fasten the Church of England tithing system upon all the colonies not protected by special charter, although Episcopalians were a minority or a small majority in every place. In the second, resistance to the militia, Quakers were, in the South, a peculiar people.

These struggles might seem to indicate a higher level of spiritual life in the meeting than John Woolman was willing, with his exacting standards, to allow. But refusal to pay a church tithe or to support a "hireling priest," or to serve in or pay for any military organization was practically compulsory on every Quaker. His conduct in these affairs was under the eye and judgment of the meeting, and he would find himself "denied" or "disowned" if he did not come up to scratch; cast out, in fact, of the Society—treatment which destroyed social prestige and in some cases a loss of credit which involved financial ruin.

Riding up through Maryland at last, up the western shore of the beautiful Chesapeake, Woolman observed a type of civilization that was more Pennsylvanian than Southern, except for the tobacco and the slaves. Maryland had towns and the settled social life that goes with group communities. There was more general culture, a thriving middle class, a variety of trade and industry. Maryland was not a helpless parasite upon one crop, or wholly dependent upon slave labour. Her intercourse was with Pennsylvania rather than with Virginia. It was already manifest, in germ, that if the unthinkable should ever happen, and there should be a cleavage between the North and the South, Maryland's interests would lie with the North.

But if a tree is to be known by its fruits there was something deeply good in the roots of the patriarchal culture of old Virginia. It had somehow given birth to, and was slowly ripening, George Washington and Thomas Jefferson.

When Woolman dismounted from his horse at his father's door on the first day of August his mind was full of the fact of slavery and its complicated evil effects.   He had left Isaac Andrews at Haddonfield and called on his sister on the way.   Now the family group at home gathered out on the grass when supper was cleared, and listened long to his stories in the warm perfumed dusk.   The bullfrog by the creek twanged his deep 'cello string, and the fireflies made stars among the leaves.   All was peace there, within and without, all harmony and loving-kindness and rest after good labour.   But they saw from their safe place the unrest of the outer world ; they felt its pain.   No slaves had run out when John had ridden through the plantation, to give him servile greeting and to take his horse to stable.   Eber, now seven years old, had joyfully seized the bridle, and Abraham, nine, had run for a bucket of water, and Jonah, thirteen, had been proud to unsaddle and curry the beast, while eighteen-year-old Uriah took the saddle-bags for his admired eldest brother, and little Rachel had bustled for warm water and a bowl of soap jelly to wash off John's own sweat and dust of travel, and Hannah had scurried to prepare more supper, and Esther had fluttered round, and the mother had called orders to Abner to kill another chicken—John was come !   How love rejoiced in opportunity to serve, and service was glorified in becoming the very will of the heart.   Something very precious, beyond the worth of its weight in tobacco—or even in rubies—was lost when all this energy of services was relegated to those who performed it per-functorily, and even through fear and with hate.

So John told them of his adventures over fifteen hundred miles and of the slave-ridden life on the great estates in the South, and his father particularly was keenly absorbed in his tale.   Then in his turn John heard about the volunteer draft, which had taken place during his absence, five gentlemen being given letters of commission authorizing them each to raise a hundred men, to be embarked immediately at Perth Amboy for New York and to join Governor Clinton.   And of a mob at Newark which had twice made riots and broken open the gaol "declaring openly their intention to throw off their Dependance on the Crown of Britain and flying in the Face of the Government."[1]

Certainly an era, pleasant, vigorous, and hopeful, was closing, and closing fast, and no one could foresee what was coming in its place.

The next day John Woolman returned to his lodging at Mount

[1] *N. J. Archives*, First Series, XV, 488.

Holly and did that tailoring job for Thos. Redman, and so began a quiet routine two months, reimbursing his exchequer, arranging his private affairs, and mulling over the notes and reminiscences of his trip.

But now that so many able-bodied men, English and Indian, had been taken out of the province there began to be a spreading fear of invasion by sea. Word came from the Council at Perth Amboy directing beacons and watches to be set at strategic high spots along the shore to look out for invasion. Squan and Deal and the Highlands of Neversink, all upon the sea coast, were to set a constant sentinel "to watch for the approach of 6 ships or more" and "if he judge them to be enemies to fire the beacon."[1]

John Woolman, sensitive to the growing panic of lonely settlements where older residents still remembered the days of the pirates, "felt an increasing concern for Friends on our sea-coast." And early in October he once more took horse and set off on a journey, this time "In Company with My friend Peter Andrews," and rode right around the New Jersey sea coast in its loneliest part—Salem, Cape May, Great and Little Egg Harbour, Barnegat, Manahockin, Squan, and so to Shrewsbury. There is no lovelier season in all the world than October in New Jersey and Pennsylvania, and no more delightful time to travel, but on this journey Woolman and his friend left behind them, after Salem, the golden and scarlet woods, and turned into the dark recesses of the pines. This region was poor and thinly settled. Wide marshes often made going difficult, and the inhabitants attempted little agriculture, depending for a sparse livelihood upon fishing and timber. It was cheering to them to have warm demonstration that Friends in the richer parts cared how they fared, taking trouble to come out to see them and comfort them, and, if necessary, share their danger. Beginning at old-established Salem and ending at the substantial settlement of Shrewsbury, John Woolman again experienced the sharp contrast between the poor and the well-to-do within the Society of Friends ; although none here were living so hard as on the frontier or so soft as on the vast estates of Virginia. Woolman's aim was not social reform ; he was not consciously the apostle of a revolution or the mouthpiece of a theory of any sort. His concern was simply to express the loving-kindness which all human creatures ought to feel for one another as children of one family, one Father. But to go on such journeys as these, often accepting hospitality

[1] *Ibid.*, 461.

one night in an environment of such insufficiency that all the human energy was exhausted in merely keeping alive, and within a day's journey, a mere fifteen or twenty miles through the pine-scented gloom, to enter the sunny clearing surrounding a well-established settlement where abundance overflowed, was to make a sensitive Shelleyan spirit fierily conscious of the need of adjustment.

Such impressions wove themselves into one fabric with those he had brought back with him from the South. There was something wrong about the sharp inequality of the human lot ; and most of the ills which he saw gathering about the civilization that he loved seemed to him to arise from this root.

He had by now seen a good many of the colonies. He had observed closely the types of life in the Quaker provinces and in the South. But one large section, one important phase of colonial civilization, he had not yet seen close to—the civilization of New England. And he began to plan a visit there.

In the meantime, however, attendance at the Quarterly Meeting at Shrewsbury ended his present advance. From Shrewsbury the two friends—who were able to keep in affectionate harmony the whole way without special help from heaven—turned homeward. "We were out twenty-two days, and rode, by computation, three hundred and forty miles." [1]

Woolman had now travelled in one year not much less than two thousand miles. The winter was a time to stay at home ; and besides he needed to earn some money. The employer's business given up and the tailoring man dismissed, John Woolman now had the sole use of the little tailoring shop. His orders were constant, his needs were small, and he was negotiating for the purchase of the business ; a steady insurance against the ugly poverty which he had seen and condemned.

A touch of circumstantial evidence that John Ogburn may have been Woolman's employer is offered in the fact that Ogburn was certainly selling off his property at this time and preparing to retire. He was the owner of business premises in Mill Street and also owner of the Three Tuns Tavern. In 1748 he sold the Three Tuns to Josiah White, who retained it—renting it to different innkeepers—for his lifetime, and left it among other real estate to his wife in his will. The tavern was owned by the Whites for sixty years.

[1] Whittier ed., p. 61.

Woolman had besides something else in view. And his father and sister knew all about it. It was, indeed, an open secret among the Burr and Woolman connexion. Courtship is hard to hide. But it met with the unforeseen delay of family sorrow. How was Elizabeth Woolman to know that this, her thirty-first year, was more important to her than any other ? And how were her visiting brothers and sisters and cousins to know that a peculiar radiance of memory would light these winter days for them in time to come, and that when they now said to her "in the summer"—"in the spring"—"next month" even, what they really said was Never ?

XVI

DEATH OF ELIZABETH WOOLMAN AND FIRST
NEW ENGLAND JOURNEY

THAT winter Elizabeth Woolman's fate overtook her. One evening
with an aching head and swimming eyes she set her needle in the last
stitch and folded up her work beside the fire. Filled with a deep depression and a sense of encroaching physical ill, she climbed the stair to the
cold bedroom where Maria hastened to warm the icy feather bed with
the warming-pan. And in the morning Elizabeth Estaugh, summoned
by the frantic Maria, found her friend delirious with fever, and sent a
horse messenger for Mrs Woolman. Before long the dread disease
declared itself, smallpox, the most horrible and the most mortal carried
in early days by the mother country to the colonies. Good Dr Ross,
graduate of the University of Edinburgh, rode over from Burlington on
the faithful black nag. The sturdy animal bore him over so wide a
practice that it often took him a fortnight to complete his rounds, even
when the season was suitable for him to sleep out by night in the fields
and woods. But neither his lavish and frequent bleeding of Elizabeth
nor the assortment of medicines in his saddle-bags could avail, nor the
famous natural simples which Josiah White eagerly brought, nor her
mother's skilled nursing. And not even the presence of her favourite
brother could give the patient any cheer. The clear, bright spirit was
clouded by the intolerable miseries of the body, and by the untimely
approach of death with all its terrors.

"The fore part of her Illness she was in Great Sadness and dejection of mind," wrote John Woolman, but "Tho she was thus disconsolate, Still She retained a hope, which was an ancor to her." And after a while the darkness passed, and the slow downward progress of her illness became a path of light. "Her disorder Appearing dangerous that her life was despaired of, Mother appeared Sorrowfull, of which She took notice And Said, Dear Mother weep not for me I go to My God."

John Woolman rode over to visit her daily, and heard her most intimate thoughts to the last, alluding to himself in his Journal for public use as "an Intimate friend." But "comeing Some miles to Se her the Morning before She died," he was able to receive her final words before she lapsed into the unconsciousness that is Nature's own anæsthetic. He "asked her how She did ; she answered, I have had a hard night, but Shall not have Another Such, for I shall die, & It will be well with my Soul : & accordingly died the next Evening."

In spite of the mystic prescience and the triumphant affirmation of her parting words, John Woolman was painfully affected by the manner of her death. The disfigurement which made her dying face unrecognizable, the stench of the closed sickroom, the husky harshness of her difficult speech, all the ignoble disguise thrown over her familiar charm by the devilish corruption of the disease, implanted in Woolman a lasting horror of the smallpox.

Perhaps this intensified his desire to paint her portrait as she really was, and so allows the reader of his Journal an unusual glimpse into Woolman's heart and into the family life.

She was from her youth of A thoughtfull disposition And remarkable Compassionate to her Acquaintance in their Sickness or Any Distress, being ready to help As far As She could.

One Instance of the Regard to the Care of her I think worth noticeing. It hapened that She and two of her Sisters being then near the Estate of Young women had agreed one first day afternoon to make A Visit to Some other young women Some distance of, whose company in All probability would have done them no good. They Expressed their desire to our parents who discouraged & Stoped them. The Same afternoon as my Sisters were toGather talking About their disopointment, Elizabeth Expressed her Satisfaction In being put by as believing it to be best for them Ading this Ryme

Such as thy companions be So will people think of thee.

Now the little home at Haddonfield was broken up. Negro Maria

I

hired herself to Mrs Woolman Senior, and John Woolman, an exact and efficient man of business, did Elizabeth his last service by settling her estate with dispatch.

Elizabeth had made her will two years before, "being at present in good health and perfect mind & memory Yet calling to mind ye uncertainty of this Life." John had drawn it for her, and John and Asher were her two executors. By May all was cleared. Her beautiful furniture and her best gowns were distributed among her sisters, with her great looking-glass for her mother, and a major share of all her furnishings for Hannah. Money legacies of six pounds proclamation money[1] were left to each of her brothers and sisters, the younger ones to have it "put out to Interest at their Proper Risque until they shall Severally arrive to ye age of Twenty one years." Her Beloved Father, Samuel Woolman, received her great Bible. And her favourite and dearest brother, John Woolman, received "the sum of Twelve pounds proclamation money and my Gold buttons."

So closed the book of a sweet life, and in the sense of bereavement suffered by the large family, none felt it like John Woolman. Business and travel are a man's natural escapes from gnawing sorrow. In the month of April John Woolman had clinched the purchase of real estate from John Ogburn described as a brick house and lot of land in Mill Street, Mount Holly. And a month later he signed the deed of purchase of eleven acres of farm and orchard from Peter Andrews, part of a larger farm which Andrews had purchased a year before from Elizabeth Estaugh. Then, with Peter Andrews as equal companion, furnished with travelling certificates from Burlington Monthly Meeting, Woolman took horse and rode north for Long Island and New England, to complete his survey of slavery and its effects throughout the colonies.

"My beloved companion and I belonged both to one meeting, came forth in the ministry near the same time, and were inwardly united in the work. He was about thirteen years older than I, bore the heaviest burden, and was an instrument of the greatest use."[2]

---

[1] The different colonies acting independently had rated the shilling—and therefore the pound—at different values. In 1706 a proclamation of Queen Anne fixed the nominal value of the pound at the existing rate. The most common coin in circulation was the Spanish dollar. Burlington decreed in 1722 "that silver pass according to the Late Queen Anne's proclamation, that Dollars pass at 5 shill according to proclamation money and that English Copper half pence shall go for pence apiece proclamation money."

[2] Whittier ed., p. 64.

Woolman rapidly sketches in the itinerary. They began with the New York Yearly Meeting at Flushing, Long Island, then met a large gathering of people "not Quakers" at Setawket, and another in a private house at Oyster Bay. Then "having visited the island we went over to the main" and took trouble to go to the back settlements in the wild country round Oblong, Nine Partners, and Milford. Then they rode through Connecticut, where the settlers were mostly Presbyterian but "generally civil to us," and after three days' riding came to the colony of Rhode Island. There they visited in and about Newport, Dartmouth, and those parts ; then to Boston, and thence eastward as far as Dover.

From Newport we sailed to Nantucket, were there nearly a week, & from thence came over to Dartmouth. Having finished our visit in these parts we crossed the Sound from New London to Long Island and . . . proceeded towards home, which we reached the 13th of seventh month 1747 having rode about fifteen hundred miles and sailed about one hundred and fifty.[1]

The earliest settlers of New England had been very loth to admit Quakers, not only because they wished to preserve unpolluted their own regimented Presbyterianism—which fined a man for not attending meeting, and set him in the stocks for kissing his wife on a Sunday—but because the Quakers were known to be dangerously liberal. Not only had the Presbyterian divines done their best to keep them out of the borders of New England, as Peter Andrews's grandmother had found to her cost, but they had made a sturdy effort to keep them out of the continent itself.

But the New England Yearly Meeting was now well established, bought by blood and martyrdom, the Quakers were numerous and prosperous, and bigotry concentrated on the Roman Catholics. For this there was a definite political reason. New England was bearing the brunt of the slow spasmodic war, the French-Canadians were Catholics and so were the praying Indians, their allies, and Jesuit priests had been known to accompany raiding parties of secret massacre. Nerves were on edge in New England, and, as often in times of intense insecurity, popular religion had got mixed up with nationalism. God was on the side of the Protestants and English, and against the Catholics and French. The famous and brilliant New England divine, Jonathan Edwards,

[1] *Ibid.*, p. 64.

wrote a letter from Northampton, Massachusetts, the summer of Woolman's visit, to a fellow divine in Scotland :

> Nor need you be informed by me of the repeated mercy of God to
> us in confounding our enemies in their renewed attempt this year by
> delivering up their fleet, on its way thither, into the hands of the
> English. In all probability that fleet was intended for a very extensive
> design against the English colonies in conjunction with the French
> forces in Canada. For there was an army lay waiting at Nova Scotia
> which, on the news of the sailing of their fleet immediately left the
> country, and returned to Canada over the lake Champlain, towards
> New England and New York ; and they attacked Fort Saratoga in
> New York government, and killed or took about fifty men that were
> drawn out of the fort, but desisted from any further attempts about
> the time we may suppose they received the news of the defeat of their
> fleet. And very soon after they received this news in Canada, the
> French there released most of our captives, and sent one ship loaded
> with them, to the number of about one hundred and seventy, to Bos-
> ton, and another ship with about sixty, if I remember right, to Louis-
> burg. . . . New England has had many other surprising deliverances
> from the French and Indians. . . . Our enemies own that the heavens
> are on our side and fight for us.[1]

Many passages in the Old Testament could be used to bear out ideas of
this kind, but the learned dialectic of Mr Edwards was at no loss to find
them also in the New. What about those mysterious prophecies
regarding beasts and Antichrist and vials in the Book of Revelation—
the pouring out of the sixth vial on the River Euphrates in particular ?

> I signified it as what appeared to me probable that one main thing
> intended by the drying up the river Euphrates was the drying up of
> the temporal supplies and income of the antichristian church and
> kingdom ; and suggested it to consideration whether God, appearing
> so wonderfully for the taking Cape Breton and the American fishery
> thereupon depending, out of the hands of the French, and thereby
> drying up so great a fountain of the wealth of the kingdom of France,
> might not be looked upon as one effect of the sixth vial. I would now
> also propose it to be considered whether God's so extraordinarily
> appearing to baffle the great attempt of the French nation to repossess
> themselves of this place be not some confirmation of it ; and whether
> or no the almost ruining the French East India trade, by the dreadful
> hand of Heaven, in burying their stores at Port l'Orient, and the taking
> so many of their ships by Commodore Barnet, and also the taking

---

[1] *Memoirs of Jonathan Edwards*, by Sereno E. Dwight, I, cxxxiii.

of so many of their South Sea ships, vastly rich, and several other things of like nature that might be mentioned, may not probably be further effects of this vial.

Indeed, the more Mr Edwards contemplated God's past dealings with England and Scotland and the colonies the more he perceived and marvelled at "what obligations he has laid those nations under," having "made his arm bare in almost miraculous dispensations of his providence in our behalf to succeed us against our enemies and to defend us from them."[1]

It was not, however, considered a baring of God's arm or a dispensation of his providence when in the following November Sir Charles Knowles, lying at Nantucket, short of men to man the fleet and in no way depending upon miracle, sent his boats up to Boston and impressed colonial seamen, mechanics, and labourers from wharves. He was not praised as helping to pour out the sixth vial. On the contrary, the angry men of Boston seized the British commanders and other officers in the town and imprisoned them as hostages for the release of their fellow-citizens. And after three days of rage and resentment an exchange of prisoners convinced the British Navy that their usual rough-and-ready recruiting would not run current in New England however righteous their cause.

Among these hardy, independent, and prejudiced people John Woolman now moved, breathed the bracing New England air, admired the surf thunder on the rocky coast (so different from the sand-banks of New Jersey), travelled the forests rich with elm and maple and the wild grape, and dwelt briefly in the isolated farmhouse and the well-ordered town. When he entered Boston he saw Boston Common, where the only Quaker martyrs in America had suffered death by hanging in the dark days of Endicott, and the governor's house, where the cynical Charles II had played a practical joke on Endicott by sending him as royal emissary the banished Quaker Shattuck with sealed orders of religious toleration. Having had the Quaker's hat knocked off him, what a bitter humiliation to the governor's pride to perceive the royal seal, to rise and stand to attention and uncover to the King's Messenger—"Give Mr Shattuck his hat !" Flesh is grass indeed, and the place thereof knew it no more. Those who now went about the streets of Boston were thinking other thoughts, indifferent to Quaker peculiarities, or were Quakers themselves. Their main preoccupation, apart from the always dominant private care

[1] *Ibid.*, cxxviii and cxxix.

of each, was the French and Indian War, and the hideous danger of a
secret, surprise raid on the lonely settlements.   They delighted in sermons
which suggested everlasting escape from this menace.   The Quakers,
holding war to be against their faith, did not expect God to be on the
side of their armies, but were not able to free themselves from the idea
that attack and disaster were a judgment of God upon the people for
their sins.   They also, Quakers, were sinners in a general way, and
accepted their share of ill luck as a chastening, but to feel that specific
wrongdoing on their part had any share in the provocative causes of war,
that was very far from their remotest imagination.   John Woolman,
seeing many among them rich, owners of ships, engaging in extensive
commerce, and owners and buyers of slaves, had many thoughts on this
subject which it was yet too soon to express.

"In this journey," says Woolman, "we were taught by renewed
experience to labour for an inward stillness; at no time to seek for words
but to live in the spirit of truth and utter that to the people which truth
opened in us."

Very different had been the visit and ministry of Whitefield seven
years before.   He had stirred the people up, indeed, in place after place,
"so that the whole room was full of nothing but outcries, faintings and
the like."   And the Reverend Mr Edwards had followed it up afterwards
in his parish of Narragansett and done his best to keep the excitement
alive.   In the spring of 1741 he had addressed the children, for instance,
to impress it on them separately, and "when they were dismissed they
almost all of them went home crying aloud through the streets to all
parts of the town."[1]   Encouraged by this success, in the middle of the
summer Edwards gathered the young people "to my house—a most
happy meeting . . . many fainted under these affections. . . . We had
several meetings that summer attended with like appearances."

But the Quakers, observing these events with an exasperating coolness,
saw the fervour die away in 1742, and the town return to its former ways
and thoughts.   John Woolman and his friend made no such tremendous
public stir.   Even in the Quaker meetings their passing is quietly noted
in an occasional undescriptive minute.   But here and there a mind was
touched, not to a passionate excitement but to a new way of thinking.
Woolman roused a question that caused a sensitive spirit to turn and
look at his own life from a new angle.   So was planted a seed that grew

[1] Edwards's Journal in *The Works of Jonathan Edwards*, p. c.

quietly and secretly, as seeds must always grow, hidden from sight in the earth.

It was on this journey that Woolman met a kindred spirit and made a close friendship for life in Thomas Hazard, of Tower Hill, Rhode Island. Hazard was one of the aristocrats of the colony and looked it, over six feet tall, handsome, and of a naturally proud bearing. The Hazard family produced, in their time, four Lieutenant-Governors of Rhode Island. The average farms in those parts ran about two hundred to three hundred acres, like those in New Jersey, but since pasturage for cattle and horses was apt to take up more space than tillable land, farms of a thousand or two thousand acres were not uncommon among the breeders of horses. Thomas Hazard's father, Robert Hazard, owned twelve thousand acres,[1] and his domestic arrangements were on such a scale that when in later life he retired from activity, and diminished his estate by giving large farms to his sons, he congratulated himself on the modest size of his reduced establishment "being only seventy in parlor and kitchin."[2] Two vessels every year sailed from Newport, laden with Robert Hazard's woollens, grain, cheese, and horses for the West Indies. And four thousand sheep yielded their annual wool, and led a fat existence on grass so rich that when allowed to grow for hay it reached to the top of the walls and fences. Outhouses and attics provided sleeping-places for an army of slaves. The horse-raising plantations reckoned equal numbers of slaves and horses, and Robert Hazard, with his large model dairy, and sheep and wool industry added, was the largest slave-owner in Rhode Island. The horses were unique. They were a remarkable breed, of Andalusian strain, noted for swiftness and easy pacing. They could pace a mile in a little more than two minutes, and had such an even pace and strength that they could travel one hundred miles in a day without injury to themselves or riders. They were saddle-horses pure and simple, never used in harness, as "draughting stiffened their limbs." In America they were called the Narragansett pacer, and in England they were imported at great expense under the name of the Spanish jennet. Robert Hazard, father of Thomas, raised one hundred pacers for export annually. When in 1742 the eldest son and chief heir to all this married a wealthy and beautiful Quaker girl her father, Governor Robinson, said, "This day by the marriage of my daughter to Thomas Hazard I have ennobled my family!"

[1] According to Mr Isaac P. Hazard, great-grandson, in Updike, p. 179.
[2] Ibid., p. 181.

Yet young Tom Hazard had managed somehow to escape the deceitfulness of riches, and after a sojourn at Yale College had come back and looked at the familiar splendours of his home with an alien eye. Presented by his father with a well-stocked farm as a wedding gift, including slaves and cattle, he had declined the slaves, and freed such as were already at his disposal, and when Woolman went to Tower Hill as his guest he found the young couple, with their first children, living in great simplicity, working the plantation with free labour. This drastic step in so prominent a citizen had roused great indignation among the neighbours, and had particularly enraged Tom's father. King of his little kingdom, he was unaccustomed to the faintest criticism, and this action of his son's struck at his heart. It was a deep, public condemnation of his ways, and he threatened to disinherit Thomas if he did not conform to current custom and use slaves. Tom Hazard found himself straitened for a while. He had paid out a considerable sum in cold cash in order to purchase himself a clear conscience, and it looked as if it might cost him dearer yet. John Woolman was one of the few who thought it cheap at the price. The young men met as men in a foreign country who speak the same language, and had warm and enheartening hours together. Thomas Hazard was of a most unyielding temper. In his maturity some one said of him, "It is a good thing that Tom usually makes up his mind right, for he never changes it!" Woolman's friendship and comprehension came at just the right time, and perhaps enabled the son to behave with respectful gentleness towards his father without any compromise of principle. It was part of Woolman's power that he "felt tenderness" towards the oppressor as well as the oppressed. He perceived that the pure universal love he longed for must include them both, as indeed it did include both in the sight of heaven. The oppressor was often like a man who had lost his way in a fog and believed himself to be travelling in the right direction when he was only weaving round upon his tracks in a great obscurity. Does one regard such a man who has lost his way with indignation or with pity? So Woolman discoursed of the great brotherhood to Tom Hazard from another angle, and with such effect that Hazard, labouring to the end of his life for the cause of the freeing of the slave, both in the Society of Friends and in the Rhode Island Assembly, never did so with the harshness and acrimony of the typical reformer, but always maintained a sweet and understanding spirit.

A family tradition has come down that the father's reconciliation with his son was so complete that he not only reinstated him in his will, but also, impressed by his argument and example, set free in that will his own slaves. A perusal of Robert Hazard's will, however, made just before his death in 1762, explodes that theory, since he left slaves itemized as part of his disposable property to his wife and to all of his children, excepting only Thomas,[1] who would not receive them. But Thomas has his right share of his father's estate, and is named sole executor of his will. The tradition is very strong, none the less, and it is possible that Robert Hazard freed some of his large body of slaves before he died.

On return to Mount Holly John Woolman stayed only long enough to see that his new property was being set in order, to make some necessary arrangements, and to pay visits to his family before he was again on the move. Visiting at Chesterfield, he found that an old friend, John Sykes, was making plans for a journey among Friends in Maryland, and Sykes invited him to go as his companion. This fitted in with Woolman's desires, and the two obtained certificates and set off together early in October, visiting Friends "in the lower counties of Delaware and on the eastern shore of Maryland," attending the Baltimore Yearly Meeting at Little Creek, and finally coming home by way of Nottingham. John Sykes was a man of sixty-five, but since he lived to be ninety, he was now merely in vigorous middle age. He was an interesting companion, full of stories and reminiscences, for he was himself an original settler. He had been born in old England, at Hull, and been brought over to New Jersey as a boy by his father in the same ship as the Murfin family. Robert and Ann Murfin had their two little girls with them, Mary and Johanna (both born in Nottingham, England), and Robert's young sister, Katherine Murfin. The latter had the very first wedding in the colony. Not even the Meeting-tent, made of a sail, had yet been put up. But Quakers did not need a sacred building or dedicated enclosure for their religious ceremonies. Every day, every hour, every place, was equally pervaded with divinity if men would pay attention. As Jacob said with astonishment in the empty valley, "This is none other but the house of God, and this is the gate of heaven." So Katherine and her bridegroom met with no delay.

The preliminaries being settled they soon after assembled a few Friends, proceeded to the nearest public place—the first cross-way

[1] See *College Tom*, by Caroline Hazard, p. 52.

they came to—and there solemnly declared that they took each other for man and wife, with mutual promises of faith and love, until death should separate them. After the ceremony they returned home to dinner and made good cheer on some fresh fish which they purchased of a party of Indians they met in the path.

The Sykeses and the Murfins took up land "near Burlington, in the woods." Where the Sykeses built their cabin was later called Bordentown and was right on the Delaware ; where the Murfins built theirs was along Crosswicks Creek, and was later called Chesterfield. "Our houses was made of palidoes and some of logs, covered with long grass. They pounded the corn by reason they had no mill in the country. There was great hardships, yet I never heard them say I would I had not come here or repine."[1]   The Indians were thick about those woods, and took a great interest in the queer ways of the white people. They were peculiarly attached to the lonely Murfin household, and the two bewitching little girls. They would often stroll in and share a meal or play with the children. And since there was no school to go to, and Mary and Johanna had schooling at home with their mother, they picked up the Indians' language. Exchange of gifts was frequent, and generally to the advantage of the settlers in the long run, but what cannot be replaced acquires extravagant value, and it was a severe trial to the Murfins when a young Indian chief took a fancy to the red bed-curtain with brass rings, and "would not be denied so brave a piece of finery though they could illy spare it." Oh, yes, he gave a field or something for it. John Sykes knew all about the Murfins' lives, because when the girls grew up he married Johanna. Daniel Smith, of Burlington, great-uncle of Woolman's friend, John Smith, married Mary. Careless Mary Murfin Smith, so trained in the lore of woods and waters, who yet lost her life by drowning, in Woolman's twentieth year, watering her horse in the high spring tides on the crumbling banks of the Delaware. Ungrateful Mary Murfin Smith, friend and playmate of Indians, rare speaker of their dialect, who wrote in her manuscript story of her life, commenting on the smallpox :

It may be observed how God's providence made room for us in a wonderful manner in taking away the Indians. There came a distemper among them so mortal that they could not bury all their dead. Others

[1] Mary Murfin's manuscript, "Burlington Smiths." Smith papers, Library Company of Philadelphia.

went away, leaving their town. It was said that an old Indian king spoke prophetically before his death and said the English should *increase* and the Indians *decrease*.

Just how much God's providence had to do with smallpox was a subject of John Woolman's secret brooding.

As to the close survey of Delaware and Maryland, overlapping and adding to some of his previous impressions of the effects of slavery upon all who practised it, and upon the Society of Friends in particular, Woolman notes, "Though our Society in these parts appeared to me to be in a declining condition, yet I believe the Lord hath a people amongst them who labour to serve him uprightly, but they have many difficulties to encounter."

Woolman estimated his first Southern journey at fifteen hundred miles, so he had altogether travelled not far short of four thousand miles in the open travelling seasons of the two years since his own release from the ties of working in another's employ. He never mentions fatigue or sickness, or any injury to his horse. The parallel journal of David Brainerd,[1] who travelled at the same time in much the same country in New Jersey and New England, and furnishes a day-to-day record of such travelling, is filled with the hourly fatigue and physical misery of a man in low health, frequently mentioning "the hideous wilderness," thanking God after each journey that he has not broken his legs, and of such poor horsemanship that on one occasion he allowed his horse to break its leg among some rocks and was forced to shoot him and continue the journey on foot.

Woolman's health was resilient, his fatigue negligible ; he was an able horseman and had the planter's care for his beast. And whether the trail led among the deep woods or up the open hillside, along the sandy barrens by the shore or skirting the treacherous morass, he looked on the changing landscape with an artist's eye. There is no word out of him about a hideous wilderness ; he speaks of "the visible creation."

When he got back from the Eastern Shore of Maryland "by the way of Nottingham" and resumed his life in Mount Holly he had had his fill of travelling for a time. A rolling stone gathers no moss. The holiday season, in the interval between an employed career and a self-directed career, was over. He turned with energy to his own affairs.

[1] Yale graduate, friend of Jonathan Edwards, Presbyterian minister and missionary to the Indians for the Society for the Propagation of the Gospel.

It was not for nothing that he had secured before he went away that spring the two small parcels of real estate on which he had set his deliberate choice.   And of all John Sykes's good stories of the early times, was there not one in particular that he loved best to hear as they accomplished their fifteen miles a day ?   The story of that first archaic wedding which John Sykes had witnessed as a boy, held under the leafy trees at the cross-roads in the primeval forest, like something from the Golden Age.   Behind John Sykes's bare words Woolman's lively imagination visualized the scene, dreamed back into that hour when poetry had for one become act, when the wind that moved the leaves, and the Spirit that moved the heart, had seemed of the same essence, when God was all but visible, and the Quaker silence had been broken by the scuffling squirrel and the simple, audacious songs of the unalarmed birds.

In these journeys of spring and fall, when he came among people Woolman was alert to the passing scene, keen to note the effects of commerce, war, and slavery ; but in the silent stretches of the forest or along the surf-resounding shore, when the travellers, single-file, communed each with his own thoughts, Woolman's secret heart was busy with the two deepest mysteries of human life—death and love.

XVII

MARRIAGE

THERE was a girl who had quietly crept into Woolman's heart. It was no stranger who had dawned suddenly and overwhelmingly upon his sight, but one familiar to him from childhood, a member of the great family clan. Her name was Sarah Ellis. Samuel Woolman's children thought of her as a cousin, but there was no blood relationship. Mrs Samuel Woolman's brother, Joseph Burr, had married Jane Abbott, and Jane Abbott's sister Mary married Benjamin Ellis. Sarah was the daughter of the latter couple. So Woolman's Uncle Joseph and Aunt Jane were also Sarah Ellis's Aunt Jane and Uncle Joseph.

Sarah was one year younger than John Woolman, and there were many things about her which made her interesting to her livelier 'cousin.' To John, who loved his father so dearly, it was incredibly touching that this poor child had never known what it was to have a father. The sweetest of mothers and the best of uncles could never make up for that.

Benjamin Ellis had come to the colonies at the age of twenty-one with the intention of settling in Philadelphia or New Jersey. He was engaged in a business, probably connected with his grandfather's goldsmith business in London, which required frequent trips to England. Chester-field Monthly Meeting minuted the granting to him of a travelling

certificate[1] directed to London Friends in August 1719 ; and he brought
one back from Hammersmith, Middlesex, London, to Philadelphia dated
"2 month [April] 1720." Either he was a man of unusually quick
action, for a Quaker, or he had obtained his lady's promise before he
sailed to England, for in November 1720 we find the record of his
marriage, and it took three of those seven months to "pass Meeting" in
preparation for a Quaker wedding.   He took his bride, Mary Abbott, to
Philadelphia, and there they had rather less than a year of idyllic happiness.   Benjamin was due for another business trip across the Atlantic, but
delayed to see his wife safely through childbirth, making all preparations
to leave as soon as his child was born, for his next certificate, from Philadelphia to London, is dated August 25, 1721, and little Sarah was born
on August 26.   Somehow this swift going and coming, this rapid
decisive action, puts an aura of romance and dash about the dim memory
of Benjamin Ellis.   He knew so exactly what he wanted ; he put it
through without fumbling or delay.   In a colony now overburdened
with marriageable young women—Peter Kalm estimated that there was
only one beau for every fourteen girls at the time of his visit[2]—Ellis
found so immediately the girl of his choice, won her, and possessed her.
But the summer of 1721, which seemed the beginning of their complete
family life, was its end.   Leaving his kisses, and perhaps his tears, on the
infant's crumpled cheek, Benjamin Ellis sailed away down the Delaware
and out to the open sea, bound for London, "he intending there on
business" ; and was never heard of more.

When it became evident that the vessel was lost the heartbroken young
widow took refuge with her father and mother at Chesterfield.[3]

Little Sarah lived, then, until she was nine years old, in the home of
her grandparents, John and Ann Abbott, and perhaps was a rather old-
fashioned little girl, the only child in the house.   She did not want for
playmates with many cousins living close at hand ; but it was a quiet,
grave house to come back to or to be left behind in, and it gave the child
quiet, retiring ways.   In the clan rallies of Burrs and Woolmans, those

[1] This was in the nature not of a certificate for travelling in the ministry, but of
introduction and guarantee.

[2] 1748–51.

[3] Abbottsville, the Abbott homestead, was actually in the township of Nottingham
(Burlington County, New Jersey), just across Crosswicks Creek from the township of
Chesterfield.   But the Abbotts were members of Chesterfield Meeting, and were
spoken of as Chesterfield Friends.   Chesterfield Meeting-house was in the village of
Crosswicks.   The Nottingham usually mentioned in this story, where John Church-
man lived, was in Bucks County, Pennsylvania.

large, vigorous groups of romping children, she was like a violet in a field of buttercups ; sweet when you noticed her, but she did not show much.

The standard of elegance and manners in the Abbott household was high. Grandmother Ann—only forty-five when her two-year-old granddaughter came to live with her, still beautiful and in her prime —was of gentle blood. If her Quaker principles had permitted her she could have used a coat-of-arms which many a duke might envy. She had been born a Mauleverer of Yorkshire, and her ancestry went back unbroken to Robert FitzWalter, Henry de Bohun, Robert de Roos, Roger Bigod, and nine other of the Barons of England whose names stand as Sureties of the Magna Carta. True, she denied all worldly pride, and would never boast of race ; yet the old consciousness of *noblesse oblige* beat in her pulse, and combined with the humility of her religion to produce a singular grace.

When Sarah was nine her mother, Mary Ellis, married again. George Williams was himself a widower with seven children. Such happiness did Mary Ellis bring into his home that the memorial minute made after her death touches an unwontedly personal note. "She was well-beloved by her husband's children, and upon her death left a sweet savour behind her." Two of her stepsons, being of the opinion that one could evidently not do better than that family, married two of her younger sisters. She "desesed her life" in April 1739, when Sarah was seventeen.

Soon after her mother's death Sarah was taken to live with her Aunt Jane, Mrs Joseph Burr. And in 1741, when John Woolman's grand-father, Henry Burr, died, his beautiful house, Peachfields, two miles out of Mount Holly, was inherited by his son Joseph. Here Sarah, accus-tomed now by her stepbrothers and sisters to a large family, became again a loved member of a lively household. The grey stone house, ample and stately, surrounded by fifteen hundred acres of its own fields and woods, looked away over the level land to the round shape of the Mount itself. The town was an easy walk. And besides the ironworks cousins and other friends, one or other of the Woolmans was always dropping in ; and among them John. Peachfields had all his life been to John Woolman a second home. So Sarah Ellis and John Woolman were near neighbours in the same town, in the free and constant inter-course of cousinship : attending the same meeting twice a week ; grouped in this corn-husking picnic or that Firstday dinner or evening circle under the trees ; leaning by moonlight together at Cousin Joseph's sawmill above the rushing waters of the dam.   For Uncle Joseph Burr had two sons, again named Henry and Joseph ; and while Henry helped on the farm, and presently settled on adjoining acres, Joseph took over the sawmill in Mount Holly, a very profitable business.   John Woolman's Account Books contain entries of "ceder rails at Joseph Burr's," "boards at Joseph Burr's."

For the first few years after Sarah came to Peachfields John Woolman's attention was very much elsewhere.   Yet they met constantly, and since John Woolman was always prominent in the group, if he did not notice her much it is pretty certain that she noticed him.   Perhaps it was for his sake that she refused her other suitors, and reached her middle twenties unengaged.   Like William Penn's wife, the fascinating Gulielma, she was kept "till he at length came for whom she was preserved."   When he was ready she was there.

No inkling leaks through Woolman's reserve of how his first awareness of her came—what grave exchange of glance across a gay company, or what sudden perception of a heartfelt listening to some speech of his. How does it ever happen ?   A door opens, a drawbridge falls, and one's personal island is invaded, the inner fortress entered, and a fire is kindled on one's very hearth.   "What, are you *here* ?" is hardly asked before the recognizing soul says, "Why, it's *you* ! "

In some such natural inevitable fashion the two came together, linked by a thousand memories from the very dawn of consciousness unto the present day.   Woolman was now seeking the subtler, more secret flowers, was attracted by fragrance, and turned away from show.   Many men in many times have thought modesty the greatest ornament of womanhood ; and Woolman held this opinion the more intensely that he esteemed humility to be the first essential of right living.   Yet this humble-hearted girl, whose sensitive face so readily reflected her keen following of the talk in which her voice was slow to join, whose dark lashes fell so quickly before his earnest glance, added to these charms the graciously serene air of the gently bred.   In her shyness she was no awkward country bumpkin ; she was a Mauleverer.   She had the courage to be herself without pretence or affectation, and in her rare speech she spoke her honest thought with the direct simplicity and ease of generations of the English landed gentry.

John Woolman tells nothing of his courtship.   The man who does not

allow us to approach too near his mother or his sister, how much more
will he guard the privacy of his wife.   Yet in the mentions of her which
occur from time to time throughout the Journal, and in the tone of such
letters from him to her as are available, a spirit breathes which suggests
that if she had a love-letter of his to cherish it might well resemble the
letter written by the great Quaker Robert Barclay (first Governor of
East Jersey, although he never came there) to the lady who became his
wife :

> Dear Friend, . . . The Love of thy Converse, the Desire of thy
> Friendship, and the Sympathy of thy Way & Humour with my
> Spirit, has often (as thou mightest have observed) occasioned me to
> take frequent Opportunities to have the Benefit of thy Company in
> which I can truly say I have often been refreshed and the Life in me
> touch'd with a secret Unity which hath flow'd from the same in thee.
> Many Things in the natural Will concur to strengthen and encourage
> my Affection towards thee and make thee acceptable unto me, but
> what is before all and beyond all is that I can say in the Fear of the
> Lord that I have received a Charge from him to *love thee*.

In the first writing of his Journal for publication Woolman did not
so much as condescend to mention his marriage.   He let it be inferred,
by occasional reference to "my wife."

At the remonstrance of a friend he added an inserted paragraph,
written in with his own hand above the lines of a copied version of
the Journal.[1]   It is a brief, curt statement, frigid in its aristocratic deter-
mination not to wear his heart upon his sleeve for daws to peck at, or
to expose his modest lady to the public stare.

> About this time believing it good for me to Settle & thinking Seri-
> ously about a Companion my heart was turned to the Lord with
> Desires that He would give me Wisdom to proceed therein agreeable
> to his Will & He was pleased to give me a Well inclined Damsile
> Sarah Ellis to whom I was married the 18th day of the Eighth month
> 1749.

"Was pleased to give me."   He had not to struggle to win her ;   he
had only to open his hand, and the shy wild bird flew in.   Perhaps she
had been watching for his hand to open, and nestled there as one who has
come home.   Sure it is that she never in her life opposed him.   He
was gentleness itself, but he had a compelling quality.   She immersed

---

[1] Swarthmore College collection.

herself in him; her thoughts became like his. The one letter of hers extant after her husband's death is filled with his phrases. A man who more than most men avoided command, who like George Fox with Margaret Fell would honour his wife as his equal, and who might very easily have linked himself with a dominant, devoted Quaker woman whose life moved with a strong tide sometimes apart from his and who would leave him frequently for long intervals while she travelled in the ministry, he was gifted instead with a wife who have him such submission that he never noticed it. He only realized with restful delight the harmony of his home and perceived that she was indeed a "Well inclined Damsile." Perhaps submission is the wrong word; it was not so much that she gave in to him as that she wanted what he wanted.

She had not a conventionally pretty face, and this had saved her from some of the temptations of feminine vanity. And in an environment where every practical man looked for health and strength in the woman he should marry, Sarah Ellis had a fragile look. But her lover had been attracted to her by observed acts of kindness, had seen her face as her mirror never showed it to her, when some child appealed, or some service was to be rendered, or when a thought of peace possessed her in the meeting-house. And it is surely her portrait he draws, with ardent tenderness and subtlest appreciation, in the lines, "Some Glances of real beauty Are percievable in their Countenances who dwell in true Meekness. Some tincture of true harmony in the Sound of that Voice to which Divine love gives utterance."

Quaker marriage regulations demanded that the couple should appear twice before the Burlington Monthly Meeting and publicly declare their intentions of matrimony. At John Woolman's second appearance his young sister Hannah, now twenty-three years old, took advantage of the moral support of her brother's presence to appear for the first time with her fiancé, Samuel Gauntt. The first time of appearance committees were appointed to inquire as to their "clearness," and the second time favourable reports of the committees were presented to the Monthly Meeting and permission for the wedding granted. A further Committee of Overseers was appointed to see that the wedding was conducted in due form.

The investigation as to "clearness" covered inquiry into previous matrimonial entanglements, character, financial stability, and consent of surviving parents. The present pair being well known in their neighbourhood, such investigation was in their case largely perfunctory, but the consciousness of its invariability and thoroughness was a deterrent to hasty or unwise marriage, and a safeguard to the State. Part of the reason why Monthly Meetings tended to disown members who got married out of meeting by agency of a justice or of a "hireling priest" was that such marriages were sometimes a cloak for irregularity. Cases on record include bigamy, sex relations between the couple before marriage, and—last and least—absence of parental consent. The secret marriage of Henry and Elizabeth Drinker's daughter is a case in point, her father having withheld his consent and thereby successfully blocked the young people's marriage in Friends' Meeting. Since their slate was otherwise clear, the meeting later accepted the young people back into membership, but the father never forgave his daughter.

John Woolman and Sarah Ellis, however, passed all requirements, and on a golden October day the Woolman clan gathered in the meeting-house at Mount Holly for the wedding.

Samuel and Elizabeth Woolman were there[1] to sit beside their son, the bridegroom. Uncle Joseph and Aunt Jane Burr sat in the place of parents to the orphan bride. John Abbott and Timothy Abbott represented her mother's people.[2] Asher and Abner and Uriah and Esther and Jonah and Rachel supported their brother. Burr cousins and Lippincott cousins and Haines cousins were present. Esther Andrews represented her husband Peter and his brother Isaac, unavoidably absent. Peter Fearon came in person to see his friend married, and so did Josiah White and his wife Esther. A happy and a homelike company, while the first falling leaves whirled gaily in the surrounding forest and scattered flakes of gold before the feet of the bridal pair. And on the bridegroom's wide-skirted coat of camlet—woven by his father, dyed dark blue by his friend Josiah, tailored by himself—gleamed sister Elizabeth's gold buttons, plain, not wrought.

The bride, eschewing hoops or any artificial aids, wore a dress so full-gathered as to stand out around her, showing off the slenderness of her waist and the round sleekness of the fitted bodice. The cut was low enough to leave the neck cool and free, and a little gauzy linen fichu matched her small dainty cap. No woman would be seen at any function bareheaded—all wore caps ; and the distinctive Quaker cap,

---

[1] Appendix X.
[2] They were her uncles, her mother's brothers.

"like a Phrygian helmet," was not yet. Aprons were part of the costume, but white aprons were only worn by the gay ; Sarah Ellis, in her soft blue dress, added a green apron, not dreaming of the time when coloured aprons would be deemed "gay" and white aprons "plain" ; and similarly with the green stockings of thin worsted which showed below her skirt.

Quietly as a flower she came in by her lover's side, and passed between the waiting, silent forms to her place on the facing bench beside Aunt Jane. That would have been her mother's seat, but her mother was in heaven. And this was a time to remember heaven, in the deep quiet, with her heart's hope realized. There was no one needed to give a Quaker maid away. She gave herself. And there was no call at any time in the meeting for any who knew cause why these two should not be joined in matrimony to speak now or for ever after hold his peace. Thorough investigation had been made beforehand, and chance interference was not allowed for.

Silence, deep and restful, deep and holy, spread above them and around them like a sea. They sank into it, with love and prayer, and felt the Presence of the Father who united the living and the dead. John Woolman at last broke the waiting silence by rising to his feet with his bride and, facing the assembly with Sarah's hand in his, he recited with his eyes on hers, "in Solom manner," the Quaker formula of marriage, "In the presence of the Lord and of these our friends I take thee, my friend, Sarah Ellis, to be my wife, promising by divine assistance to be unto thee a loving and faithful husband until death shall separate us."

With his deep, harmonious voice and the instinctive pitch of a practised speaker, he was well heard to the back of the room. And now it was her turn, and she must speak her part, returning equal vows. Under the battery of eyes she blushed and trembled. It is always the bride who is most stared at. But her bridegroom's hand was strong on hers, and he saw the beauty of her upturned face. She read in his glance the message that never failed her, "Thou art lovely, my beloved !" And she commanded her voice and spoke like a Mauleverer, clearly and well.

"In the presence of the Lord and of these our friends I take thee, my friend, John Woolman, to be my husband, promising by divine assistance to be unto thee a loving and faithful wife until death shall separate us."

Then they sat down together, hand in hand, never again to be parted.

Distance might do its worst on many journeys, and ocean seas, and even Death itself ; but their bond was of a kind not to be put asunder.

To what kind of home did John Woolman bring his bride when he swung down from his horse and lifted her from her saddle in the bright moonlight of the autumn night ? John Woolman's wife could trust him for her dignity and her comfort. A pleasant white frame house, sufficiently remote from the village for seclusion, yet conveniently near the King's Highway,[1] standing among shade trees of oak and elm, and surrounded by eleven acres of orchard and garden ; and this was all their own, bought and paid for, to keep if they wished "for ever" and to hand down to their children. The bride, only daughter of her mother, had inherited much of her mother's own furniture from that first home in Philadelphia, and it had been conveyed by wagon from its long sojourn in the Chesterfield homes and set in place during the months of the engagement. Wedding gifts from the large family circle supplied other pieces, and there was in particular a handsome chest of drawers, the only piece individually mentioned and bequeathed long years later in Sarah Woolman's will. Perhaps it was an heirloom from the old Mauleverer manor-house, and carried with it memories of a grander past.

Grander, but not happier. John Woolman, twenty-nine years old, the heats and impulses of first youth over, but still in the full vitality of young manhood, had planned a life of serenest happiness. Observing, judging, and weighing, he shaped circumstances to his ends, and laid down his keel for the kind of vessel that he wanted, leaving nothing to chance. His theory of life did not involve living like the birds and taking no thought for the morrow. The days of life insurance were not yet, but unencumbered real estate was a good substitute. Had John Woolman died within a week or a year of his marriage his wife would have been well provided for. And this practical common sense and thrifty business foresight never made war in his mind with his mystic faith in God.

As my mind was often inward Meditateing on God's Providence Manifested in the Visible world I was more & more confirmed in my Judgments that to place my whole trust in him Was best for me, and laboured from one month to Another to come into that Condition of

---

[1] Which ran from New York to Philadelphia, via Springfield and Moorestown.

Trusting in God with all my heart And not to Lean to my own understanding.

Yet from one month to another he collected his dues and paid his bills, bought advantageously, and kept his accounts straight, as a necessary part of the upright life.

His business premises in Mount Holly were about half a mile from his home. Waking in the early morning to the singing of birds, the sun-saluting crow of his own rooster, and the clucking of the laying hens, how cheerful it was for John to walk down for an early dip in the ice-cold waters of Buttonwood Run, next to his orchard, while Sarah washed herself all over in the shady bedroom. Cleanliness, in a grubby age, was a passion with those two. Then the husband brought in eggs, warm from the nest, and milk of last night's milking, cold from the spring, while the wife made tea and set out the pretty china, and bread of her own baking, and honey from the hives which stood under the apple-trees. Then John Woolman left Sarah to her round of homely duties, redding the house, feeding the ducks and chickens, baking and sewing, and in any spare hour carrying her wheel, perhaps, outside to sit and spin, or on a wet day spinning in the quiet room to the cheerful rhythm of the rain.

It was not lonely, because friends and relatives were within easy reach. Hardly a day would pass without a visitor, calling "on purpose" or pausing to turn aside for a half-hour on the way to or from Springfield or Philadelphia. On Thursday and Sunday the pair walked about a mile down through the market-place and up to the right along the Burlington Road to the cross-roads in the forest where the meeting-house stood, and there joined in peaceful worship followed by cheerful converse "in the company of other people." Monthly Meeting took them on horseback to Burlington, and Quarterly Meeting to Burlington or to Chesterfield, and the Spring General Meeting took John to Philadelphia, and September summoned them both to Yearly Meeting in Philadelphia or Burlington alternately. No, life was far from dull, at any time. And in the first spring woman's greatest adventure came to Sarah, the adventure of motherhood. She expected her child in December, and the forward movement of the year, the slow ripening to harvest, was one with the mysterious rhythm of her body.

John came home late in the afternoon and often used the remaining hours of daylight in outdoor tasks, the care of orchard and livestock ;

but reading and writing were a necessary part of his day, and he demanded also leisure to savour the visible creation, the world in which he lived, the movement of events. A life of constant toil was never part of his plan. He hired a labourer to do the heavy work on his land ; and he kept a careful eye on his wife to see that she did not do more than was wholesome or pleasant. Your "woman's work is never done" theory would not do for him. He had seen plenty of that in his own home, with his vigorous bustling mother ; and he had seen what seemed to him the better part chosen by his sister Elizabeth, who had refused to submerge her mental life in the practical, and had preserved in all her industry the art of leisure.

That was a peaceful interval all over New Jersey, all over the valley of the Delaware, all over the colonies. Just as the tide of the great ocean moved every day beside the Mount Holly wharf, lifting up the boats or laying them down upon the mud, so the Peace of Aix-la-Chapelle, signed far away in Europe,[1] brought back the Mount Holly and Burlington men from the borders of Canada, relieved tension, and spread an eddy of happiness and hope. Just to have war stop was a relief, even if the New Englanders did not like giving back Louisburg to France, and foresaw fresh trouble along the unsettled boundary line. The Spaniards began to negotiate to buy back the *asiento* and so remove the opportunity for smuggling and the provocative search of ships ; and so they did, at last, but the *asiento* had done its work. Mr Edwards's vial was being poured out, and was by no means emptied yet.

But the wise man takes peace where he finds it, and enjoys it while he may. And the first months of John Woolman's married life were halcyon days. The new charm of the most intimate form of human love, the sympathy of the beloved's way and humour with his spirit, the deep satisfaction of all the needs of his nature, released his powers. He rewrote and completed the long essay upon slavery which he had projected and roughed out years before ; and though Sarah was a sympathetic listener, it was his father, Samuel Woolman, who was his valued critic. Many an evening John and Sarah rode over to the home farm, or Samuel Woolman, a vigorous man in his sixtieth year, got on to his sorrel mare Bonny and rode to Mount Holly to enjoy the quiet of his eldest son's home, and look at his manuscripts, and share his thoughts on public and private matters, on slavery, business, and war.

[1] August 1748.

Business was prosperous. Mount Holly was becoming more and more a centre for the neighbourhood. The *Pennsylvania Journal* of August 30, 1750, opens a window on to a lively bustling scene.

Notice is hereby given That there is to be given gratis at Mount Holly in the county of Burlington on Wednesday the 19th day of September, Twenty Pistoles to be run for by as many Horses, Mares or Geldings as any Person or Persons shall see fit to put in. They are to be put in twenty shillings for every Horse, Mare or Gelding, & enter them four days before the Day of Running. They are to run three heats, one mile at a heat, on a straight course, & to carry weight for inches.

Any one that shall win two heats & save the distance the third shall win the prize & the next Day the Betts shall be run for . . . the Horses to be entered at John Budd's or Caleb Shinns.

A Quaker trader would have nothing to do with a horse-race, but he could not help benefiting by any affairs which drew visitors to the town. One did not ask a would-be customer whether he had come to Mount Holly that day in order to indulge in the sin of betting and gambling.

John Woolman's private thoughts were full of hope and life, looking forward to the birth of his child. But with the shocking unexpectedness of human life the next family event was a major bereavement. Autumn set in chilly and damp, and an epidemic of influenza passed through the Delaware region. Such an illness often attacks the healthy and brings them down with surprising suddenness. And Samuel Woolman was fatally stricken. Some one—perhaps motherly Aunt Jane Burr, or perhaps competent young sister Hannah, who had married Sam Gauntt very near the time of her brother John's wedding—stayed with Sarah in the Mount Holly orchard while John Woolman placed himself unreservedly at his father's service for the last short stretch of travel down to the river's brink. The wife and mother was the chief nurse by day, centre and pulse of Samuel Woolman's home for forty-six years, mother of his thirteen healthy children, and love of his youth. And all his children took their turn to come to his bedside, thankful to do some service or errand, confident in his especial affection for each one of them. But to his eldest son he turned for a close companionship, a kinship of mind and soul, not common, and dearly held by both.

In the fall of the year 1750 died my father Samuel Woolman of a fever, aged about sixty years. . . . After my return from Carolina in

1746 I made some observations on keeping slaves which some time before his decease I showed to him ; he perused the manuscript, proposed a few alterations, & appeared well satisfied that I found a concern on that account. In his last sickness as I was watching with him one night, he being so far spent that there was no expectation of his recovery, though he had the perfect use of his understanding, he asked me concerning the manuscript & whether I expected soon to proceed to take the advice of friends in publishing it ? After some further conversation thereon he said, "I have all along been deeply affected with the oppression of the poor negroes, and now at last my concern for them is as great as ever."

The son who could act as tender nurse and equal friend to his father could also act as lawyer and man of business. And a composed foresight of the inevitable end, without fuss or sentimentality, was common to them both.

"By his direction I had Wrote his will in a time of health, and that night he desired me to read it to him, which I did, and he said it was agreeable to his mind." And that disposed of, the document folded and put by, the feverish brows and hands bathed again, the parched lips refreshed with a cooling drink, Samuel Woolman murmured to his son, in all simplicity and candour, some of his deepest thoughts.

He then made mention of his end, which he believed was near, and signified that though he was sensible of many imperfections in the course of his life, yet his experience of the power of truth and of the love and goodness of God from time to time even till now, was such that he had no doubt that on leaving this life he should enter into one more happy.

That intimate midnight talk was their last.

The next day his sister Elizabeth came to see him, and told him of the decease of their sister Ann who died a few days before ; he then said, "I reckon sister Ann was free to leave this world ?" Elizabeth said she was. He then said "I also am free to leave it" ; and being in great weakness of body said "I hope I shall shortly go to rest."

This sister Elizabeth, John Woolman's aunt, who made her brother thus a last farewell, had been married three times and was now Mrs John Harvey. The sister Ann who had gone before so recently had been Mrs John Buffin.

Again, as in the case of his own sister Elizabeth Woolman, John

Woolman found immediate outlet for his sorrow in the expeditious settlement of his father's estate. Asher was his fellow-executor. Samuel Woolman died on the fifth of October, 1750, and the will was probated on the seventeenth of December.

On the eighteenth of December, with all due care and attendance, Sarah Woolman gave birth to a daughter, and her parents named her Mary.

XVIII

WOOLMAN'S FATHER'S WILL

SAMUEL WOOLMAN must have owned before he died close to a thousand
acres. By the terms of his will he gave :

> to my loving wife Elizabeth Woolman one half of the improve-
> ments, half the barn, half the orchards, half the marshes on both sides
> the Creek, with firewood and fencing to supply her said half of said
> improvements where I now dwell during the term of Four years and
> three months from the date hereof.

Also, "my sorrel Mare called Bonny and one colt," and

> the two brick rooms below stairs and the least brick room above
> stairs and half the cellar and half the kitchen during her Widowhood.
> I will that my son Asher enjoy the remaining half of my improvements
> and buildings where I now dwell and also that he enjoy all the improve-
> ments on north end of my land until my son Jonah arrives at full age.
> My land at Evesham I will that it be divided into three equal parts. . . .
> The Eastern part bounded on Mason Creek I give to my son John
> Woolman his heirs and assigns forever : the Western part bounding
> on Freedom Lippincott I give to my son Jonah Woolman his heirs and
> assigns forever. The middle part and all the marsh on the north end
> and also the meadow ground I give to my son Asher. . . .

Also :

> I give to my son Asher all the South Side with buildings and I will
> that son Asher pay out of the same twenty pounds (money) to my
> son Uriah in 1 year after I die. . . . And to my son Abraham fifty
> pounds and to son Eber thirty pounds. All North End of lands and

house thereon to son Jonah, he to pay son Abraham thirty pounds and Thirty pounds to son Eber.

My lands in Morris County of 388 Acres I give to my sons Abraham and Eber. My Cedar Swamp called Old Swamp I give to my seven sons. Land I bought of James Southwick I give to my son Eber.

A lot of land in Bridgetown I give to my loving Wife Elizabeth Woolman. After the 4 years and 3 mos expire I will that my son Asher pay out of the profits of plantation the sum of five pounds to Wife Elizabeth yearly and Every year during her widowhood pasture for horse, cow, and necessary wood.

I give to Uriah one hundred eighty pounds . . . to daughters Sarah Elton, Patience Moore and Hannah Gauntt each five shillings. To my son Asher fifteen pounds to be held in trust for my daughter Sarah Elton to be used at his discretion for her or for her children. To my daughters Esther and Rachel Woolman fifty pounds when full age or marry. I will that my sons Abraham and Eber be put at trade for fourteen years.

To my sons Uriah and Jonah 1 flock bed and bolsters, 3 blankets and one coverlid. To my sons Abraham and Eber 1 chest, 1 flock bed and like furniture with the others.

All residue after debts and funeral expenses are paid and Legacies I give to Wife for her support and to enable her to educate my children. I wish my wife to have care of Jonah and to have benefit of his labour until he is of age.

The witnesses to his signature and seal were Thomas Green, Daniel Wills, Jr., and Joseph Green.

Jonah was seventeen at the time of his father's death, so the four-year interval covered his minority. Asher was twenty-eight and unmarried. Abraham and Eber were thirteen and eleven respectively. With those two youngest bound out apprentice, and Uriah, now twenty-two, still working out his apprenticeship in Burlington, the household at the old homestead on the Rancocas was boiled down to Asher as the head of the house, young Jonah, Mrs Woolman as mistress, and Esther and Rachel, the two remaining daughters, with the Negro servant, Maria. Rachel was a mere girl of fifteen, and twenty-year-old Esther was already being courted by Zebulun Gauntt, the brother of Hannah's husband, whom she married in 1752. Abner in the same year married Mary Aaronson, whose Dutch ancestor, Derek Arenson, had come from Amsterdam. It seems a little odd that Abner alone gets no mention in his father's will, except as receiving a seventh share in the cedar swamp. But it is probable that Abner had received his share in some other way, perhaps in

being started in life independently, since his relations with his family
remain continually cordial. He named his eldest son after his brother
Asher, and he was particularly intimate with his brother John.

Asher and Jonah were for some reason slow to marry. Perhaps such
eligible young men found themselves faced with too large a choice, and
became fastidious. Certainly Jonah, who came into control at twenty-
one of an independent house and estate, might have been expected to
find himself a wife before he reached his thirties. But he was thirty-
one when he married Màrtha Mullen in the fall of '64. Asher's longer
delay, becoming at last a bridegroom at the staid and sober age of forty-
seven, might have had some connexion with the strange terms of the
will, which gave the mother such a dominant share in her son's house.
A daughter-in-law might well hesitate to undertake housekeeping in a
home where her husband's mother owned half the kitchen. The fact
that that clause got into the will shadows forth a suggestion that Mrs
Woolman's superabundant energy expressed itself, even though affectionately, in a certain overbearingness. She must have her way. As
long as her husband lived she was assured of her queenship ; he would
see to it. Was not John Woolman's one memory of being in disgrace
with his father due to a boyish flare-up with his mother ? Did young
Elizabeth Woolman take up an independent career outside her home for
nothing ? And why was it that Rachel, the youngest girl, left behind
at home alone at seventeen to be a companion and caretaker to her
mother, never married ? Did she find the dominant influence absorb
her quite, with no one to share it, no one to stand between her life and
it ? Shadows only ; but Samuel Woolman, preparing in health for his
death, took care to safeguard his wife's authority as well as her material
comfort. And that thoughtfulness about the kitchen, the core of
domestic life, would hardly arise unbidden in a man's brain. Not to
mention Mrs Woolman's ownership of three other rooms in the house,
for her lifetime (unless she remarried).

Mrs Asher Woolman in 1769, moving in with Mrs Woolman, Rachel,
and the two domestics, had only three years to share the house with
them. But that it was death alone which took Mrs Woolman away
from her familiar home by the Rancocas seems certain by the phrase in
her will in 1772, "I give to my grand daughter Elizabeth Elton my bed
in the back room below stairs with the bedstead, boulster, curtains, one
coverlid, two sheets and two pillows." This surely refers to one of the

"two rooms below stairs" bequeathed her by her husband, and needing no other description.

John Woolman, by the terms of the will, became possessed of another parcel of real estate, the land at Evesham bounded on Mason Creek. He now had three separate lots, the other two being the eleven acres on which he lived, outside Mount Holly, and the house and shop in Mill Street. Knowing his desire to avoid much cumber, and his dread of the temptation of riches, it is not surprising that we find him almost at once proceeding to sell one of them. The new lot at Evesham would seem the obvious one to part with. But the one he sold was "the Brick house and the framed shop and all the lot belonging to them on Mill Street, Mount Holly"; and it is hardly less surprising that he sold them to his mother. How could John Woolman part with those excellent business premises, and what did Mrs Samuel Woolman want with them on May 16, 1753?

A partial answer to the first question is that John Woolman could not live in two houses at once. There is no record as to who had been living in the Mill Street house all this time. John Woolman probably had a clerk or an apprentice there, living, as he had once done, in the empty house. Certainly some one had to be on the spot, by night as well as by day, to take care of perishable merchandise, and to guard against theft and fire. The answer to the second question might dovetail into this.

In 1753 Mrs Woolman and her principal business adviser, her eldest son, were looking forward to a possible marked change in her affairs the following year. Then the four probationary years mentioned in the will would be up. Mrs Woolman could no longer be in receipt of half the produce of Asher's farm and half of Jonah's; and Jonah's labour would no longer be at her disposal. It would seem a good time for her to move and take a cosy house somewhere with Rachel. True, she already owned, under the will, a lot of land in Bridgetown (Mount Holly), but that was in New Street, too far out of the current of affairs. John and Asher well knew that their mother's lively temperament could only content itself with such a modest scale as would be within her income if she could be in a central place so as to feel the pleasant stir of the town about her, and have the consolation of frequent casual visitors. Mrs Woolman herself was attracted by the position of the Mill Street house, agreeably near to her brother, John Burr, and the Whites, and other friends. John's apprentice, or clerk, could be added to her household as a boarder to the benefit of her exchequer, and John would pay her rent for his shop. So she made the purchase. But when the four years were up, and Asher was not married, or even engaged, there seemed no hurry about moving. She was very well where she was. She did not there notice any difference in income. No doubt the prospect of a small house, two women together, seemed intolerably dull to Mrs Woolman, accustomed to the spaciousness of a large farm, liberal housekeeping, and abundant hospitality. With all her married children and her grand-children to visit her, it appeared natural and even necessary, and what her husband would have wished, for her to keep up the family headquarters on the old lines, in the house which was now technically Asher's, but which seemed hers and Samuel's still.

But she retained ownership of both the lots in Mount Holly, leasing the Mill Street shop to John as long as he wanted it and then without difficulty finding other tenants. Property there was a good investment. In her will she left :

my brick house in Mount holly with the framed shop, and all the lot of them belonging . . . to my daughter Rachel Woolman to hold to her, her heirs and assigns forever, on condition that she pay ten pounds proclamation money to my grand daughter Elizabeth Elton.

And "my lot of land in New street in Mount holly, I give to my grandson Asher Woolman son of Abner Woolman dec. to hold to the said Asher his heirs and assigns forever."

There is no evidence that even Rachel Woolman ever lived in the Mill Street house. Such traditions as are available suggest that she leased it to tenants on a long lease, and at the expiration, three years before her death in 1795, sold it. It was not much of a house for a maiden lady. The framed shop, however, a lean-to at the side, where Woolman had done his tailoring, had been bought separately by Josiah White before this time and moved to his own house across the way.

Rachel's probable destiny was to finish out her life as a useful aunt in the home of one of her married brothers or sisters. And such a career often provided, to a warm nature, a rich experience of vicarious mother-hood.

For a while yet, however, John Woolman continued to maintain the shop in Mill Street, and to rent it from his mother.

XIX

MERCHANT IN MOUNT HOLLY

WOOLMAN'S chief function in the town at present was that of a merchant and shopkeeper, and so it was for sixteen years after his first coming to Mount Holly. Seven of these years at least he had spent in service for his original employer ; then he had had a year of comparative leisure, largely spent in travel, during which he had been acquiring his employer's premises[1] and stock and preparing to start in business for himself. A year before his marriage he had opened the shop in Mill Street and conducted his trade there ever since. Among his various occupations and interests this was the one that showed the most. The average citizen of Mount Holly, if anyone should inquire about John Woolman, would have answered, "Oh, yes, he's a shopkeeper. I know his shop." They might have also added that he was a tailor. There they could find him during business hours every day, and through his open door he could observe the increasing stir of the town life, the passers-by to the taverns and to the mills ; he could see down the street to the west the Market-house and Town Hall which had occupied the centre of the market-place since 1746, and the whipping-post and stocks established by law at its nearer end. Now on wet days the produce of the incoming planters

[1] At least, we suppose it was his employer's premises which he bought. All evidence points that way.

160

was covered from the rain, and on hot days from the sun ; though in summer it was still necessary to open the market at four o'clock in the morning to get perishable stuff—fruit, vegetables, meat, milk—all away and back to the purchasers' homes before the sun was an hour high. The Market-house was the ground floor, made with open arches all round ; the upper floor was the Town Hall, a closed room with a fire-place and sturdy windows, where all the year round, in all weathers, town meetings were held, committees could meet, and the affairs of the township be taken due care of. Elections also were held there, and as long as Quakers were in control both men and women voted. Before this building was erected the town meetings met more or less alternately at two other places—"ye meeting-house near mont holey" and "ye Saw Mill and Grist Mill near Mount holley." Now Northampton Town-ship had a permanent centre, and it all gave dignity to Mount Holly and drew custom. Farmers riding in with their families to market or coming in to town meeting would often stop for a meal at the Three Tuns, the Cross Keys, or the Black Horse, the nearest taverns to the Market-house, where they could get a "Common hott family dinner with a pint of Beer or Cider" at the modest price of eightpence a head, or "a Dinner ordered extraordinary for one shilling" ; or, if they merely needed passing refreshment, a quart of Common Strong Beer within doors cost fourpence, and they could treat their wives and children to a nice little snack of Bread and Butter with Tea or Coffee for eightpence each, or with Chocolate for fourpence—both including loaf Sugar. Woolman was most strategically placed for all such visitors coming and going. "I must just run in to Woolman's for that riband for Sally's cap as soon as I've finished my chocolat. It won't take but a minute," Or "We can get the coffee, nails, and molasses at Woolman's and get it into the wagon just before we take dinner at the Inn. Then it won't delay us afterwards, and we can get home before dark."

Woolman knew this very well ; he had planned for it. He could not help applying common sense and foresight. Nor could he help buying intelligently, and with a knowledge of his neighbours' needs, or keeping most careful and exact accounts, and continually avoiding debt. His business, run on these infallibly sound lines, began to show a distressing tendency to increase.

His first intention had been to run the shop simply as an adjunct to his tailoring. "I had begun with selling trimmings for garments, and from

L

thence proceeded to sell cloths and linens,"[1] but the pressure of demand, working on his sound business instincts, caused him presently to get "a considerable shop of goods." As, for instance, "tea, thread, rum, molasses, butter, coffee, knitting needles, snuff, earthan dishes, chocolat, check, sheeting, tape, indigo, powder and shot, mettle buttons, silk, buckram, gloves, ceder board."[2]   The last was evidently a product of the valuable cedar swamp which Samuel Woolman had divided between his seven sons ; and one entry shows the influence of family give-and-take on business :   "1000 foot half-price Ceader board Deliv. at Jos Burr's Mill."[3]   John Woolman frequently took himself to task, examining his goods to see if they were really useful, trying not to buy things that "chiefly served to please the vain mind in people." Far from persuading customers to buy, he was earnestly concerned that they should get what they really needed, what was suitable for their purpose, and that they should not pay more than they could afford. He practised the same sort of responsibility that he had in former days recommended to the innkeeper.   But instead of customers being frightened away, they were attracted.   It was a delightful place to visit. Woolman, taking a close personal interest in each purchase and each purchaser, concerned over their choice of goods as if he were the buyer rather than the seller, had unconsciously discovered the great modern business slogan, "Service."   Not only were Woolman's customers certain of value received, sure that he would never overcharge or under-measure, but they were warmly gratified by the nature of his relationship with them.   Each one felt himself especially "liked" ; how else could one explain the shopkeeper's attitude ?   And indeed Woolman did like them, and his interest in their welfare was not a cold moral principle but a warm fellow-feeling.

Mary Bennett, buying such a lot of materials for clothes—"shalloon and check and buckram and holland and cambrick and ribond"—would find herself engaging in a discourse on the beauty of simplicity, and the charms of a tranquil life with few needs.   And Lemuel Sheldon perhaps would find himself most tactfully advised against buying too much on credit and running himself up a bill which he would find too big when time came to pay.   And Ann Smith, her mind set on mohair, would

---

[1] Whittier ed., p. 78.
[2] Various items in Woolman's Account Books.
[3] *Ibid.*

leave the shop with fustian, having been charmingly persuaded by this peculiar salesman that it would serve her purpose just as well at half the price.

Yet success dogged his footsteps. "My trade increased every year," says Woolman, "and the way to large business appeared open, but I felt a stop in my mind."

His views on riches had not changed. Years and experience had confirmed him in his early estimate. He had laid his plans for a modest business "without much cumber," but he found it growing cumbersome. He kept his profits moderate. Yet with his almost self-supporting home, and his returns in rent from some of his inherited land, and the modest way of living which he and his wife preferred, he found himself with increasing money in reserve, and all the while fresh orders coming in and more help needed in the shop and more accounts to keep. The worst of it was that he enjoyed it. He argued with himself that "trading in things Usefull is an honest employ." He tried to moderate his business. He gave up this and that line of merchandise—after due warning to his customers, so that they "might consider what shop to turn to." But some men seem to succeed as easily as others fail. Woolman had the qualities which commanded success in spite of his desire not to pursue it. "The increase of business became my burden ; for though my natural inclination was towards merchandise, yet I believed truth required me to live more free from outward cumbers; and there was now a strife in my mind between the two."[1]

In this strife Woolman shared an experience common to many idealistic business men, especially in youth. Andrew Carnegie had it, and Josiah White's grandson Josiah, and Woolman's friend, John Smith. Andrew Carnegie and Josiah White III each settled the struggle by planning to retire from business as soon as they had made a certain sum, and to give themselves for the rest of their lives to altruistic pursuits. Josiah White III set his mark at forty thousand dollars, which he determined to get before his thirtieth birthday, and sure enough got by the time he was twenty-eight.[2] "My aim," he says in his Journal :

had been to lose no time until I had acquired enough, and then to appropriate the balance of the life a good Providence allowed me in such a way as would give me the most comfort. No morning, I

[1] Whittier ed., p. 78.
[2] As a hardware merchant in Philadelphia.

thought, ever opened more clearly than mine now presented, having realised by industry and integrity my best anticipations, escaped the pollutions of trade, having an abiding feeling to do what was right in the sight of my Maker and fellow-man with a desire to be useful to the latter . . . with good hopes to rely on for a peaceful, pleasant, and moderate journey through life, so as to step from a calm journey through this world into that which never ends.

But the no-margin habits of fourteen years were too strong for him. In sheer boredom he found himself forced to start again with some form of business enterprise, just as a hobby, and one thing led to another ; he discovered the use of anthracite coal, he became concerned in making the first American railway, and he died a multi-millionaire. As for Carnegie, he found himself unable even to retire when his mark was reached ; his snowball was on the roll, and he was bound to go with it, in the intoxication of undreamed-of power.

John Smith settled the struggle with himself by putting the responsibility entirely on the shoulders of Providence. So long as he himself was honest and energetic and used his common sense, then it was for God to decide whether he should be rich or poor.

> *Twelfth month* 21*st*, 1746. Heard as soon as I came down Stairs that our ship *Friendship* had put into Antigua, having sprung a Leak at Sea, and the Vessel was like to be Condemned there, her upper work being rotten. . . . This very great disappointment I bear with Resignation and Cheerfulness Considering that I know not whether it's best for me to be Rich or poor.

And

> 1747, 17*th Fifth month*. Heard as I returned home the Certainty of our ship *Bolton's* being taken at our Cape by a privateer Sloop who has likewise taken several Vessells. Endeavoured to be Resigned in this great Loss and disappointment and to say without murmuring Shall we receive Good and shall we not also receive Evil.[1]

That he did become rich was the evident intention of Providence.

But John Woolman, in his clear-cut uncompromising way, did not think it sound to set some future date for one's practice of ideal theory. To-day was what one had. Nor was it logical to pursue a course designed to lead to riches, and then challenge Providence to prevent it if advisable. He had decided for himself against a cumbered life. He could find no way of keeping his business within the moderate and

---

[1] John Smith's MS. diary.

easily handled limits which he had determined on ; so he reluctantly gave it up altogether.

I had in a good degree learned to be content with a plain way of living. I had but a small family ; and on serious consideration believed truth did not require me to engage much in cumbering affairs. . . . And in a while I wholly laid down merchandise, and followed my trade as a tailor by myself, having no prentice. I also had a nursery of apple-trees, in which I employed some of my time in hoeing, grafting, trimming, and inoculating.[1]

One of the things which Woolman found particularly against the grain in the running of a merchant's business was the collecting of bills.

In merchandise it is the custom where I lived to sell chiefly on credit, and poor people often get in debt ; when payment is expected, not having wherewith to pay, their creditors often sue for it at law. Having frequently observed occurrences of this kind, I found it good for me to advise poor people to take such goods as were most useful and not costly.

Woolman suspected this credit system, and took pains to sift it to the bottom.

In the Course of my Trading being somewhat troubled at the various Lawsuits about collecting mony which I Saw going forward ; On applying to a Constable he gave me a list of his proceedings for one year, as follows, To wit, Served 267 warrents, 103 Summonses, and 79 Executions. As to writs Served by the Sherrif I got no Account of them.[2]

Woolman's feeling about the payment of bills was as strict as that of a Smith or Pemberton, and his belief in the great universal brotherhood did not prevent him from collecting what was due to him. There were many ways, however, of removing this from hardship, accepting produce or labour in place of cash and practising the utmost patience and consideration where people were in a difficulty. The produce or labour was set down in the accounts with a money value attached, as "By work in my Meadow 2 shillings, By Henry Choping wood at Door one shilling six pence, by weeving nineteen shillings one penny," and so the account was gradually balanced to mutual satisfaction. But if there were any indications of evasion Woolman did not hesitate to exact justice.

"I had once had a Warrant for an Idle Man who I believed was about

---

[1] Whittier ed., p. 78.   [2] Folio MS., p. 39.

to run away, which was the only time I applied to the Law to recover Money."[1]

This action gave Woolman no remorse. But there was one phase of his business which later on did cause him severe regret. In 1769 he confesses :

> Some years ago I retailed rum, sugar, and molasses, the fruits of the labour of slaves, but had not then much concern about them save only that the rum might be used in moderation ; nor was this concern so weightily attended to as I now believe it ought to have been.

So "it hath seemed right that my small gain from this branch of trade should be applied in promoting righteousness on the earth."[2]

The Account Book shows that rum was much in demand, retailed by Woolman by the quart or by the gallon. The idea of total abstinence had not made its appearance even in the most puritan sects, nor did it until the middle of the next century. Elizabeth Fry, the prison reformer, who died in 1845, was persuaded by straitlaced opinion to give up music on religious grounds, but was afraid to give up stout and ale in case this should weaken her ; and her brother-in-law, Sir Thomas Fowell Buxton, made a great fortune as a brewer without a thought of criticism from his Quaker relatives. Drunkenness was dealt with, as we have seen, but the use of alcohol was taken for granted. Woolman did not regard rum as an evil in itself or even as a "superfluity." He regarded it rather as something which was easily misused. When, in his fiftieth year, he gave up the use of rum for himself he equally gave up sugar and molasses, and for the same reason—he had discovered about the cruel conditions of the slaves in the West Indies, where these things were produced. His discussion of the use of liquor is moderate and cool and interwoven with his universal theme.

> In time of trading I had an opportunity of seeing that the too liberal use of spirituous liquors and the custom of wearing too costly apparel led some people into great inconveniences and that these two things appear to be often connected with each other. By not attending to that use of things which is consistent with universal righteousness there is an increase of labour which extends beyond what our Heavenly Father intends for us. And by great labour and often by much sweating, there is even among such as are not drunkards a craving of liquors to revive the spirits ; that partly by the luxurious drinking of

[1] Folio MS., p. 39.   [2] Whittier ed., p. 206.

some, and partly by the drinking of others led to it by immoderate labour, very great quantities of rum are every year expended in our colonies, the greater part of which we should have no need of did we steadily attend to pure wisdom.

When men take pleasure in feeling their minds elevated with strong drink, and so indulge their appetite as to disorder their understandings, neglect their duty as members of a family or civil society and cast off all regard to religion, their case is much to be pitied. . . . Every degree of luxury hath some connexion with evil. . . . As I have sometimes been much spent in the heat and have taken spirits to revive me, I have found by experience that in such circumstances the mind is not so calm nor so fitly disposed for Divine meditation as when all such extremes are avoided. . . . Did those who have the care of great estates attend with singleness of heart to this heavenly Instructor which so opens and enlarges the mind as to cause men to love their neighbours as themselves, they would have wisdom given them to manage their concerns without employing some people in providing the luxuries of life, or others in labouring too hard ; but for want of steadily regarding this principle of Divine love, a selfish spirit takes place in the minds of people which is attended with darkness and manifold confusions in the world.

This throwback to his young manhood, the years on the farm, haying or harvesting under the pitiless hot sun, his bones melting in the humid exhausting heat that will visit for days at a stretch the Delaware Valley, makes one look twice at those strong words "craving" and "extremes," and question whether this is another light on the nature of the youthful follies which he regretted. Woolman, however, is not the man to make a luxury of self-blame. He has said all he means to about that closed past.

John Woolman did not think of rum as the only thing passing across his counter which could be put to a wrong use. Almost anything could be made to do harm as well as good. A woman could come in for nothing else but knitting-needles, and go away and ruin her eyesight and her temper by working far into the night by the dim candle, making clothes for her children with immoderate labour. A man could buy some nails and cedar-board and make himself into a surly father and a sullen husband by tiring himself out building a pig-pen after the hard farm day, instead of fishing the stream or sitting with a book under the trees, and restoring his soul.

In the same way, although Woolman retired from business to prevent himself from growing rich and to give himself more time for living, he did not condemn business as such, or advise others against its pursuit ; he merely warned :

> yet through the great number of superfluities which are bought and sold, and through the corruption of the times, they who apply to merchandise for a living have great need to be well experienced in that precept which the Prophet Jeremiah laid down for his scribe : "Seekest thou great things for thyself? seek them not."

He had felt for himself and observed in others the two great dangers of the business life—hurry and compromise.

> In the love of money and in the wisdom of this world, business is proposed, then in the urgency of affairs pushed forward, and the mind cannot in this state discern the good and perfect will of God concerning us . . . if we give not up those prospects of gain which in the wisdom of this world are open before us, but say in our hearts, "I must needs go on ; and in going on I hope to keep as near the purity of truth as the business before me will admit of," the mind remains entangled, and the shining of the light of life into the soul is obstructed.[1]

Through all Woolman's thoughts about trade runs the constantly developing theme of his theory of happiness. He does not speak of self-denial but of "Customs contrary to pure wisdom which tends to change agreeable employ into a Toyl." He does not speak of this world as a vale of tears in which we may well expect the worst, consoled by thoughts of heaven, but instead expresses his robust and never-failing pleasure in the daily human contact, "For Brethren to Visit each other in true Love I believe makes part of that happiness which our heavenly father intends for us in this life." He offers counsel of worldly wisdom "To be well acquainted with the Affairs we are interested in, with the dispositions of those with whom we have connexions, to have outward concerns within proper bounds, and to shun doubtful disputes about property" ; and urges "content with that true simplicity in which no wandering desires leads on to Strife, where no treasures possessed in a selfish spirit tends to beget ill-will in other selfish men."[2]

But when Woolman says, "I had but a small family," in that tone of finality, though still a young man and only a few years married, he confesses, with the completest of reserve, an intimate tragedy. Himself

---

[1] Whittier ed., p. 227.
[2] From Woolman's essay, *Serious Considerations on Trade* (1758, Gummere), pp. 398–401.

one of so large a family, he had no doubt looked forward to a large family group in his own home, and Mary, with all her engaging baby charm, was to be but the first, the forerunner, of all the laughter and life and eager stir of a houseful of children. In the summer of '53 the natural hope of another child had received promise of fulfilment ; and John Woolman stayed closely at home to take care of his wife, whose fragility was now manifest as a reality. On the twenty-first of July, 1754, a son was safely born, and the delighted father named him William,[1] after the great-grandfather whose bones had been the first of any Woolman's to rest in American soil. But little William had arrived with difficulty, had almost slain his mother in his coming, and his own life, flickering feebly in the summer heat, faded out when the leaves began to turn. Not only was he lost, but with him went all hope of a successor. There was no longer any need to save up for future children. There would be only Mary to provide for.

So deep and bitter was the blow that the father passes it over in complete silence. Not in his Journal, nor on the fly-leaves of his Account Book, does he mention little William's name or make the slightest allusion to his two months' struggle to inhabit this world. No words of pious resignation are necessary or fitting. John Woolman silently readjusted his life.

So there are no descendants of John Woolman who bear his name. Mary, however, was a vigorous child, grew up and married and had ten children, seven of them sons. She died of smallpox at the age of forty-seven.

[1] Minutes of Burlington Monthly Meeting, Register of Births and Deaths.

XX

LAW AND MEDICINE

ONE of Woolman's friends was a Frenchman, Anthony Benezet, seven years his senior, a teacher in the Penn Charter School, of Philadelphia. Benezet was an ugly man with courtly manners and a warm human charm. Though he was a Quaker and a strong supporter of his adopted country, the English colony of Pennsylvania, his house was none the less a centre of French culture and a port of call for foreign visitors. To him John Woolman could go to share conversation about the mystics of Port Royal, near Paris, whose practice of silent prayer at all times and places, and cultivation of the inward life, seemed often identical with Quakerism, Catholics though they were. Their persecution and dispersal had given them some publicity and roused a demand for the writings of Fénelon in particular. Certainly Woolman had borrowed and read, perhaps owned, Fénelon long before his marriage. Perhaps even it was Fénelon he was reading, the "pious author," on the winter night which to him was "memoriable" in his nineteenth year.

Now John Woolman turned his attention from little Mary's first tooth and first gurgles of recognition to hear from his French-born friend of the publication in France of Volume One of Diderot's *Encyclopædia*, whose thirty-four volumes were to continue to appear throughout the rest of Woolman's life, and to be completed in the very year of his death. It was an attack, by historical survey and cool exact information, on all the rooted superstitions, cruelties, injustices of society, freeing people's minds from preconceived ideas and preparing the way for unthought-of revolution and republicanism. "If we allow negroes to be men it will begin to be believed that we ourselves are not Christians," said Montesquieu. And while Woolman doubtless heard from Benezet of this new ferment, the "enlightened despots" of Europe—Frederick of Prussia, Catherine of Russia, Maria-Theresa of Austria—were reading Montesquieu as they had read Pascal and Voltaire, and were stirred to thoughts of social and political reform. They had godlike powers, those three, and each dreamed of using his power to establish a perfect working order within his own orbit where every citizen would be good and happy. The dictum of Diderot echoed everywhere, "If laws are good morals are good" ; and of Helvetius, "It is the good legislator who makes the good citizen."

The benevolent despots were unable to keep the peace long enough to complete their experiments (Frederick was after all chiefly an artist in the art of war, and had to keep in practice) ; but obscure John Woolman in Mount Holly, living under liberal laws and glad of it, was aware, as he observed himself and his fellow-citizens, that laws alone would not make morals good, but that goodness must begin in the individual, and was of its essence voluntary. Pure universal love, as he called it—closely following the phrase of Fénelon—would result in spontaneous right action ; but one could begin the practice of right action before having attained the rare state of universal love. And there was one particular form of right action which seemed elementary, the avoidance of which maintained so glaring and obvious a wrong that to tolerate its existence, even, must harden the heart.

Voltaire, the great Frenchman, dominant thinker of the world in the eighteenth century, more powerful than any other, spoke much of liberty in the abstract. Woolman, possessing most of the freedoms of which Voltaire spoke, was consumed with a passion for liberty in a concrete sense, the freeing of his fellow-Americans, both white and black, both owners and owned, from the burden of slavery. Had he believed in the power of laws to change bad customs at the root he might have become a political agitator. Thomas Hazard laboured in the Rhode Island Assembly to wipe out slavery by law. But Woolman knew of abortive laws now on the statute-books of Pennsylvania, New Jersey, Virginia, which could not operate owing to almost universal non-consent of the governed, or because of interference by the home authorities.   So he chose the slow, deep way of working : the changing of individual opinion.   His method was that of personal suasion ; not like the demagogue or the public preacher, attacking crowds, but in the close man-to-man dealing of friend with friend.

One very direct channel for this lay along his legal practice, especially in the writing of wills.   He consistently refused to include any clause bequeathing slaves.   This sometimes gave offence, as the testator not unnaturally thought the contents of the will was none of the writer's business.   Those who took the trouble to make a will were usually solid citizens, well seasoned in life, and they disliked the implied criticism. Woolman was very sensitive to their point of view.   "Offending sober people was disagreeable to my inclination," he confesses.   He also lost money by it, both by loss of legal fees and by withdrawal of custom.

> Tradesmen and retailers of goods who depend on their business for a living are naturally inclined to keep the good-will of their customers ; nor is it a pleasant thing to young men to be under a necessity to question the judgments or honesty of elderly men and more especially of such as have a fair reputation.

But, having faced the consequences and prepared his mind for them and thought out the logic of his position, he was forearmed, lost neither his temper nor his manners, and constantly maintained the only tenable position—that he must keep his own conscience clear.

To the argument that it was not his business what went into a will he replied, "It is the duty of all to be firm in what they certainly know is right for them," and, "I had a scruple in my mind against doing writings of that kind."   To the argument most cogent and most frequently used in a community where each owner held very few slaves and felt a very personal relation to them, that the slaves were part of the family, that it was a kindness to bequeath them in the family and a cruelty to turn them loose in a world with which they were untrained to cope, Woolman—remembering Grandfather Burr and the Honourable Richard Smith—replied with care.

> A charitable benevolent man, well acquainted with a negro, may, I believe, under some circumstances, keep him in his family as a servant on no other motives than the negro's good ; but man, as man, knows not what shall be after him, nor hath he any assurance that his children will attain to that perfection in wisdom and goodness necessary rightly to exercise such power ; hence it is clear to me that I ought

not to be the scribe where wills are drawn in which some children are made sale-masters over others during life.

Was there a barb in that reply when they thought it over afterwards ?

An ounce of action is always worth a pound of theory. Woolman's positive and well-mannered refusal to draw wills in which slaves were bequeathed stirred up a good deal of feeling. This is a matter in which Woolman is prepared to be explicit, and he gives several incidents in detail, affording a clear exposition of his method and its results.

About this time a person at some distance lying sick his brother came to me to write his will. I knew he had slaves and asking his brother was told he intended to leave them as slaves to his children. . . . I told the man that I believed the practice of continuing slavery to this people was not right and that I had a scruple in my mind against doing writings of that kind ; though many in our Society kept them as slaves, still, I was not easy to be concerned in it and desired to be excused from going to write the will.

Again :

About this time an ancient man of good esteem in the neighbourhood came to my house to get his will written. He had young negroes and I asked him privately how he purposed to dispose of them. He told me ; I then said, "I cannot write thy will without breaking my own peace," and respectfully gave my reasons for it. He signified that he had a choice that I should have written it, but as I could not consistant with my conscience he did not desire it, and so he got it written by some other person. A few years after, there being great alterations in his family, he came again to me to write his will. His negroes were yet young, and his son, to whom he intended to give them, was, since he first spoke to me, from a libertine become a sober young man, and he supposed that I would have been free on that account to write it. We had much friendly talk on the subject and then deferred it. A few days after he came again and directed their freedom, and then I wrote his will.

A great deal of tact was needed on such occasions not to feel them as a contest for personal victory, but Woolman's entire sweetness and modesty made the way easy, and his relief at being able to perform the other's wishes left his visitor's *amour propre* as undamaged as possible.

Near the time that the last mentioned friend first spoke to me a neighbour received a bad bruise in his body and sent for me to bleed him, which having done he desired me to write his will. I took notes, and amongst other things he told me to which of his children he gave his young negro. I considered the pain and distress he was in and knew not how it would end, so I wrote his will save only that part concerning his slave and carrying it to his bedside read it to him. I then told him in a friendly way that I could not write any instruments by which my fellow-creatures were made slaves without bringing trouble on my own mind. I let him know that I charged nothing for what I had done, and desired to be excused from doing the other part in the way he proposed. We then had a serious conference on the subject ; at length, he agreeing to set her free, I finished his will.

These incidents, besides their main information, give an insight into the variety of services which John Woolman practised—not only a smattering of law but a smattering, it appears, of medicine, too.

Woolman's friend, Josiah White, had a great reputation as an amateur doctor, but his skill lay along the lines of natural remedies—herbs and simples and fomentations of leaves, some learned from the Indians and some discovered by himself. White was a skilled botanist, and to roam the woods with him was an education. Even on horseback he would ride slowly, his eyes on the tangled edges of the path, and often would suddenly dismount and dig some precious specimen to put in his case. He combined the curiosity of the scientist with the rather blurred pre-science of the mystic. On one occasion a companion—John Pemberton— asked him what medical use the unfamiliar plant had which White was at that moment pulling up. "I don't know yet," said White, "but I shall some time find a use for it." And there are many stories of White's entering a strange house unbidden, on some sixth-sense warning of critical sickness there, and even refusing to leave (peacefully seating him-self in the parlour, with every courtesy) until he had been allowed to see and minister to the patient. As an amateur physician he quite rightly never charged for medical advice or remedies, nor would receive any kind of disguised payment. When once a grateful patient who had taken a lot of his time in many visits succeeded in persuading him at next slaughter to accept a quarter of mutton it worried Josiah White for weeks. "I see that quarter of mutton always before me when I am gathering herbs !" he complained. This is not to be confused with the superstition of the witch-doctors that the magic of their gift of healing would be broken if they accepted reward for it. There was no magic or superstition about White's undoubted gift. He used the methods of the scientist, learning by experiment with natural remedies, and Wool-man's final theories on medicine and health were rationally influenced by his much older friend.

The practice of bleeding, however, is the touch of the professional physician, and it is probable that John Woolman had been taught how and where to open a vein and measure a regulated amount of blood into a basin by good Dr Alexander Ross, who moved from Burlington to live at Mount Holly in 1752. When the doctor was away on the fortnightly rounds of his large and extended practice emergencies at home often had to be met. Bleeding was an almost universal panacea for all ills, injuries, fevers, whatever, and a person capable of doing it in the doctor's absence was a boon to any community. John Woolman possessed the qualifications : he was tender, scrupulous, exact, firm ; he inspired confidence ; and though germs were unknown, dirt was partly understood, and he was delicately clean in his handling. So he could on occasion behave as a first-aid expert, a bleeder of the sick.

Few enter more deeply and quickly into the intimacy of any household than the lawyer and the doctor, who come primed from the start with a man's consent to talk about his most private matters. Only one other can compare with them ; and that is the priest. Mount Holly had no resident priest, clergyman, minister—whatever the sectarian name for the office might be. It was a Quaker community, and Quaker ministers were different, non-professional, 'amateur' if you wish, with responsibilities which were undefined. A Quaker minister did not necessarily undertake what other churches know as pastoral work. It was the appointed Overseers of the Meeting who were responsible for visiting families, and their duties were rather to inquire into reasons for absence from meeting, financial difficulty, misdemeanour, and the like, rather than to minister to a mind diseased. But from time to time a Friend who had been recorded as an elder or a minister felt a leading, or "concern," to visit families in a priestly sense. When such an impulse came upon him, and deepened into a duty, he laid it before the Quarterly Meeting of Ministers and Elders exactly as if it entailed a distant journey, and only entered upon it after obtaining the sanction and support of the meeting in the form of a minute. So a visiting minister was, in a sense, reordained for the service every time, and a human busybodyness, which might go with a loose use of the amateur status, was guarded against.

John Woolman was convinced that his chief service as a minister was not in the speaking in meeting—upon which he kept a very close watch lest he should run before the call—but in the less public, less praised, humble, family visiting. There was none more difficult, none which went so deep when rightly done. Of the thirty-eight times in his life on which John Woolman applied to his meeting for a minute, twenty-four were for visiting of families. Families in the Great Meadows, the upper part of New Jersey ; families in Bucks County, Pennsylvania ; families in Burlington Monthly Meeting, families in Chesterfield, families in Mount Holly, families in Philadelphia, families at Haddonfield, families at Ancocas[1]; deep, deep his influence sank, as the family group gathered in silence in the largest room and felt themselves led into the impersonal presence of God to look at their lives and their problems from a new perspective. This was all very well until their visitor, in private conversation afterwards (conversation in which they had expected the luxury of highly personal religious talk, sin, salvation, death, and everlasting life), pointed out that the logic of the new perspective meant getting rid of some of their encumbrances, particularly— if they had them—slaves. It was painful and disconcerting, and Woolman's Journal often ruefully comments on "searching laborious exercise among the inhabitants of that place" or records that "strength was given to go through the trials which in the course of our visit attended us," though he generally concludes that he "found inward peace." This and this alone was his pragmatic test as to whether or not he had truly obeyed the mysterious influence of the will of God. It alone gave him "fresh confirmation that acting contrary to present outward interest in regard to truth and righteousness, and thereby incurring the resentments of people, opens the way to a treasure which is better than silver, and to a friendship exceeding the friendship of men."

[1] Copying the minute ; the same as Rancocas, remember.

XXI

AUTHORSHIP; THE ESSAY ON "SOME CONSIDERATIONS ON THE KEEPING OF NEGROES"

But besides these instruments of personal approach John Woolman had another tool at his command which it is evident that he considered more important than any other, and which he took peculiar pains to keep supple and trimmed. That was his pen. If a word fitly spoken is like apples of gold in pictures of silver, how much more a word fitly written —written and printed and held and kept, read slowly and at leisure, reread, perhaps—learned, marked, and inwardly digested. Woolman knew how much the written word meant to him as a reader, and from early youth he had the born writer's impulse to set down his thoughts in writing for himself to read. The transition from keeping a personal notebook to writing for others is readily made. Jonathan Edwards did the same, and so did David and John Brainerd, and John Smith, and Samuel Fothergill, and John Churchman, and many others of Woolman's contemporaries and friends. The ink on their pens was free, their writing flowed along. It is grammatical, competent, sometimes racy, but it finds no place among future generations on the college curricula of students of English prose style. As the first biographer of Jonathan Edwards, the most famous of these men, remarks :

His inattention to his style is certainly to be regretted. . . . He appears . . . to have sent his works to the press very much in the state in which they were first written. Let it here be remembered that the cultivation of style was not then attended to in the colonies, and that it is extremely doubtful whether, in the then existing state of the country, it would have been possible for him to have devoted much attention to style.[1]

Mr Edwards, his biographer adds, took more pains in his latter years after reading Richardson's novel *Sir Charles Grandison*, which gave him some ideas on English prose which he had never had before.

How then did it come about that John Woolman had ideas on style, that he devoted himself to the art of writing, and that he hardly wrote anything which does not rank as a classic? Some Quakers to whom the word 'art' is suspect (though there are many Quakers in the modern world, from the late Roger Fry down, who hold art dear) have suggested, with naïveté, that it was Woolman's clear and honest spirit which made him take care to make his writing clear and honest. But what turgid writer would not be clear if he could? By what test is a man to know when his writing is clear, and when it is not? That clarity which holds the crystal sentence up to the light and lets the meaning untarnished through is the hardest achievement of all. That Woolman secured it is no accidental accompaniment of an honest mind, and though it is partly a gift of fortune—an eye for form, and an ear, which came at birth—it can only finally be wrought by labour. This kind cometh not forth but by prayer and fasting.

John Woolman's first publication, the essay on *Some Considerations on the Keeping of Negroes*, took place about three years after his father's death, the fruit of long preparation, of many experimental hours. Woolman says it was published in 1753, but the earliest copies of it bear the imprint of 1754.[2] It was passed for publication, and issued by the Overseers of the Press of the Society of Friends of Philadelphia, and therefore carried their authority, and was widely distributed among all the Quakers in the colonies. It was also read by numbers of others, unconsciously moved by the beauty of its language and the sweetness and loftiness of its thought.

Woolman began this document by putting forward his theory of the general brotherhood of all mankind, and quoted the golden rule in its support.

I take it that all men by nature are equally entitled to the equity of this rule. . . . One man ought not to look upon another man or

---

[1] *Works of Jonathan Edwards*, I, ccxxix.
[2] Appendix XII.

society of men as so far beneath him but that he should put himself in their place in all his actions towards them and bring them to this test, viz How should I approve of this conduct were I in their circumstances and they in mine ? . . . If I purchase a man who hath never forfeited his liberty, the natural right of freedom is in him ; and shall I keep him and his posterity in servitude and ignorance ? To act continually with integrity of heart above all narrow and selfish motives is a pure token of our being partakers of that salvation which God hath appointed . . . and is beyond all contradiction a more happy situation than can ever be promised by the utmost reach of Art and Power united not proceeding from heavenly wisdom.

. . . The highest delights of sense or most pleasing objects visible ought ever to be accounted infinitely inferior to that real intellectual happiness suited to man in his primitive innocence and now to be found in true renovation of mind.

. . . It appears by experience that where children are educated in fulness of ease and idleness, evil habits are more prevalent than is common among such who are prudently employed in the necessary affairs of life. And if children are not only educated in the way of so great temptation, but have also the opportunity of lording it over their fellow-creatures, and being masters of men in their childhood, how can we hope otherwise than that their tender minds will be possessed with thoughts too high for them, which by continuance gaining strength will prove like a slow current gradually separating them from (or keeping from acquaintance with) that humility and meekness in which alone lasting happiness can be enjoyed.

Man is born to labour, and Experience abundantly sheweth that it is for our good : but where the powerful lay the burthen on the inferior without affording a Christian education and suitable opportunity of improving the mind, and a treatment which we, in their case, should approve, that they themselves may live at ease and fare sumptuously and lay up riches for their posterity, this . . . I doubt not is sometimes the effect of a perverted mind : for while the life of one is made grievous by the rigour of another it entails misery on both.

Throughout this essay, afterwards called Part I, there is very little mention of the sufferings of the slaves, except in the most general terms ; chiefly that they have been deprived of the "sweetness of freedom" and the benefits of education and religion. Woolman's appeal was to the masters, chiefly for their own sakes, or at least equally for their own sakes. There was no anger-provoking blame in it, nor even a misunderstanding of the owners' case. Woolman realized with what complicated bonds they were tied into the system, he did not belittle the "inconveniences" that would attend their breaking loose. He did not even make the error of recommending a specific course of action, which they might spend their time refuting and so blind themselves to the great principle which lay behind. No, he was sorry for them, because they "do miss the true foundation of happiness and wander in a maze of dark anxiety." And he offered them the best he had, fragments of splendour which remained for his own illumination from his hours of prayer, and could be carried with them like jewels in the hand up to the very throne of God Himself.

> How deeply soever men are involved in the most exquisite difficulties, sincerity of heart and upright walking before God, freely submitting to his providence, is the most sure remedy. He only is able to relieve not only persons but nations in their greatest calamities. Tis a truth most certain that a life guided by the Wisdom from above agreeable with Justice, Equity and Mercy, is throughout consistent and amiable, and truly beneficial to society ; the serenity and calmness of mind in it affords an unparalleled comfort in this life, and the end of it is blessed.

This is not the language of controversy. It could not be denied. Like Scripture itself, it wore upon the heart and turned the will. There was a universal ring about the whole essay which made it apply far more widely than merely to slave-owners. How wide its application was the discreet Overseers of the Press did not at first recognize. A little uneasiness was felt by some at such phrases as "intellectual happiness" and "renovation of mind"—not quite in accord with current orthodoxy, which gave the intellect little place in religion, and was inclined to accuse Woolman's point of view of being too ethical ; but the amount of gunpowder that lay in such sentences as the ones about labour and riches was not perceived, except as it attacked the system of slavery. And Woolman was by this time a man of weight in his community. In 1752—the year the calendar had received a violent jolt, by astronomical recommendation and Act of Parliament, and January had been made the first month, and December, in spite of its name, had been made the twelfth[1] to catch up, as it were, with Time—that year John Woolman had been appointed the Clerk of the Burlington Quarterly Meeting of Ministers and Elders, in place of the Honourable Richard Smith, deceased. In that capacity he presided over the meetings and wrote the minutes until 1769. The only position weightier than that in the gift of the

[1] Act of Parliament for all British dominions. The difference was actually eleven days.

Society of Friends was to be made Clerk (that is, presiding officer) of the Yearly Meeting. This position Woolman never held. Whether he was offered it or not is impossible to say. But he certainly had more liberty to express his concerns in the Yearly Meeting, and persuade Friends to their adoption, if not hampered by the neutrality of the Clerkship. The duty of the Clerk in any Quaker business meeting is to introduce matters of business, listen to the discussion, see that it is conducted in order, and sympathetically detect and record the judgment of the meeting. This is not so simple as merely counting the majority. A vote is never taken. A majority may not necessarily be right. Should not one man of character and judgment and spiritual enlightenment outweigh several of lighter calibre? Hence the phrase "weighty Friend," a phrase independent of age or sex, since years do not always bring wisdom. In case of difference of opinion, if the "weight" of the meeting is all on one side the Clerk is at liberty to make a minute accordingly, and the contrary opinion may be content to be guided. But if the dissenters are not content they are not roughly overruled. All may express themselves, and the meeting sometimes grows warm. John Smith notes in his diary for 11th month 26th, 1749 :

> Our business was some of it difficult, and we had abundantly too much heat and haranguing. I did not meddle much with it, but once spoke a little ill-natured, which I was uneasy for, thinking nothing but Love and meekness ought to preside in assemblies for Religious services.

A spell of silence at such times is a great healer. The Clerk will probably appeal for a committee to be appointed to have the disputed matter gone over carefully, and perhaps certain objectors approached individually in order to ascertain their exact objection or alternative proposal. The committee will in any case report to the next meeting, and the whole matter will be again opened. By this exercise of patience and forbearance and mutual search for the right decision there is no such thing in the Quaker system as a suppressed minority or a dominant oligarchy. But there is sometimes a lack of unanimity.

That was certainly the case in the "Yearly Meeting for the Provinces of Pennsylvania and New Jerseys held at Burlington by Adjournments from the 14th Day of the Ninth Month 1754 to the 19th Day of the same inclusive," when John Woolman prepared and presented an *Epistle of Caution and Advice concerning the Buying and Keeping of Slaves,* and succeeded in persuading the weight of the Yearly Meeting to send that epistle out.

The epistle was (and is) a message prepared each year during the sittings of any Yearly Meeting of Friends to send out in greeting to all other Yearly Meetings ; and an item in every Yearly Meeting's business was the reading and consideration of the epistles received from other Yearly Meetings. The Yearly Meetings in existence in 1754 were London, Dublin (or Ireland), Philadelphia, New York (New York and Connecticut), New England (Massachusetts, New Hampshire, Maine, and Rhode Island), North Carolina (North Carolina, South Carolina, and Georgia), Virginia, and Maryland. Although no organization subordinated any Yearly Meeting to any other, all looked up to London as their parent Yearly Meeting, and based their procedure on the London Discipline, prepared by George Fox. But in the colonies Philadelphia Yearly Meeting, which was "the Yearly Meeting for the provinces of Pennsylvania and New Jerseys," was the leading Yearly Meeting. Indeed, Samuel Fothergill, visiting the colonies in 1755, said "it was the largest in one Meeting-House in the world."[1] Its opinion and advice were often asked by the others, and its words carried great weight. As a rule the Philadelphia Epistle had consisted of words of pious exhortation, based rather on the obscurer style of the Apostle Paul as rendered in the King James Version, and not stimulating any uncomfortable exercise of thought. A soothing and comfortable sensation of brotherly feeling and of being all together in the right way in a rather more special sense than other people was the usual result of the reading of the epistles.

So this Epistle of 1754 went through the Society of Friends like a trumpet blast. It began straight away to the point without beating about the bush ; it was on a definite theme ; it spoke clearly without scriptural phraseology or obscure metaphor ; and it dealt with a subject which affected, in a deep and concrete way, many a life. It demanded two of the hardest exercises of the spirit—thought and decision. Everywhere it was read—in the Monthly and Quarterly Meetings throughout New England, throughout the South—it roused people.

DEAR FRIENDS

It hath frequently been the Concern of our Yearly Meeting to testify their Uneasiness and Disunity with the Importation and Pur-

---

[1] *Memoirs and Letters of Samuel Fothergill*, p. 188.

chasing of Negroes and other Slaves, and to direct the Overseers of the several Meetings to advise and deal with such as engage therein.

The Characteristic and Badge of a true Christian is Love and good Works ; our Saviour's whole Life on Earth was one continual Exercise of them ; Love one another, says he, as I have loved you. How can we be said to love our Brethren who bring, or for selfish Ends keep them, in Bondage ? Do we act consistent with this noble Principle, who lay such heavy Burdens on our Fellow Creatures ? Do we consider that they are called, and sincerely desire that they may become Heirs with us in Glory, and rejoice in the Liberty of the Sons of God, whilst we are with-holding from them the common Liberties of Mankind ? Or can the Spirit of God, by which we have always professed to be led, be the Author of those oppressive and unrighteous Measures ? Or do we not thereby manifest that temporal interest hath more Influence on our Conduct herein than the Dictates of that merciful, holy and unerring Guide ?

. . . How fearful then ought we to be of engaging in what hath so natural a Tendency to lessen our Humanity and of suffering our-selves to be enured to the Exercise of hard and cruel Measures, lest thereby we in any Degree loose our tender and feeling Sense of the Miseries of our Fellow Creatures and become worse than those who have not believ'd. . . .

. . . Signed, by Appointment, on behalf Yearly Meeting, [by twelve Friends].

Although most epistles are necessarily the work of one person (some-times advised by a committee), when they are publicly read and adopted by the Yearly Meeting they rightly become anonymous. The document is not to be received as the message of an individual but as the message of an important body—so John Woolman's name is not attached to this epistle. His friend, John Smith, and his friend, Abraham Farrington, were on the committee. And the internal evidence of authorship is overwhelming. One has only to compare this epistle with the essay on *Some Considerations on the Keeping of Negroes* which Woolman had been brooding over and writing and rewriting for several years past, and which was published just before this time, to be convinced that Woolman wrote both. But it happens that we have proof. The year before, Woolman had been appointed by the Yearly Meeting to write the Epistle to Virginia. He did so, lifting passages from his *Essay on Negroes*, both Part I—already in the hands of the Overseers of the Press—and Part II, still only in rough form on his table. This epistle went down to Virginia in the fall of '53, and when the Virginia Yearly Meeting met in May '54 they were so struck by it that the Clerk was ordered to "spread it on the Minutes"—that is, copy it out in full. A comparison of the Virginia Minute Books with the document circulated in some of the meetings in the Philadelphia area during the spring and summer of '54, and adopted by the Yearly Meeting in September for widespread circulation to all Friends, will demonstrate that the Philadelphia document[1] was Woolman's Epistle to Virginia verbatim.

This Epistle of 1754 is only one of the very many which Woolman wrote for the Yearly Meeting, and for which he gave himself no credit, even in his Journal, except by sometimes copying the epistle in. If he inadvertently mentioned his authorship he deleted the sentence in the copy he intended for the printers. Such a deleted passage in March 1755 describes his method :

It came upon me to write an Epistle to Friends which I took to our General Spring Meeting and passed to some Elderly Friends to have it inspected and signed by a number of the brethren on behalf of the meeting which with some amendments was agreed to and is as follows[2] . . .

and so forth

Woolman crossed this out, and substituted the sentence : "and an Epistle to Friends went forth from our general Spring Meeting which I thought good to give a place in this Journal."[3]

So John Woolman wielded an influence far wider than his fame.

---

[1] Anthony Benezet was one of the Overseers of the Press, and had therefore been one of those who had prepared Woolman's *Essay on Negroes*, Part I, for the press in '53. He, Woolman's intimate friend, urged forward the adoption of the Epistle to Virginia for wider circulation by the Philadelphia Yearly Meeting. He did not call it the Epistle to Virginia. It was brought forward as an independent document, quite rightly. Benezet himself presented and read it to the Philadelphia Monthly Meeting (of which he was a member, as Woolman was a member of Burlington M. M.) in January '54, and that M. M. made a minute recommending that it should be brought before the forthcoming Yearly Meeting. Since this was eight months before the Philadelphia Yearly Meeting met in Burlington and adopted the Epistle, some have deduced that Benezet was the author. But Benezet acted in good faith, and made no claim of authorship. Probably there were many present—certainly the other Overseers of the Press—who knew that John Woolman was the author. Benezet was most likely presenting it at Woolman's own request. It was good Quaker politics to prepare the way well beforehand for such a startling document.

[2] Folio MS. Journal, p. 32, Historical Society of Pennsylvania.

[3] Whittier ed. of Journal, p. 70.

XXII

LITTLE NEGRO JAMES

YET in that same year 1754, when Woolman's mind was white-hot on the subject of slavery, and he was marshalling his best energies to its destruction, he became responsible for the sale of a little Negro boy. It arose out of one of his executorships, administering the will of a deceased, part of whose property was an orphan slave boy, nine years old. There was another trustee, and together they talked over what had best be done with this child, who would need protection and shelter and a provided home for many years to come. It was finally agreed between them that they should put the boy into service with a kindly master or mistress for a definite limited period of time, on a guarantee of board and lodging. And a suitable employer was willing to take him on that understanding if the time should be set until the boy was thirty—that is, for twenty-one years.

John Woolman had recently bound two of his own brothers apprentice for fourteen years apiece, according to the dictates of his father's will, which had left him no choice. The terms of indenture were fresh in his mind. And they did not seem to differ materially from the arrangement made for the little slave boy. A typical indenture form—sometimes binding the apprentice for sixteen years—included the undertaking that during the time of learning the master's

Art, Trade and Mystery, he shall not Commit Fornication nor Contract Matrimony, at Cards, Dice or any other unlawful Games he shall not play, whereby his Master may have damage.   He shall not absent Himself Day nor Night from his said Masters Service without his Leave ; nor haunt Ale-houses, Taverns or Play-houses.

In return for these undertakings he was to get "sufficient Meat, Drink, apparell, Lodging and Washing, fitting for an Apprentice . . . and Twelve months day schooling."[1]

More could hardly be exacted from little James or less returned— with the exception of the schooling.   So John Woolman agreed to the plan, and, having agreed to it, characteristically assumed full responsibility for it.   In an index leaf of his Account Book he noted the memorandum "Negro James, bound 2nd da, 1 mo, to Serve 21 years, that is till 2nd. 1 mo. 1775."

But when money passes from one hand to another the direction in which it goes is the crucial test as to who is regarded as the one to benefit from the transaction.   In the case of Abraham and Eber Woolman their guardians had had to pay out money to their employers.   The labour they would perform, even in the latter part of their fourteen years, was not considered by either party as equivalent to the value received in instructing them in their trade.   But in the case of little Negro James it was the employer who paid down a lump sum for his twenty-one years of service, that is to say for the complete control, for that length of time, of James's arms and legs, to perform what the master's mind and will directed entirely for the master's benefit.

Let the apprentice's lot be never so hard, he was never really a slave.

That John Woolman could have become so befogged, and at a time, too, when his mind was steeped in the evils of slavery, is just one more evidence of the inconsistency of human nature.   It would be agreeable to put most of the blame on the other trustee—to assume that he was somebody who had exceptional influence with Woolman, and persuaded him with specious arguments against his better judgment.   But such an excuse was scorned by Woolman himself.   He knew himself sensitive to influence, was on his guard against this 'weakness,' and if he found that he had fallen into error by following another's advice he logically shouldered the full responsibility of his choice.   But the following sentences occur in a letter to a friend written not long after :

I have painfully felt the force of conversation proceeding from men deeply rooted in an earthly mind, and can sympathise with others in

[1] Woodward and Hageman, p. 213.

such conflicts, because much weakness still attends me. I find that to be a fool as to worldly wisdom and to commit my cause to God, not fearing to offend men, who take offence at the simplicity of truth, is the only way to remain unmoved at the sentiments of others.[1]

The disturbing incident of Negro James and the dissatisfaction which he felt about it were part of the background of this confession. Certainly Woolman repented bitterly in time to come. It was fourteen years later that the thorns of remorse began to torment his rest. Perhaps in the journey that he made in May 1768 to Philadelphia, Concord, and Maryland he had seen Negro James again, now a young man of twenty-four, driving his master's horses or waiting at his master's table ; not unhappy, perhaps, but a man, capable now of earning for himself, of marrying and settling in a cosy little home, and experiencing the simple joys of family life. He was not mistreated, he probably felt loyal affection for his master's family, exercising the Negro's gift for finding pleasure in the small things of the present ; but certainly a man retained in childish dependence, whose initiative was being destroyed, and whose desires thwarted.

Abraham and Eber had recently completed their apprenticeship and were starting in life for themselves, full of hope and ambition. But Negro James had yet seven more years to serve.

It seemed to Woolman at first an irrevocable error, and he does not record it in his Journal until he has thought of a concrete way of making partial amends.

Eleventh of sixth month, 1769 . . . as my meditations have been on universal love, my own conduct in time past became of late grievous to me. As persons setting negroes free in our province are bound by law to maintain them in case they have need of relief, some in the time of my youth who scrupled to keep slaves for term of life were wont to detain their young negroes in their service without wages till they were thirty years of age. With this custom I so far agreed that being joined with another Friend in executing the will of a deceased Friend, I once sold a negro lad till he might attain the age of thirty years, and applied the money to the use of the estate.

With abasement of heart I may now say that sometimes as I have sat in a meeting with my heart exercised towards that awful Being who respecteth not persons nor colours and have thought upon this lad I have felt that all was not clear in my mind respecting him . . . and it hath appeared to me that I should make some restitution ; but in what way I saw not till lately, when being under some concern that I might be resigned to go on a visit to some part of the West Indies and under close engagement of spirit seeking to the Lord for counsel herein, the aforesaid came heavily upon me, and my mind for a time was covered with darkness and sorrow.   Under this sore affliction my heart was softened to receive instruction, and I now first perceived that as I had been one of the two executors who had sold this lad for nine years longer than is common for our own children to serve, so I should now offer part of my substance to redeem the last half of the nine years ; but as the time was not yet come, I executed a bond, binding myself and my executors to pay to the man to whom he was sold what to candid men might appear equitable for the last four and a half years of his time, in case the said youth should be living, and in a condition likely to provide comfortably for himself.[1]

In a later essay John Woolman made a full statement of the thirty years' system and his mature judgment concerning it—another instance of the way in which he did not jump to conclusions, but was even conservative in first estimates, and by slow and logical degrees, in the coolest weighing of one thing with another, arrived at his often revolutionary deductions.

> To keep Negroes as Servants till they are Thirty years of age and hold the profits of the last nine years of their labour as our own on a Supposition that they may some time be an expense to our States is a way of proceeding which appears to admit of improvement.
> Reasons offered.   1st. Men of mature age who have walked orderly and made no contract to serve, that they are entitled to freedom I expect is generally agreed to ; and to make them serve as Slaves Nine years longer may be to keep them slaves for term of life.   They may die before that age . . . and may leave Children to whom with reason they might in their last sickness desire to give the monies they had earned. . . .
> 2nd.   The Labour of a healthy Industrious Negro Man for nine years I suppose at a moderate computation may not be less than fifty pounds proclamation money besides his Diet and Clothing. . . .

So he talks in the quiet tone of a business man, dealing with a specific instance in terms of facts and figures, and does a little sum on fifty pounds at 3 per cent. compound interest ; and it is all local and past, and our minds are easy.   Then suddenly he disperses the clouds of the local with one of his brilliant flashes of that light which is not for a day but for all time.

[1] Whittier ed., p. 202.

Though through gradual proceedings in unrighteousness, dimness hath come over many minds, yet the nature of things is not altered. Long oppression hath not made Oppression consistent with Brotherly Love, nor length of time through several ages made recompense to the posterity of those injured Strangers.[1]

[1] *A Plea for the Poor*, by John Woolman (Gummere, pp. 432 and 436).

XXIII

SAMUEL FOTHERGILL'S VISIT AND THE WAR TAX

IN the spring of 1754 John Woolman's first printed publication had been
on the subject of slavery. His next, in the spring of 1755, was on a very
different subject. John Woolman never made a public impress on the
world as a reformer, because he had not a single-track mind. His
"obedience to the voice of the true Shepherd" led him to attack evil
wherever he encountered it. And the next form in which he encountered
it was war.

The year 1754 carried large shadows of things to come. "Our Indians"
who had gone away to the valley of the Ohio had expected to live there
secure from white interference. But roving Indians, following moving
game, required a great deal of room, and roving white men, ambitious
of wealth and land, were laying claim by right of use and settlement to
immense tracts, regardless of the recurring tribes whose claim was
merely that of first-comers. And the perplexities of the Indians were
increased by the fact that there were two rival sets of white men. Their
complaints were now becoming heard. "Where is the Indians' land?
The English claim all on one side of the river, the French all on the other.
Where does our land lie?" They sent deputations to both the English
and the French, asking both to move out of the Ohio Valley. And
indeed the young Washington was sent to ask the French what they were

doing there, since they obviously belonged in Canada, and had no business down so far. The French treated both remonstrances with equal levity, and proceeded to make it hot for English settlers. Fort after fort was established. The French troops were well drilled and active. They had a large body of Indian allies. If the English wanted the Ohio and the undiscovered West they must fight for it. The colonies were prepared to face the fact that if this must be a fight they were all in it. A joint scheme of action was necessary, and a congress met at Albany on June 19, 1754, gathering all the governors together from Massachusetts, New Hampshire, Rhode Island, Connecticut, Maryland, New York, Pennsylvania, and New Jersey; Virginia and Carolina to be regarded as 'present.' The business before the congress was to unite the colonies for defence and renew the pact with the Six Nations. The Six Nations were anxious and reproachful. "Look at the French; they are men; they are fighting everywhere. But, we are ashamed to say it, you are like women, without any fortifications. It is but one step from Canada hither."

A Plan of Union—drawn up by Benjamin Franklin—was taken back by the governors to be discussed in the Colonial Assemblies, and each colony was pledged to a quota for an immediate joint army. The home government in London was startled when the news of these proceedings reached it, and hastily dispatched General Braddock, with some thousands of British regulars, to organize colonial defence and beat the French on the Ohio. But Governor Shirley, of Massachusetts, a British official observing affairs on the spot, calmed their worst fears. "Apprehensions have been entertained," he wrote home:

that the colonies will in time unite to throw off their dependency upon their mother country, and set up one general government among themselves. But if it is considered how different the present constitutions of their respective governments are from each other, how much the interests of some of them clash, and how opposed their tempers are, such a coalition among them will seem highly improbable. At all events they could not maintain such an independency without a strong naval force, which it must for ever be in the power of Great Britain to hinder them from having. And whilst his majesty hath seven thousand troops kept up within them, with the Indians at command, it seems easy, provided his governors and principal officers are independent of the Assemblies for their subsistence, and commonly vigilant to prevent any step of that kind being taken.

A young schoolmaster, also in Massachusetts, recently graduated from Harvard College, was writing in his diary near the same time, "If we can remove the turbulent Gallics, our people, according to the exactest calculations, will in another century become more numerous than England itself. All Europe will not be able to subdue us. The only way to keep us from setting up for ourselves is to disunite us." The young diarist's ambition in life was to become a Presbyterian minister. His name was John Adams.

In the autumn of 1754 Woolman's friend, John Churchman, returned from a four years' visit to England, bringing with him the now stately, wealthy English Quaker, Samuel Fothergill. His brother, Dr John Fothergill, was a close friend and scientific correspondent of Benjamin Franklin.[1] Woolman was almost certainly among the Friends who gathered at Israel Pemberton's to meet them, to exchange news, and to offer the advice of experience with regard to Samuel Fothergill's projected travel. Fothergill presently possessed himself of a good horse and accompanied by Israel Pemberton set out on an extended journey South, following Woolman's route, across the Susquehanna beyond Lancaster, and on through Maryland and Virginia. This quiet, casual, undefended travel proceeded day by day through the lovely autumn woods. Maryland and Virginia had been crossed, North Carolina and South Carolina and Georgia were in prospect, when sharp news reached the travellers that they were no longer in a land at peace. A man met on the road had an eyewitness story of an outbreak of the Indians in the back parts of South Carolina, sixteen English murdered, nine carried off, mostly women. "Some Northern Indians were seen to march through the back settlements of Virginia and Maryland. It is generally thought," wrote Fothergill to his brother and sister in England, "the English were settling themselves very fast on a piece of fine hunting land belonging to the Indians, without giving them satisfaction for it. . . . It is remote from the settlements of Friends," he reassured them, "and far from my route."

By April he was back in Philadelphia, and wrote home, "A considerable number of Indians have come down hither to remain until the hurries are over, but I am not dismayed by any appearance of danger."

There was indeed no appearance of danger in Philadelphia that spring.

---

[1] In 1751 Dr John Fothergill had written the preface to Franklin's *Experiments and Observations on Electricity made at Philadelphia in America.*

From March 29 to April 4 was the general Spring Meeting of Ministers and Elders for Pennsylvania and New Jersey, and the influx of the weightiest Quakers from the two provinces strengthened the hands of the peace party in the Assembly. If Quakers no longer had a majority in the Government they at least had a powerful and compact minority. But some of that minority was willing, if not to fight, at least to pay for fighting, salving their consciences by a strict keeping of the letter of the pacifist law. Washington's diary for May 11, 1754, notes that "Pennsylvania had raised ten thousand pounds to pay the soldiers raised in other colonies, as that Province could furnish no recruits." John Woolman had spent several weeks that winter visiting families round Burlington and round Chesterfield ; part of the time with "two Friends from Pennsylvania," and part of the time alone. The Quaker peace principle and its implications in a time like this were much under discussion, in a way which seemed to Woolman not clear-headed. The majority were not wondering at all about their active duty, but, feeling comfortably far from the scene of pressure, were stuffing up their ears with the cotton wool of a traditional faith. John Woolman reasoned that a man could not work for peace with his left hand and for war with his right. The so-called "peace-testimony" was not so simple as a mere refusal to bear arms. It involved one's whole attitude towards life. Few people seemed to realize that to be peaceful might involve their business life, their system of profits, and personal ambitions. So, fresh from many conversations, John Woolman put his thoughts into writing, shaped them into the form of an epistle, and so had them distributed, anonymously but with all possible weight behind them, throughout the Quakers in all the provinces of North America. He did not, like Fothergill, minimize the war.

"From a disagreement between the powers of England and France," he writes in his Journal,

it was now a time of trouble on this Continent and it came upon me to write an Epistle to Friends the which I took to our General Spring Meeting and proposed to some elderly Friends to have it inspected and signed by a number of brethren in behalf of this Meeting which with some amendments was agreed to and is as follows :

An Epistle from our general Spring Meeting of ministers and elders for Pennsylvania and New Jersey, held at Philadelphia from the 29th of the third month to the 1st of the fourth month inclusive 1755.

N

To Friends on the Continent of America
[signed by fourteen Friends]

. . . We have found it to be our duty to cease from those national contests which are productive of misery and bloodshed, and submit our cause to him, the Most High, whose tender love to his children exceeds the most warm affections of our natural parents, and who hath promised to his seed throughout the earth as to one individual, "I will never leave thee nor forsake thee.". . . By which operation that spiritual kingdom is set up which is to subdue and break in pieces all kingdoms that oppose it, and shall stand for ever. In a deep sense thereof, and of the safety, stability and peace that are in it, we are desirous that all who profess the truth may be inwardly acquainted with it and therefore be qualified *to conduct ourselves in all parts of our life as becomes our peaceable profession. Let us constantly endeavour to have our minds sufficiently disentangled from the surfeiting cares of this life, and redeemed from the love of the world, that no earthly possessions nor enjoyments may bias our judgments.* And if for the further promoting of his most gracious purposes in the earth he should give us to taste of that bitter cup of which his faithful ones have often partaken, Oh that we might be rightly prepared to receive it ! . . . With respect to the commotions and stirrings of the powers of the earth at this time near us, we are desirous that none of us may be moved thereat. . . . For the worldly part in any is the changeable part, and that is up and down, full and empty, joyful and sorrowful, as things go well or ill in this world. . . . But they that are single to the truth, waiting daily to feel the life and virtue of it in their hearts shall rejoice in the midst of adversity.[1]

Samuel Fothergill was at that Spring Meeting, heard that epistle read, and undoubtedly helped in the discussion of it, for he was not one to sit by and not be heard from. Woolman's part in the discussion was no doubt very modest ; he had expressed himself fully in the writing of the epistle ; but his authorship was very generally known, and must have attracted Fothergill's attention and cemented the foundation of their friendship. John Churchman was also present. William Logan, son of James, was there too. He was much attached to Fothergill, and had shared part of his recent journey. Israel Pemberton was Fothergill's chief host. These five must have been the nucleus of many searching

---

[1] This epistle is printed in full in Woolman's Journal, Whittier ed., pp. 70-73, but Woolman crossed out in his manuscript the acknowledgment of authorship given above, and substituted the words, "and an epistle to Friends went forth from our general Spring Meeting which I thought good to give a place in this Journal," which appear in the usual printed versions.

conversations between sittings. Logan was a prominent member of the Pennsylvania Assembly, and a realist, like his father. Fothergill, like most Englishmen, had the haziest idea of colonial affairs, and as a Quaker was anxious to keep his mind detached from "outward" things as he travelled, though his natural intelligence and curiosity were often too much for him. But at the best he had a very limited conception of the causes of the rising war. Churchman was most concerned that Quakers should keep themselves clear of any involvement. Woolman, saying little in a group of such brilliant, positive, and articulate men, had opinions to express which if not carefully worded would cut too deep. Again he might repeat, "My inclination is to persuade and entreat and simply give hints of my way of thinking." And he strove with himself to be certain that "the hints are given in as general terms as my concern would allow ; I know it is a point about which in all its branches men that appear to aim well are not generally agreed." All he desired was to stimulate to "a close thinking on the subject." England and France had, in fact, not yet declared war. There was a body of opinion in the colonies which believed that negotiation was still possible, that a compromise might be effected, a satisfactory boundary drawn which would leave Canada to the French, and perhaps something else—something not now used, "out west." In so big a country there might be room for all. And the Indians' grievances were certainly open to settlement on the old tested lines of treaty and purchase.

Woolman's question was, If the colonies go to war what are they fighting for ? Logan might answer, The safety of our homes and our possessions, now threatened by the Indians and the French. Woolman pointed out that our homes had in the past been secured by treaties ; and that the trouble might lie in our greed of possessions. "Wealth," said he,

is attended with Power, by which bargains and proceedings contrary to Universal Righteousness are Supported, and here oppression, carried on with worldly policy and order, clothes itself with the name of Justice, and becomes like a seed of discord in the soil. So the seed of war swells and sprouts and grows and becomes strong.[1]

Logan and Pemberton urged that this was very true in a general way, but that Pennsylvania and New Jersey could boast of a clean slate. These Quaker provinces had not quarrelled with the Indians or with the French ;

[1] Essay, *A Plea for the Poor* (Gummere, p. 419).

on the whole their bargains and proceedings had been pretty good. Yet they now found themselves in danger of unprovoked attack !

Woolman had a most painful way of exploding this self-content. He turned upon it with warmth, almost with passion, so deep did he feel it went into all that was wrong.

> Oh ! that we who declare against wars and acknowledge our trust to be in God only may walk in the light and therein examine our foundation and motives in holding great estates : may we look upon our treasures and the furniture of our houses, and the garments in which we array ourselves, and try whether the seeds of war have any nourishment in these our possessions or not.[1]

The son of James Logan could not deny a logic so similar to his father's, though so differently applied, but was convinced that the seeds of war did not lie in his possessions any more than in other people's ; John Churchman thought pride was a great danger, and drunkenness and profane swearing—he had noticed much among airy young men—sure indeed to draw down the wrath of God. And Fothergill—with the visitor's detachment, unfamiliar with colonial problems—was concerned that Quakers must prevent their minds from being embroiled and pay as little attention to these stirrings as possible. John Woolman listened with great respect, and then asked advice upon a concrete question. If a war tax was imposed could Quakers pay it ? With one accord Fothergill, Logan, Pemberton, upheld obedience and payment. Fothergill said that Friends in England frequently paid taxes when the money was applied to such purposes. Woolman was open to advice, and he genuinely admired these men, and believed them more likely to be right than himself. The argument about Friends in England was very powerful with them all. Friends in England were so enlightened.

The Assemblymen pointed out that refusal to pay the tax if it became law would be impossible anyhow. The tax would be collected by distraint if not paid voluntarily. They ignored conveniently the fact that Friends in Virginia, Carolina, and Maryland were making just such a refusal and enduring just such a penalty with regard to the tithes of the Anglican Church, established by law in those provinces. But Woolman tried to feel convinced, and for a while was "easier."

John Churchman took Samuel Fothergill away to his native town of Nottingham to a large Annual Meeting there to preach on more accept-

[1] Essay, *A Plea for the Poor* (Gummere, p. 419).

able matters ; William Logan wrote a letter of news to Samuel Fothergill's wife away in England ; and General Braddock worried for his wagons, and proceeded slowly through Pennsylvania and Maryland towards the Ohio to show the raw colonials how the British regulars would clean up their enemies for them. John Woolman went back to Mount Holly to go on with the gradual winding up of his business,[1] and began to put down some thoughts in writing on trade, riches, and the roots of war, and to seek light for himself on the subject of the expected tax.

In July the news of Braddock's disaster reverberated through the colonies. Fothergill heard of it up in Boston, where he had gone with William Logan, and wrote home to his brother, Dr John :

With respect to martial affairs, as they are remote from my business, I meddle not with them, but endeavour rather to draw out of that fire and bustle too prevalent amongst the people. An express arrived here last night [August 1st] with a confirmation of the news of General Braddock's total defeat with the loss of about 700 men killed, himself and sixty officers amongst them, and the train of artillery, baggage, etc. belonging to the army ; he took along with him 1500 picked men and kept them together in the European manner ; the French and Indians skulking behind the trees and logs of wood destroyed the English, who stood collected as a mark for some time and then left their officers and ran away. It is said the enemies were not above 300 in all—150 Indians and as many French.[2]

Another report said that Braddock's aide, young Washington, had four horses killed under him. When Fothergill got back to Philadelphia for the autumn Yearly Meeting he could no longer write home that there was no appearance of danger. Instead :

very distracted is the state of this province ; several cruel murders have been committed on the frontiers and sixteen people destroyed about the ninth inst [September] within less than 90 miles of this city, which was done by a gang of banditti, part Indians with some Irish among them. I was at the place about 5 weeks ago but do not understand any Friends were hurt.

Woolman rode to Philadelphia to the Yearly Meeting in the soft September weather with his mind made up. The consternation and terror that was flying all over the country places was the best possible

---

[1] From which he retired the next year (1756).
[2] Fothergill, p. 209.

breeder of the war spirit. He foresaw the war-tax levy as inevitable, and paying it seemed to him exactly on the same level as volunteering to join the militia. Leaving for the moment the causes of the war out of the question—and Woolman understood them as well as Logan, and far better than Fothergill or Churchman—war was a wrong way of settling any matter of dispute. If a man condemned war, as Woolman condemned slavery, as being against all reason, humanity, and religion, then he could neither fight nor pay for fighting. "I believed," wrote Woolman,

> that there were some uprighted-hearted men who paid such taxes, yet could not see that their example was a sufficient reason for me to do so, while I believe that the spirit of truth required of me, as an individual, to suffer patiently the distress of goods, rather than pay actively. To refuse the active payment of a tax which our Society generally paid was exceedingly disagreeable. . . . When this exercise came upon me I knew of none under the like difficulty.

Sarah, who foresaw a possible straitening of her circumstances when her husband should have given up his business, now saw herself in danger of losing the cow or her precious chest of drawers by distraint for the war tax. But she did not object or entreat. Her husband could not be wrong. She rode up to Yearly Meeting at his side, staunchly ready to endure whatever his clear judgment required of them both. Yes, even for Mary too. So when John Woolman handed her from the saddle at the door of the Women's Meeting, and presently went himself into the Men's Meeting in the great new Meeting-house at Second and Market,[1] he carried with him, warm at his heart, the support of her love and faith. He always had it. It never failed him.

In that Yearly Meeting Woolman spoke with power, though always with guarded brevity, against the payment of a war tax. It was a disagreeably concrete, ethical, almost worldly subject, not serving to detach the mind from thoughts of business and account books ; there were many eloquent, religious speeches made, much more to the liking of Friends. Samuel Fothergill, the noted English Friend, with his handsome presence and lovable, vigorous eloquence, was the star performer. Yet it was Woolman's concern that gradually laid hold of the meeting. Two committees were appointed, one to correspond with the Meeting for Sufferings in London about it, and the other to carry the concern

---

[1] Ready 1755.

to the Monthly and Quarterly Meetings in Pennsylvania and New Jersey. The Meeting for Sufferings, appointed in England in the time of George Fox to help Friends who were suffering for their faith, had become the standing executive of the Society. John Woolman and his friend, John Sykes, a particularly congenial companion in the absence of Peter Andrews, who was away visiting in England, fulfilled some of the duty of the latter committee in the New Jersey meetings around Shrewsbury ; and were at the annual Shrewsbury Quaterly Meeting in October[1] and heard their fellow committee member, John Churchman, give an impressive speech, which he mentions in his Journal as a spontaneous concern.

> As the sound of war and publick commotions had now entered the borders of these heretofore peaceful provinces, some solid thoughts attended my mind at Shrewsbury respecting the nature of giving money for the king's use knowing the same to be intended for the carrying on of war.[2]

John Woolman, hearing the matter well expressed by Churchman, did not feel it necessary to speak.

In November a conference of the two committees met at "the Friends' School in Philadelphia," the Penn Charter School. The Assembly was then in session, "in the Town Hall in the western part of the town," and it was decided to draw up a last-moment appeal from the Committees in conference not to impose a tax which it was now evident that some people would scruple to pay.

It seems highly unlikely that Woolman could be on a committee which was drafting an appeal to the Government on a subject which he had been the original one to introduce, and not be one of the principal writers of the appeal. The document read in part :

> To the Representatives of the Freemen of the Province of Pennsylvania, in General Assembly met. The Address of some of the People called Quakers in the said Province on Behalf of themselves and others. . . . Although we shall at all times freely and heartily contribute according to our circumstances either by the payment of taxes or in such other manner as may be judged necessary towards the exigencies of government . . . yet as the raising sums of money and putting them into the hands of committees who may apply them to purposes inconsistent with the peaceable testimony we profess and have borne to the world appears to us in its consequences to be destructive

---

[1] Whittier ed., p. 70.   [2] John Churchman's Journal, p. 231.

of our religious liberties, we apprehend many among us will be under the necessity of suffering rather than consenting thereto by the payment of a tax for such purposes ; and thus the fundamental part of our constitution may be essentially affected and that free enjoyment of liberty of conscience for the sake of which our forefathers left their native country and settled in this, a wilderness, by degrees be violated.

A sympathetic expression of unwillingness to give the Assemblymen trouble and an awareness of their difficulties were included, and the fervent desire that "you may be enabled to secure peace and tranquillity to yourselves and those you represent by pursuing measures consistent with our peaceable principles." Twenty-eight of the thirty-six members of the Assembly that year were Quakers. John Churchman and several others were chosen to take the document in person to the Assembly. But though courteously received, "a bill was however brought in by the committee of the assembly, and a law enacted for granting a large sum of money proposed to be sunk or called in by a general tax." Even the "Committee of Friends thus met were not all of one mind in relation to the tax, which to those who scrupled it made the way more difficult," says Woolman.

To refuse an active payment at such a time might be construed into an act of disloyalty and appeared likely to displease the rulers, not only here but in England ; still there was a scruple so fixed on the minds of many Friends that nothing moved it. It was a conference the most weighty that ever I was at,

wrote Woolman, and it finally came to an agreement in disagreement. Those who were in favour of paying the tax withdrew, and those who were not remained and drew up another epistle to send out to the Monthly and Quarterly Meetings and all Friends in the affected provinces, to the following effect :

. . . We . . . think, as we cannot be concerned in wars and fightings so neither ought we to contribute thereto by paying the tax directed by the said act, though suffering be the consequence of our refusal, which we hope to be enabled to bear with patience. And though some part of the money to be raised by the said act is said to be for such benevolent purposes as supporting our friendship with our Indian neighbors, and relieving the distresses of our fellow subjects, who have suffered in the present calamities, for whom our hearts are deeply pained . . . and we could most chearfully contribute to those purposes if they were not so mixed that we cannot, without at the same time assenting to practices which we apprehend contrary to the testimony which the Lord hath given us to bear for his name and truth's sake. . . . We earnestly exhort friends to wait for the appearing of the true light . . . and beware of the spirit of the world that is unstable and often draws into dark and timorous reasonings, terrors and fears that are not known to the inhabitants of that place where the sheep and lambs of Christ ever had a quiet habitation.

And as to our fidelity to the present government, our willingly paying all taxes for purposes which do not interfere with our conscience may justly exempt us from the imputation of disloyalty.

As usual with Woolman's writing, his phrases, however generally expressed, are loaded with the weight of a definite event. When he says "for whom our hearts are deeply pained," when he speaks of "dark and timorous reasonings, terrors and fears," he is reflecting feelings that had been violently stirred in Philadelphia while the committees were in session.

The people in the back parts, dwellers in lonely farms or small hamlets imbedded in forest, helpless before the sudden swooping attack of the raiding Indians, had an indignant sense that the Philadelphia Quakers as a whole were cultivating an attitude of indifference, hugging their own safety. Some of the relatives of the slain conceived a drastic method of rousing dormant imaginations. Woolman and Churchman were walking one afternoon in the street during the committee sessions. A horse stood peacefully with his nose-bag at a hitching-post ; a Negro slave went by barefoot, walking queenly with a basket of clean laundry on her head ; a stout gentleman puffed along, well wrapped against the cold with a wide-caped coat that twinkled back the sun from extra buttons, and a gold-headed cane that he set down firmly, stamp, stamp, like a third foot ; and a young cat tried to pounce and catch some sparrows that were pecking flecks of grain at the horse's hoofs. All was calm in the winter sunshine. But a sudden noise of shouting, yelling, howling, broke on their ears. In a moment the street became full, as people ran from house and shop to see the cause ; and round the corner came slowly an angry mob, milling about something in the centre. They stopped constantly that what they had there might be well seen. Woolman and Churchman, stepping back into the doorway of a friend's house, elevated on the step, saw it well and sickened at the sight. An open wagon and, within, a stiff and livid corpse with the scalped head hideously exposed. The mob, every moment augmented, was "cursing the Indians, also the Quakers, because they would not join in war for the destruction of the Indians."[1]

Churchman groaned, "What will become of Pennsylvania ?"

But there was something else equally terrible to be seen that winter in the streets of Philadelphia, though it drew no mob : wreckage of depredations not committed by Indians, nor threatening Pennsylvania. In September the forced evacuation of the so-called neutral French in Acadia, on the vexed Canadian border, had been carried out with extraordinary cruelty : first the young men driven into the ships (from ten years old upward) ; then the old men ; last the women and children— taken off at different intervals in different ships. Those left behind herded together on the shore without shelter until the last ship sailed ; and the last ship did not come until December. Some of the Acadians were brought to Philadelphia and were taken care of by the Quakers. Benezet, their countryman, was particularly active on their behalf ; but they were a broken-hearted people. Their benumbed and sorrowful presence was a continual reminder of the results of that hardening of the heart which Woolman dreaded above all other things for himself and his fellow-creatures.

> Thus oppression in the extreme appears terrible : but oppression in more refined appearances remains to be oppression ; and where the smallest degree of it is cherished it grows stronger and more extensive : that to labour for a perfect redemption from this spirit of Oppression is the Great Business of the whole family of Christ Jesus in this world.[2]

[1] Churchman, p. 239. Also see Woolman (Whittier ed., p. 112) and Fothergill (p. 232). Churchman dates the incident wrongly.

[2] Woolman's Essay, *A Plea for the Poor* (Gummere, p. 427).

XXIV

QUAKERS, ASSEMBLY, AND DRAFT

AND now far away across the world the action of one man, Frederick of Prussia, affected every man and woman in the colonies.

In January the Convention of Westminster had formed an alliance between England and Frederick the Great to maintain peace and to guarantee the neutrality of "Germany" as regarded the invasion of the Austrian Netherlands. France was an ally of Austria—a rather queer arrangement, since not many years before Austria had been given the French province of Lorraine against France's will to make up for the stealing of Silesia by Frederick. No doubt an undercurrent of the French-Austrian alliance included a readjustment of this unsatisfactory settlement. At any rate Frederick was suspicious, and his army was in first-rate condition. The father's religious theories combined with his cruelty had produced a complete cynicism in the son. By June Frederick "began to regard war as inevitable," and in September 1756, without warning, he marched his unparalleled troops into the Austrian province of Saxony and took the undefended city of Dresden, for no reason except that he happened to want it ; and so touched off the gunpowder mine of the Seven Years War.[1] That war turned into the final phase of the world-wide struggle between England and France for control of North America and India, while Frederick, concentrating upon extension of his European territory, amused himself by snatching his particular chestnuts out of the fire.

[1] For confirmation of this view, see H. A. L. Fisher, *History of Europe*, p. 766 onward.

But why should the colonists care about Europe? Why should Silesia affect New Jersey? Most of them did not even know where Silesia was, or dream that a man called Frederick of Prussia could alter the shape of their lives. Their unconscious independence of thought was already so great that they saw their own war as their own affair, and were prepared to fight it on its own merits, for themselves rather than for England. But there was a great tide rising behind the waves that broke on the Pennsylvania frontiers.

This, then, was war. No longer merely possible, and sporadic, but real, continuous, and near. Samuel Fothergill gave up trying to be indifferent, and plunged into a last-moment effort for peace. "The Assembly have sold their testimony as Friends to the people's fears," he wrote, "and not gone far enough to satisfy them." And he feared that the war would "reduce this pleasant, populous province to its ancient wilderness condition." In April he went in company with John Pemberton to visit the former Governor of Pennsylvania, Mr Thomas, and the present Governor, Mr Morris, to urge peace. "They received us with candour, but our labour was ineffectual," for the next day the Governor declared war upon "our" Indians and delivered the hatchet into the hands of the waiting messengers.

"Many thousand pounds of the province's money,"[1] wrote Fothergill, "have been laid out in erecting forts upon the frontiers and placing men in them; a step as prudent," he thought, "as an attempt to hedge out birds or deer." Provocative, too. The neighbourhood of the forts became "scenes of the greatest barbarity; in contempt and mockery eleven people being destroyed a few days ago within a mile of one of their forts."[2] "And the frontiers of Pennsylvania continue to be harassed by the barbarous Indians, who destroy man woman and child; all attempts to defend themselves against them seem vain." Fothergill, detachment and neutrality quite lost, his mind "embroiled" in spite of himself, his efforts "to prevent a cruel Indian war" all vain, hastened to take passage for home, leaving as his urgent parting advice that Quakers should withdraw from the Government in these times of violence, and resign from the legislatures of the Quaker states. They could "scarcely keep the Truth and its testimony inviolate and retain these places." James Logan had urged the same step years before for a different reason.

[1] Raised previously by Franklin through lotteries, etc.
[2] Fothergill, p. 256.

Benjamin Franklin, organizing the militia, was keen to get the Quakers out, and had his own wily way of working for it. Recruiting officers once more encouraged indentured and bound servants to enlist in spite of their masters' protest, and sometimes to their masters' ruin, as they had done years before. Franklin was at this time Clerk of Assembly. "The pointed style of the Assembly's reply to the Governor" about the recruiting was indiscreet, vexatious, and "inconsistent with their religious profession. I found many pained about it and sensible it is wrong," wrote Fothergill. "It is altogether imputed to B. Franklin, their principal penman ; who, I have sometimes thought, intended to render the Assembly contemptible, and subject our religious society to the imputations of want of respect to authority as a factious sort of people ; and I fear he has gained his point."[1] From this time onward Fothergill used all his influence—which was great—to persuade Friends to withdraw from the Government.

John Woolman did not express himself as to Quakers retiring from the legislatures of the two provinces. But he used the difficulty which Quaker Assemblymen and magistrates had in being consistent as another argument for the rank and file keeping clear of the war tax.

> Some of our members who are officers in civil government are, in one case or other, called upon in their respective stations to assist in things relative to the wars ; but being in doubt whether to act or to crave to be excused from their office, if they see their brethren united in a payment of a tax to carry on the said wars, may think their case not much different, and so might quench the tender movings of the Holy Spirit in their minds. Thus by small degrees we might approach so near to fighting that the distinction would be little else than the name of a peaceable people.[2]

In May John Woolman went on a journey to carry his concern in this matter into the more warlike province of New York—now experiencing its own war levies. The New York Yearly Meeting met at Flushing, on Long Island, and after visiting a number of local meetings, both on the island and on the mainland, John Woolman ended up at the Yearly Meeting. His rank as a member of the Ministers' and Elders' Meeting of Philadelphia Y. M. gave him entrance to the heart of the deliberations, the New York Meeting of Ministers and Elders, and in that gathering he spoke with the plainness and incisiveness that went strangely

---

[1] *Ibid.*, p. 247.   [2] Whittier ed., p. 111.

with the ease and gentleness of his private manner. "The exercise of my mind at this meeting," he says,

> was chiefly on account of those who were considered as the fore-most rank in the Society. . . . I saw that if I was honest in declaring that which truth opened in me, I could not please all men ; and I labored to be content in the way of my duty, however disagreeable to my own inclination.[1]

He saw clearly that the ordinary successful man was more responsible for war than he was ready to suppose, and that it was illogical to do all the things that led up to war, and then refuse the final fighting. The connexion between war and wealth became continually plainer to him, and all this time—looking closely to his own duty, careful not to preach what he did not practise—he was gradually closing down his own mercantile business in Mount Holly.

In July Peter Andrews died, far from home, at Norwich in England, and John Woolman, with Esther Andrews, the widow, and the young son Benajah, executors, once more performed for a man he loved the prosaic service of efficient business settlement of his estate. Woolman's Ledgers make it plain that he was by this time an expert land surveyor and conveyancer, and from the year '54 onward he did an increasing amount of this kind of business, to supply the gap in his income left by the giving up of his shop. "To Attendance Viewing Sundry Lands for Sale and at Both Days of the Land Vendues, ten shillings." "To Employing my Brother to go to Borden Town to Speak with John Sykes Ex^r of Matters Champin Concerning Wm Earle's estate, five Shillings." "To Examining old Writings halfday Searching for papers relateing to Earle's estate, two shillings." "To going again to measure the Triangle piece lying on the Northerly Side of Bisphamps and making a draft of the whole with an Essay on paper dividing it into lots."

The complete picture is that of a vigorous and active man, trusted in business matters by his equals, influential in his community, thorough, no procrastinator, and no sentimentalist. As a young man he used to do "a day's work" for one shilling ; he now charged five or six times as much, approximating the charges of his neighbours. "One day in the Appraisement and writing and Assisting in putting up Advertisements for the Sale of the goods, six shillings." "Attending Vendue and writing

[1] Whittier ed., p. 77.

as Clerk, five shillings." "Attending the Sale of the Plantation, collecting moneys, signing deeds, taking up bonds, five shillings."

In order to clear the title to the Andrews land he bought it and resold it to the wife and son in two lots, one of 195 acres, and the other of 21 acres, and also a dwelling-house and barn. So young Benajah and his mother were well provided for. But the death of Peter Andrews left in Woolman's life an irreplaceable loss, an equal companion whose judgment he trusted, whose sympathy was never-failing, and whose comradeship was almost daily. Among Woolman's many friends there was no one to take his place.

One of his friends, however, moved nearer to him this summer. John Smith with his lovely wife Hannah and their rapidly increasing family of children left Philadelphia permanently and took up residence in Burlington. It was a simpler and more wholesome place to bring up their children, it was farther removed from the war, and it had always been the place above all others which John Smith loved. He had decided that his peace principles demanded that he should withdraw from the Assembly, and it seemed natural to come back to his old home. Any fine afternoon he and his wife could be seen—John Smith back in good time from the wharf or counting-house—taking tea under the trees in front of their house ; and any passer-by, riding or walking down the street, might be hailed and summoned to join them. It is on record that they once so hailed a perfect stranger, liking his looks, and the man, dismounting and staying with them an hour, decided to buy land and settle in Burlington, bewitched by such gracious neighbours.

Hannah Logan Smith was that year made a minister of the meeting at Burlington—perhaps at the instance of John Woolman, who was presiding Clerk of the Burlington Monthly Meeting of Ministers and Elders. Hannah, feeling that much was now demanded of her, tried hard to be worthy, to shut out from her mind all worldly vanities, and —for one—refused to ride any more in the four-wheeled "Chaise with the Driver" and horses, preferring to go horseback like a true country-woman. But there was room for all sorts in the Society, and Mrs Israel Pemberton still drove in her chaise unblushing.

That autumn the Yearly Meeting met in Burlington, so Quakers were drawn out of the unwholesome area of Philadelphia, where a smallpox epidemic had raged all summer. In face of Indian ravages on frontier farms, war tax, and militia recruiting, it was obvious that some

Quakers were going to get into trouble, so after stern and soul-searching sessions a Meeting for Sufferings was appointed to take care of the possible sufferings of Friends.

Woolman had already suggested, in the memorial which had gone to the Assembly the year before, that a good alternative to the war tax would be a tax to raise money for promoting friendship with the Indians (by means of just purchase for lands illegally occupied) and for relief of those colonists who had already suffered from the raids. He now proposed that Yearly Meeting stock should be raised for these purposes without delay. This would do good in itself in the directions mentioned and would prove that Quakers did not wish to shirk their share of public expense. This proposal was adopted and minuted in September 1756, and the Meeting for Sufferings in London was written to in December about it and all the other matters which had necessitated the formation of the new Meeting for Sufferings. Stirred with sympathy for their American friends, they promptly sent over two of their members to confer with and advise them. John Hunt and Christopher Wilson were the two. English Quakers were none of them accustomed to Friends in government. Only members of the Church of England could sit in the English Parliament, and the debarred Quakers had decided that such activities could be classed as "worldly." Hunt and Wilson had seen Fothergill since his return from the colonies, and heard him deplore that Quakers were members and office-holders in the Pennsylvania and Jersey Assemblies. They came with their minds on that matter made up. Surely Quakers should never be in any position which required any form of "strife." They had better withdraw voluntarily and with dignity, resigning their offices as a last protest. John Hunt, we remember, was always "safe and very correct." The firm advice of the English Friends convinced many waverers, and the Quakers resigned from office. By 1757 there were few left in the Pennsylvania Assembly.[1] So easily and so completely did the first determined opposition to their dominance overthrow them, lest in the very effort to resist war they might be false to the spirit of peace.

But in New Jersey they held on longer. In January Governor Belcher asked the New Jersey Assembly to raise a quota of one thousand men. They answered, by a vote of twelve to seven, that they would only guarantee to raise five hundred, and that "they were determined not to

---

[1] Israel Pemberton, for one, could not see his way to leave.

oblige or compel any of the inhabitants to serve as soldiers."[1]   New Jersey was not only the most liberal of the provinces, but it lay securely behind the great Delaware, far from fighting Indians or hostile French. Its five hundred volunteers marched cheerfully away under Colonel Parker, and finally joined the garrison of Fort William Henry, on Lake George.

In August a frantic horseman reached Amboy with news that the Marquis of Montcalm, most dashing, most successful, and most chivalrous of the French, was besieging Fort Henry, and its state was desperate.

In that news the war crossed the Delaware.   New Jersey roused itself to help its own.   On August 9, under the crescent moon, the rapid hoof-beats of an urgent comer brought Mount Holly people from their beds ; and a call to arms, the word 'militia,' men's anxious voices in question and answer, drowned the familiar chanting of the katydids. A few days after Mount Holly market-place saw new volunteers from all Northampton Township drawn up in review, and the fathers and mothers, wives and sweethearts, who watched saw their dear ones chosen or rejected before their eyes.   The tests were not exacting.   "A number of men were chosen," says Woolman, "and sent off under some officers."[2]   A thousand men, all over New Jersey, were so raised and dispatched, wearing their own clothes, those that had them taking their own rifles ; expecting to be paid by the Crown, armed and fed by the province.   Of drill they had had little or none.   "Shortly after," says Woolman, "there came orders to draft three times as many, who were to hold themselves in readiness to march when fresh orders came."   The casual volunteer system had begun to break down.   The demands were too large and too quick.   "On the 17th there was a meeting of the military officers at Mount Holly, who agreed on draft."   Presumably the town council provided names of men of likely age in their neighbourhood, and so a list was drawn up from which the commander made choice, trying to spread them out fairly, and to avoid widows' sons and cases of especial hardship, with the advice of the local men who knew the prospective soldiers personally.

Orders were sent to the men so chosen to meet their respective captains at set times and places, those in our township to meet at

[1] *New Jersey Archives*, under date.
[2] Whittier ed., pp. 112-114.

O

Mount Holly, amongst whom were a considerable number of our Society. . . . In this time of commotion some of our young men left these parts and tarried abroad till it was over ; some came and proposed to go as soldiers ; others appeared to have a real tender scruple in their minds against joining in wars. . . . I had conversation with several of them to my satisfaction.[1]

Perplexed young men found John Woolman extremely easy to talk to. His apple orchard was only a few minutes' walk from the centre of town, and it was really better to talk there than it had been in the shop. There was a great sense of leisure under the apple-trees beside the pleasant Run. And John Woolman would sit down with them in the shade with an air of being able to give them all the time in the world. It was easy ; but it led to hard conclusions. If they were going to object to the draft Woolman made them see clearly that there was only one way to do it—the open, direct way. No running away—the act of a coward ; and no getting some one else to plead for them. They must go straight to the officers and make their own statement. Then, having made it, stick to it, whatever comes ; as the man who chooses the army will stay by his choice under fire.

There was another way of escape, besides running away, and that was to pay some one else to take one's place. The officers were only concerned with the number of their quota ; Tom would do for them just as well as Jim ; and if Jim had a 'conscience' and Tom had not why not make an exchange to Tom's financial benefit ? John Woolman gave this argument short shrift. He pressed home the question, What is it that you are objecting to ? Do you just object to you yourself being drafted ? Or do you object to the whole method of war ? If it is the first you cannot logically claim a religious motive. If it is the second you cannot put another man into the ranks in your place.

And there were a few times when a young man who had claimed a religious objection to war found himself met with a question that was almost sardonic—why this sudden interest in religion ? This awareness of your duty to God and to your fellow-man has never been noticeable in you before, has it ? There was in times of crisis, Woolman pointed out,

an advantage in living in the real substance of religion, where practice doth harmonise with principle. . . . But where men profess

[1] Whittier ed., p. 114.

to be so meek and heavenly minded and to have their trust so firmly settled in God that they cannot join in wars, and yet by their spirit and conduct in common life manifest a contrary disposition, their difficulties are great at such a time.[1]

Woolman well perceived and sympathized with the difficulties of the officers, too, likeable and honest citizens, performing as best they could an irksome and unpopular task.   Among them, Woolman said,

> are men of understanding who have some regard to sincerity when they see it ; and when such in the execution of their office have men to deal with whom they believe to be upright-hearted, it is a painful task to put them to trouble on account of scruples of conscience, and they will be likely to avoid it as much as easily may be. . . . When officers who are anxiously endeavouring to get troops to answer the demands of their superiors see men who are insincere pretend scruple of conscience in hopes of being excused from a dangerous employment, it is likely they will be roughly handled.[2]

So the men advised by Woolman either went away sorrowful and tried for some easier mentor or took the boldest course possible, the fairest dealing with the draft officers.   "When the captain came to town," said Woolman,

> some of the last-mentioned went and told him in substance as follows : That they could not bear arms for conscience sake ; nor could they hire any to go in their places, being resigned as to the event. At length the captain acquainted them all that they might return home for the present, but he required them to provide themselves as soldiers and be in readiness to march when called upon.[3]

But every message from the front was a week old, and even as the first call for help arrived the cause was lost.   The fort surrendered after a six-day siege, and the Indian allies of the French, not knowing or disregarding Montcalm's safe-conduct, massacred hundreds of the prisoners before Montcalm could return to save them.   The first thousand men of the fresh New Jersey draft, marching to the relief, turned back ; and the three thousand more who were drafted and got in readiness to march were not needed.   It was too late to save Fort Henry ; but the news of the reinforcements checked the enemy. The captured New Jersey regiment, with other prisoners who survived, were released on their parole not to fight for eighteen months.   They came back to their farms

---

[1] *Ibid.*, p. 113.   [2] *Ibid.*   [3] *Ibid.*, p. 114.

and villages in a fierce recruiting spirit, and from then on New Jersey readily provided a thousand men in arms each year. Arms, tents, and equipment to be provided by the Crown, a bounty of twelve pounds per man, and food and pay to be provided by the province, as long as the war lasted.

Meanwhile, seeing England's troops spread thin, some in America, some in India, and her Navy having to provide transport to these far-distant places, France resolved on a bold invasion of England itself. Transports and fighting fleets were prepared in the French Channel ports. Fifty thousand Frenchmen were to be landed in Essex, twelve thousand in Scotland, and a raid simultaneously to be made upon Ireland. Many of the Catholic Scots and Irish, it was thought, would rally to the invader. Such a threat as this encouraged the French and roused the English all over the provinces of North America.

What could the Quakers do in Pennsylvania and New Jersey, influential as they still were ? What answer could they make to the arguments of their neighbours who urged the reasonableness, the inevitableness, of fighting in such a case of common danger ? John Woolman said :

It requires great self-denial and resignation of ourselves to God to attain that state wherein we can freely cease from fighting when wrongfully invaded, if by our fighting there were a probability of overcoming the invaders. Whoever rightly attains to it does in some degree feel that spirit in which our Redeemer gave his life for us.[1]

[1] Whittier ed., p. 111.

XXV

SOLDIERS BILLETED IN MOUNT HOLLY

When the New Jersey men were mustered again in the spring they went to join the British regulars under Abercrombie to attack Fort Ticonderoga, and they went heartily, in a good cause as they saw it, eager to take the forefront of the attack. The forced draft was no longer necessary, and the authorities were glad to drop it in a Quaker province. But as the winter camps broke up and troops were moved to concentration points for the march north, occasional billeting on private houses was resorted to as the easiest way of providing healthy food and shelter for English colonials among their own people. The billeting was arranged for in a courteous and personal way by local officers who knew local conditions and house capacities ; and it was adequately paid for. So in April 1758 "orders came to some officers in Mount Holly to prepare quarters for a short time for about one hundred soldiers. An officer and two other men, all inhabitants of our town," says John Woolman, "came to my house. The officer told me that he came to desire me to provide lodging and entertainment for two soldiers, and that six shillings a week per man would be allowed to pay for it."[1]

They found John Woolman in his apple orchard, with his daughter Mary, now eight years old, prancing about helping him, making a

[1] *Ibid.*, p. 114.

bonfire of the winter brush. Their voices and laughter carried no burden of the world's darkness. "Clear air is food for the lungs ! " said Woolman, and he encouraged his daughter's tomboy ways. "Youthful years and a lively motion."[1]

A couple of sheep kept short the greening turf, their lambs gambolling beside them ; and a heifer with a young calf was tethered in serenest rumination at the far end, within reach of the swollen, ice-cold water of the Run.

John Woolman welcomed the visitors with his usual cordiality, and invited them into the snug house for a glass of cider, leaving Mary with the important responsibility of minding the bonfire. "Fire is good—in its place ! " her father reminded her.

Sarah was sitting at her spinning-wheel indoors, and after she had risen and curtsied her gentle welcome she went back to her spinning, and only looked attentive and inquiring when she heard them state their business. Soldiers in the house would not be very nice ; but John would know what to do about it. She looked at him and saw the lively warmth of his face clouded with thought. He turned away from his guests and sat silent for several minutes. The silence fell powerfully on all of them, and none broke it. The officer, who had experienced Woolman's understanding of his difficulties with regard to the draft, knew that this was not a moment for arguments and reasons. At last Woolman spoke with a little hesitation. On the one hand, as they well knew, he was against all war, did not wish to help to fight the war even indirectly, and therefore felt it would be inconsistent to take money for keeping soldiers in his house ; on the other hand, though it would be rather awkward "to entertain men who were under pay as soldiers," he did not want to refuse hospitality to any fellow-creature, or to deny the right of the State to ask it. So, he concluded, "I believe I shall not refuse to admit them into my house, but the nature of the case is such that I expect I cannot keep them on hire."[2] One of the guests was rash enough to say that he thought Mr Woolman might accept hire consistently with his religious principles. To which impertinence Mr Woolman, who alone was able to judge what his religious principles demanded, restrained himself from making any reply.

"Though they spake of two, there came only one, who tarried at my house about two weeks, and behaved himself civilly." And it is certain

[1] From the Account Book.   [2] Whittier ed., p. 115.

that John Woolman did not try to argue his peculiar guest out of the course which he had chosen. Every man to his own duty. Yet the young soldier could hardly have gone away from that two weeks' visit unmarked. The simple daily pleasures of the family are reflected in the copies which John Woolman set for Mary in her writing lesson. "Winter, a fire and a good room." "Some labour and some rest." "Motion the friend of health." "By useful motion the soil is prepared."

But he saw to it that she got plenty of outdoor life, giving her little tasks to do for him as if she had been a boy, not confining her only to girl's work in the house. If Sarah made a little demur at a below-zero frost he would laugh away her fears. "Hard frost refines the air!" he would say; or, if it was a blowing wind, "North wind refines the air!" And he would take care that Mary's dress did not bundle her up past free movement, and that she did not stand about and get chilled. "Lively motion warms the blood," he said.

Then when they came indoors, with glowing cheeks and hearty appetites, Sarah found her husband ready to take pleasure in her savoury meal. "In hard labour good feeding is good," said he. "Light food for an easie life." And with his arm about her waist, she got his carefully understated, almost teasing praise (so as not to replace her sweet modesty with vanity, the easiest sin of woman), "A good cook is very helpful!"

He was as careful to protect them all from laziness as from overwork. "Moderate labour tends to our health," he said. But on the other hand "content with a little prevents much toyl." And if in the winter, when diet tended to become monotonous, Mary got fussy about her food—apple pie, made with dried apples, may be good eating, but who would want it for supper every day?—there was no scolding or remonstrance. Her father's calm unanswerable law was, "Let the dainty man try abstinence."

He was on guard lest he and Sarah should spoil Mary, and he knew that his affection for these two he so tenderly loved might tempt him, like many other husbands and fathers, to selfish action on their behalf. He was at any rate determined that they should never come to want, and as he said to Sarah when they discussed the fine demands of what Woolman called the just balance it was true that gold often corrupts the mind, but "to provide for old age may be honest."

John Woolman's delight in his only child, whom he never knew as otherwise than young, is expressed in the words, "A Rose in the spring

smells sweet. Innocent youth excels the fragrance of roses." Şarah's
delicate, gentle charm pervaded the house and, guarded by her husband,
remained a charm and never wilted into peevish ill-health. Not only
would he bring in for her all needed water from their own well, and
keep an abundant stack of firewood in the box beside her hearth, he was
alert to see that she did not overtax her strength ; he gave her leisure.
As he needed for himself every day some quiet to read, muse, and shape
his thoughts in writing, so he saw to it that his dearest had quiet too.
Often it took the form of gathering round the fire in the evening with
idle hands, relaxed, at rest, even the quiet spindle laid aside, while John
read to them aloud some book that was feeding his soul. That particular
winter John was reading Thomas à Kempis, and while 'Roman Catholic' was synonymous with Devil in almost every home in the British
colonies John Woolman and his wife and child were proving once more
that sincere, simple, and devout souls are everywhere of one religion.[1]

"I have been informed," said John Woolman in his Journal,

> that Thomas à Kempis lived and died in the profession of the Roman
> Catholic religion ; and in reading his writings I have believed him
> to be a man of a true Christian spirit, as fully so as many who died
> martyrs because they could not join with some superstitions in that
> church. All true Christians are of the same spirit, but their gifts are
> diverse.[2]

In this life the soldier guest was perforce a sharer, and—like other
billeted men—beguiled his idle hours by helping with the daily tasks
of wood and water, teased Mary good-naturedly as she learned to milk
the cow, whittled a doll for her out of soft wood, and was pleased to
see her housewifely skill in making a dress for it—she sewed as well as
his own little sister of full two years older. For was she not a tailor's
daughter ? And in the evening round the fire, driven in by darkness
from the sweet scents of the April evening, he listened to the reading,
half asleep. Then one evening when he came in the house was full of
a pungent odour, and the family were all busy together with a witch's
brew upon the hearth. "More beeswax ! More beeswax !" cried
Mary, and he grabbed the yellow lump off the shelf and shaved it off
for her into the pot, pleased to be one of them. "Four parts rosin, two
parts beeswax, one part tallow !" chanted Mary, looking at her father
for prompt affirmation. When it was all melted together they dumped

---

[1] William Penn.   [2] Whittier ed., p. 116.

the hissing mass into a pan of cold water, and then all of them with laughter pulled it out among them like toffee, until the smooth, grained, light yellow stuff was declared by the master of the orchard to be perfect, and it was divided into little parcels of oiled cloth and put by on the shelf for use as needed. The next day the soldier watched John Woolman grafting his apple-trees with neat clean strokes, Mary eagerly pressing on the grafting wax over the wound, softening it in her little fingers like putty.

And when word suddenly flew about the village that Indians had raided over the borders of New Jersey and surprised a peaceful family at tasks just such as this, "at two o'clock in the afternoon," and gone again like devil shadows into the forest, leaving behind them blood and fire and death and ruin, the soldier felt certain of his duty to protect people who were too gentle to protect themselves. Yet perhaps he carried away, as well as the indelible impress of a singularly happy way of living, a maxim which would serve him in the berserk aftermath of battle—one which Woolman impressed on little Mary, and wrote for her in her copy-book—"A hard heart is a bad companion,"[1] and "Take no hard-hearted pleasures."

The officer in charge made one more effort to pay Mr Woolman for his billet. Going round the town paying the hosts, he came out towards Woolman's house on the Springfield Road and met Woolman on horseback, riding from home on some conveyancing business. He stopped him with a salute, and after exchange of courtesies offered him the money as if it were a matter of course. But Woolman decidedly refused it, and turned his horse away on his journey. As he turned and put the horse to the trot he heard the officer, on foot, saying that he was obliged to him. And it struck Woolman that he was being regarded, in a mild way, as a benefactor to the army, giving a soldier board and lodging for nothing ; a very nice patriotic example. So he took an early opportunity of calling at the officer's house to put his point of view so clearly that there would be no possibility of misunderstanding it. The hospitality to the soldier was to be regarded as a forced distraint upon his goods. Yet, harsh as that sounded, it was said without offence ; for Woolman liked the soldier personally, and they all knew it.

There was a Frenchman, presumably a Catholic, of another kind than Fénelon or Thomas à Kempis, in Mount Holly, a living witness to the

[1] MS. Ledger.

fact that cruelty is terrible to suffer but worse to perform. He had arrived furtively, skulking through the woods two years before, wearing the uniform of a French soldier. He knew no English. He had dug out a hole under a large white oak brought down by a storm in a wood belonging to Joseph Burr on the Peachfields estate. The hole was barely long enough to stretch himself in at full length, and not high enough to sit up in, but he could be persuaded to no other shelter. When he was discovered he was half dead from starvation, and the kindly Aunt Jane would have taken him into her house to revive him, but he resisted like a madman. He accepted food, however, gratefully, and after that some one took food to his cave every day. Colonel Charles Read, who knew French, was brought to him, and he answered intelligently a few questions. His name, he said, was Francis Phyle, native of Lucerne in Switzerland ; he came with the French troops to Canada, and was in distress because of his sins. Having said that, he would say no more, and nothing more of him was ever learned. The neighbourhood grew used to him, as to any determined eccentricity, called him the Hermit, and could hardly remember the woods without him. Mary went once or twice with her big boy cousins to take his dinner. He might be invisible inside his hole, nothing showing (when one stooped down to look) but his hair, like an animal's fur. Or he might be sitting outside in the leaf-checkered sunshine, as motionless and irresponsive as a tree-stump, his blank eyes fixed on vacancy. What was it he was always seeing which veiled from him the beauty of the woods and filled his heart with torture ? One more feature of his penance, or of his inward horror, soon became apparent, and was itself too suggestive to be dwelt upon. He would never look at, or make use of, fire.

Death, which avoided the Hermit, struck down one more member of Woolman's intimate circle that summer. Esther Andrews did not long outlive her husband. Woolman was away from home for only a fortnight that year, taking two weeks in August to pay visits in Chester County and Philadelphia County around Philadelphia, leaving a man to take care of his orchard and stock. He was home again when Esther fell ill, and Peter Andrews would have been glad to know that his friend and his friend's wife were with his Esther to supervise the nursing of her, and cheer her spirit right up to the great boundary.

John and Hannah Smith were getting ready for meeting in Burling-on on a fine September Sunday when a rider in urgent, unsabbatical haste shattered the silence of the quiet street before their door. John Smith, hastily meeting him, received an express from John Woolman, a short but intimately worded note :

                                    10 of 9 mo and first of the week. 1758
BELOV'D FRIEND

               JOHN SMITH

   Our friend, Esther Andrews departed this life about eight o'clock this morning. They propose to bury her corps to-morrow in the afternoon to meet at the house where she lived at 2 o'clock. If thou would please mention it in your meeting this afternoon with a general Invitation to friends, it will be acceptable to those who have the Care of the burial.

                          thy loving frd

                              JOHN WOOLMAN[1]

So private grief and public distress took their turns, and Woolman received each to the full, but steadily maintained the hope and confidence of one always conscious of "that Almighty Being who inhabits eternity and preserves and supports the world."[2]

It might have been argued, as some did, that the war was by now beyond control ; that the efforts of the Quakers at Easton and at Burlington that year to renew their old treaties with the Indians, and make an Indian peace, locally at least, were in vain and showed ignorance of the larger issues ; and that all individual resistance to war, in any form, was like trying to turn back the tide when it rose up the Delaware from the sea. But John Woolman maintained that each individual was responsible for his own action, and that the faithfulness of a single person had far-reaching effects.   Above all, as he thought of his own father and as he thought of Mary, the duty of parents loomed large to him as the very heart and kernel of all progress in the right life.   Duty of education, of heritage, of example.

   Our own real good and the good of our posterity in some measure depends on the part we act. . . . Many of our fellow-subjects have suffered on and near our frontiers, some have been slain in battle, some killed in their houses, and some in their fields, some wounded and left in great misery, and others separated from their wives and little children, who have been carried captives among the Indians. We have seen men and women who have been witness of these scenes of sorrow, and being reduced to want have come to our houses asking

¹ Original in Friends' Reference Library, Friends' House, London.
² Whittier ed., p. 133.

relief. It is not long since many young men in one of these provinces were drafted in order to be taken as soldiers ; some were at that time in great distress, and had occasion to consider that their lives had been too little conformable to the purity and spirituality of that religion which we profess. . . . Many parents . . . in that time of trial were led to consider that their care to get outward treasure for them [their children] had been greater than their care for their settlement in that religion which . . . enableth to bear a clear testimony to the peaceable government of the Messiah. . . .

Do we feel an affectionate regard to posterity ? and are we employed to promote their happiness ? Do our minds, in things outward, look beyond our own dissolution ? and are we contriving for the prosperity of our children after us ? Let us then, like wise builders, lay the foundation deep, and by our constant uniform regard to an inward piety and virtue let them see that we really value it.[1]

[1] Yearly Meeting Epistle, written by Woolman in 1759. Printed in full in Journal, pp. 131–132.

XXVI

SECOND SOUTHERN JOURNEY

JOHN WOOLMAN began writing his major book—his Journal—the year that he gave up his business. It was one fruit of his increased leisure. That is to say, he was more in command of his time. By the year 1757, having covered the first thirty-six years of his life in a record which fills not more than fourteen small pages of print, he has caught up with himself, and though we in no case get his first daily draft, he is making his notes with the knowledge that he is going to use them as material for a published work. The result is a marked increase in detail ; and he has besides warmed to the task. This accounts for the difference in vividness between the story of his first journey to the South and his second.

Ever since his first journey, made before his marriage, it had been on his mind to go back again and labour some more for the slaves and the slave-holders on the tobacco plantations. In May 1757 he felt that the opportunity had come. It was before the fall of Fort William Henry, and there was no thought of his family being in danger. Uncle Joseph Burr would have an eye to them—not to mention Aunt Jane, always like a mother to Sarah. And he got a reliable man to take care of his orchard and keep Sarah supplied with water and wood. So with necessaries in his saddle-bags, he rode through the gateway in the snake fence on a fine spring morning, and turned to wave to his dear ones and carry the last glimpse with him in his mind's eye.   The little white house stood embowered in apple-blossom, under the flickering shadow of two ancient forest trees in the dooryard—red-budded sugar maples, already robbed of their sweet running sap.   A blue wood-smoke went straight up from the chimney.   And Sarah and Mary waved wistfully to him from under the apple-trees at the very verge of the Run, dressed in their full gathered skirts and green aprons, the one a little replica of the other. It was with a wrench that John Woolman turned his back on them and, splashing through the ford of Buttonwood Run where it crossed the highway, went away through Mount Holly town along Race Street beside the mill-race to the Philadelphia Road, leaning from the saddle to shake the hand of many a friend as he passed, because every one knew where he was going.   His "concern" had gone through the Burlington Monthly and Quarterly Meetings in due form, and he had their certificate in his pocket.

He had thought of going alone, because he remembered difficulties with his companion on the last Southern journey on account of his own unconventional behaviour, and that was nothing to what he contemplated on this.   But his brother Uriah unexpectedly offered his company, since he was going South on business.   Uriah, now a man of twenty-nine, had recently set up for himself in Philadelphia on "the east side of Front Street," perhaps as a tobacco merchant ; certainly he wished to make a good many contacts in North Carolina, and his elder brother would not only be good company, but he knew the road. John Woolman was at first rather embarrassed.   Their purposes of travel were so different that he doubted if they could be combined.   And since a Quaker travelling with a certificate of religious concern was not allowed to use it as a business opportunity—which would lead to endless corruption of motive—it seemed a little invidious for such a person to take a man who was on a business errand as a travelling companion. They straightened all this out however with brotherly candour, took the advice of some elderly experienced Friends, and Uriah obtained for himself "a certificate suitable to the occasion."   He was, after all, a Quaker and had a right to Quakerly introduction, so long as every one knew his motive was secular ; and it was so stated on his minute.

John Woolman picked up Uriah in Philadelphia, and they went on together.   This time Woolman took a different route, aiming at the western shore of the Chesapeake. They did not go to Lancaster but to Nottingham, and spent a night there at John Churchman's house. Then they crossed the Susquehanna by ferry, and went down through Maryland. They made pretty good speed, not pausing for any meetings—which must have been gratifying to Uriah, though he was perfectly at his brother's disposal as long as they were together—because Woolman was determined to be at the Yearly Meeting in Virginia. And on May 11 John Woolman specifically states that "we crossed the rivers Patowmack and Rapahannock and lodged at Port Royal,"[1] a statement remarkable because a page or two before he rashly embarked on a definite date and set down in writing—checked over by him at least three times, because he copied it twice—that he was at a friend's house in Burlington, New Jersey, on the night of May 13, and had an extraordinary dream there.[2]

Passing this over for the time being, however, and returning to the itinerary of the Southern journey, we learn that Woolman and his brother "came amongst Friends at Cedar Creek in Virginia on the 12th." They parted company here, and Uriah went on about his business to Carolina,[3] and next day Woolman rode, in company with several of the Friends, a day's journey to Camp Creek, stayed overnight and attended Monthly Meeting there on the fourteenth ; then rode to the mountains up James River, as before, and had a meeting at a Friend's house. Then to Fork Creek, and back to Cedar Creek, had a meeting there, then to Swamp Meeting and to Wayanoke Meeting, then crossed the James River to Burleigh Meeting, then Black Water, and thence to the Virginia Yearly Meeting at the Western Branch. After delivering himself at the Yearly Meeting and also at the Meeting of Ministers and Elders with painful pungency on the subject of slavery, "I went to Carolina, and on the 1st of sixth month was at Wells Monthly Meeting."[4] Here he met Uriah again, no doubt by pre-arrangement, and that first of June was a happy day. Uriah was now ready to return home, indeed pressure of business compelled him to do so, but John Woolman was not yet ready, so Uriah joined with some Friends from New Garden who were going homeward, and John Woolman continued alone to Simons

[1] Whittier ed., p. 88.
[2] Ibid., p. 84.
[3] Up to Cedar Creek Woolman says "we," after that "I." The brothers joined up again at Wells, when John Woolman, after weaving about in Virginia, went down to Carolina. See Whittier ed., p. 102.
[4] Ibid. p. 101.

Creek, Newbegun Creek, Little River, the Old Neck, and Piney Woods —"the last meeting I was at in Carolina"; and then back again into Virginia, where—no longer pressed to get on to the Yearly Meeting— he paid a large number of visits; then a few in Maryland; and so back home to Mount Holly in time for the apple harvest. He had been out about two months, and travelled eleven hundred and fifty miles.[1]

He was away from home as long as this only twice again in his life— once on his second visit to New England, three years later, and once on his visit to England itself. And he never again went to Virginia or Carolina.

Before setting out on this second and last trip to the real South Woolman had prepared himself in a peculiar way. He was going into conditions he had seen before and which he loathed, he was going to engage in personal contacts of the utmost difficulty; and as he frequently told himself, "conduct is more convincing than language." He had therefore resolved on a piece of conduct which he shrank from to the uttermost; one so unconventional and gauche that the prospect of it hurt him in advance more than it could hurt even those whom he knew it would deeply wound and offend. He was carrying with him a certificate which would guarantee him hospitality in a region where lavish and generous hospitality was a byword; and he was going to offer to pay. Offer? He was going to insist on paying; no slave-owner should give him a free meal.

He explained all this to Uriah at the very first, and Uriah none the less stuck to it that he would like to go along, evidently valuing the charm of his brother's society much above any awkwardness which it might entail. So John Woolman provided himself with plenty of small silver, that he might never be at a stand for lack of change, and when they arrived among the aristocracy of the South he carried out his difficult intention. It was indeed "a trial both to me and them." To the proud and touchy planters he offered the last insult—he compelled them to take money for his entertainment. He would not live "free-cost," even for a single night, on the labour of slaves. Yet he never left anger behind him. Often a stupefied planter gazed at the coins in his hands and marvelled how he could have been so reduced, so conquered. But there was the tangible evidence.

Woolman was exercising again the power and grace of his personal

[1] Whittier ed., p. 107.

intimate approach. Not crudely or publicly did he offer those shaming coins. "I spoke to one of the heads of the family privately, and desired them to accept of those pieces of silver and give them to such of their negroes as they believed would make the best use of them."[1] A searching conversation was the inevitable result.

I used much plainness of speech with him, and he appeared to take it kindly.

Many of the white people in those provinces take little or no care of negro marriages ; and when negroes marry after their own way, some make so little account of those marriages that with views of outward interest they often part men from their wives by selling them far asunder, which is common when estates are sold by executors at vendue.

Many whose labour is heavy, being followed at their business in the field by a man with a whip, hired for that purpose, have in common little else allowed but one peck of Indian corn and some salt for one week, with a few potatoes ; the potatoes they commonly raise by their labour on the first day of the week. The correction ensuing on their disobedience to overseers or slothfulness in business is often very severe, and sometimes desperate.

Men and women have many times scarcely clothes sufficient to hide their nakedness, and boys and girls ten and twelve years old are often quite naked amongst their master's children.

Some Quaker masters and others made attempts now and then to teach their Negroes to read, but

in common this is not only neglected but disapproved. These are the people by whose labour the other inhabitants are in a great measure supported and many of them in the luxuries of life. These are the people who have made no agreement to serve us, and who have not forfeited their liberty that we know of. These are the souls for whom Christ died, and for our conduct towards them we must answer before Him who is no respecter of persons.[2]

To Woolman as a young man conversation had been a glittering ornament. Now, small talk and frivolity long forsworn, he had made of conversation an instrument that was both a weapon and a tool. Not only his hosts but fellow-travellers, met on the road, fell under the spell of his talk.

On the way we had the company of a colonel of the militia who appeared to be a thoughtful man. I took occasion to remark on the

[1] *Ibid.*, p. 88. [2] *Ibid.*, pp. 94–95.

P

difference in general betwixt a people used to labour moderately for their living, training up their children in frugality and business, and those who live on the labour of slaves ; the former, in my view, being the most happy life.

The colonel agreed. The Negroes were a peck of trouble, a lazy, shiftless lot. "One of your labourers, sir, would do as much in a day as two of our slaves."

"Free men," said Woolman, "whose minds are properly on their business find a satisfaction in improving and cultivating their land and providing for their families. But negroes, labouring to support others who claim them as their property, and expecting nothing but slavery during life, have not the like inducement to be industrious."

The colonel presently said, "Well, sir, after all, the lives of the negroes are so wretched in their own country that many of them live better here than there. What with their wars and one thing and another, I reckon they're happier here."

"If compassion for the Africans on account of their domestic troubles is the motive of our purchasing them," replied Woolman, "that spirit of tenderness would incite us to use them kindly, that, as strangers bought out of affliction, their lives might be happy among us." This sardonic tone silenced the colonel. And Woolman presently urged with great warmth the argument that appeared to him as strong as any, the harm done to the white. "The present circumstances of these provinces," he said, "appear to me difficult. The slaves look like a burdensome stone to such as burden themselves with them. And if the white people retain a resolution to prefer their outward prospects of gain to all other considerations, and do not act conscientiously toward them as fellow-creatures, I believe that burden will grow heavier and heavier until times change in a way disagreeable to us."[1]

Another day, when he was riding with a company of Quakers, one of them—perhaps Woolman's host of the night, smarting under the reception of forced payment—bethought himself of a grand Biblical argument in favour of the slave trade, and rashly walked into the lion's den. "The negroes," said he, "are well understood to be the offspring of Cain, and their blackness is the mark God set upon Cain after he murdered Abel. It is the design of Providence that they should be slaves, as a condition proper to the race of so wicked a man as Cain was."

[1] Whittier ed., p. 90.

A second rider, perhaps primed beforehand, spoke up heartily in sup-port of this view. Woolman demolished them easily, hardly turning in his saddle. According to Scripture, he reminded them, all of Cain's race, and indeed all the sons of Adam, except Noah and his immediate family, were drowned in the Flood. "The love of ease and gain," he told them, "are the motives in general of keeping slaves, and men are wont to take hold of weak arguments to support a cause that is un-reasonable." And then that warmth rose within him that could have made him an orator, had he not constantly been on the watch to keep it in check, wanting to keep his words simple and few. He stopped his horse in the forest path to burn his thoughts into the hearts of those dark-hearted men. "I believe liberty is their right, and as I see they are not only deprived of it, but treated in other respects with inhumanity in many places, I believe he who is a refuge for the oppressed will in his own time plead their cause, and happy will it be for such as walk in uprightness before him. And thus," he says, "our conversation ended."[1]

Woolman allowed his Journal to carry the confession, "it was a time of inward suffering." But there were hours and days of happiness. Some of these were in Carolina, where new settlements were breaking the wilderness, and had not yet reached the stage of being able to use slaves. Their energy and enterprise and simplicity made him feel a unity with them, a "fervent love" for them, and he appealed both in speech and in a written epistle[2] that they would keep themselves clear of using slaves, for their own sakes.

Where slaves are purchased to do our labour numerous difficulties attend it. To rational creatures bondage is uneasy and frequently occasions sourness and discontent in them, which affects the family and such as claim the mastery over them. Thus people and their children are many times encompassed with vexations which arise from their applying wrong methods to get a living.

He did not, however, urge them to be content with poverty, as Saint Francis might have done. He had the American acceptance, one might say respect, for the material side of life, and encouraged them to believe that they could without using any wrong means obtain the ample sufficiency which would ensure the enjoyment of life.

[1] *Ibid.*, p. 92.
[2] The Epistle to Friends in the Back Settlements of North Carolina, from which these quotations are made in slightly abbreviated form, is printed in full in the Journal, Whittier edition, pp. 98-101.

Where people let loose their minds after outward things . . . and are more engaged in pursuing profits than to be inwardly acquainted with the way of true peace, they walk in a vain shadow, while the true comfort of life is wanting. . . . Treasures though small attained on a true principle of virtue are sweet, and while we walk in the light of the Lord there is true comfort and satisfaction in the possession ; neither the murmurs of an oppressed people, nor a throbbing uneasy conscience, nor anxious thoughts about the events of things, hinder the enjoyment of them.[1]

As usual, except where he actually speaks of the purchase of slaves, his thoughts transcend the local issue and remain applicable to the conduct of life in a social order where Negro slavery has become a thing of the past.

Another cause of happiness on the Southern journey was in the making of new and congenial friends. At Newbegun Creek in Carolina, for instance, there was a Quaker, Samuel Newby, who "laboured for his living having no negroes," who came to where Woolman was staying on purpose to ride a piece with him, and "as we rode together he signified that he wanted to talk with me concerning a difficulty he had been under." The difficulty turned out to be about the war tax. Virginia and Carolina, not being Quaker colonies, had gone in for war tax and militia draft several years before, when trouble first started. Quakers had consistently resisted the draft—in the person of drafted individuals of their sect, who often bought themselves off by paying some one else, in tobacco, to go in their place—but had paid the tax. This Newby "had a scruple in his mind in regard to paying it, and chose rather to suffer distraint of his goods ; but he was the only person who refused it in those parts and knew not that any one else" anywhere had any similar objection. His neighbours had made him feel that he was peculiar and obstinate, a cranky individual ; but, says Woolman, "From a sympathy he felt in me yesterday in meeting, he found freedom thus to open the matter with me in the way of querying concerning Friends in our parts." What a delightful unity and mutual reassurance was there discovered in the forest.

Another time was when, on his way down to Virginia Yearly Meeting, he had stayed briefly at Cedar Creek in the house of James Standley, whose son William, it turned out, had suffered imprisonment at Winchester last summer along with some other clear-headed young men who,

[1] Whittier ed., p. 101.

when drafted, had refused to buy another man in their place. Woolman discussed this with immense interest, and the young man, who had never heard his own groping thoughts stated as Woolman could state them, and who was reassured as to the eternal values of his choice, took pains to meet Woolman again on his return through Virginia. He met him somewhere near Black Creek and offered himself as guide on a three-day journey through the woods to Goose Creek, where Woolman wanted to go. This leisurely journey through the forest solitudes, a respite from jarring contacts, surrounded by beauty and in the congenial company of young William Standley, was the high-water mark of Woolman's happy experiences in the South. It was about one hundred miles. "We lodged the first night at a public-house ; the second in the woods ; and the next day we reached a Friend's house at Goose Creek.[1] In the woods we were under some disadvantage," says Woolman, because— perhaps having missed the way to some expected lodging—they had with them nothing to make a fire. It seems odd that so experienced a traveller, and a man of such foresight, as John Woolman, should be caught in the woods without his tinderbox, to say nothing of William Standley, who had the responsibility of guiding a stranger. However, so it was ; and we may thank that lost tinderbox.

They had no bells for their horses, so they could not let them loose as usual to graze. However :

we stopped a little before night and let them feed on the wild grass, which was plentiful, in the meantime cutting with our knives a store against night. We then secured our horses, and gathering some bushes under an oak we lay down ; but the mosquitoes being numerous and the ground damp I slept but little. Thus lying in the wilderness and looking at the stars [2]

Woolman began thinking about Adam and Eve after they got turned out of Eden, and what the wilderness was like when no one improved and cleared and cultivated it, and what men would be able to do if they had only their bare hands and no tools, and what a good thing inventions were which made for the progress of mankind. The preachers of original sin seemed to think that the Almighty intended Adam and Eve and all their descendants to be unhappy, as a punishment for that first disobedience in the Garden, but it seemed to Woolman otherwise. He thought, on the contrary, "how the Almighty, though they had been

[1] *Ibid.*, pp. 105-106.   [2] *Ibid.*, p. 105.

disobedient, continued to be a father to them, and showed them what tended to their felicity as intelligent creatures." And so, as Orion sank smoothly down the sky, his dreamy thoughts turned to the everlasting problem of human life, the relationship of the ideal with the practical, the balance between the right foot and the left which must be made if a man is to move forward and not stand still among the brutes. "To provide things relative to our outward living in the way of true wisdom, is good, and the gift of improving in things useful is a good gift, and comes from the Father of Lights." But when the motive of invention is evil the effects are evil.

It is therefore as necessary for us at this day constantly to attend on the heavenly gift, to be qualified to use rightly the good things in this life amidst great improvements, as it was for our first parents when they were without any improvements, without any friend or father but God only.

Woolman got home in July to find Mount Holly stirring with war alarms, and had to give his time and mind to the questions of draft and tax. But in the slow, careful, meditative writing up his Journal of his trip South he enunciated a great axiom which was independently shaping itself, with unforeseen implications, in the minds of his contemporaries, Washington, Adams, and Jefferson. "I believed," wrote John Woolman in 1757, "that liberty was the natural right of all men equally."[1]

[1] Whittier ed., p. 89.

XXVII

CONTROVERSY ON SLAVERY AT PHILADELPHIA

BEFORE Woolman went South he had written for the Press a set of short essays under the general title of *Considerations on Pure Wisdom and Human Policy*, the sub-heads of the four pieces being "On Labour," "On Schools," "On the Right Use of the Lord's Outward Gifts," and "On Trade." On his return he submitted these to the Quaker Overseers of the Press, and they were published under their auspices in 1758[1]— all except the short essay "On Trade," which was indefinitely postponed.

Woolman began to prepare a new essay on Slavery, but to make a thorough job of it he intended some solid reading and a second visit to New England ; in the meanwhile he dealt with the slave system, as opportunity served, in his own neighbourhood. There was little to complain of in New Jersey and Pennsylvania as to the treatment of the slaves, but "oppression remained to be oppression." The mere name SLAVE had become to Woolman horrible.

"Placing on Men," he said :

the ignominious title SLAVE, dressing them in uncomely garments, keeping them to servile Labour in which they are often dirty, tends gradually to fix a Notion in the mind that they are a sort of people

[1] Gummere, p. 382.

231

below us in nature, and leads us to consider them as such in all our Conclusions about them.[1]

The best masters found themselves unable to plead innocence of this ; and Woolman, spending two weeks in August '58 "visiting" meetings and families in Chester County and Philadelphia County—riding two hundred miles around and about before he had finished—was often unhappily conscious of giving pain.   His constant prayer was for strength that he might not be tempted by a false compunction to let those off easily whom he liked and respected, but remembering the wrongs of those others, so bitterly wronged, he might be uncompromising, "setting aside all views of self-interest and the friendship of this world."[2]

The Quaker conscience was not really comfortable about slavery. There were individuals—such as Anthony Benezet—who went as far as Woolman ; and a very general feeling was rising against the *buying* of slaves, so much so that a Query had been formed on the matter—one of the list of piercing questions, officially issued by the Yearly Meeting, the reading and answering of which in the meetings at set times kept Friends up to the mark of a uniform standard.   When John Woolman attended the Virginia Yearly Meeting he found them reading there the Queries issued by Philadelphia, but when they came to the new one about buying slaves they altered it to say "trading in slaves," and though Woolman got up and protested it, so it remained.

Some Friends in the Philadelphia Monthly Meeting—that is, in Philadelphia County, and the city itself, among those visited by Woolman—had in the summer of '58 been guilty of buying some more Negro slaves ; and instead of showing repentance, they sent in a formal objection to the condemning Query, and asked to have it reconsidered by the Yearly Meeting.   John Woolman attended a committee in Philadelphia in which this was discussed, and so went up to the Yearly Meeting in the fall with the foreknowledge that the fight about the Query would be on.   It came up towards the end of the several days' sessions.   John Woolman let all other subjects pass, and waited to give his whole weight to this one.   "The case of slave-keeping lay heavy upon me, nor did I find any engagement to speak directly to any other matter before the meeting."   When at last it was broached division of opinion was considerable, and feeling ran high.   "Though none did openly justify the

---

[1] *Considerations on Keeping Negroes*, Part II (Gummere, p. 363).
[2] Whittier ed., p. 118.

practice of slave-keeping in general," yet some opposers hesitated to go to an uncomfortable extreme which would give "uneasiness" to various influential Friends. Two suggestions seemed to emerge on which a compromise might be effected. One was the favourite one in any disturbing Quaker gathering—namely, that Friends would be patient and not hurry matters ("the Lord in his time might open a way for the deliverance of these people"). The other—suggested and supported by many who "had negroes"—was that a "rule might be made to deal with such Friends as offenders who bought slaves in future."

John Woolman rose and spoke.

"Many slaves on this continent are oppressed and their cries have reached the ears of the Most High. . . . He cannot be partial in our favour. In infinite love and goodness He hath opened our understanding from one time to another concerning our duty towards this people and it is not a time for delay. Should we now . . . through a respect to the private interest of some persons, or through a regard to some friendships which do not stand on an immutable foundation, neglect to do our duty in firmness and constancy, still waiting for some extraordinary means to bring about their deliverance, God may by terrible things in righteousness answer us in this matter."

As to the second point, that buyers of slaves should be disciplined while holders of slaves remained approved, Woolman disposed of that fallacy.

"The root of this evil would never be effectually struck at until a thorough search was made in the circumstances of such Friends as kept negroes, with respect to their motives in keeping them, that impartial justice might be administered throughout. . . . The case is difficult to some who have slaves, but if such set aside all self-interest, and come to be weaned from the desire of getting estates, or even from holding them together when truth requires the contrary, I believe way will so open that they will know how to steer through those difficulties."[1]

To this high stand at length no opposition was publicly made. And a committee was appointed for personal visits to those who kept slaves, to try the wise way of touching the individual conscience, with the authority of the Yearly Meeting behind them. Of this committee John Woolman was one, as well as his friends John Sykes and John Churchman. During the rest of the year 1758 and 1759 John Woolman made a number of visits on this committee work, chiefly around or in

[1] *Ibid.*, pp. 119–120.

Philadelphia, where the toughest work was to be done, but also including Salem and parts nearer home.

"Some whose hearts were rightly exercised about them [their slaves] appeared to be glad of our visit, but in some places our way was more difficult." At such times Woolman was careful to avoid provocative heat. Clinging fast to the impeccable justice of his case, he took embittering argument down to "the root from whence our concern proceeded," and breathing there again the serene air of the Presence of the Most High, it "preserved my mind in calmness under some sharp conflicts, and begat a spirit of sympathy and tenderness in me towards some who were grievously entangled by the spirit of this world."[1]

Yet he did not escape without offence and estrangement. And his method of dealing with these was characteristic of the open, warm flow of a naturally bold and vigorous nature, schooled to the gentlest of methods by natural sensitiveness as well as by religion. He became aware that a coolness was arising between him and some of his friends "of considerable note." That intangible rift in friendship is hard to deal with. There is nothing to put the finger on. Pride dictates that, being conscious of having given no just cause for offence, one should wait until the other "comes round." So a new habit of avoidance gradually grows up and replaces the old habit of mutual seeking out ; discomfort replaces the old pleasure when accidental meeting takes place ; and friendship, life's best gift, dies of starvation. Woolman thought it over, then took horse—took obvious trouble—rode to the house of an estranged friend, and without excuse or beating about the bush told him privately "that I had a desire to have an opportunity with him alone. To this proposal he readily agreed . . . and things relating to that shyness were searched to the bottom, and we had a large conference which I believe was of use to both of us, and I am thankful," says Woolman simply, "that way was opened for it."[2]

This is the action of a man of superb mental health.

He was away from home during this period—from the fall of 1758 to the spring of 1760—seven times in all, sometimes only for a few days, seldom longer than a fortnight. Most of his time was spent as usual at Mount Holly, with his wife and child, his orchard, his animals, surveying, tailoring, teaching, writing ; the quiet life that he loved the best. Meanwhile, the war continued. A thousand New Jersey men had lost their

---

[1] Whittier ed., p. 124.   [2] *Ibid.*, p. 125.

lives ; a thousand more were mustered. Barracks to hold three hundred were built at Burlington, and another at Elizabethtown, and at Trenton, and at Perth Amboy. The cost of the war to the population of New Jersey was estimated at five dollars a year for every living being in the province. The Quakers continued to suffer distraint for their war tax, and the Meeting for Sufferings continued to help the poorest members in distress thereby, and to raise funds at the rate of a thousand pounds a year for the Indians and for relief of war victims.

When the Yearly Meeting met again in 1759 the point of view regarding slavery was markedly changed for the better. The year's personal remonstrance by Woolman and others had borne fruit. "It was recommended to Friends to labour against *buying* and *keeping* slaves." Woolman, seeing this recorded and sent out by the meeting, and the whole meeting apparently under the concern, when "at times in some meetings I have been almost alone therein,"[1] felt a joyful sense that progress was really being made, and that action would follow. At this Yearly Meeting he left what was well alone, and devoted his attention to the war and its ravages, with his disconcerting habit of finding the roots of war not in the wicked acts of the Catholics or the Indians or the French or the English Government, but in everybody's private life—"that spirit of selfishness and exaltation which stands in opposition to real peace and happiness."[2]

The two noblest living exponents of the art of war[3] were at grips before Quebec ; both chivalrous, both brave, both gentle—when not on the field of battle—and both religious. The Protestant General Wolfe fought the Catholic Montcalm ; and Quebec fell. "Who run, who run ?" said the dying Wolfe ; and when they told him said, "Now God be praised, I die happy !" While William Pitt, hearing the news, remarked, "The more a man is versed in business the more he finds the hand of Providence everywhere."

If it was the hand of Providence which gave Quebec, and with it Canada, pouring them out—as Mr Edwards thought—in the seventh vial, there was an ingredient in the bottom of that vial which was very unexpected. The difficulties of raising a war tax and a militia in the most powerful of the colonies, Pennsylvania, and its sister province, New

---

[1] *Ibid.*, p. 126.
[2] *Ibid.*, p. 133.
[3] I think of George Washington more as a statesman.

Jersey, had not gone unnoticed, and Benjamin Franklin was even then in London as Agent for Pennsylvania to obtain the assistance of the Proprietors, Thomas and John Penn, or of the trusted British Government itself, to settle the dispute between Governor and assembly as to which of them carried the right of taxation. The English generals and governors in America had reported other difficulties in other provinces—there was no uniform tax system, or uniform way of raising an army. The Congress of Albany, dangerous as a symptom, was right in so far as that a united standing army and a general fund for war purposes were necessary to the permanent defence of the English colonies in America against their joint enemies. So the idea had already taken root in England that at the peace "acts of parliament will be moved for amendment of government." One popular plan was centralization under a Viceroy, with a council composed of representatives from all the provinces, "and a standing force in America." "This," wrote Calvert in January 1760, "will occasion a tax." And he prepared to give suggestions as to the safest and simplest method of imposing a light uniform tax on the English colonies—for their own defence—by British Act of Parliament.

The Quaker Dr John Fothergill was showing Franklin the warmest friendship, introducing him to suitable people, and giving him the best advice he could. William Pitt, confident that Providence was favourable to the British (and he included the British colonials in the term), could not find time to see Franklin ; but the latter saw the Attorney General. That shrewd lawyer, too clever to be perceptive, thought he could see through Franklin's cordial professions. "For all what you Americans say of your loyalty," he said, "and notwithstanding your boasted affection, you will one day set up for independence."[1] "No such idea," said Franklin sincerely, "is entertained by the Americans, nor ever will be, unless you grossly abuse them."

John Woolman had just written, and had published in Philadelphia, one of those many sentences of his which have a strangely prophetic ring.

"Contending with one equal in strength is an uneasy exercise, but if the Lord is become our enemy, if we persist in contending with him who is omnipotent, our overthrow will be unavoidable."[2] Contending with him who is omnipotent meant, as Woolman had frequently pointed

[1] Lord Camden.   See Bancroft's *History of the United States*, IV, 380.
[2] Whittier ed., p. 132.

out, practising the spirit of self-interest and oppression ; and to have the Lord on our side required not belonging to any specific sect, creed, or nation, but feeling "a deep attention to the Divine Councellor, and an ardent engagement to promote, as far as we may be enabled, the happiness of mankind universally."[1]

[1] *Consideration on the True Harmony of Mankind* (Gummere, p. 449).

XXVIII

SMALLPOX IN MOUNT HOLLY

IN the year 1759 there were two excitements at Mount Holly, one quite exhilarating, the other dismal indeed. One was the coming of the first stage-wagon. This advertised its intention of carrying goods and passengers once a week to Philadelphia,[1] a tedious and jolting journey, but more convenient to many than horseback. Curtains would shut one up snugly from the rain, and give some protection from winter cold. And the best seats had cushions. It delivered and called for passengers at Cooper's Ferry, came on at a good pace with four horses, changed horses at Moorestown, continued on with refreshed speed to Mount Holly, and called all the inhabitants to the street—or at least to the window—to watch its magnificent passage along those favoured streets which were on its route. Competition for its favour was so keen that it had to make two stops in the town, one at each of the chief taverns —the Three Tuns and the Black Horse, the keepers of which were partners in the ownership. Coming from Burlington it came first to the Black Horse ; coming from Philadelphia it came first to the Three Tuns. So all was fair, turn and turn about. The Three Tuns, owned by Josiah White, was now rented and run by Daniel Jones, brother of the Rebecca Jones who had just been admitted into membership with Friends in

---

[1] It really ran all the way from Philadelphia to "the bay near Sandy Hook" by stages, and there connected with a boat to New York. According to my map (1765) there is no through road from Mount Holly to Middletown and Sandy Hook except via Burlington. But its owners, of course, required it to come round by Mount Holly.

Philadelphia at the age of seventeen.   The lively Zach Rossell, a colourful and influential citizen, was still host at the Black Horse, and it was
above his mantel that the chilled incoming guest was glad enough to
find, writ fair :

> All ye who stand before the fire
> Pray sit ye down—'tis my desire
> That other people as well as you
> Shall see the fire and feel it too.[1]

Whoever was now running Woolman's former shop—of which Woolman regularly collected the rent for his mother—had the added advantage
of being right on the spot for the going and coming of the stage.   And
possibly advance information of this was in Woolman's mind when he
confided to his Journal that "the way to large business appeared open,"
as one good reason for giving up his shop altogether.

The other event was an outbreak of smallpox in Mount Holly that
winter, and suffering and fear fell upon the town.   It was worse even
than the Indians, and one never knew where the dreaded secret foe
would strike next ; the mother of the family, the baby at the breast,
the father upon whose exertions all depended, were equally vulnerable,
equally defenceless.   The barred door and shuttered window might not
keep it out, but shut it in.   John Woolman, ever since the death of his
sister, had regarded smallpox with a peculiar loathing, as most to be
dreaded of mortal ills.   With his customary healthy-mindedness he had
faced this feeling out, analysed, examined it, refused to let it inhabit a
separate compartment from that of his religious faith, tested both his
dread and his faith by each other.   He was not ignorant of medicine
or of the laws of health, and he was not indifferent to either.   Some
medical recipes appear in his Account Books, written in for casual
reference.   And his strong common sense was all on the side of using
the resources of science to battle any sickness.   Yet there was no disaster
which could befall a man, even smallpox, which could not be turned
to his good.   And therefore the existence of sickness and evil did not
necessarily discount the love and the goodness of God.

The more fully our lives are conformable to the will of God, the
better it is for us ; I have looked on the small-pox as a messenger
from the Almighty, to incite us to consider whether we employ our

---

[1] George de Cou, *Historical Sketches*, etc., No. 1, p. 10.

time only in such things as are consistent with perfect wisdom and goodness.[1]

Such a standard seems at first sight inhumanly severe, but Woolman hastens to reassure himself by enumerating what some of those things may be in a modest, ordinary life, lived not in the warm climate of the East—where a man does not need two coats—nor in medieval Europe, but in eighteenth-century America, with its particular conditions of climate, social obligations, business habits, and the common give-and-take of neighbourly intercourse. And the cheering practical nature of his conclusions again avoids the extreme of the doctrinaire.

> Building houses suitable to dwell in, for ourselves and our creatures ; preparing clothing suitable for the climate and season, and food convenient, are all duties incumbent on us. And under these general heads are many branches of business in which we may venture health and life as necessity may require.[2]

This brings him to another consideration—how far may a man go out of his way to avoid infection, or is it right to go on just as usual and take the risk of infection as it comes ? He saw among his acquaintance every extreme—some closing their houses and fleeing the place during the epidemic, regardless of severe business loss ; others shutting themselves up in unnatural seclusion, with frequent bleedings and dosings and burning of suphur as preventatives, while making themselves sick with fear ; and others again going about their doings with a reckless exposure to disease, in a fatalistic "what is to be will be" mood which had as little to do with science as with courage. Woolman could not help a certain scorn of cowardice, and perhaps he liked the reckless people best, however little sense they showed. But for himself he thought out a test by which to check the activities which might justify him in risking health and life (a risk which involved his dearest also).

"This disease being in a house and my business calling me to go near it" (as in the writing of a will, for instance, it might call near indeed), "incites me to consider," says Woolman,

> whether this is a real indispensable duty ; whether it is not in conformity to some custom which is better laid aside, or whether it does not proceed from too eager a pursuit after some outward treasure. If the business before me springs not from [what] perfect wisdom

approves, to be brought to a sense of it and stopped in my pursuit is a
kindness, for when I proceed to business without some evidence of
duty I have found by experience that it tends to weakness.

If I am so situated that there appears no probability of missing the
infection, it tends to make me think whether my manner of life
. . . has nothing in it which may unfit my body to receive this
messenger in a way the most favourable to me.

For instance, is diet sensible and suitable ?   Is vitality being lowered
by overwork on the one hand or inactivity on the other ?

Social life is a necessity, but "this infection, which often proves mortal,
incites me to think whether these social acts of mine are real duties."
Woolman again here almost ruefully confesses his love of company, and
goes on to examine his civic duties.

Do affairs relating to civil society call me near the infection ?   If I
go it is at the hazard of health and life, and it becomes me to think
seriously whether love to truth and righteousness is the motive of my
attending . . . or whether ought of narrowness, party interest,
respect to outward dignities . . . do not stain the beauty of these
assemblies, and render it doubtful, in point of duty. . . . That which
is a means of stirring us up to look attentively on these blemishes and
to labour according to our capacities to have health and soundness
restored in our country, we may justly account a kindness from our
gracious Father, who hath appointed that means.

And, knowing in his own heart the yearning, tender, and protective love
of a father for an only child, Woolman reiterates his faith in the deepest
terms of his experience.   "The care of a wise and good man for his only
son is inferior to the regard of the great Parent of the universe for his
creatures.   He . . . doth not afflict willingly, nor grieve the children of
men."[1]

Dr Ross, going in and out among the infected families as was his
obvious duty, strongly recommended inoculation, and Woolman did
not carelessly reject the idea.   Inoculating people in health with a mild
form of smallpox was very popular with the medical profession.   It had
been observed that those who had had smallpox never had it again, and
it was a selling point in the sale of slaves that they "had had the small-pox
favourably."   Philadelphia doctors had such a reputation for skill in
successful inoculation that the young Jefferson was sent to Philadelphia
for the express purpose of being inoculated, and came through it very

[1] *Ibid.*, pp. 137, 138.

Q

satisfactorily with a mild illness. The great expert in England was a Quaker, Dr Dimsdale, and when in 1767 Catherine the Great sent for an English doctor to come to Russia and inoculate herself and her son and heir, the Grand Duke Paul, Dr John Fothergill recommended Dimsdale for the job. In case of accident—for the element of risk was recognized—Catherine had relays of post horses prepared for him all along the line from St Petersburg to the border, to ensure his escape from misguided vengeance ; but the inoculation turned out successfully, and Dimsdale received a reward worthy of a great Empress. He was given the title of Baron, with a fee of ten thousand pounds, travelling expenses of two thousand pounds, and an annuity of five hundred pounds for life.

But Jonathan Edwards, summoned in 1757 to become President of Princeton in succession to his son-in-law, Aaron Burr—who had been practically killed by preaching the funeral oration of the founder of the college, Governor Belcher, when in a high fever—found an outbreak of smallpox there when he arrived in the spring of '58, and consented to be inoculated as a preventive. "He had it favourably," said his doctors, "and it was thought all danger was over, but a secondary fever set in" and he died in a few days. His daughter, Mrs Burr, and her children were inoculated at the same time, and had "recovered" when he died ; but alas, Mrs Burr also had a curious and fatal relapse, which the physician said he could call by no name but "that of a messenger sent suddenly to call her out of the world."[1]

Woolman, with a wife and child also to think of, was not, in the face of these facts, convinced of the value of inoculation. He remarks that many in Mount Holly were inoculated, "of whom a few died." He decided not to risk it, but his reasons had no relation to fatalism or contempt for preventive medicine.

> Had He endowed men with understanding to prevent this disease [the smallpox] by means which had never proved hurtful nor mortal, such a discovery might be considered. . . . But as life and health are his gifts . . . to take upon us by inoculation when in health a disorder of which some die, requires great clearness that it is our duty to do so.[2]

Woolman had an increasing conviction, shared—or perhaps inspired—by his friend Josiah White, that inward health, the health of the spirit,

[1] *Works of Jonathan Edwards*, I, ccxiv, ccxx, and ccxxi.
[2] Whittier ed., p. 139.

had a great effect upon the body. Not long after his sister's death—
perhaps conscious that he had himself succeeded at that time in throwing
off an infection to which he had certainly been exposed—he had written
to a friend, "Being unclothed of our own wisdom and knowing the
abasement of the creature, we find that power to arise which gives
health and vigour to us."[1]

By 1803 Elizabeth Fry was accepting the advice of her doctor to allow
the newly discovered practice of vaccination—neither hurtful nor mortal
—to be performed upon her first child.

The terrible winter of '59 wore away at last, and the spring returned ;
the apple-trees budded, and the bees began their honey business ; the
chlorophyll, life's slender bulwark against death, returned to the grass ;
those weakened with illness stole out to sit in the sun ; and those others
heartbroken with sorrow once more put the seed into the ground that
it might die for life's sake, and prepare another harvest. And John
Woolman, his family uninjured, got ready reluctantly for a long absence
from home, a four months' visit to New England on behalf of the slaves
and their owners.

[1] *Ibid.*, p. 83.

XXIX

SECOND JOURNEY TO NEW ENGLAND

WHATEVER pleasures the changing scenes of travel might bring or the new friends and human contacts on the way, it always made John Woolman sad to leave home. This visit to New England had been long intended and must be carried through, but the constant presence of Death in the streets of Mount Holly that winter had reminded John Woolman again of the shortness of life and its uncertainty, and his wife and child clung to him wistfully as he bade them farewell.

The letters which he wrote on the eve of departure to his two friends, John Pemberton and John Smith, reflect this feeling, as well as the practical care which ensured that Sarah and Mary should at any rate have no removable anxieties over "outward things" while the husband and father was away.

Woolman's chosen companion for this journey was Samuel Eastburn, a landowner in Bucks County, Pennsylvania, and a member of Buckingham Meeting. Eastburn had been born in England of the noble family of the de Estburns, who had come over with William the Norman and received at his hands one of the first Norman manors, later called East-bourne, on the Sussex coast. He had been brought by his parents to Philadelphia at the age of two, and was now a man of fifty-eight. His breeding and charm rendered him a fit companion for Woolman, while his point of view was so sympathetic that at the end of four months of close association of the most exacting kind Woolman named him "my beloved companion and true yoke-mate."

Woolman's letters to his wife did not give much information as to his doings in New England, but that was characteristic of his letters at any time. He was making full notes as he travelled—a sort of daily journal —from which when he got home he would compose a finished account of his trip for the Journal which was to be printed some time in the future, with all experiences and impressions worth remembering ; and Sarah would share in and read all these, both the rough and the finished, enlivened by his spoken commentary, and filled in by her questions, on many an evening of the coming fall and winter.

The first week-end at Newport, about May 11, had made a painful impression on Woolman. "The great number of slaves in these parts and the continuance of that trade from thence to Guinea" involved all the leading citizens, many of whom were Quakers.

It is a strange thing to look back at the eighteenth century and observe that with the vast rich continent of Africa open to trade, and busy merchants plying there—already marking off the Gum Coast, the Grain Coast, the Ivory Coast, and the Gold Coast—it was the traffic in slaves which predominated. The total export some years rose to 100,000, and the English alone carried over two million Negroes to America between 1680 and 1786, "the chief and fundamental support of the American plantations." Yet in spite of the immense private fortunes made in this traffic the African Company was rocking. In 1730 Parliament granted it a ten-thousand-pound annual subsidy towards the maintenance of its forts and factories (as they euphemistically called the slave-concentration places on the coast). But the Company did not recover, and Parliament, "fearing the injurious results of a declining Negro trade," in 1750 liquidated the African Company monopoly and substituted a Regulated Company including all merchants trading to Africa. The trade by American merchants leapt forward, and the New England seamen made quick and easy money by supplying the large Southern slave market. Boston and Salem merchants were well to the fore in this traffic, but Newport was the acknowledged leader.

When a century later the industrial North, engaged in war with the agricultural South, made a fervent battle-cry about the freeing of the slave, the South, miserably conscious of a bad cause there, had some right to feel bitter resentment at a holier-than-thou attitude on the part of men whose great mercantile houses had many of them been founded on the capital made by their fathers in the slave trade.

The involvement of the Quakers, all of whose theories of life and religion were so obviously against the slave system in any form, was what Woolman could not bear. In New Jersey and Pennsylvania they had already got as far as being uncomfortable about owning slaves and still more about buying new ones ; in the South—Virginia, Carolina, and Maryland—they were mostly unable (in their opinion) to avoid owning and buying, but were ready to condemn "trading in slaves." But in New England, where in many ways the standard of moral living was so high, the Quakers—more numerous and more influential than in the South—were deeply involved, directly and indirectly, in the slave trade itself.

As to their numbers, a Mr Fayerweather, minister for the Society for the Propagation of the Gospel in Narragansett, complains in 1761 that Quakers, Deists, and Infidels swarm in that part of the world, and pleads that many good books are wanted in the Narragansett country for the suppressing of Deism, Infidelity, and Quakerism. Headquarters at home advised him to heat his church in winter.

Another missionary of the S.P.G., the notable Reverend Dr MacSporran, was scandalized at first coming over in 1741 to discover an island near Rhode Island, "with 400 or 500 inhabitants who had never had the Gospel preached to them in any other shape but Quakerism." It hardly surprised headquarters that he should write of such a country "Here liberty of conscience is carried to an irreligious extreme."[1]

The S.P.G., with ministers throughout the colonies, were consciously enlightened on the Negro question, urging their flock everywhere to regard their slaves not just as slaves but as *men* slaves and *women* slaves, and to baptize them whenever possible. A bit of a flurry arose on the question of baptism, some simple-minded owners fearing that to recognize a Negro thus not only as possessing a soul but as a fellow-Christian might introduce an awkward element of equality—at least before God— and might result in a mutual conviction that it was wrong to keep them slaves. It took a special pamphlet issued by the Bishop of London and the Attorney General to allay this misapprehension. And it was a Congregational minister in Rhode Island who afforded the star example of emancipation from such superstition when he baptized his two Negro servants into church membership, had them in to morning prayers every day, married them himself by Church ritual ; and then,

[1] Updike, appendix, p. 514.

against their passionate entreaties, sold the wife away to a distant purchaser.[1]

Stories such as these were known to the travellers, and made part of the background of their thought and their message. But every one knew such incidents. Woolman did not pause to record them in his Journal. In one form or another, more blatant or less so, they were the commonplaces of every day. They rested, one and all, on a fundamental point of view, and it was that to which Woolman devoted his attention ; particularly among Quakers, whose language he could speak, and who, freed from the tyranny of the verbal inspiration of the Scriptures—by which, since slaves were in the Bible, it was customary to justify slavery—had no excuse for being in darkness.[2]

Going on to Boston and then eighty miles to the eastward, they found things no better, and Woolman, always made stern by stubborn opposition, "had some hard labour with the disobedient, by laying things close and home to such as were stout against the truth." On return to Boston they had an unexpectedly comfortable visit, perhaps associating with "those who were meek," or having cowed them into becoming so ; and they rode away from Boston to pay one more visit in those parts, conducted by a fat and heavy guide. It was a hot day, and we have seen Woolman before put in charge of a slow guide and know that his patience could not endure it. As the fat Friend steamed and perspired and came heavily along on his overladen horse, "my companion and I," says Woolman, "expressed our freedom to go on without him, to which he consented and we respectfully took our leave of him ; this we did," Woolman courteously explains, no doubt repeating what he had said to the guide, with kind care not to hurt his feelings, "as believing the journey would have been hard to him and his horse."[3]

They got back to Newport for the Yearly Meeting with a very depressed sense of what the Society of Friends was like in those parts, entirely hardened on the question of slavery ; but they were not prepared for what happened. During the actual sittings of the Yearly Meeting itself, while pious utterances were being rolled forth with great unction in the meeting-house, amid hundreds of well-to-do Friends, including visitors with certificates from England and other parts, a slave ship came

[1] Goodell, p. 13.
[2] See George Fox on the Bible, *George Fox's Journal*, edition by Rufus Jones (pp. 102, 103).
[3] Whittier ed., p. 144.

into Newport harbour. Immediate unloading and sale were essential, and the owner, a Quaker, was summoned out of the Yearly Meeting.

Woolman was literally sickened by it. "Understanding," he wrote, "that a large number of slaves had been imported from Africa into that town, and were there on sale by a member of our Society, my appetite failed, and I grew outwardly weak." Like Habakkuk ("When I heard, my belly trembled; my lips quivered . . . : I trembled in myself. . . .") "I had many cogitations and was sorely distressed." It was impossible to stop the sale, or to imagine that any persuasion could cause a merchant to set free several hundred raw Negroes, fresh from their native jungles. Impossible to imagine what such poor creatures could do with freedom, away from all that was familiar in life, unacclimatized, untaught, without the English language.

Woolman did not go down to the wharf to see the horror. The imaginative recognition of it was enough. Nowhere in all his record is there any indication that Woolman was ever an eyewitness of the worst brutalities that slavery could show. But the son of Governor Robinson, Rowland Robinson, Tom Hazard's brother-in-law, went down once to see a cargo of his own brought in, and was so unable to bear the sight that he burst into tears, set free all his share of the miserable wretches and provided for them, and took pains to purchase and set free as many as he could find of those whom he had previously imported. Such was the impact on an emotional and unimaginative nature of the perception of the physical torments of the middle passage. But Woolman's sensitive imagination did not need arousing, and he avoided rather than sought scenes of physical distress.

He used his time and strength instead for a strong immediate attack on the slave trade.

"I was desirous that Friends might petition the Legislature to use their endeavours to discourage the future importation of slaves, for I saw that this trade was a great evil, and tended to multiply troubles. . . ." No doubt he consulted with his friend Thomas Hazard,[1] who was at the Yearly Meeting. Hazard was deeply sympathetic, but knew the procedure of the Assembly and the difficulties in the way of presenting a petition. Woolman then began to wonder if he ought to try to get an

---

[1] Woolman characteristically does not betray his consultant to perhaps unwanted publicity. "I inquired of a friend" (p. 145, Whittier ed.). But Hazard was certainly the natural, almost the inevitable, one to consult.

opportunity to "speak a few words in the House of Assembly then sitting in town," and had a sleepless night meditating about it, finally going to sleep on the decision that he would do it if it seemed right in the morning. But in the morning it became clear—on consulting Tom Hazard again—that the Assembly was expecting to be prorogued that day or the next ; one could not therefore both go to the Assembly and attend the Yearly Meeting. Woolman had come a long way to attend the Yearly Meeting, his natural avenue of influence was through the Society of Friends, and if he left them to go to the Assembly he might not after all be permitted to speak ; so his "mind settled," and he attended the Yearly Meeting, but prepared a document in the form of a petition to present to the Legislature (probably written during the sleepless night). This he showed to Tom Hazard and a few others, and with their approval brought it before the Yearly Meeting in the following speech—short, emphatic, direct :

I have been under a concern for some time on account of the great number of slaves which are imported into this colony. I am aware that it is a tender point to speak to, but apprehend I am not clear in the sight of Heaven without doing so. I have prepared an essay of a petition to be presented to the Legislature if way open ; and what I have to propose to this meeting is that some Friends may be named to withdraw and look over it, and report whether they believe it suitable to be read in the Meeting. If they should think well of reading it, it will remain for the meeting to consider whether to take any further notice of it, as a meeting, or not.[1]

"After a short conference " some Friends went out and looked over the document, and reported that they thought it might be read to the meeting, which was done. Many of them expressed "unity" with the proposal to present it to the Legislature, and it was agreed that those who were willing to sign it should do so "out of Meeting."

This was probably the beginning of Thomas Hazard's work in the Legislature against the importing of slaves, and presently against the buying and selling and use of slaves in the colony.

Fourteen years later an Act was passed by the Rhode Island Legislature which prohibited the importation of Negroes, spoke of the right of personal freedom, and enacted that, although all citizens and residents retained legal ownership of such slaves as they had, all slaves entering the state from outside would become automatically free men. And in

[1] Whittier ed., pp. 145-146.

1787, in the ardour of the new liberty, an Act was passed to prevent the trade itself, which imposed a penalty on every citizen who as master, agent, or owner of any vessel shall buy, sell, or receive on board his ship any slave.

Woolman's comment on his successful stirring up of Rhode Island Friends on the matter is, "My heart yearned towards the inhabitants of these parts, believing that by this trade there had been an increase of inquietude amongst them."[1] As usual his contribution was anonymous. It was others who signed his document ; and those looking through the archives without the necessary clue would not attribute authorship or initiative to John Woolman, resident as he was of a far-distant province.

One instance of the "inquietude" of New England Friends was their curious point of view with regard to lotteries. It has always been a *sine qua non* with Quakers—as, indeed, with Methodists and Baptists and other prominent sects—that they should not take part in obvious forms of betting and gambling, of which certainly lotteries are one. When Franklin got up a lottery in Philadelphia as a means of raising war funds the Quakers did not subscribe ; though there were plenty of others to do so. But in New England the Government lotteries were supported by a number of Friends, and wildcat lotteries also—as once you got the lottery habit, why miss the chance of a good prize ? A discussion on these lotteries and Quaker participation arose in the Yearly Meeting, some Friends wanting all use of lotteries condemned as "gambling," others hotly maintaining that Friends should be "excused for participating" if they only patronized the Government lotteries, the legal ones.

Woolman could hardly believe his ears at hearing such a point of view, selfish, confused, and dark, advocated in a Quaker meeting, and he got up and spoke to the point without premeditation and with considerable heat, demolishing a misguided "ancient Friend" in that sardonic style of which he was a master, and which he was always keeping in check. After he sat down and cooled off he was sorry to recollect that his words had not been enough "seasoned with charity." On the other hand, he did not want to weaken their impression in the midst of a warm debate. He waited in discomfort and regret until a minute was safely made to be sent down to the Quarterly Meetings advising Friends against all use of lotteries whatsoever. Then he arose and apologized, saying that he did

[1] Whittier ed., p. 146.

not withdraw from the matter but regretted the manner of his speaking, "believing milder language would have been better."[1]

This is the only case on record where John Woolman lost his temper. And it is interesting to notice that he lost it on what was to him a side issue, not to be compared in importance with the two main themes of his attention—slavery and war. On these two subjects he was accustomed to exercise over himself an iron control, lest he should injure the cause by his rash presentation of it. He would patiently listen to muddle-headed statements, peevish self-justification, rationalized self-interest, and would often meet them with the utmost gentleness, in order that by all means he might save some. On these subjects he could not be caught napping. But all that suppressed fire of indignation and disgust, recently especially aroused—and controlled, except as it made him sick—with relation to the Quaker slaver, was ready to break out if it could find another outlet. Besides, Woolman had been suffering for weeks under a double nervous strain, first on account of his wife and child, and second on account of the exceptionally difficult work in which he was engaged on this journey ; and the letters and news he had just had from home—making vivid to him his delicate wife's difficulties and her longing for him—were not altogether of a nature to soothe. So he let off steam over the lotteries and was all the better for it. The wreckage of the ancient Friend was a small sacrifice to pay.

He needed all his serenity for the task he had next set himself. It was nothing less than to visit all the leading Quakers of Newport who were slave-holders, on the subject not only of trading in but of keeping slaves. These were wealthy and important men, living like princes. Robert Hazard, father of Thomas, was not a Quaker, but there were Quakers who lived his way. Woolman, reflecting on his friends at home, the Logans and the Pembertons and the Smiths, considered how a stranger might best approach them, and he decided on a careful formality, such as a visiting ambassador might use. First he mentioned his wishes to two elderly Friends "who came out of the country," but who were acquainted with and respected by the Friends in and about Newport. Then one of these country Friends accompanied Woolman to consult one of the most noted elders of Newport Meeting. This elder owned slaves, and Woolman had already "had a private conference with him and his wife concerning their slaves," near the beginning of the

Yearly Meeting. The elder now "in a respectful manner, encouraged me to proceed to clear myself of what lay upon me." Woolman explained fully, and requested advice on the "manner of proceeding." Perhaps a conference with all the leading Quaker slave-holders together in a private house :

> or if he thought they would take it unkind to be asked to come together and to be spoken with in the hearing of one another, I was free to spend some time amongst them and to visit them all in their houses. [The elder] expressed his liking to the first proposal, not doubting their willingness to come together ; and . . . he named some others whom he desired might also be present.

If Woolman had realized what a complete conquest he had made of this elder in that almost forgotten talk with him and his wife near the beginning of the Yearly Meeting he might not have bothered with the two country Friends as introducers. When the next question arose as to how it was to be explained to the Quaker aristocracy of Newport what was expected of them the elder (characteristically nameless) forsook the rôle of friendly adviser to enter wholly into partnership with Woolman. "A careful messenger being wanted to acquaint them in a proper manner, he offered to go to all their houses to open the matter to them—and did so."

This conference of the wealthy Quakers of Newport took place about eight o'clock the next morning in the meeting-house chamber ; and Woolman especially mentions that the kind country Friend, and the visitor from London Yearly Meeting, John Storer, and his own companion, Eastburn, were present. They sat awhile in the restful, healing Quaker silence, and then John Woolman told them his thoughts on the subject of slave-catching, slave-buying, and slave-keeping with simplicity, brevity, and special reference to its ill effects on themselves and their children ; admitting at the start all they had to say about kind treatment, good food, and so on, as possibly true but irrelevant to the main issue.

> He that hath a Servant, made so wrongfully, and knows it to be so, when he treats him otherwise than as a free Man, when he reaps the Benefit of his Labour without paying him such Wages as are reasonably due to free Men for the like Service, Cloaths excepted ; these Things, tho' done in Calmness, without any Show of Disorder, do yet deprave the Mind in like Manner and with as great Certainty, as prevailing Cold congeals Water. These Steps taken by Masters and their Con-

duct striking the Minds of their Children whilst young leave less Room
for that which is good to work upon them . . . and they from thence
conceiving Ideas of Things and Modes of Conduct, the Entrance into
their Hearts becomes in a great Measure shut up against the gentle
Movings of uncreated Purity.

Through the paternal feelings of his hearers, similar to his own,
Woolman tried to rouse the imaginations dormant by long habit.

Our Children breaking a Bone ; getting so bruised that a leg or an
arm must be taken off ; lost for a few hours so that we despair of their
being found again ; a Friend hurt, so that he dieth in a day or two ;
these things move us with Grief.   And did we attend to these Scenes
in Africa, in like Manner as if they were transacted in our Presence,
and sympathise with the *Negroes* in all their Afflictions and Miseries as
we do with our Children or Friends, we should be more careful to
do nothing in any Degree helping forward a Trade productive of so
many and so great Calamities.   Great distance makes nothing in our
Favour.   To willingly join with Unrighteousness to the Injury of
Men who live some Thousand Miles off is the same in Substance as
joining with it to the Injury of our Neighbours. . . . Now when our
minds are thoroughly divested of all prejudice in relation to the difference of colour, and the Love of Christ in which there is no partiality
prevails upon us, I believe it will appear that a heavy account lies
against us as a Civil Society. . . . If Christ is our Shepherd and feedeth
us and we are faithful in following him, our lives will have an inviting
language.

So he spoke the thoughts which habitually burned within him. "We
then proceeded to a free conference upon the subject."   Undoubtedly
these men, who could have bought up not only Newport but half New
England, had never heard the business of slavery put upon such a level,
nor listened, fascinated, to such clear, unworldly talk.   It was so different
from what they were accustomed to on the subject that somehow it
"wrought a tenderness amongst us ; and the subject was mutually
handled," says Woolman, "in a calm and peaceable spirit.   At length
. . . I took my leave of them in a good degree of satisfaction,"[1] and
indeed he learned afterwards that many of them went away and made
wills by which their slaves were to be set free.

Then he went back to his lodging and poured out his heart in a letter
to his wife. "I find at times a disposition to hasten for thy Sake.   But

[1] Whittier ed., p. 149.

Such is the weight of the work I am engaged in and Such the baptisms with which I have been baptized that I see A Necessity for all nature to Stand Silent. . . ." And gathered her to his heart with close and comforting arms and told her to make her life as comfortable as may be and spare no cost. . . .

The happiest time of John Woolman's visit to New England was the trip to Nantucket. They sailed from Dartmouth, he and Samuel Eastburn and several other Friends. "The wind being slack we only reached Tarpawling Cove the first day, where, going on shore, we found room in a public house, and beds for a few of us—the rest slept on the floor." Which probably means the women had the beds. "We went on board again about break of day, and though the wind was small" they got to within four miles of Nantucket ; and then "about ten of us got into our boat and rowed to the harbour before dark." Woolman was one of this first batch. He was not patient, in travelling, with avoidable delay. "A large boat went off and brought in the rest of the passengers about midnight." The next day but one was their Yearly Meeting, which lasted four days. Woolman admired the beautiful speaking of Samuel Eastburn, and himself enjoyed a quiet life, with the exception of his visit to the women's meeting. The beauty and peace of the island, the wild seas breaking, the simplicity of the hard-working people—"few or no slaves on the island"—gave a healthy happy respite from too prolonged mental and spiritual struggle with an age-old evil. It was a relief to enter into conversation with sailors and whalers and farmers about the salty concrete problems of their hardy lives. To give no good advice and to receive none. To let the Name of God lie silent. Many of these men hazarded their lives every day just to get firewood and food. They were clear-eyed, grim, and fundamentally humble.

I observed many shoals in their bay which make sailing more dangerous, especially in stormy nights ; also that a great shoal which encloses their harbour prevents the entrance of sloops except when the tide is up. Waiting without for the rising of the tide is sometimes hazardous in storms and by waiting within they sometimes miss a fair wind. . . . There was on that small island a great number of inhabitants and the soil not very fertile, the timber being so gone that for vessels, fences, and firewood they depend chiefly on buying from the Main. . . . They depend principally upon the whale fishery. . . . I understood that the whales being much hunted and sometimes wounded and not killed grow more shy and difficult to come at.

The visitors had practical experience of the difficulty of wind and tide that made life interesting for the islanders. "When Meeting was over we all agreed to sail the next day if the weather was suitable . . . and being called up the latter part of the night about fifty of us went on board a vessel ; but the wind changing, the seamen thought it best to stay in the harbour till it altered, so we returned on shore."

Woolman looked forward to a holiday of solitude and peace, but alas ! one of the visiting Women Ministers insisted on a meeting, and one was held to which Woolman and the others faithfully went to support her, and she satisfied her heart with a long sermon ; no doubt appreciated by the islanders, whose entertainments were few.

"The next morning about break of day going again on board the vessel, we reached Falmouth on the Main before night, where our horses being brought, we proceeded towards Sandwich."[1] Then Newport, Greenwich, and on down to New York, pausing there to visit Friends ; then back to Flushing and Rahway. Here, their roads parting, the two friends took leave of each other, having shared an unmatched comradeship for four months ; and Woolman proceeded home alone across New Jersey as fast as his horse could reasonably travel.

But in all the joy of the reunion, all the days that followed under the deep blue August sky, with the united cheerful business of the apple harvest, the cider-making, and the apple butter, with blue wood-smoke under the trees, Woolman's heart was often heavy. The problem and the burden grew larger instead of smaller. He had taken up the burden, and now he could not lay it down. He might have said with Hamlet,

> The time is out of joint ; O cursèd spite,
> That ever I was born to set it right !

He wrote down in his Journal the suspicious words, "I do not repine at having so unpleasant a task assigned to me" ; and murmured to himself, like Milton, that God appoints to his servants their respective employments.[2]

---

[1] Whittier ed., p. 152.   [2] Ibid., p. 143.

XXX

THE CHANGE

IN the winter—the hard, intense, severe American winter—the only
war men could conduct was the war against cold. The armies huddled
into camps ; such men as could got to their homes. There was a sort
of tacit armed truce until spring once more unlocked the rivers and
melted down the barriers of snow from the forest paths.

Winter in Mount Holly was the cosy season, the indoor season. John
Woolman no longer had to fight his way through sleet and storm to his
shop in the village. He could adjust his occupation to the weather. In
the bright, sharp frost he was out pruning his apple-trees ; in rain or
fog or snow he was indoors at his tailoring or at somebody's accounts
or getting on with his writing—this winter it was the second *Essay on
Keeping Negroes*, as well as his Journal. And people no longer having
to avoid each other, there being no epidemic abroad, there were happy
social gatherings—in the familiar spaciousness of Peachfields, or at
Josiah White's modest but comfortable house, or the home of Woolman's
neighbouring brothers, or the Bisphams, the Haineses, or any of "my
dear fr'ds about home." One such party, in December, was held at the
old Woolman homestead on the Rancocas by Asher Woolman and his
mother. The occasion was the arrival of a guest, an English Quaker
lady from the beautiful Westmorland Lake District. Her name was

Jane Crosfield. There she sat with serene face in the candlelight, a woman of forty-nine, having left behind her husband and children, her comfortable, substantial home, and all the responsibilities of household cares, and come in a little ship across a winter sea in war-time at the bidding of the mysterious inward call. The ship had been the *Philadelphia Packet*, a member of the first line of ships to sail regularly between Philadelphia and London, started eight years before by a Quaker shipowner, Joshua Fisher, in Front Street.[1] This time the *Packet* had come over in a fleet of thirty-six ships under convoy. Yet, though Quakers sometimes balked at accepting armed protection, Jane Crosfield's call would not be denied. John Woolman had met her already in Philadelphia at James Pemberton's, where she had been first entertained ; and now he inquired as to her further plans. When he heard she was intending to go on to New England at that season of the year he was dismayed for her. No woman ought to attempt it. He looked at Sarah and ten-year-old Mary, in their warm winter dresses and soft white kerchiefs, sitting cosily beside the fire in the large circle of friends and relatives, absorbed in silent admiration of the stranger. And he thought of either of them—even robust Mary—pitting their feminine strength against such bitter travel. He had never been to England, but he had more than a suspicion that the Englishwoman, even though she boasted of being a North Countrywoman, did not in the least foresee what was ahead of her. MacSporran had written to England recently from Rhode Island :

Last winter in February, which begins the spring with you, I rode 30 miles upon one continued glaze of ice upon the land. . . . With a horse well caulked and frosted 'tis fine travelling for one that can sometimes 'light and run to bring the blood into his feet and increase the checked circulation. As from my lands I can see the Atlantic Ocean I have seen it froze as far as the human eye could reach ; and 'tis common in a beautiful lake of salt water that fronts my farm to have the ice three feet thick every winter.

Commonplace to the colonist, but inconceivable to the native of England. Yet Woolman hesitated to interfere. She was as clear about her duty, to all seeming, as he had on similar occasions been himself. Josiah White and his daughter Hannah were of the party, and as the talk progressed it was evident that Hannah White was completely under the spell of the vigorous, lively newcomer, and that Mrs Crosfield presently

---

[1] In 1753 (family records of Mrs Edward Wanton Smith, of Germantown).

R

began to single her out, and once or twice addressed her especially, charmed by her youthful enthusiasm and earnest response. The talk became serious and spells of deep silence fell.

The next day there was a meeting in the old meeting-house of Woolman's childhood, Rancocas Meeting, and Jane Crosfield preached with power. And then after a hearty meal the English Friend made her thanks to her hosts and rode to Mount Holly, escorted by Asher to the house of Josiah White, where she was to spend the night of December 12. The Whites gathered their friends in to meet her that evening, and among them again John Woolman and his wife and daughter. And at this gathering it was solemnly announced that twenty-one-year-old Hannah was to be Jane Crosfield's companion on her journey to New England. There seemed to John Woolman no chance to utter a word of warning, and he did not want to introduce a note of discouragement. But after going away he wrote Mrs Crosfield a letter and sent it round before she left in the morning. And it is noteworthy that in all her travels she kept that letter with her.

12th day, 12th mo, at night, 1760

Since I understand thy draft[1] toward New England at this season of the year [wrote John Woolman], I have felt a near sympathy in my mind toward thee, and also thy new companion, H. White. Looking seriously over the stages and waters and thinking on the hard frosts and high winds usual in the winter, the journey has appeared difficult. But my mind was turned to him who made and commands the winds and the waters and whose providence is over the ravens and sparrows. I believed thou understood his language . . . and in that there is safety. . . . "He that believeth maketh not haste," and there seemed to be a hint in my mind to give thee that thou take a sufficient portion of that doctrine along with thee this journey. Should frozen rivers or high winds or storms sometimes prevent thy going forward so fast as thou could desire, it may be thou may find a service in tarrying even amongst a people whose company may not be every way agreeable. . . .

Farewell, my dear Friend.

JOHN WOOLMAN

The want of a suitable opportunity this evening occasioned me to take this way.[2]

---

[1] Thy drawing—thy leading. The powerful inward sense of being *drawn* in a certain direction.

[2] Copy of letter and extracts from Jane Crosfield's diary furnished me by her descendant, Bertram Crosfield, of London. The letter is also printed in full, Gummere, p. 61.

So spoke a traveller who was himself much irked by delay.

Fortunately Jane Crosfield survived her travels, and sailed back to England in October 1761 with a most amazing outfit of gifts to make her return voyage comfortable—"23 Bottles of English Beer, 6 Bottles of Claret, 1 cag of Rum, 1 Jar Coffee, 2 lb. Chocolate, nuts, onions, preserved crabs, 2 barrels of apples, 1 Barrel of Potatoes & Turnips, 2 hams, and many other goodies, as well as a Mattress, 3 pillows, 2 Blankets, a Coverlid, 1 Pewter chamber pott, and 1 iron candlestick." And for "Loose in the Cabbin," sugar candy, liquorice, one stone drinking cup and saucer. Evidently the bed and bedding she came with had been sent back on the ship, as too cumbersome to keep or store during a year of travel.

One of Woolman's small but exacting jobs that winter was the settling of Negro Maria's little "estate," for whom he and Asher were joint trustees ;[1] and then the establishing of another Negro maid with his mother. A girl named Isabella was found in the Burr household, well trained in the excellent home ways, familiar with the family habits ; and cousin Henry Burr, son of Joseph, brought her over to the Rancocas farm one day, and John Woolman had to be there in conjunction with Asher to look her over and legally settle the terms of her residence, all the more important for a free Negro. The arrangement turned out well, and Mrs Woolman mentions "negro Issabel" in her will, and also another "negro Maria"—"Thirty shillings to her sister Maria who lived with me, all in goods at the appraisment." Evidently in Mrs Woolman's later years a second maid was added for her day and night attendance.

"While our spirits are lively we go cheerfully through business," said Woolman. And his native cheerfulness had a good deal to feed upon in his private life. His wife and child were a perennial source of delight ; and as long as he could stay at home he enjoyed the things he did. He had achieved what he had clearly formulated to himself as an ideal pattern of living. He was one of those men "not rich" but who, "released from too close an application to business, are enabled to hire assistance, to provide well for their cattle, and to find time to perform those duties among their neighbours which belong to a well-guided social life."[2]

But his mind was sore with his recent experiences in New York and

---

[1] Appendix IV.
[2] Whittier ed., *A Plea for the Poor*, p. 276.

New England and the insidious ramifications of the slave system.   And the continuing war with the French and Indians—only delayed by weather, waiting to burst forth hideously like a devil's plant in the spring—was another branch of the same deadly root, human selfishness ; "the miseries of many of my fellow-creatures engaged therein ; some suddenly destroyed, some wounded and after much pain remaining cripples ; some deprived of all their outward substance and reduced to want ; and some carried into captivity."[1]   It preyed upon his heart— in those small hours of the morning, when life is at its lowest ebb ; in hours of solitude and reverie by day, at some mechanical task or sitting with his pen—the overwhelming darkness of the world.   And a bitter question gnawed at him—he to whom the unpleasant task had been assigned of remonstrating with his friends about their habits and methods, was he himself clear of blame ?   He, who was so ready to say to a great estate-holder that if he could not keep his estates together without slave labour then he ought to give up the estates—was there no equivalent sacrifice to sincerity demanded in his own life ?   Seeing how subtle the entanglements were, how one thing led on to another, had he not taken even a few steps which led in the wrong direction ?

In visiting people of note in the Society who had slaves, and labouring with them in brotherly love on that account, I have seen, and the sight has affected me, that a conformity to some customs distinguishable from pure wisdom has entangled many . . . and greatly opposed the work of truth.[2]

Were there no such customs that in a small and moderate way he was conforming to himself ?

This undercurrent of harsh self-examination, new to him since the time when he had closed the dark months of his adolescence, ran through the winter, and lowered his usual excellent health.   Since those youthful years when, though middling healthy, he was often weary, overstrained by the too heavy farm work for which he was not fitted, he had scarcely had a day's illness.   Gruelling travel in all weathers, sleeping in damp woods, being wet to the skin in exposed boats or beaten upon by the torrid summer sun, eating poorly cooked food at unusual hours, or again being too much and too richly fed in wealthy houses, exposure to infection at the beds of the sick or dying—including two smallpox epidemics—had not shaken his health more than to make him say once to his wife, in a

[1] Whittier ed., p. 160.   [2] Ibid., p. 159.

letter from New England, that he was not at the moment so hearty and healthy as he had been sometimes. But on May 31, 1761, he was taken ill of a fever, accompanied by deep depression and great physical misery. It sounds like a bad attack of influenza. Perhaps good Dr Ross further reduced him by bleeding ; certainly Josiah White must have hurried round with some nasty-tasting decoction of herbs. But they did not seem to help the body much, and they could not touch the mind, which lay wrapped up in its secret sorrow, its torturing circle of questions and self-blame. Blame, because it had occurred to Woolman that there was just one way, and only one, still open to him by which he could cut clear from the entanglements of customs which had their roots connected with slavery and war. The dyes used in cloth came from the West Indies slave plantations. He could give up the use of anything that had been dyed. Woolman had thought already of this drastic step ; and his basic common sense and his hatred of being conspicuous had united to wrestle with the inward strain that sought release in such a form.

Thinking often on these things the use of hats and garments dyed with a dye hurtful to them, and wearing more clothes in summer than are useful, grew more uneasy to me, believing them to be customs which have not their foundation in pure wisdom. The apprehension of being singular from my beloved friends was a strait upon me, and thus I continued in the use of some things contrary to my judgment.[1]

In his illness this struggle represented itself to him as a resistance to what was required of him. So he says :

I felt all the powers in me yield themselves up into the hands of Him who gave me being. . . . There was now no desire in me for health until the design of my correction was answered . . . and as I felt a sinking down into a calm resignation so I felt, as in an instant, an inward healing in my nature, and from that time forward I grew better.[2]

Every one has experienced the sudden peace which comes from the solution, in any direction, of a mental conflict which has been long and hard. Woolman was a resolute man, accustomed to carry out his decisions, and, having made up his mind on this awkward subject, he never looked back from it. As soon as the clothes he had in use wore out, he replaced them with others "the natural colour of the cloth."

---

[1] *Ibid.*, p. 161.   [2] *Ibid.*

It took about nine months to attain this end, and he was ready with a suit of the new kind at the time of the Spring General Meeting in Philadelphia in 1762 ; but even at that he had "several dyed garments fit for use" still, so that presumably the shock given to his friends was gradual, in keeping with his usual moderation.   The hat, curiously enough, was the worst trial ; and even Woolman delayed getting himself a hat of the natural colour of the fur until after he returned home from the Spring Meeting.   What made it worse was that white beaver hats had suddenly been adopted by dandies as the height of a new fashion, and when Woolman came out in one he was regarded by Mount Holly friends and Burlington friends as having suddenly turned "worldly."   When he added the undyed coat and knee-breeches and natural-coloured stockings, and even shoes of untanned leather, his appearance was—as he was all too well aware—"singular."

Woolman had ten years yet to live in the world, and for all that time he maintained this style of dress.   The result was that as far as visual impression was concerned, no one could see anything else.   To his own contemporaries he was the man who wore undyed clothes ; and in the vista of two hundred years that has been the first thing to catch the eye. Every private conversation of John Woolman's from then on, and every public utterance, had to work against and to have subtracted from it the preliminary handicap of his peculiar dress.   Those whom he influenced and impressed—and they were many—had to say "in spite of" before they acknowledged his power.

One of the attendant drawbacks of adopting a distinctive costume is that it is very hard to abandon it.   A big public defiance of convention has been made, and if the reasons for it were valid they must be shown to have ceased to exist ; otherwise the first step was a grave error.   If a kind of protest against slavery and war was intended, as Woolman at first obscurely felt, those causes were hardly likely to die before he did. And in the last year of his life there is an indication (I think) that the first reasons—which seemed valid—had ceased to hold water, and Woolman reassures himself with something very like a little rationalization, explaining that his motive was partly cleanliness.

> Having of late often travelled in wet weather through narrow streets in towns and villages where dirtiness under foot and the scent arising from the filth which more or less infects the air of all thickly settled towns was disagreeable . . . I have been where much cloth hath been

dyed,[1] and have at sundry times walked over ground where much of their dye-stuffs has drained away. This hath produced a longing in my mind that people might come into cleanness of spirit, cleanness of person, and cleanness about their houses and garments. Some of the great carry delicacy to a great height themselves, and yet real cleanliness is not generally promoted. Dyes being invented partly to please the eye and partly to hide dirt, I have felt . . . a strong desire that the nature of dyeing cloth to hide dirt may be more fully considered. Washing our garments to keep them sweet is cleanly, but it is opposite to cleanliness to hide dirt in them . . . hiding that which is not clean by colouring our garments seems contrary to the sweetness of sincerity. Through some sorts of dyes cloth is rendered less useful. And if the values of dye-stuffs and expense of dyeing and the damage done to cloth were all added together, and that cost applied to keeping all sweet and clean, how much more would cleanliness prevail.[2]

However, first reasons and last were written in his Journal, not to be published until after his death. Woolman did not make a crusade about undyed clothes. On the contrary, his pained and offended friends found that he regarded his dress as his own private affair, and he did not intend to discuss it. If they rebuked him for "affected singularity," or if they "grew shy of him," he let the matter alone ; "those who spoke with me in a friendly way I generally informed, in a few words, that I believed my wearing it was not in my own will." Here was a ready-made test of, and protection against, that "superficial friendship" to which Woolman was conscious that he had always been too prone. He was a bit tempted to try to explain himself to his most intimate friends, but the subject appeared difficult ; one can see that it would be hard not to make any reasons sound priggish ; it was in fact a sort of symbolic act, and only in terms of act could it register or find a base. So Woolman took what was after all the boldest course, that of a steady, good-humoured silence, "trusting that if I kept my place the Lord in his own good time would open the hearts of Friends towards me." And this sound policy had its reward.

Woolman's unfailing tact, however, caused him to restrain for the time of probation all his public activity. "I felt my way for a time shut up in the exercise of the ministry."[3] But the hours of deep, silent submission in the meetings were precious and satisfying.

[1] At Kendal, England. See Chapter XLII herein.
[2] Whittier ed., p. 243.
[3] *Ibid.*, p. 162.

Like all Woolman's actions, even this one, thought by some to be unreasonable and extremist, was strictly logical. Some ten years after his death John Hunt, of New Jersey (not the London Hunt), reports :

> Slavery now begins to be generally abhorred. Even the public newspapers manifest a dislike to the practice. A query in one of them says, 'and why is this cruelty practised ?—Why, that we may have sugar to sweeten our tea, that debilitates us, and rum to put in our punch, which intoxicates us, and indigo to dye our clothes. In short, great part of the human species are dragged into slavery to supply the luxuries of the rest.' [1]

During the winter of '61, before his illness—the winter of Jane Crosfield's visit—John Woolman was finishing his long essay, Part II of *Considerations on Keeping Negroes*. In November he took it up to Philadelphia to submit it and discuss it with one or two friends before submitting it to the Overseers of the Press. John Churchman had already had it to read, taking it home with him after a visit to Mount Holly. There is some evidence that Churchman was a little jealous of Woolman. His way of telling things in his journal sometimes seems to steal John Woolman's thunder. Woolman on the contrary admired Churchman, and gave great weight to his opinion. The reception by Churchman of Woolman's essay was cold. But Woolman's feelings were not noticeably hurt. He tried to improve his product and took it next to Israel Pemberton. There was smallpox in Israel's house, so Woolman left the essay with a note :

17da. 11 mo. 1761

BELOVED FRIEND

The piece J. Churchman took home he perus'd but being taken poorly made no remark in writing on it. My brother Asher being at their last Monthly Meeting, and I writeing to J. C. about it, he sent it, and George, I expect by his agreement [George was John Churchman's brother] sent a letter to me refering it to me carefully to review and transcribe it. Since which I have spent some time therein, and am now come to Town in order that if way should open for Friends to meet again upon it, I may be near in Case they should want to speak with me. I am a little Cautious of being much at thy House on acct. of the Small pox, but would gladly meet thee at Such house as thou thinks Sutable, to have a little Conversation with thee.

---

[1] *Friends' Miscellany*, IV (1787), 276.

I have not yet offered it to any of the Committee. I lodge at Reuben Haines', and am mostly there.

I remain thy loveing fr'd

JOHN WOOLMAN

Endorsed, "For Israel Pemberton when he comes home."

The careful Pemberton filed it away, again endorsed, "From John Woolman, about his treatise. I.P."

It is evident in all their relationships that Israel Pemberton's respect for Woolman was very deep. He perused the document with care, went to Reuben Haines's house and discussed it with Woolman, made some suggestions, and left it with Woolman to take to the Committee of the Overseers of the Press. Woolman was himself a member of that committee. The Overseers handed it to Anthony Benezet to look over, with a message to Israel Pemberton—probably giving those two Friends the responsibility of final revision and preparation for the press. Pemberton's call on Woolman and the meeting of the committee took place on the same day—perhaps for Woolman's convenience, since he was in town on purpose, and there was smallpox about. Thanks to Pemberton's care in keeping letters, we have Woolman's note to him, written "Same Evening, after we met."

BELOVED FRIEND ; As I expect to go out of Town (if well) in the Morning, and it's likely may not Se thee, I thought it best to Acquaint thee That I remain Well satisfied with what thou propos'd relating to the preface, and though I have look'd over the piece with Some care and done according to the best of my understanding, I have all along been apprehensive that if it be made publick There was a further labour for some other person necessary, and if thou can feel liberty from thy other concerns and freedom to Spend some time in a deliberate reviewing and correcting of it, and make such alterations or additions as thou believes may be usefull, the prospect of it is agreeable to me.

In true brotherly love I

remain thy fr'd

JOHN WOOLMAN

The Committee gave it to Anthony, with a message to thee. J. W.

Israel Pemberton endorsed it "From John Woolman, a^{bt} his Treatise, 1761."

This correspondence gives a picture of the attitude of John Woolman's friends towards his authorship. They recognized that he had a gift for writing, and year after year they appointed him to write epistles for the Yearly Meeting. Many of them, among whom were the Pemberton brothers, were very much struck by the quality of the things he said. He was never trite, never commonplace ; he was extraordinarily uplifting. They felt he would really be an unusually good writer—equal to Benezet or Churchman—if he would only pay more attention to his style. His sentences did not "roll" right. And his carelessness—and he a schoolmaster—was beyond belief. He would split an infinitive on occasion ; he would even end a sentence with a preposition. Well, it was difficult to say exactly what was wrong, but it was different from the writing of other people who were of recognized excellence. They laboured with him, and he took it with the utmost good humour and humility. He took his things home to revise, went over them phrase by phrase with utmost care and with the best intentions. But alas ! his idiosyncrasy was too strong for him. He could not write their way. All he could do was to offer to allow some friend he trusted to edit and revise at pleasure. Israel Pemberton was probably the most modest at this task. He was no author, he did not know about your niceties, but he could recognize a good thing well said.

When in years to come John Woolman's Journal was published the first edition of it, which remained for a long time the standard text, was very heavily edited, chiefly by Anthony Benezet. Yet Benezet loved Woolman. Speaking one day of friendship, he said, "A little sincere friendship is indeed all that this world can afford that is truly great and worth regard," yet he comments sadly on the touchiness of even "the best of those who profess friendship—except one or two who are in some degree of John Woolman's spirit."

The Publication Committee were ready to accept Woolman's essay on *Considerations on Keeping Negroes;* but at the last Woolman had another thought. If it was printed by the committee it would cost him nothing, and it would be given away free among Friends ; but some who subscribed liberally to the Yearly Meeting stock out of which this was paid for were slave-holders. Woolman decided that he would prefer to pay for its publication himself, and sell it at a small price. It would then be clear of taint, and probably attract more attention, since "they who make a purchase generally buy what they have a mind for." So he finally took it to Benjamin Franklin, and it was published in the spring of 1762 by Franklin and Hall. Hundreds of people were thus reached by Woolman's thoughts in the more permanent medium of print during the months when his adoption of undyed clothing had closed his mouth for a while.

XXXI

INDIAN JOURNEY (I)

THE winter truce of the year 1762-3 had not worn to an end when the welcome news arrived that those authorities in far-distant Europe upon whose erratic will the making of peace in America depended had decided to stop the Seven Years War. England and Prussia had 'won,' France and Austria had 'lost.' The Treaty of Paris in February wound it all up, laying a sound foundation for future wars, and carrying in addition the seeds of two revolutions. For though the pattern of Europe looked very much as before—Frederick of Prussia still keeping the rich stolen province of Silesia—France had lost her navy, had lost her grip on India and on America, and was financially near ruin, with a social order rotten to the core. "It will last my time," said Louis XV, in words that became a proverb for the cynicism of selfishness. "After me the deluge." As for the King of Prussia, his fortunes were on the rise. He had proved himself a brilliant general. He was admired by such different men as George Washington and the Reverend Mr Whitefield, who both saw him through a haze as the champion of Protestantism against the wicked Catholics. And, himself an able writer, he made his private cold and accurate comment on the war which he had won, in a strain which would have made a text for John Woolman. Frederick wrote :

> Prussia's population had diminished by 500,000 during the Seven Years War. On a population of 4,500,000 that decrease was con-siderable. The nobility and the peasants had been pillaged and ran-

somed by so many armies that they had nothing left except the miserable rags which covered their nudity. They had not credit enough to satisfy their daily needs. The towns possessed no longer a police. The spirit of fairness and order had been replaced by anarchy and self-interest. The nobility and the merchants, the farmers, the working-men and the manufacturers had raised the price of their labour and their products to the utmost. All seemed intent upon ruining each other by their exactions. That was the terrible spectacle which the formerly so flourishing provinces offered after the conclusion of the war.

Frederick looked upon suffering with indifference. His father long ago had killed his heart. But his arid mind endured a frightful ennui. In his secret journal he wrote, "Meanwhile life is passing, and when all things are weighed and considered, what has it been but care, trouble, sorrow, and tribulation ? Was it worth the trouble to be born ?" He composed in his spare moments an Apology for Suicide, and carried poison always about with him.

But these two sad men, the Kings of France and Prussia, who—not altogether through their own fault—were so far divided from "the true felicity of man in this life"[1] and so gifted in destroying the felicity of others, were unknown to the Indians of North America both in their peace and in their war. The Indians, stirred up, were not so easily allayed. They had taken sides with the French or with the English for their own simple purposes. And the Treaty of Paris had nothing in it about the Indians' land. So the war in America did not stop quite on time, though there was a hiatus while the Indians paused to see what they were going to get out of it. They then started again on their own, united under their genius Pontiac, with redoubled fury against the victor English. Against the English because they remained in possession of disputed territory, while the French withdrew.

Ever since the start of the wars the Quaker-dominated Assemblies of New Jersey and Pennsylvania had never ceased to take account of the Indians' point of view, and to try to continue to treat with them in the old tradition of William Penn, regardless of French and English strife or European complications. They had tried to isolate, as it were, the Indian part of the war and to deal with it separately, at least as it related to "their own Indians," the Delawares, and the grievances of the Delawares within the limits of the Quaker provinces. The Indians

[1] Woolman.

would always come to meet the Quakers, and conferences were held at Burlington, at Crosswicks, at Easton, and even in Philadelphia between Quakers and Indians throughout the seven years of the war, with constant and honest effort to make at least that much peace.   The Governor of Pennsylvania might be vexed at non-official intervention and call it meddling, but there is no question that it did good, that it had effects ; temporary local treaties were arranged and were better than none. They saved a very large proportion of the settlers from the worst effects of Indian guerrilla war.   The Conference at Burlington was called immediately after those murders in New Jersey which occurred in 1758 "at two o'clock in the afternoon" ; and there were no more attacks in New Jersey.   Governor Bernard of New Jersey took a prominent part in the Easton Conference, with his entire Council, and the results kept New Jersey quiet within her borders until the final general peace.   It was a consolation to the Delawares to feel that they were being seriously and courteously listened to, and at the Easton Conference they stated their case fully, both their difficulty in loyalty when the French came to the Ohio region to which the Delawares had retreated, and also their troubles about tracts of land taken from them which they were not aware they had sold :

> the English settling so fast they were pushed back and could not tell what lands belonged to them . . . but we trust to you, the Governor of New Jersey, to take our cause in hand and see that we have justice done us. . . . You deal hardly with us ; you claim all the wild creatures and will not let us come on your land to hunt them.   The cattle you raise are your own, but those which are wild are still ours, or should be common to both.[1]

The temporary solution arrived at was to form a New Jersey Association for Helping the Indians, of which Woolman was one of the founders and charter subscribers.   And the first action of the new society was to arrange for the immediate settlement of some of the dispossessed Indians in New Jersey.   "A tract of upwards of 300 acres was purchased, in Burlington county, in which is a cedar-swamp and a sawmill, adjoining many thousand acres of poor uninhabited land suitable for hunting, and convenient also for fishing the sea-coast."[2]   The Commissioners named it Brotherton, and deeded it in trust to the Indian natives for ever.   This

---

[1] *History of New Jersey* by Samuel Smith, pp. 469–470.
[2] *Ibid.*, p. 483.

was the first Indian reservation in America. John Brainerd was presently appointed to take charge of it by the Governor, and the local situation was thus dealt with. The confidence of the Indians was regained, and what fighting any New Jersey men had to do was done far afield from their own homes. A multiplication of such arrangements, and where would have been the war ? This was an instance of that active democratic initiative which Thomas Penn (joint Proprietor of Pennsylvania with his brother John) so disliked in the Quakers, as he wrote to Governor Hamilton in 1760, "their levelling republican system of government so much adopted by them."

One of the Indian conferences in Philadelphia was held at the house of Anthony Benezet. Woolman was present and took notes—yielded for publication after his death by his wife, who wrote at the bottom of the page, "This writing is my dear Husband's own hand if friends think them worth a printing I am willing if not I Desire Content." And below that a little afterthought by itself, in her delicate, pretty handwriting modelled as closely as she could on John's, "its Impared but I think a good Scholer May read it I would hold nothing Back that will be useful."

As he added the impressions of this conference to memories of his boyhood a desire to express human brotherhood by visiting the Indians where they lived began to take hold of Woolman's heart. As he explains it :

Having for many years felt love in my heart towards the natives of this land who dwell far back in the wilderness, whose ancestors were formerly the owners and possessors of the land where we dwell, and who for a small consideration assigned their inheritance to us, and being at Philadelphia in 8th month 1761 on a visit to some Friends who had slaves, I fell in company with some of those natives who lived on the east branch of the river Susquehanna at an Indian town called Wehaloosing, two hundred miles from Philadelphia. In conversation with them by an interpreter, as also by observations on their countenances and conduct, I believed some of them were measurably acquainted with that Divine power which subjects the rough and froward will. . . . Love was the first motion and thence a concern arose to spend some time with the Indians that I might feel and understand their life and the spirit they live in, if haply I might receive some instruction from them, or they might be in any degree helped forward by my following the leadings of truth among them.

While this project ripened in his mind he mentioned it to no one "except my dear wife." But in the winter of 1762 he had come to a decision to make this dangerous venture without further delay, and obtained a certificate from his Monthly Meeting and had it endorsed, for added weight, by the Quarterly Meeting, and also by the Spring General Meeting in March (the one at which he wore his old black hat for the last time). He now had to find a trustworthy Indian guide. In May one of his friends—probably Israel Pemberton—sent him word by letter that a man and three women of the Delawares who came from a little beyond Wehaloosing were in Philadelphia on business. Woolman rode up to town and met them, liked and trusted them—as did his friends—and made arrangements to hire the man as his guide and accompany the party when they were ready to go back. They agreed to meet on June seventh "at Samuel Foulk's at Richland[1] in Bucks County," Pennsylvania.

Sarah had, as usual, made no opposition, but as she got his things ready, repeating to herself his reasons for going in convincing words learned verbatim from him, her distress was evident. Tears fell upon the change of linen, upon the long stockings she had knitted that winter, according to his wish, in undyed yarn. No one could deny that it was a time "when travelling appeared perilous," and Woolman confessed that for him too "the thoughts of the journey were often attended with unusual sadness." About a week before he expected to set out he went to a meeting for young men at Chesterfield—the Youths' Meeting, which he and John Smith and Peter Andrews and others had attended when they were young, where they had heard Samuel Fothergill's father speak with his loud voice. Woolman now spoke to the young men, all of whom, looking forward to their future, were making up their minds about the part they should take, if any, in government and in public affairs generally. He chose the vigorous subject, "I pray not that thou shouldst take them out of the world, but that thou shouldst keep them from the evil." And he pointed out that being kept from evil did not necessarily mean being kept safe. The apostles and martyrs had not escaped cruel death. But "it appears that whatsoever befals men while they live in pure obedience to God certainly works for their good, and may not be considered an evil as it relates to them." On the Sunday he and his wife and daughter went as usual to the Mount Holly

<hr>

[1] Now called Quakertown.

Meeting, and afterwards "in true love and tenderness I parted from Friends, expecting the next morning to proceed on my journey." He was tired, and there must be an early start in the morning, so the family went to bed early, and with the sweet June air blowing in upon their fatigue they were soon asleep.

"After I had been asleep a short time," says John Woolman, "I was awoke by a man calling at my door and inviting me to meet some friends at a public house in our town, who came from Philadelphia so late that Friends generally were gone to bed." Perhaps the man was Daniel Jones, brother of Woolman's young friend Rebecca, inviting him to the Three Tuns Tavern. Woolman dressed hastily, with a soothing word to his wife, who thought the message was only from somebody come to say a late farewell ; and walked rapidly down the leafy moonlit street. The only sounds beside his own footfalls were the mew of a swooping owl and the cool splash and chuckle of the millrace. The sleeping houses spoke of security and peace, with casual windows open to the night. Who were the friends who had ridden out so late to catch him at the eleventh hour before he went ? Their saddled horses at the hitching-post beside the inn brought hint of danger somewhere on the road ahead. Why go to meet it ? Was not his first duty here to his family and home ? Was there not plenty of work to do where he was without going into outlandish places ?

In a thoughtful and questioning frame of mind, not obstinate, holding himself ready to change his plans if need be, he went into the tavern. The room looked strange at that time of night, dim and tidy and empty. His friends—now seen to be the Pemberton brothers, Israel and John— sat at a table by a window, with two candles that made a little island of light in the surrounding shadows. They rose to greet him with affectionate handclasps. The innkeeper served them with cold beer and cider, and left them to their business.

These Friends informed me that an express had arrived the last morning from Pittsburg and brought news that the Indians had taken a fort from the English westward and had slain and scalped some English people near the said Pittsburg and in divers places. Some elderly Friends in Philadelphia, knowing the time of my intending to set off, had conferred together, and thought it good to inform me of these things before I left home that I might consider them and proceed as I believed best.[1]

[1] Whittier ed., pp. 164–185, for account of the Indian journey.

The conference did not take very long.   Woolman absorbed all possible
facts, thanked his friends warmly, and returned home with a mind in
doubt.   Sarah had fallen asleep, and he was studious not to wake her.
But he himself lay long awake seeking for the inward orders that would
clear his mind of indecision.   His chief anxiety was that he might not
cling to his plans out of a spirit of bravado.   Like every brave man, he
shrank from making any parade of courage.

"Going to bed again," he says,

> I told not my wife till morning.   My heart was turned to the Lord
> for his heavenly instruction. . . .   When I told my dear wife she
> appeared to be deeply concerned about it ; but in a few hours time
> my mind became settled in a belief that it was my duty to proceed
> on my journey, and she bore it with a good degree of resignation.
> In this conflict of spirit there were great searchings of heart . . . that
> no motion might in the least degree be attended to but that of the
> pure spirit of truth.   The subjects before mentioned on which I had
> so lately spoken in public were now fresh before me.

He reminded himself of them, and comforted Sarah with them—poor
comfort they gave her human heart, but she resigned herself to John's
conviction—took final leave of his family and friends, picked up the
Pembertons at the inn, and rode to Burlington, where there was Monthly
Meeting that day.   After taking leave of friends there—the bereaved
John Smith and others—he crossed the river by the Burlington ferry
"accompanied by my friends Israel and John Pemberton" and spent the
night at Israel Pemberton's house in Philadelphia.   "Parting the next
morning with Israel, John bore me company to Samuel Foulk's, where I
met the before-mentioned Indians ; and we were glad to see each other."

Samuel Foulke was a Quaker prominent in politics, two years younger
than Woolman.   At a time when political action on the part of Friends
was becoming unorthodox he stood for election to the Pennsylvania
Assembly, was elected in 1761, and retained his seat there for seven years.
He then resigned it to his brother John, who held it until the Revolution.
Samuel Foulke was a vigorous defender of the charter, of liberty of conscience and government, and steadily resisted the encroachments both of
the Proprietors and of the home officials.   When the majority of Quakers
withdrew from the Assembly in '57 and refused to stand for re-election
they were inclined to regard as "wrong" those who remained.   But
Samuel Foulke succeeded in making the best of both worlds, and showed

his good standing with Friends by the fact that while in the Assembly he was simultaneously serving—as he did for thirty-eight years—as Clerk of the Richland Monthly Meeting.

His promotion of Woolman's Indian visit was more than personal friendship. He evidently regarded it as an excellent idea, and the kind of thing that might have far-reaching good effects.

In the evening of happy sociability at Samuel Foulke's house a heart-warming surprise awaited John Woolman, which was almost enough in itself to confirm him in feeling that he had done the right thing. Among those present were two of his attractive friends, William Light-foot—the same who had brought him news of Sarah when he was at Newport—and Benjamin Parvin, both men in their middle thirties, young enough to be adventurous and old enough to be good company. These two had not come, like some others, to bid Woolman farewell, but to offer to go with him all the way. Woolman, deeply touched and pleased, none the less felt it his duty to try to reason them out of it. He dreaded the responsibility of taking them into danger—if there should be danger—and he urged that it was not worth the risk, unless they had some better motive for going than just to be with him ! These argu-ments were successful with Lightfoot, and he decided he would only come part way ; but not so with his cousin Benjamin. Every reason advanced seemed to Benjamin an argument for going with Woolman instead of the reverse. And indeed he had written before to suggest it, though John Woolman even then had demurred at accepting it.

"Here [at Foulke's]," says Woolman,

my friend Benjamin Parvin met me and proposed joining me as a companion—we had before exchanged some letters on the subject—and now I had a sharp trial on his account ; for as the journey appeared perilous, I thought if he went chiefly to bear me company and we should be taken captive, my having been the means of drawing him into these difficulties would add to my own afflictions ; so I told him my mind freely and let him know I was resigned to go alone. But after all if he really believed it to be his duty to go on, I believed his company would be very comfortable to me. . . . Benjamin appeared to be so fastened to the visit that he could not be easy to leave me ; so we went on, accompanied by our friends John Pemberton and William Lightfoot, of Pikeland.

They lodged at Bethlehem the first night, scene of a terrible Indian raid a few years before ; and from there in the morning John Pemberton reluctantly went back, having clung to his friend far longer than either of them had expected, business and public duties awaiting him at home. He carried back with him a letter to Woolman's wife.

8da: 6mo: 1763 about Sunset

I am now at Bethlehem, a Moravian Town, and midling well, in company with John Pemberton, Wm Lightfoot and Benjamin Parvin. Iohn expects to go home in the morning (it being very near night). William and Benjamin Expect to go forward to fort Allen on the Frontier. Then William Expects to turn home. And as to Benjamin —His mind at present seems so Engaged that he Shews no Inclination to leave me. I have had Some weighty Conversation with Him and let him know that I am quite free to go alone if his way does not appear clear to Him. My Indian Companions appear friendly and shew I think quite as much regard for me as they did at our first meeting at Philada. There is nothing to me appears aniways discouraging more than what Thou knew of when I was with thee. I am humbly Thankfull to the Lord that my mind is so supported in a Trust in Him that I go cheerfully on my Journey and at present Apprehend that I have nothing in any way to fear but a Spirit of Disobedience, which I Trust through Divine Help I may be delivered from.

That Pure Light which Enlightens every man coming into the World to me appears as Lovely as Ever, To the guidance of which I hope thou and I may Attend while we live in this world, and then all will be well.

With Endeared love to thee and my Daughter & my Dear friends and Neighbours I conclude thy most Affectionate

HUSBAND JOHN WOOLMAN

In the margin he added, "My Companions Express a Sympathising Love to thee." Endorsed, "For Sarah Woolman."

From Bethlehem : "William and we went forward on the ninth of the sixth month and got lodging on the floor of a house about five miles from Fort Allen. Here we parted with William."

William Lightfoot, riding home just on the edge of the adventure, felt very much like the sister-in-law of Ruth who turned back in the famous story. He was quite right to do it, he was very sensible—John Woolman himself had said so, and had urged and approved his going ; but there was a little element of playing safe about it which made him feel on the defensive. He did not go to see Sarah Woolman when he got home, but he wrote her a letter, and here it is :

PIKELAND *6th moth. 13, 1763*

ESTEEMED FRIEND,

　　SARAH WOOLMAN

　　I may hereby Inform thee that I met thy Husband at Samuel Foulk's last 3rd day Evening, and in Discourse Concerning the Journey he exprest a Close Exercise which the News of the Troubles to the Westward had brought upon him. Signifying that in Case the Journey should be attended with Danger from an Enemy, he thought he could be much easier to go alone than to be Instrumental in bringing any into danger, who had no weightier motive to undertake it than to Accompany him, and as I never had resolved on going, it seem'd most easy for me to Decline it. Tho' not much on the account of Danger, having heard these reports some Time before without any great apprehensions of that, and am in Hopes that thy Husband & Benj. Parvin (who is gone with him) may Return safe again. I went with them about 20 Miles beyond Bethlehem and when I parted with them (which was last 6th day Morning) they seemed well and Cheerful.

　　And tho' the journey may [illegible] . . . Occurence, which perhaps may be a Close Exercise to thee on thy Husband's account, yet I hope thou may be Enabled to bear with Patience and Resignation the Dispensations that Providence may Permit thee to pass through.

　　I conclude thy Sympathizing Friend,

WILLIAM LIGHTFOOT, JUR.

P.S. B. Parvin not having time to write thee, desired me to Remember his Love to Thee.[1]

Benjamin Parvin was a grandson, on his mother's side, of that Michael Lightfoot, Treasurer of the Province of Pennsylvania, who had advised John Smith, in the throes of a hesitant courtship, to go in and win his adored lady. He had done it with great delicacy and without mentioning any names, but the encouragement had been unmistakable and very precious to John Smith. There was a connexion by marriage between the Smith and the Lightfoot families, Michael's son Thomas having married Mary Smith, the granddaughter of Daniel Smith, of Burlington, and of Mary Murfin Smith, his wife. In the complicated system of "Quaker cousins," Smiths, Lightfoots, Parvins, and Pembertons all mingled together in intimate family groups.

Benjamin Parvin and William Lightfoot were first cousins, but it was Benjamin who was a man after Woolman's own heart. And though John Woolman may have felt that the motive was inadequate, it is to

---

[1] Originals of both these letters are in care of the Pennsylvania Historical Society.

others an endearing trait that Benjamin undertook that journey for no
better motive than love of his friend. He had no special call himself
to visit the Indians, he would leave that to John ; but he had a call, a
very distinct one, not to let his friend go alone into danger. Like John
Woolman he was a man who knew his own mind, and smilingly set
aside John's scruples, "so fastened to the visit that he could not be easy
to leave me." A man of thirty-six and a man of forty-three are equals
in age. And in that unconscious phrase "William and we" it may be
discerned that, though it was nice of William to come so far, he would
not be much missed, and it is more than possible that he knew it. The
other two were so obviously, uncontrollably *en rapport ;* "comfortable"
together. The last he saw of them, as he turned to look back at them—
with a dash of sulkiness—riding down to the water's edge to cross to the
Indians' country, they were in high spirits, "well and Cheerful."

But the night before in the public house, which was so crowded that
Woolman and his companions could only get lodging on the floor, they
had made their first contact with the Indians, and Woolman's easy way
of entering into conversation with chance-met strangers bore considerable fruit.

> At this place we met with an Indian trader lately come from Wyo-
> ming. In conversation with him I perceived that many white people
> often sell rum to the Indians which I believe is a great evil. In the first
> place they are thereby deprived of the use of reason, and their spirits being
> violently agitated, quarrels often arise which end in mischief, and the
> bitterness and resentment occasioned hereby are frequently of long
> continuance. Again their skins and furs, gotten through much
> fatigue and hard travels in hunting, with which they intend to buy
> clothing, they often sell at a low rate for more rum when they become
> intoxicated ; and afterwards, when they suffer for want of the neces-
> saries of life, are angry with those who for the sake of gain took
> advantage of their weakness. The chiefs have often complained of
> this in their treaties with the English.

In thinking over this conversation, familiar in detail but impressive as
first-hand experience, Woolman compared this kind of cheating with the
making of counterfeit paper money, then so prevalent that it had been
made into a capital offence in New Jersey. "Where cunning people
pass counterfeits and impose on others that which is good for nothing
it is considered as wickedness ; but for the sake of gain to sell that

which we know does people harm and which often works their ruin, manifests a hardened and corrupt heart. . . ."

But what made their hearts so hard and corrupt? Was it not the unendurable misery of poverty, and the sight of others in luxury? Here was another flower of evil from that same old root. "While my mind this evening was thus employed," says Woolman,

> I also remembered that the people on the frontiers, among whom this evil is too common, are often poor, and that they venture to the outside of a colony in order to live more independently of the wealthy, who often set high rents on their land. I was renewedly confirmed in a belief that if all our inhabitants lived according to sound wisdom, labouring to promote universal love and righteousness, and ceased from every inordinate desire after wealth and from all customs which are tinctured with luxury, the way would be easy for our inhabitants, though they might be much more numerous than at present, to live comfortably on honest employments without the temptation they are so often under of being drawn into schemes to make settlements on lands which have not been purchased of the Indians, or of applying to that wicked practice of selling rum to them.

No war or treaty could get down as far as that. There was no short cut to such a solution. But though for the human race the way to it might seem almost as long as Time, the way to it for the individual was short. Woolman had himself traversed it ; and he kept himself happy and hopeful by dealing with the individual. Far away in France a man named Rousseau had a similar point of view. Woolman himself might have written the key sentence of the famous *Contrat Social*, published the year before in Paris, "The good state is one in which every member agrees to act for the common good, to do as he would be done by."

In the inner content created by the consciousness of acting according to that precept the two friends, having said good-bye to William, set off with their three Indian guides in the misty early freshness of the morning, both being of the temperament which accepted to the full the good of the passing hour, and did not allow the "still, sad music of humanity" to quench the joy of sunrise, the pearly reflections in the river, the singing birds, the dew.

> *Tenth of sixth month.* We set out early this morning and crossed the western branch of Delaware called the Great Lehie, near Fort Allen. The water being high, we went over in a canoe (swimming the horses). Here we met an Indian, had friendly conversation with

him and gave him some biscuit ; and he, having killed a deer, gave some of it to the Indians with us.   After travelling some miles we met several Indian men and women with a cow and horse and some household goods who were lately come from their dwelling at Wyoming and were going to settle at another place.   We made them some small presents, and as some of them understood English, I told them my motive for coming into their country, with which they appeared satisfied.   One of our guides, talking awhile with an ancient woman concerning us, the poor old woman came to my companion and me and took her leave of us with an appearance of sincere affection.   We pitched our tents near the banks of the same river, having laboured hard in crossing some of those mountains called the Blue Ridge.   The roughness of the stones and the cavities between them, with the steepness of the hills, made it appear dangerous. . . .

A heavy rain added the last touch to their perils and discomforts.

However, after the better part of a day of this hard, rough, and dangerous travel Woolman was not in the least exhausted.   Their tents were pitched on an Indian site, and he tells :

Near our tent, on the sides of large trees peeled for that purpose were various representations of men going to and returning from the wars, and of some being killed in battle.   This was a path heretofore used by warriors, and as I walked about viewing those Indian histories, which were painted mostly in red or black, and thinking on the innumerable afflictions which the proud fierce spirit produceth in the world, also on the fatigues of warriors in travelling over mountains and deserts ;   on their miseries and distresses when far from home and wounded by their enemies ;   of their bruises and great weariness in chasing each other over the rocks and mountains ;   of the restless, unquiet state of mind of those who live in this spirit, and of the hatred which mutually grows up in the minds of their children,—the desire to cherish the spirit of love and peace among these people arose very fresh in me.

This was the first night that we lodged in the woods, and being wet with travelling in the rain, as were also our blankets, the ground, our tents, and the bushes under which we purposed to lay, all looked very discouraging. . . .

But he and Benjamin had camped out from their boyhood, and knew better how to be comfortable than the Indians.   "We kindled a fire, with our tent open to it, then laid some bushes next the ground and put our blankets upon them for our bed, and lying down, got some sleep." In the morning Woolman felt a little unwell, it is true, but the river flowed inviting, and he decided not to forgo his morning dip. "I went into the river ; the water was cold, and soon after I felt fresh and well."

When John Bartram, the Quaker botanist, came this way twenty years before with Conrad Weiser and some Indian guides he spoke of it as "the terrible Lycoming wilderness." The Lehigh Valley railway now bears cushioned travellers on shining rails of steel along the ancient Indian trail.

About eight o'clock we set forward and crossed a high mountain supposed to be upward of four miles over, the north side being the steepest. About noon we were overtaken by one of the Moravian brethren going to Wehaloosing[1] and an Indian man with him who could talk English ; and we being together while our horses ate grass had some friendly conversation ; but they travelling faster than we, soon left us. This Moravian, I understood, had this spring spent some time at Wehaloosing, and was invited by some of the Indians to come again.

Bethlehem, the last town of civilization that way, was itself a Moravian settlement, and the Moravians, an active missionary church, had had many missions among surrounding Indians. Wyalusing was rather far, but they had it on their list of visiting missionaries, and the chief was said to be a convert. The haste of this present missionary, Pastor Zeisberger, with his Indian companion, Anthony, was owing to a fear—aroused when it got about in Bethlehem that some Quakers were going up to Wyalusing—that the tribe might turn Quaker instead of Moravian. Woolman's keen perceptions gathered this without difficulty from what the good Zeisberger had supposed to be his guarded conversation by the way, and he took care to give the Moravian plenty of start. Not at this time nor at any other was he out to make converts for the Quaker sect. The next day being pouring wet again, and a Sunday to boot, he gave orders, as leader of the party, that they take a quiet day of rest from travel. "We continued in our tent," and Woolman took the opportunity to examine himself afresh as to his reason for coming, expressing his chief purpose in words that must surely be unique in the annals of civilized Christian approaching pagan savage, to wit, "that I might feel and understand their life and the spirit they live in, *if haply I might receive some instruction from them.*"

The delay was even greater than Woolman had anticipated, though

---

[1] Wyalusing.

no harm in that. "Our guide's horse strayed, though hoppled, in the night, and after searching some time for him his footsteps were discovered in the path going back, whereupon my kind companion went off in the rain" for it was still raining on Monday "and after about seven hours returned with him." They went on their way as long as it was light, however, and then "here we lodged again, tying up our horses before we went to bed, and loosing them to feed about break of day.

Thirteenth of sixth month. The sun appearing we set forward, and as I rode over the barren hills my meditations were to the alterations in the circumstances of the natives of this land since the coming of the English. The lands near the sea are conveniently situated for fishing ; the lands near the rivers, where the tides flow, and some above, are in many places fertile, and not mountainous, while the changing of the tides makes passing up and down easy with any kind of traffic. The natives have in some places, for trifling considerations, sold their inheritance so favourably situated, and in other places have been driven back by superior force ; their way of clothing themselves is also altered from what it was, and they being far removed from us have to pass over mountains, swamps and barren deserts, so that travelling is very troublesome in bringing their skins and furs to trade with us. By the extension of English settlements, and partly by the increase of English hunters, the wild beasts on which the natives chiefly depend for subsistence are not so plentiful as they were, and people too often for the sake of gain induce them to waste their skins and furs in purchasing a liquor which tends to the ruin of them and their families. . . . I had a prospect of the English along the coast for upwards of nine hundred miles where I travelled, and their favorable situation and the difficulties attending the natives as well as the negroes in many places were open before me. . . . Here I was led into a close and laborious enquiry whether I, as an individual, kept clear from all things which tended to stir up or were connected with wars, either in this land or in Africa. . . . In this lonely journey I did greatly bewail the spreading of a wrong spirit. . . . And here luxury and covetousness with the numerous oppressions and other evils attending them, appeared very afflicting to me, and I felt in that which is immutable that the seeds of great calamity and desolation are sown and growing fast on this continent. Nor have I words sufficient to set forth the longing I then felt that we might . . . labour to check the growth of these seeds that they may not ripen to the ruin of our posterity.

These meditations, with their dark prophetic climax, as the five travellers rode single file on the Indian trail, were recorded, at any rate in the rough, during the rest periods and evening halt, in the notebook which Woolman always carried. They are interesting in themselves, and also interesting as an evidence of the serenity of mind, the complete detachment from present danger, which Woolman and his friend maintained over the lonely barren hills and the dense forest. The terror of Indian warfare lay in its silence, its swiftness, its secrecy, its caprice. Already, without warning, men going to the sawmill with their team had been found next day by searchers, dead in the forest beside their dead oxen. Many times the solitary house in the clearing, peaceful and somnolent, had never heard the padding moccasined feet, nor seen the well-camouflaged approach, until noontide silence or midnight quiet was rent by the ear-splitting screech of the high-pitched Indian yell. And of those prisoners who saw the dawn, one might be slowly killed at the stake with torments too horrible to name, while another might be made blood brother of his capturing brave. As the two white men, Englishmen, rode into the wilderness with one Indian man and two women, any hilltop might contain a watching spy, evil with many cheatings on his furs ; any forest thicket might conceal a murderer out for scalps and eager for revenge upon the English. Woolman, knowing all this and specifically warned into the bargain, was absorbed in an almost academic discussion as to the relations, past and present, of the red man, the white, and the black, and a dark foreboding of calamity—not personal, but continental. However, personal danger was presently to make itself unmistakably felt.

XXXII

INDIAN JOURNEY (II)

ON the evening of that sunny day, the thirteenth of June, they arrived at the Indian settlement at Wyoming,[1] and their arrival evidently produced consternation. The Indian guide, with his two women, riding in first, had some close conversation with some of the villagers in the Indian tongue, and there was no gesture of welcome towards the strangers. On the contrary, the Indians disappeared, and the guides, beckoning them into "the house of a very ancient man," passed on disturbing news. "An Indian runner had been at that place a day or two before us, and brought news of the Indians having taken an English fort westward and destroyed the people and that they were endeavouring to take another" ; worse, the very night before another Indian runner had come in the middle of the night from a town about ten miles from Wyalusing, and roused up the village with the news that some Indian warriors from distant parts had come to that town with two English scalps and told the people that it was war with the English. So did the great Pontiac, the first Indian chief to make effective combination of all the tribes against the white men, have his messengers running through all the forests and villages along the whole of the western frontier ; and so did the news spread out fanwise from centre to centre, as the local messengers carried it instantly to their scattered neighbours. And no one knew how widespread it was, or thought of it as more than local trouble.

Here it was at Wyoming—the first preliminary call—just as Woolman

[1] Then on the vaguely defined frontier of Pennsylvania, the "back parts."

arrived. "War with the English" was the slogan ; and here were two of the English—a suggestive coincidence. The wrinkled ancient host, the guides, and the white men sat thinking this over, when through the open door Woolman saw an Indian coming towards the hut. The panther-like tread of an Indian brave at twilight is not reassuring ; and this man's actions were suspicious. Instead of coming frankly in to see the strangers, he paused outside the door in the shadow, alert, furtive, watchful. .

Of the few things that could have been done in that crisis, the most obvious was to ask one of the Indians, preferably the guide, to go out and negotiate, and pacify the newcomer, offer him presents and so on. Woolman had brought along some little things suitable for gifts, as we see by his giving some to the hunting party he had first met. Or they might have asked the host to invite the man in, where he would have been one among many. A timid man, or one of quiet, subdued disposition whose blood ran thin and slow, or even one in whom a steady sober caution was the prevailing mood, would certainly have made one of these choices.

But Woolman did not hesitate. He at once rose and went out. And when the Indian saw him coming he snatched a hatchet out from under his match coat, with the startled threatening gesture of a wild animal, and the bright steel gleamed between them. But there was no answering steel from the white man. Nor was there a contemptible gesture of fear, a tremor, a turning to flight—which would have been equally provocative and equally too late. An Indian could throw a hatchet faster than the eye could follow. Instead there was an open hand extended in a grave gesture, "for the Indians love not to be smiled upon," and the white man came steadily, leisurely on.

"I went forward," Woolman casually explains, "and speaking to him in a friendly way, perceived he understood some English." By this time Benjamin had come out to stand by his friend—he had scrambled to his feet and followed out as quickly as he could, but Woolman's action had taken them all by surprise. "My companion joining me we had some talk with him concerning the nature of our visit in these parts." What could be more mollifying than to tell an Indian that a white man had come to see what he could learn from Indians about the Great Spirit ? He could hardly believe that he had understood aright. He needed to have it corroborated in his own tongue. The Indian "then went into the house with us, and talking with our guides soon appeared friendly, sat down and smoked his pipe." Woolman had a kindly explanation about the hatchet, that no one might think the Indian disagreeable. "I believe he had no other intent than to be in readiness in case any violence were offered to him."

The Wyoming Indians now frankly discussed with Woolman the news of the Indian runners, and pointed out that not only was travel going to be dangerous for himself and his friend, but that they themselves were going to evacuate the village and remove, bag and baggage, to a safer place. The decision now rested with Woolman—should they two go on against all hazards, or should they accept the situation and go back ? Benjamin, that charming companion, gave Woolman affectionately to understand that it would be all right with him either way. He had only come to be with Woolman through thick and thin.

That night, lying in the hut "after a hard day's journey," Woolman reviewed and weighed all the reasons that had led him to come thus far, searching for the right judgment. It had seemed right to come on against the Pembertons' warning, was it not still right now ? He knew that not only his own life but his companion's might rest on his decision.

In this great distress I grew jealous of myself, lest the desire of reputation as a man firmly settled to persevere through dangers, or the fear of disgrace from my returning without performing the visit, might have some place in me. Full of these thoughts I lay great part of the night while my beloved companion slept by me, till the Lord, my gracious Father, who saw the conflicts of my soul, was pleased to give quietness. Then I was again strengthened to commit my life and all things relating thereto into his heavenly hands, and got a little sleep towards day.

In the morning the word was forward, as Benjamin had rather supposed it would be. They had a friendly talk with about twenty of the local Indians, telling them that they had come to see the Indians and "visit them in their houses" in a spirit of love, and for no other purpose ; and then took leave of them and went up the Susquehanna river about three miles to the house of an Indian called Jacob January. Here again they found the bustle of preparation to get away to safety, consequent on the news of war. Jacob January had slaughtered his hog and was cutting it up while his women were making store of bread and packing their goods to move up the river. Woolman's guides had left their canoe here when they came down in the spring, and were calling to pick it up. "Lying dry, it had become leaky" and had to be repaired ; "this detained us some hours," says Woolman with evident pleasure, "so that we had a good deal of friendly conversation with the family." They ate dinner, made their hosts some small presents, then, "putting our baggage into the repaired canoe, some of them pushed slowly up the stream while the rest of us rode our horses. We swam them over a creek called Lahawahamunk, and pitched our tent above it in the evening." And that night they all slept well.

The next day they went forward in the same way until the afternoon, when a violent storm rolled up, and they made camp early, meeting the canoe at one of the appointed places. The rain all night was so heavy that it "beat through our tent and wet both us and our baggage." And in the morning a wreckage of fallen trees greeted their eyes. Fortunately they had camped in a sheltered valley, but their travelling all day was rendered strenuous and difficult by the number of fallen trees that continued to block the way and by the slippery mud underfoot. "We seldom saw our canoe but at appointed places, by reason of the path going off the river," so they did not see the event that afternoon when their own canoe, heavily laden and pushing against a swollen current, met another canoe coming downstream loaded with furs, paddled by several Indians. Greetings and news were exchanged, and the men coming downriver, understanding where camp was to be pitched, pushed back upstream six miles to the place, and surprised Woolman and Benjamin and their guide after dark, waiting the others by the camp fire. Their leader was named Job Chilaway, and he was an Indian from Wyalusing "who talks good English and is acquainted with several people in and about Philadelphia." He was in fact one of the Delawares who had been born in New Jersey and had migrated west. They had hardly finished the preliminaries of making acquaintance and speaking of mutual friends when the baggage canoe arrived, and the tents were put up ; then over supper Job Chilaway told his white friends the rest of his news. An Indian runner had come to Wyalusing the day before and told them that three warriors from a distance had lodged in his village a few nights past, and that these three were going against the English at Juniata. There seemed every likelihood of Woolman's party meeting them on the trail, as Job Chilaway earnestly warned them. Job was himself on the way down to the province store at Shamokin, a place of call for traders and mails ; and by the light of the camp fire

Woolman seized the chance to send a letter to his wife, enclosed in care of Israel Pemberton. There was no reassuring news to give her at the moment. It might very well be the last letter she would ever receive from him. He did not wish to alarm her by any suggestion of that or of the danger that was around him, but at the same time he longed to give her comfort if this should be the last word.

My DEAR AND TENDER WIFE

A sence of Alsufficiency of God in supporting those who trust in Him in all the Dispensations of his Providence wherein they may be tryed feels Comfortable to me in my Journey.

My Daily Labour is to find a full Resignedness to Him and may say with thankfullness he Remains to be my Gracious Father.

To Him I recommend thee, my Dear Companion, greatly Desiring thy mind may be Resigned to Him for I Veryly believe if we keep in this Frame all will End well.

I write in Haste but Remember my Dear Daughter & fr'ds.

JOHN WOOLMAN

In margin, "Please sent this to Wife."

Addressed, "For Israel Pemberton, in philada. to the Care of the Storekeeper at Shamokin. pr Job Chilaway."

The note to Israel Pemberton on the same sheet read :

16: 6.1763

DEAR FR'D

We are now well near Wahalowsing in Company with Job Chilaway & Several Indians from Wahalowsing and Some from Else where who appear Civil & kind.

JOHN WOOLMAN

The Company of B. Parvin is Comfortable to me.[1]

In the morning, now the seventeenth of June, Woolman bade farewell to Job Chilaway, and the parties continued their separate ways. Woolman was feeling unwell. The thorough drenching the night of the storm, and the day of hard scrambling travel over fallen trees and débris, had made him feverish, but not so much so as to make him content not to travel ; so they pressed on to the last lap of the trail. Eleven days had passed since Woolman had ridden away from Mount Holly. Tension had steadily mounted as they grew near the frontier, and every turn in the trail the last forenoon might have brought them face to face

[1] Original in Pemberton Papers.

with the three braves who were out on the warpath against the English, and who would have been proud to take a pair of fresh scalps along to Juniata. But now the high June sun at the end of the forest path shone on the cleared fields of rich corn and yams belonging to the Susquehannas, and on the neat communal houses by the riverside, about forty in number, "some about thirty feet long and eighteen feet wide—some bigger, some less. They are built mostly of split plank," said John Woolman, "one end being set in the ground and the other pinned to a plate on which rafters are laid, and then covered with bark." This at length was Wyalusing. The guide asked them to wait there on the edge of the forest "while he went to the town to tell the people we were come." But as he tied the horses for them before going an Indian appeared through the trees. "The first Indian that we saw was a woman of a modest countenance, with a Bible, who spake first to our guide, and then with a harmonious voice expressed her gladness at seeing us, having before heard of our coming." After the exchange of courtesies the woman passed on, and Woolman and his friend sat down on a log, preparing themselves in the quiet beauty of that place for the unknown tasks that lay ahead, and fell into spontaneous silent worship. Then a beautiful thing occurred. The woman, lingering on the way, looked back and studied what they were doing. "My companion and I sitting thus together in a deep inward stillness, the poor woman came and sat near us ; and great awfulness coming over us, we rejoiced in a sense of God's love manifested to our poor souls."

The vitally shared silent communion was broken by the distant blowing of a conch shell, and presently two Indians, one of whom, John Curtis, Woolman had met at Anthony Benezet's, appeared up the path to welcome them and invite them into the town. They took the travellers into a house where the conch-shell signal had already summoned the people together. About sixty people were sitting there in silence. The Chief, Papunahung, and the Moravian missionary who had passed them on the road were present, and Anthony the Indian, whose sister was the wife of Job Chilaway, and herself born in New Jersey. It is not unlikely that it was Anthony's sister, eager to greet a New Jersey Friend and able to speak some English, who had come to meet them, with her Bible, in the forest. The Bible seems an indication that she could also read a little English, a rare accomplishment indeed for an Indian woman.

T

Papunahung knew the Quaker ways. He had attended Friends' Meeting in Philadelphia, had himself spoken there, and had been at conferences with Quakers on Indian affairs, notably the recent one at the house of Anthony Benezet. He offered the visitors the best greeting he knew, a meeting after the Quaker fashion. No banalities of common-place greeting or formal introduction marred the lofty courtesy of the occasion. The visitors were guided softly to the places reserved for them in the dim, crowded house, and sat down with hardly a rustle. "After sitting with them a short time," said Woolman, "I stood up and in some tenderness of spirit acquainted them with the nature of my visit." Anthony—or another—rose with him and interpreted for him sentence by sentence. Woolman then showed his certificate, knowing they would value it as a sign that he represented, as it were officially, a large body of Quakers ; in fact, the whole Philadelphia Yearly Meeting (the Friends of New Jersey and Pennsylvania). The interpreter repeated his explanation. And there were manifest signs of pleasure. Now was the time for official welcome, and Papunahung rose and made his stately gesture of greeting, while the Moravian pastor, David Zeisberger, made a gracious speech in the Indian tongue.

As the meeting dispersed Papunahung drew Woolman aside, beckon-ing the interpreter, and broached a problem which had been giving all the Indians some perplexity, and which they were proposing to solve in a way which demonstrated the fine manners of all concerned. It was the problem of sectarian competition. Papunahung was himself a Moravian convert, and David Zeisberger was there at his invitation. Had the Quakers happened to come at a time when Zeisberger was not there the population would have been entirely at their disposal. But as it was, the regular gatherings for worship morning and evening would be held under Zeisberger's control, and he would be the main speaker. They therefore offered to come together at any other time that Woolman wished, to hold Quaker meetings and listen to him and his friend. Left to get on by themselves for months at a time, the Munseys at Wyalusing were suffering from an embarrassment of riches.

John Woolman appreciated the situation and their suggestion to the full ; but he had a better idea, one which Zeisberger, as first on the field, could not have suggested without patronage. Woolman went to the Moravian pastor, suggested that it would be an unnecessary tax on the people to ask them to come together for extra meetings, and would David Zeisberger allow him and his friend to attend the Moravian meetings and to take subordinate part in them ? "I told him . . . my belief that no ill effects would follow if I sometimes spake in their meetings when love engaged me thereto." David Zeisberger could meet liberality with liberality. "He expressed his good will towards my speaking at any time all that I found in my heart to say."

Perhaps it goes without saying that Woolman did not abuse the privilege or steal any of Mr Zeisberger's thunder. Except as a Quaker is to be defined as a man who feels the Presence of God in his heart (with its inevitable corollary of love for his neighbours), Woolman was not there to make Quakers. And he was quite contented to have such a man call himself a Moravian or a Catholic. They arrived on the afternoon of Friday the seventeenth and stayed until Tuesday morning the twenty-first. Woolman sat in silence through the Saturday morning meeting, but spoke on Saturday evening ; was silent on Sunday morning, spoke in the evening meeting ; on Monday was silent at both meetings ; and spoke on Tuesday morning, the last meeting before they left.

Language proved an unexpected difficulty. Zeisberger could speak the Indian dialects fluently, but his native language was German. Anthony had to be the go-between when Woolman and Zeisberger conversed. And Woolman soon discovered in the meeting on Saturday evening what a complicated business it was to try to express unfamiliar ideas through the double medium of interpreters "none of whom were quite perfect in the English and Delaware tongues ; so they helped one another, and we laboured along, Divine love attending." Woolman tried to help them out by using very short sentences, but his style was naturally succinct and packed with ethical content. It was different from the sort of sermons the Indians were accustomed to, which elaborated endlessly on the Bible stories and the theme of the sacrificial atonement of the divine Son of God. Phrases in this connexion were ready-made, they could quickly have rendered them ; but John Woolman kept their minds on the stretch and taxed their powers of understanding and of language to the utmost to try to render his close-packed and lofty thought into an equivalent in the Indian speech. There were also two dialects represented among these Indians, the Delaware Valley Indians and the Susquehannas, although both belonged to the great

Algonquin group, subordinate to the Six Nations. John Woolman felt this halting and almost disputed delivery very trying ; it was worse than being delayed by a slow-riding companion on a journey. At his second attempt :

> I spake to them awhile by interpreters, but none of them being perfect in the work and I feeling the current of love run strong, told the interpreters that I believed some of the people would understand me, and so I proceeded without them. . . . After I sat down one of the interpreters seemed spirited to give the Indians the substance of what I said.

And practice was making perfect. At his last meeting, on the Tuesday, "In short plain sentences I expressed several things that rested upon me, which one of the interpreters gave the people pretty readily."

But John Woolman had more to give the Indians than poorly interpreted addresses. On that Saturday evening when the laborious efforts of various interpreters had torn the sacred feeling of the meeting to ribbons Woolman said :

> Afterwards, feeling my mind covered with the spirit of prayer, I told the interpreters that I found it in my heart to pray to God, and believed, if I prayed aright, He would hear me ; and I expressed my willingness for them to omit interpreting ; so our meeting ended with a degree of Divine love. Before our people went out I observed Papunehang . . . speaking to one of the interpreters, and I was afterwards told that he said, "I love to feel where words come from." When the last mentioned meeting was ended, it being night, Papunehang went to bed ; and hearing him speak with an harmonious voice, I suppose for a minute or two, I asked the interpreter, who told me that he was expressing his thankfulness to God for the favours he had received that day, and prayed that He would continue to favour him with the same which he had experienced in that meeting.[1]

Going in and out among the Indians, observing them and feeling for them, Woolman gave them an affectionate and admiring sympathy which must have been pretty new to them from a white man. "The affectionate care of a good man for his only brother in affliction does not exceed what I then felt for that people. . . . In my own eyes I appeared inferior to many among the Indians." The chief, Papunahung, with his noble presence and harmonious voice was one who had commanded Woolman's admiration from the start, ever since their conversation,

---

[1] Whittier ed., p. 181.

through an interpreter, at Benezet's, and they were lodged in Papuna-hung's own communal house, where each subsection of the family—married sons and daughters, cousins, and so on—had their own quarters and their own fire, with neat sleeping-bunks and semi-partitions.

After Woolman's farewell speech on Tuesday morning the Indians lined up to shake hands with him, in ceremonious and cordial adieu.

So the visit was all over, and the Englishmen departed. And no one could tabulate or measure what they had done.

The return trip had loomed formidable ; but when they were ready to go they found that a number of Indians who wanted to take their furs down to Bethlehem to trade were all anxious to go with them. They had two canoes loaded with the furs, and a number of horses. Their suggestion was that the two white men should travel comfortably in the canoes, "since the waters were so raised by the rains that the horses should be taken by such as were better acquainted with the fording-places. We therefore," says Woolman,

> with several Indians, went in the canoes, and others went on horses,
> there being seven beside ours. We met the horseman once on the way
> [that day] by appointment, and at night we lodged a little below a
> branch called Tanhannah, and some of the young men, going out a
> little before dusk with their guns, brought in a deer.

Travelling by canoe, going with the current, swift, silent, easy in motion, is the most restful travel possible, when expert paddlers at stern and bow relieve one of apprehension at tricky spots. The first two days were delightful, and they reached Wyoming before sunset on Wednesday. The village was deserted, and they went up a small creek and made camp, pitched the tent, and carried out baggage before the slower horse party arrived. But from here on they had to part with the River Susque-hanna, and "next morning the horses being loaded and our baggage prepared we set forward being in all fourteen"—so five more horses had turned up from somewhere—"and with diligent travelling" got half-way to Fort Allen. That night, Thursday, they camped on low ground among rising mist, chosen by the Indians because it afforded grazing for the horses in the midst of poor grazing country. Woolman "had sweat much in travelling, and being weary slept soundly," so he caught a chill, but pressed onward, and it soon "got better." Next day they passed Fort Allen and lodged near it in the woods. Going up they had laboriously crossed the Blue Ridge Mountains between Fort Allen and

Wyoming, but coming back the Indians showed them a shorter way by which they slipped between the mountains, crossing the curls of the "westerly branch of the Delaware, or Great Lehie," three times by fords. Shorter, but not so very much safer. "In the second time of fording, where the river cuts through the mountain, the waters being rapid and pretty deep, my companion's mare . . . was sundry times driven back through the river."

As they approached civilization it became clear to Woolman why so many Indians had wanted to come with him, instead of just the two guides he had engaged for the return journey.

> The troubles westward and the difficulty for Indians to pass through our frontier was, I apprehend, one reason why so many came, expecting that our being in company would prevent the outside inhabitants being surprised. We reached Bethlehem on the 25th, taking care to keep foremost and to acquaint people on and near the road who these Indians were. This we found very needful, for the frontier inhabitants were often alarmed at the report of the English being killed by Indians westward.

At Bethlehem on Saturday night Woolman and his companion paid the Indians for their services and left them to their business, finding their own separate lodging in an inn ; and early on Sunday morning they set off to Richland, arriving in time for meeting. Their arrival caused a sensation, and they went for Sunday dinner to Samuel Foulke's house, escorted by eager friends. After dining Woolman and Benjamin Parvin took horse in different directions, and Samuel Foulke, unable to part soon from his restored friend, rode with John Woolman to Abington to the house of John Cadwallader—also a former member of the Pennsylvania Assembly. Here more friends were gathered to an evening meal ; and early in the morning Woolman rode on through Philadelphia to Burlington. His eagerness to reach home did not allow him even to call on Israel Pemberton on his way, but at Burlington he paused for lunch at John Smith's and—perhaps while lunch was getting ready— he wrote Israel Pemberton a letter from there.

BURLINGTON, *27da. 6mo. 1763 1 o'clock*

DEAR FRIEND,

Through the Mercies of the Lord my Belov^d Companion and helpmate B. Parvin and I were helped to perform our Journey to Wahalousing and came back to Bethlehem on Seventh day night was yesterday at the Swamp Meeting and I lodged last night at John Cadwaleders and am now hasting home—Our Journey though attended with much deep Exercise hath been greatly to our Satisfaction. We were at seven Religious meetings with the Indians many of which people I believe were in these troublous times greatly Comforted in our visit and they all appeared kind and Loving to us—I saw nothing amongst any of them in that place which to me appear^d like disaffection to the English—but our Conversation was mostly with the soberer sort. The Moravian Preacher who was there when I went and contin^d there while I stay^d appear^d Kind and courteous from first to last and I believe his intentions are honest.

In a humbling sense of His goodness in whom my Soul has trusted, I remain with kind love to thee and family and all my Dear fr^d

JOHN WOOLMAN

For

Israel Pemberton in Philad^a

And so on home, down the shady, familiar Burlington Road, past the cross-roads in the woods where the meeting-house stood, on down past the Black Horse and the Cross Keys to Mount Holly market-place ; then to the left through the market-place, along by the mill-stream, past his old shop and the Three Tuns, and on up the Springfield Road, to splash through the Buttonwood Run, and ride up the grassy knoll to his own fair little house in the orchard ; his hair upon his own head, and not at an Indian's belt ; his movements free at his own will, and not bound to a captive's heavy tasks ; his wife and child safe under his own roof, their soft cheeks against his own, and their tears upon his hand.

What a store of tales he had for them now. "Tell again how you met Job Chilaway ! . . . Tell how it was when the interpreters argued with each other about a word, in the middle of the meeting ! Tell about the man with the hatchet !" A shuddering tale that, for Sarah. But to Mary the worst of all was about the snakes, and how suddenly one came upon them in the narrow path, "much grown up with bushes —rough stones—a difficult road to travel ; and the more so because rattlesnakes abound here, of which we killed four." Indeed, "people who have never been in such places have but an imperfect idea of them."

XXXIII

UNREST

IT seemed a small matter for one white man, maintaining strict neutrality, to take his life in his hands and go a long distance into the back parts and spend a week-end with a group of quiet Indians. But so it was a small matter when a few years later a Boston street boy called a British redcoat a lobster. Yet the one, backed and increased and taken up by others, ended in an outbreak of suppressed irritations which touched off a revolution unparalleled in its results. And what a profound revolution the other might have touched off—a revolution in human behaviour and the relationships of races—if there had been as many of John Woolman's kidney to go on friendly visits to the Indians as there were teasing youths in Boston to upset the tempers of the British.

Now Woolman found himself in demand as a purveyor of information. News in Philadelphia was scanty and uncertain, rumours were on the wind. Now he was in a delicate situation, not unforeseen by him. He had gone among the Indians as a friend ; he was in danger of being used as a spy. Even his trusted friends, the Pemberton brothers, though they had been affectionately anxious that he should not endanger his life, had regarded his visit as possibly useful to find out what the Indians were up to. Conestoga was the edge of Pennsylvania proper, and beyond that the country, though under the general jurisdiction of the Pennsylvania Assembly, was vaguely lumped together as the Ohio wilderness. Woolman had been quite a way into this wilderness.

There was a lot he could tell of immediate use or future use about whether all the Indians around those parts were disaffected or only a minority ; which was which ; were they coming down in numbers from that direction, or did they seem to be going westward ? He was a reporter from the front. But he would only be so used as far as his report could contribute to safety or peace. He would not give military information. He had gone in good faith, been received in good faith, and he would steadily maintain it. He was not so unworldly that he could be innocently used to tell what might turn to the disadvantage of his hosts when it came to the ears of their enemies of any colour.

On July 2, 1763, John Pemberton wrote from Burlington to his political brother Israel :

DEAR BROTHER,

Yesterday, Mother and myself Spent with our friend John Woolman at his house : He looks better for his journey and is well satisfied that he went. I asked him Several Questions respecting the Indians etc, and he gave me what accounts he could, but he found in his Journey his Mind closely engaged to attend to the concern he was engaged in, and cautious of questioning the Indians. . . . [One reason Woolman gave had that edge to it with which he often punctured take-for-granted self-content. The Indians might have asked questions in return "that he could not say anything to without casting some blame on the English." John Pemberton remarks privately that perhaps they could get more out of B. Parvin. However, John Woolman is ready to let his friends have his own notes.] He allowed me the liberty to preserve his Remarks on his Journey and to enclose them for thy Perusal, with this request—that thou show them to no other person, as he intends to Survey them again etc, and please to return them speedily if thou forwards them here, directed either to him or me, they may get to his hands. Thou wilt perceive that Alarms had been sent among the Indians ; they were preparing to leave Wyoming when he got there. Capt Bull (or *Jacob*) he understood, intended up the Western branch of the Sassquehanagh and the others proposed to scatter themselves, some in One part and some in Another. [But Woolman "could not" tell of "what nation or who those Runners were that advertised the Indians near Wyalousin," though he warned his friends that they were carrying the war signal, the bloody scalp. Job Chilaway, whom they all knew, "expressed much sorrow that he was obliged to be absent," but his trading errand was evidently partly a blind for an errand of warning of those warriors to the inhabitants.] The Indians seemed as much concerned as any of us would be (as Jno thought) and he tho't would join any endeavour that could be th't on to prevent the Spreading this Calamity. . . . On his Return to Wyoming, all the Indians Except an Old Man were gone. [Woolman was cautious about revealing the identity of this old man, probably left behind for a purpose, to let his brethren know how the war moved.] He was very Friendly, and asked after thee—but Jno: did not enquire his name. [As to new-come white settlers in those wild parts, Woolman had seen some and had warned them of their danger —though he says nothing about it in his printed account. To John and Israel he confides.] There were about 20 men and boys from Connecticut. He did not understand what they proposed in General —One Man Expressed his Intentions of returning and tho't to set homewards the next day. . . . He did hear (but knows not that it is more than conjecture) that some Indians had a design to come in their Canoes to take them by Surprise.

In fine, it is not by accident that he has not called on Israel. John told me if thou desired it he would come to town, but as he was particularly Cautious of entering into Enquiries, and heard little, he apprehended his Intelligence would be of little Service and would rather avoid it. Thou may perceive from the Inclosed that he was fr'dly rec'd. In every place where they understood his Errand were rejoyced and very kind, and he did not Perceive in any an Evil disposition towards the English. He desired his love to thee.

I am thy affectionate Bro.

JOHN PEMBERTON

Papuna, Jno. Curtis, etc. Desired Love to the Friends in Philadelphia.[1]

By "the English," neither Woolman nor Pemberton was referring to the professional British troops. They meant "us." They themselves and their fellow-colonists in Pennsylvania, New Jersey, Connecticut, New England, Virginia, and the rest—they were the English. They had never thought of themselves as anything else. Born on the soil of the New World, they were born English.

Woolman came back to find that that rising of the Indians which like a breeze in the forest had blown across his pathway had in other places risen to a hurricane, before which the white frontier settlers had scattered in terror to seek refuge where they could. Many were shelterless in the woods, and some of those fell a prey to scalp-hunters hurrying to join Pontiac's forces, like those three braves whom Woolman had just missed. Others, remaining, were murdered in their homes and

---

[1] Pemberton Papers, XVI, 109.

their harvest fields as the summer wore on. The Indian rising was more general, more widespread, more determined and controlled, than any before known. A panic spread through the provinces. Sir Jeffrey Amherst, British general, marching past burned and smoking ruins and the bodies of scalped woman and babies, said that the Indians were the vilest race of beings that ever infested the earth ; to rid the earth of them would be a meritorious act ; and sent out orders to kill all prisoners. To which the Indians, experts at secret and revengeful war, replied by ambushing a convoy near Niagara Falls and getting away with more than seventy scalps. The Delawares were Pontiac's shock troops, and fought alongside their old enemies, the Six Nations. Nothing like this Indian unity had been imagined. By strategy, by treachery, or by force, they mastered fort after fort. Virginia, Maryland, Pennsylvania, New Jersey, were all in danger.

When the Indians approached the River Delaware Governor William Franklin, of New Jersey, ordered out the militia, remanned the fortifications, built more blockhouses. Yet some Indians crossed the river and massacred several families. The Assembly voted two hundred men for the defence of the province, and ten thousand pounds ; and presently raised six hundred more volunteers to join the main body of troops under Bouquet and Bradstreet.

At such a time as this, when the Swiss professional soldier, Bouquet, with his grim talent for Indian war, was marching with his first troop of ragged Highlanders towards Bushy Run for the relief of Fort Pitt, some printed advertisements appeared in Mount Holly. They were to the effect that on a certain day at a particular public house a juggler would be present to perform some remarkable tricks of sleight-of-hand. Woolman regarded this frivolity with scorn. Some Mount Holly men had gone off with the troops to defend their neighbours. Others were scrimping themselves to give generously to the relief of those who had suffered loss of all they had in exposed places. Was this a time for any men to waste their hours staring at this foolish fellow, or to waste their money in supporting him in a disgracefully useless existence ? When the juggler arrived Woolman went to the innkeeper and ceremoniously obtained permission to spend part of the evening at the inn, otherwise than as a customer. Two of the possible innkeepers, Zach Rossell and Daniel Jones, were on very friendly terms with Woolman, serving on town committees with him and using his expert services in real-estate deals, and appraisement of land and goods. When the time came for the juggler's second performance Woolman was sitting by the door, well placed for catching all who came in, and expressed his opinion in his usual outspoken manner, both privately to those whom he knew best, and in a general speech when a good number had assembled. One man tried to answer him with some texts of Scripture, but after "calmly debating the matter, he gave up the point." Woolman stayed about an hour—to the great detriment of the juggler's business—and then he went away and left them to their own devices. As a collector for the Quaker relief fund and for the New Jersey Society for Helping the Indians at Brotherton, he was a good judge as to which of his fellow-townsfolk were finding it easy to pay for their own trivial amusement when they found it so hard to pay for public-spirited enterprises. He judged it selfish and indifferent in so burdened a world, and therefore "contrary to the nature of the Christian religion." Hard words indeed. But with his customary justice he did not scold the juggler, a poor misguided creature.

The juggler himself was only a straw which showed the direction of the wind. Woolman's severe judgment was not only his own. Such entertainments were generally despised. Dr Johnson thought that actors and mountebanks were no better than performing dogs. And Mount Holly was full of Quakers who refused military service and war tax. All the more reason for them to show a sense of serious responsibility for the troubled times.

Woolman's sympathy for the Indian as a fellow-creature was severely tested that fall, not only by the horrors of Pontiac's war, but by an example nearer home. "Having hired a man to work, I perceived in conversation with him that he had been a soldier in the late war on this continent ; and he informed me in the evening, in a narrative of his captivity among the Indians, that he saw two of his fellow-captives tortured to death in a very cruel manner." Sickened and depressed, Woolman went to bed under the dark cloud, the sense of the terrible indifference of heaven, which such stories bring in their train ; and fell asleep miserable, the problem unanswered. But he awoke in the bright fall morning, the scarlet maples dazzling against the blue sky, the air wine-sweet, and "a fresh and living sense of Divine love" flowed into him like breath. He got up and seized his pen to write before breakfast the thoughts that crowded to comfort him.

. . . Doth vanity form imaginary wants ? Do these wants prompt men to exert their power in requiring more from others than they would be willing to perform themselves were the same required of them ? Do these proceedings beget hard thoughts ? Do hard thoughts when ripe become malice ? Does malice when ripe become revengeful, and in the end inflict terrible pains on our fellow-creatures and spread desolation in the world ?

And on the other hand :

Do mankind, walking in uprightness, delight in each other's happiness ? And do those who are capable of this attainment, by giving way to an evil spirit, employ their skill and strength to afflict and destroy one another ? Remember then, O my soul ! the quietude of those in whom Christ governs, and in all thy proceedings feel after it. . . . Accept of the strength freely offered to thee and take heed that no weakness in conforming to unwise, expensive and hard-hearted customs, gendering to discord and strife, be given way to.[1]

It is the evil that cannot be prevented that brings despair. John Woolman could always trace particular evils to a preventable root, and, like one of the world's gardeners, devoted himself joyfully and hopefully to weeding it out. But before he began weeding in a general way he always looked first with a careful eye over his own garden patch.

As to the Indians being no devils but human beings, driven, like other human beings, to hideous cruelties on occasion by a gradual conformity to hard-hearted customs, the end of Pontiac's war bore singular witness. Chief clause of Bouquet's dictated peace was that all the captives in Indian hands must be brought in within twelve days to Fort Pitt—"all the prisoners, without exception ; Englishmen, Frenchmen, women and children ; whether adopted into your tribes, married or living amongst you under any pretence whatever." And in October 1764 Bouquet and his army—the New Jersey men among them—stood under the splendid banners of the trees receiving the returned prisoners. Day after day they came from near and far ; and from near and far came the fathers and the mothers, the wives and brothers and sweethearts of the lost to claim their own. Then were the white prisoners glad to be taken from those devils ? Some were indeed ; but they were mostly among the newly captured. Those others who had spent years with the Indians loved them and were loved in return. The children clung to their

[1] Whittier ed., pp. 190-191.

foster-mothers, wife clung to husband, and friend to friend. Many had to be dragged away by force ; not a few of the young wives escaped later and fled back to their Indian husbands and the wild, free life of the stream, the wigwam, the canoe.

Before Pontiac's defeat, however, in the winter of the Indian terror, there is a curious entry on the side leaf of Woolman's Ledger. "*December 1763.* Removed to Asher Wollman's to live the first day of the twelfth month 1763 and left household goods with Several Neighbours." The household goods do not include furniture (except some bedding). They are evidently small odds and ends, packed mostly in a "large black-leather Trunk and a ceader box painted read." No chairs, tables, and such, though there is one keg of "puter" and some surveyor's steel rules. In spite of the misspelling of the family surname, in no other case committed by Woolman, it looks as if John Woolman made this entry, and it seems to convey the information that he closed his own home that winter and moved his wife and daughter to the old homestead on the Rancocas. Perhaps he did this so that if he were away at any time they might not be left alone, nervous and unguarded, when every one was dreaming of wild Indians every night. On the other hand, he did not go much away that winter. Such family visiting as he did was done in and around Mount Holly. As far as ordinary safety went, Mount Holly, as a town, offered more protection than the comparatively lonely farm. But there is another alternative. Perhaps Asher felt the responsibility of being alone there with his elderly mother and timid sister ; perhaps he was himself nervous—and small blame to him. He might have asked his eldest brother to move in there for the winter and help keep up the household morale. Whatever the reason for the move, if it did apply to John Woolman it is quite clear that it was temporary. Woolman's Account Book for 1764, Journal entries regarding his orchard and so forth, and all traditions regarding his residence put it beyond question that before the fall of '64 they were back again in their Mount Holly home. In the winter of '64 Woolman mentions obtaining a minute for "visiting families in our own Meeting, and especially in the town of Mount Holly, the place of my abode."[1]

But not all outrages were committed by Indians, and the winter of '63 carried another danger to Philadelphia and its environs in the anti-Indian outbreak by the roughly organized frontiersmen who called

[1] Whittier ed., p. 191.

themselves the Paxton Boys. This mob was headed by a group of Irish[1] who coveted the rich land round Conestoga, the Indian "Council fire" for immemorial generations. The high ground sloped steeply to the place where the brown stream of the little, swift Conestoga flowed into the broad blue waters of the Susquehanna, near the Mennonite settlement of Lancaster, some forty miles from Philadelphia. The Paxtons had made more than one effort to snatch the unfarmed land away from the Indians by illegal settlement, broken up eventually by the sheriff's posse. Now they took advantage of the public terror and of such pronouncements as that of Amherst, got a riotous bunch together, surprised Conestoga, and murdered fourteen Indians of the many peaceful Delawares who, like Woolman's friends, had not joined Pontiac or been unfriendly to the English. The rest of the Conestogas fled to Lancaster and demanded protection. "For their better security" they were locked up in the town prison ; but at midday the Paxton Boys rode in on horseback with fierce yelling and gun-firing, broke open the prison, and murdered all the Indians there, men, women, and children, in cold blood. The news of this flew among the Indians, and those at Wyalusing and round about, whom Woolman's visit had assured once more of Philadelphia's attention and interest, thought they could do no better than trust that friendship and hurry down to Philadelphia as fast as they could travel. Their Moravian teacher, David Zeisberger, approved the plan and came with them. They were just in time. They were actually in the city, protected and welcomed by the Quakers, when the roaring Paxton Boys reached the outlying village of German-town. There a determined band of armed citizens met them, headed by Benjamin Franklin, and Franklin's diplomacy and firmness, backed by the obvious threat, persuaded them to go home. Meanwhile the Indians were without shelter in the December cold, and William Logan and Israel Pemberton hurried about to get blankets for them, and to try to persuade the barracks to house them—in which they at last succeeded. After some months of stay, sick with the city air, the Indians summoned courage to return to their distant settlements, and with their faithful Moravian pastor returned via Bethlehem to Wyoming and Wyalusing. Unquestionably their friend, John Woolman, must have been one of those who helped take care of them and raise subscription for them during

[1] Or Scots-Irish. They were called Irish at the time, but some of their graves are to be found in the churchyard of the Presbyterian Church at Harrisburg.

their time of exile in the city of Philadelphia, as well as Anthony Benezet, though both are silent, and the Quaker meeting records are most concerned with disciplining those hotheaded Quakers who, in the excitement of the hour and the danger of the Indians and the city, took up arms to back Franklin.

This flurry may have been part of the reason why Woolman's family joined households with Asher's that December.

As to whether there was any excuse of fear or suspicion for killing off the Conestoga Indians in the middle of the Pontiac war let one of their neighbours bear witness.   One Susanna Wright mourned in a letter :

> The cruel murder of these poor Indians has affected and discomposed my mind beyond what I can express.   We had known the greater part of them from childhood ; had always been intimate with them. Three or four of the women were sensible and civilized, and the Indians' children used to play with ours and oblige them all they could.   We had many endearing recollections of them. . . . The brutal enormity so affected us that we had to beg visiters not to speak of it.   But it was still the subject with everybody.

In the various difficulties negotiated and patched up between the Indians and the white settlers in Pennsylvania and New Jersey from the beginning—including the first murder of all, in 1727, done by drunken Minisinck Delawares at Wyoming—the favourite Indian phrase had been, "This is but a little cloud ; the sun has not set."   But now the sun had set.   The hatchet, drenched in both white and Indian blood, was never again buried.   The most dangerous of human emotions, fear, had been let loose.   The Quakers, with their fearless friendly policy, the fundamental precept of which was settlement by Indian consent, had withdrawn from their dominating position in the government of the leading colony.   That bulwark removed, the way was clear for unmitigated violence and militarism in Indian dealing.   Useless for the Quakers to salve their consciences with their Friendly Associations, their Indian reservation, their beautifully worded letters of protest to Governor or general.   They had taken their thumb out of the dike.

Pontiac was beaten, but confidence was destroyed.   Neither side trusted the other ever again.   The lonely frontiersman on the edge of the Quaker provinces built his house within running distance to a fort, and lay down with his loaded gun ready by his side.   The solitary

Josiah White's House in Mount Holly

Reproduced from a water-colour drawing by kind permission of the owner, Walter Rhoads White

Indian hunter watched out for other dangers than those of wolves or snakes. Fear begot hate, and hate begot cruelty. Ten years after John Woolman's death a sudden panic unprovoked struck the white settlers in the wilderness round Wyalusing, and they came down like the Paxton Boys upon the peaceful Indians and their noble chief Papunahung and massacred them every one among their standing corn. The settlement which John Woolman had seen prosperous and quiet in the afternoon sunlight was left a black and bloody ruin. And in the hearts of the murderers was left a haunting memory of a hundred Indians who had not lifted a finger in their own defence, or tried to run away, but had accepted passively the sharp blow of the hatchet and the knife, singing to the last their Indian hymns.

Papunahung, who had found God, the Great Spirit, all alone in the forest long before he knew any Christians, and had become inwardly "fully persuaded that when God made men he never intended they should kill and destroy one another," had said, after learning Christian doctrine, "I have often thought it strange that the Christians are such great warriors." And there is no room for doubt that in the last scene of his life, as in all others in which he was observed, "his deportment was such as manifested his mind to be quiet and easy."[1]

To the raw new settlers he was just another Indian devil because of his dark face ; it was a benefit to rid the world of him and his kind ; but John Woolman found in him a kindred spirit, one whom he was proud to hail as his superior.

Meanwhile Pontiac's war also brought to a head the conviction of the home government that the American colonies must have a properly organized, properly equipped standing army. Loudon had written a few years before :

> In the Jerseys and in Pennsylvania the majority of the Assembly is composed of Quakers ; whilst that is the case they will always oppose every measure of government and support that independence which is deep-rooted everywhere in this country. The taxes which the people pay are really so trifling that they do not deserve the name ; so that if some method is not found out of laying on a tax for the support of a war in America by a British Act of Parliament, it appears to me that you will continue to have no assistance from them in money, and will have very little in men, if they are wanted.

[1] Benezet, p. 482.

U

Here again the withdrawal of the Quakers left the coast clear. And a scheme long projected, apparently innocent, passed the House of Commons without much dissent and became law—the Stamp Act, by which, in the purchase of stamps required for the legalizing of various documents—wills, receipts, bills of lading—a moderate tax would be painlessly imposed upon those citizens best qualified to pay ; the money so raised to be used within the colonies for their own defence. Such a stamp duty was already in use in England, and nobody minded. That the colonies minded so much—resented it so hotly—discerned such a big principle at stake—was a real astonishment to many people in England. Were not the colonists Englishmen ? Indeed, they had left themselves so hitherto, and still did. But at the Congress of New York, summoned to ensure a united front of all the colonies against the stamps and a uniform action of repudiation—a Congress this time not of governors, but of representatives from the elected Assemblies—a new name had arisen. It was not meant to be an anti-British word ; it was only to supersede a narrow local nomenclature, like Pennsylvanian or Virginian ; but none the less it rang bell-like in the mind. It was the word "American."

The shouts of liberty in the colonies roused an echo in great-hearted Englishmen, led by Pitt and Burke, and the Stamp Act was repealed in February 1766. But it left behind that unity and that word. And it had incidentally provoked two noteworthy utterances which fitted neatly into Woolman's theories on slavery and war. The first was made at the Congress of New York by the representative from South Carolina.

We are a very weak province, yet a rich growing one . . . and a great part of our weakness, though at the same time 'tis part of our riches, consists in having such a large number of slaves amongst us ; and we find in our case, according to the general perceptible workings of Providence, where the crime slowly yet surely draws down a similar and suitable punishment, that slavery begets slavery.

The second, more striking still, was made by that clearheaded gentleman, Benjamin Franklin, being questioned at the bar of the House of Commons regarding the Stamp Tax. "May not a military force carry the Stamp Act into execution ? " he was asked. He replied, "Suppose a military force be sent into America ; they will find nobody in arms ; what then are they to do ? They cannot force a man to take stamps who chooses to do without them."

On the twenty-seventh of July, 1764, John Woolman had a dream which he wrote out in full under the heading "Dream of Visit to a Dictator in War-time on Mission of Peace." It exists in a separate fragment and has not been bound up with his Journal. But it belongs to his thoughts at this period, when the strands of the recently accomplished Indian visit mingled with the slowly forming intention to travel to Europe. Perhaps Frederick the Great, George III, and Pontiac all are shadowily projected in the figure of the Dictator.

At Night I dreamed I was abroad on a Religious Visit beyond the Sea, and had been out upward of two months and that while I was out on the visit the people of the Country where I was & those of a Neighboring Kingdom having concerns together in affairs abroad had difference which arose so high that they began to fight and both parties were preparing for a General war. I thought there was no Sea between them, but only bounded by a line, and that the Man who was Chief among the other people lived within a Day's Journey of where I was. I being troubled at these things felt a desire in my mind to go and Speak with this Chief man and try to prevail on him to stop Fighting that they might enquire more fully into the grounds of their disagrement and endeavour to accomodate their difference without sheding more Blood. So I set of having one man with me as a pilot and after travelling sometime in the woods we came in sight of a few of those people at Labour having Guns with them ; I being foremost came near them before they saw us, and as soon as they discovered that we were from their Enemies Country they took up their Guns and were preparing to fire on us, where upon I hastily approached them holding up both my Arms to let them see that I had no warlike weapons. So I Shook hands with them and let them know the cause of our coming, at which they appeared well pleased. In the surprise at our Meeting my Pilot held forth a small Gun he had with him which I knew not of before but they so soon understood our Business that none fired : After which I saw my Pilot no more : But one of these people offering to Conduct me to their Chief Man, He and I set forward & Travelled along a path through woods & Swamps near SouthEast and on our way my new Pilot who could talk broken English Spake to me with an agreable countenance & desired that when I came before their Chief I would speak my mind freely, & signified their Salutation at meeting was to Speak to each other but not to Shake hands. At length we came to the House of this Chief Man, whom I thought had the Command of the Soldiers and was at the head of the affairs of their Country but was not called a King. His House stood by its self & a good Garden with green herbs before the Door In which garden I stood, while my pilot went to tell this Chief man that I

wanted to speak with him.   As I Stood alone in the Garden my mind
was Exercised on the Affair I came upon and presently my Pilot
returned and passing by me said he had forgot to tell me that I had
an invitation to Diner.   Soon after him came the Chief man, who
having been told the cause of my coming looked on me with a Friendly
Countenance, and as I was about to enter on the business I awoke.

John Woolman

This is the world of dream and fairy-tale—or of the Indian—where
a Dictator may be met in a green garden and talked to amiably on
thoughts of peace ; yet the dream turns into a sort of parable of Woolman's philosophy.   Arms are more of a danger than a protection ;
fear, flight, or a supine submission will get you nowhere ; the only real
basis for settling international or racial differences is a steady and active
good will.   And a victor in war, no matter how 'good' the cause, is
not the man to make a peace ; "for it is unfit for a Person to sit as Judge
in a Case where his own personal Resentments are stirred up."
In his waking hours Woolman set down his thoughts on the subject
of the Dictator, the Tyrant of any kind.

He whose will is a law to others, and can enforce obedience by
punishment ; he whose wants are supplied without feeling any
obligation to make equal returns to his benefactor, his irregular
appetites find an open field for motion, and he is in danger of growing
hard and inattentive to their convenience who labour for his support,
and so loses that disposition in which alone men are fit to govern.[1]

[1] Gummere, p. 363.

XXXIV

LIFE IN MOUNT HOLLY

MEANWHILE the pattern of life in Mount Holly was becoming continually richer. Not distracted by political dissension or by border danger, with few slaves and no great fortunes, it was like a maturing apple-tree, rooted in the soil and bearing year by year a more abundant harvest of ripe fruit. Yet its atmosphere was far from crudely rustic. Mount Holly was proving the meaning of such words as "civilized," "polished," and "urbane," the community words of the charm and value of the settled life. Had John Woolman ever written an autobiography in the ordinary sense this kind of life would have filled most of its pages. The Journal, carefully recording all the journeys and not much else, gives a false impression of restless movement. Woolman was actually away from home not more than a total of twenty-eight months in thirty-two years, counting from the time he first came to Mount Holly until he went away on his last journey. An average of less than a month a year. After all, he had a living to earn, and that takes up most of a man's time. And he revelled in the life of home, town, and community. It never bored him, he was never "uneasy" in it, never felt his neighbours uncongenial or himself out of place. When away he never fails to ask to be remembered to all his dear friends about home. And though his own house was modest and small—even smaller than

Josiah White's, and Josiah, though well-to-do, lived in a very modest house—he had, from the worldly point of view, the dignified background of the ample Woolman homestead on the Rancocas and the stately Burr house near Mount Holly. Many a Sunday afternoon or summer evening he and Sarah and Mary spent on the wide lawns of Peachfields, with Uncle Joseph and Aunt Jane, with Joseph Junior and his wife, and Henry, and their children, looking away through the trees over the flat fields to the hedgehog shape of the Mount, squatting cosily on the landscape. A friendly hill, but not exactly a tame one. The children of Henry and of Joseph Junior were Mary's contemporaries, and prevented her from getting that only-child feeling. It was with them she sometimes went to take the Hermit his rations in her great-uncle's woods ; and from time to time some of the cousins came to share her lessons in John Woolman's school. For, although as far as Woolman is concerned it is off the record, he "several times opened a school at Mount Holly for the instruction of poor Friends' children and others" ;[1] and the Account Books carry items charging various people "for school-ing thy children." He sometimes had a niece in the house as a boarding pupil and sisterly companion for Mary. Brother Abner is not only charged for "schooling thy daughter" but also "To expence of keeping and teaching thy daughter" for a couple of months ; and another time Asher's daughter is the one.

The very year of Woolman's marriage Mount Holly had advertised in the *Pennsylvania Gazette*, November 2, 1749, "Any schoolmaster or schoolmistress that shall come well recommended to be of a sober behaviour and can spell well and write a good common hand may find encouragement for keeping of a school by applying to William Foster." Whether this advertisement produced a teacher, and whether, if so, he held school in William Foster's house, is not told. But ten years later a schoolhouse was erected in Mount Holly by a group of public-spirited citizens, who entered into Articles of Agreement to raise a stock fund for the purpose of the education of youth. Twenty-five shares of stock were issued, the holders, including Josiah White, Zacariah Rossell, John Budd, and Dr Ross, to purchase a school lot, take title to same, and establish a school. In September 1759 they purchased a lot on the north side of New Street, and the schoolhouse was erected—twenty-four feet

---

[1] Memorial of Burlington Monthly Meeting, on John Woolman. Printed in full, Journal, Whittier ed., pp. 259-263.

long by twenty feet wide and eight feet high to the eaves ; having an arched ceiling, ten feet high in the centre.   There was just the one room, with a front door and a back, fireplace, and windows ; and it stands there still.   Perhaps the Reverend John Brainerd, on his periodical visits to the town, sometimes held his catechism there ; for why should he not have the loan of it ?   But perhaps not, since it was dominated by a Quaker majority who did not like the catechism ; for two years later, in '61, he bought himself a piece of land near the school in New Street,[1] and gradually built himself a small church and house.   And in '69 he moved in from lonely Brotherton, and made Mount Holly the centre from which he radiated out over his scattered parish.   But he had nothing to do with the building or running of the first school, which, though not under the control of the meeting, was established by citizens who were mostly Quakers, and run by them until the Revolution.

Whether John Woolman ever taught in this schoolhouse or not is hard to say.   But just as the tradition which connects this school with Brainerd is untrue, so the tradition which connects John Woolman's school with the Little Meeting-house in Mount Holly seems equally ill-founded.   The Little Meeting-house was built in 1763 in a little lane leading into Mill Street.   The site was a few hundred yards back from John Woolman's former shop, and the tradition that he ever used the meeting-house to teach in appears to have arisen from a feeling that it would be so handy for him.   But since he had severed connexion with the Mill Street premises fully half a dozen years before this date, that reason will not hold water.   Meeting-houses were occasionally used for schools, "in the care of Meeting," as a temporary measure, but the arrangement of a meeting-house with close-ranked benches and Ministers' gallery was not convenient for a school.   There was no room for desks or tables.   Certainly the Burlington Monthly Meeting Records, though they contain the minutes permitting the new meeting-house to be built in Mount Holly town, "for the convenience of Friends," and the later minutes of its use, contain no suggestion of its ever being used as a school. And Woolman's school was not "under the care of the Meeting."   After the Revolution, when Mount Holly had increased enough in size and importance to be established as a Monthly Meeting—instead of, as

---

[1] Then called School Lane, and later called Brainerd's Street.   The transition to erroneously calling the school "Brainerd's School" is obvious.   See George de Cou, Pamphlet No. 1, *Historical Sketches of Mount Holly and Vicinity* (p. 12).

heretofore, being under the wing of Burlington Monthly Meeting—and sectarian feeling had increased in the town, a school was started under the care of the meeting, and a Friends' Schoolhouse was built. Woolman's son-in-law, John Comfort, was one of the trustees for the purchase of a lot for school purposes and bought a lot from John Brainerd on December 21, 1779. A minute 8th mo. 5, 1784, states "that a school-house and dwelling-house were established at Mount Holly, but no school held at the time." By 1788 the Friends' School was in operation.[1]

Woolman might have held school in his own small house—the phrase "opened a school" might seem to suggest it ; or more probably, owing to the double lack of a regular supply of scholars and of regular teachers, the little arched schoolhouse kept irregular term, and Woolman might have been one of those who opened it from time to time ; not salaried by the trustees, but charging each individual scholar according to the parents' means. The Memorial written after his death implies that he taught some children for nothing, "being concerned for their help and improvement."[2] His friend, Anthony Benezet, was a salaried teacher. The city schools had already been established on the English public school system, with salaried teachers hired and regulated by a board of governors, and regular terms and curriculum. The Board of the Penn Charter School agreed, through Israel Pemberton Senior, to "allow Benezet the use of the School, and the sum of Fifty Pounds out of the Publick Stock [of the Yearly Meeting] for one year in consideration of his teaching fifteen poor children." He had now given up his teaching at Penn Charter to start a progressive Girls' School which, like Penn Charter, was established and paid for by the Philadelphia Yearly Meeting. Benezet was hired by the Board "to keep a morning school for teaching poor girls. It is agreed to employ him on twenty pounds to teach twelve poor girls."[3] He could add as many paying pupils as he wished, and wrote to a friend about "my school, which its with difficulty I keep from being too large." Elizabeth Drinker was one of his paying pupils and, a little later, wild Becky Jones (as Rebecca Jones was called in her youth). The former gives a vivid glimpse of a school which, though larger, must have closely resembled Woolman's, for Woolman modelled his upon it. "Read to-day Parnell's Hermit," she wrote in her diary, "a poem, and

---

[1] See George de Cou, *Historical Sketches of Mount Holly and Vicinity* (No. 2, p. 3).
[2] Burlington Monthly Meeting Memorial.
[3] George S. Brookes, *Friend Anthony Benezet*, p. 271.

an essay on Creation added. This little book, most of which I had by rote : the reading revived old sensations—we used to read it at A. Benezet's school, standing in a row,—four lines at a time." And again— the entries several years apart—" 'Every moment of time is a monument of mercy,' was a copy we used to write at A. Benezet's school." The writing of copies was an important part of the curriculum, not only teaching penmanship but influencing character. Woolman and Benezet worked together sometimes on producing suitable mottoes for their pupils to copy. A number of Woolman's are written out in his Account Book. "Take good measures to obtain good ends." "Brace not up a tale-bearer—A whisperer separateth friends." "Steel too soft may turn. Steel too hard may break." "Anger clouds the judgment. If anger burns, stand still." "Hay once eaten and there an end"—perhaps to be interpreted as meaning the same as the old proverb about spilt milk. In copying the sentence over and over to cultivate a good clear even handwriting, according to the standard of the eighteenth century, the copied phrase sank deep into the mind, and might float up again to render good advice in time of need, and help to shape a life. But a great many of Woolman's copies, strange to say, have no moral content, all the same, but are simply delighted expressions of joy in life, especially country life—about air and frost and rain and the scent of flowers and the pleasure of rapid movement and of agreeable employ. Things he evidently liked to speak of, but thought too light to put into a published Journal.

When Rebecca Jones took over her mother's school for girls—and made a great success of it—there were then three friends together, Benezet, Woolman, and Rebecca, all interested in educational theory and experiment. Rebecca was a good deal the youngest, but she kept her end up. One winter day when Woolman was spending a week-end in Philadelphia with his cousin Reuben Haines, the wealthy brewer—Reuben's mother was a Burr[1]—there was a heavy snowfall, and people woke on Sunday morning to find themselves imprisoned by drifts before their doors, and their windows blind with snow. Rebecca and her woman partner gave up all hope of getting to meeting ; but at breakfast-time there came a resounding knock at the door. First thing that morning when Rebecca had peeped out no one could have got near to knock— Drinkers Alley, where she lived, was waist-deep and more. But now, when she ran to open, there was John Woolman, like a snowman,

<hr/>

[1] Sister to Woolman's mother.

banging down his shovel and stamping the snow off his feet. He suggested that she should invite him to breakfast—he thought he'd earned
it ! And he had dug her out a path all the way to the Bank Meeting-
house in Front Street. He sometimes visited her school, and would
pleasantly write copies for them in his peculiarly clear, free handwriting.

Woolman wrote two brief essays on schools.[1] His theme is the
natural innocence and sensitiveness of children and the importance of
getting the right tutors for them, so that their minds may expand under
right influences. "That Divine Light which enlightens all men, I
believe, does often shine in the minds of Children very early." No
tutor should undertake the teaching of too many children at once,
because then problems of authority and discipline arise. Besides,
individual attention gets the best results, both in scholarship and in the
more important matter of character. Children are not all alike, and
"require diligent observation of their several tempers and dispositions.
A large number of children in a school is often a heavy weight on the
mind of an honest tutor." Here again the problems of poverty and
wealth enter in.

> Where the straitness of a man's circumstances, joyned with the
> small wages set on teaching children proves a temptation and so enters
> his heart that he takes charge of too many . . . or where the desire
> for wealth so corrupts the heart of any that they take charge of too
> many, here the true order of a Christian education is frustrated.

On the other hand, if all people lived modestly and avoided superfluous
luxuries, and labour was wanted only for things consistent with that
modest standard, there would be so much money to spare for education
that teaching might be better paid, and a man could make a decent
living by teaching a small number of children, and the temptation to
overcrowd his school might be lessened. Moreover, it is the responsibility of parents to demand something more in tutors than mere ability
to teach by book, not to "send our children to men to get learning who
we believe are not influenced by the Spirit of Truth."

His interest in education probably started in Mary's earliest years,
and he composed a *Primer or First Book for Children*, which was popular
enough to go through three editions. On one occasion his Account
Book records selling a hundred of them at once. Anthony Benezet
also speaks of a different and revised *Spelling Book and Primmer* on

[1] One in *A Plea for the Poor* and one in *Considerations on Pure Wisdom and Human Policy*
(Gummere, pp. 427 and 390).

which he and Woolman collaborated, and which was published after Woolman's death.   Benezet explains "that the end proposed by myself and our dear friend J. Woolman, who had the work much at heart," was not only to make learning easy to the children, but to arrange it by such easy stages that "good mothers, situate in lonely places where instruction cannot be procured, may be enabled to instruct first themselves and then their children."[1]   Another fruit of Woolman's sympathetic observation on his journeys in the "back parts" of nine provinces.

Regarding the payment of schoolmasters, Benezet remarks in one of his letters—advising a young man not to "come over" in expectation of having "encouragement" as a schoolmaster :

> Several have sought employ that way without success, the country people, as well friends as others, are shamefully penurious ; sometimes by chance a Schoolmaster has met with that is just worth a single man's while ; but that is uncertain and such that the better he does his duty, so as to bring on the children, so much the sooner is he likely to be out of employ.[2]

This all tends to indicate the probability that John Woolman's teaching was done from time to time in the little arched schoolhouse, which had no resident teacher, no regular term system or curriculum, no salary attached to it, and whose trustees were his intimate friends.   If a teacher came in from outside he came at his own risk, his "wages" entirely depending on the number of his pupils.   And the pupils were often considered to be brought on far enough when they could read, write, and do simple sums.

Josiah White sometimes kept school—surely in the same schoolhouse— and Mary Woolman was one of his pupils.   Woolman's Ledger contains an entry crediting Josiah White's account five shillings and threepence "For schooling Mary," to be reckoned against "Boards had by thy tenant (80 foot)," and "A small house taken from Mother's lot," which together left Josiah indebted to the amount of some six pounds.   Since Mary was in her late teens at the time, it is likely that she was having lessons in botany and the medicinal use of herbs, such as would be invaluable to any future wife and mother.   But advanced students who wished special tutoring could be taken at the same time and in the same room with babies who were struggling with the alphabet, and youngsters of eight and nine learning to read and cipher.   So long as there were not

[1] Brookes, p. 328.   [2] Ibid., p. 317.

too many, mixture of ages and subjects could be handled, and was expected.

As for school supplies, they were billed to the parents—ink powder, quill pens, paper, the "Primmers," and printed books for the older ones, such as "J. Griffith's Books," and "Eliz. Jacob's Epistles." The inconvenience of keeping a school, even a small and irregular one, in the single living-room of a small house would seem to rule it out when a schoolhouse was available less than a quarter-mile away. John Woolman hated a cluttered-up life. The peaceful atmosphere of learning would mix very ill with the banging of the iron pots, the cooking over the open hearth, the necessary kitchen work of even the simplest civilized housekeeping. It was different when Mary was small, and they could take a quiet mid-morning hour, with perhaps another neighbour's child, to teach her her letters ; or, later on, give her brief tasks of reading and writing. But when John Woolman's concern for his daughter's education led him inevitably on to a concern for poor children of the neighbourhood who were not being taught, and with his usual impulse to do something about it he started a "school," where some children paid and some did not, he surely made use of the best conveniences available. And what was available was a rent-free building where an approved schoolmaster was "encouraged" to hold school for as many children as he could get to come or liked to be responsible for.

It was both an evidence of improved education in the district and an encouragement of it when in 1765 the "Bridgetown Library Company" was formed, and obtained a royal charter by the interest of Governor William Franklin. The Governor's summer home was near Mount Holly (which was at present going through the Bridgetown phase of its existence), a mile west of the Rancocas. The books were housed on the second floor of the market-house, and Benjamin Franklin's son would have a flying start in selecting and obtaining a good first choice. Travel books, voyages, life and customs in foreign parts, were particularly popular. They provided a romantic element missed, but desired, by those who shied at fiction. But the establishment of a library is an important landmark in a town's history, offering an almost free entry to all the world's culture for those too poor to buy their way in. Woolman always urged all his pupils, boys and girls, to arrange their adult days in such a way as to ensure time to read.

There was a certain free-and-easy casualness about the life, which

seemed actually to create more time. When it was convenient to hold
school one held school. But since payment was precisely for service
received, with no contract on either side, it was a simple matter for
either teacher or pupils to take time out. When the cow calved, when
the calf was slaughtered, when the haying had to be done, when the
apple harvest was ripe, or when a journey was projected, school was
"out," and might or might not resume, according to demand. And the
ever-revealing accounts balance one occupation against another. Aaron
Barton has to pay John Woolman for some schooling, and for a spelling-
book, for making lichen breeches buttons, for five shillings' worth ("I
believe") of grass in the meadow eaten by his cow, and again for the
"pastureing of the Cow Some part of Sum^r" (eighteen shillings' worth
that time). But John Woolman owed him for "work in my Meadow,
work in Nursery, for Henry [a son?] Choping wood at Door etc,
Henry mowing 2 mornings, 'self' helping about one load Hay, Henry at
work a little on the Road [one shilling and threepence worth], 'self'
and Isaac [another son?] helping Stop the Water, and [the largest
amount of money] for Weaving." When the accounts were balanced
Aaron was only two shillings in debt.

Very little money changed hands. William Cox at Ferry bought
sixteen shillings' worth of "Stone at my Quarry," and Woolman used
the ferry twice in part payment. William Calvert bought of Woolman
a brindle cow, cost five pounds, and also owned two quarters' rent at
fifteen shillings each. He was Woolman's tenant for the Mill Street
shop and house, now owned by Mrs Woolman Senior ; against his
debt Woolman sets a credit for "1500 feet of boards, 6 yds of Camblet,
1 ivory Comb, and a Looking Glass."

Mary Woolman now had suitors—one very favoured one—and it
is to be feared she was prinking. Her indulgent father, trying to steer
a difficult course between his pleasure in seeing Mary admired and his
apprehension of making her vain, submits to credit Aaron Smith with
two shillings and sixpence for Work at Mary's hat ; and Richard Perry
"Made shoes for Mary and Souled a pair for Wife." So Mary was
smart in new hat and shoes, had an ivory comb to smooth her hair, and
to set off the apple-blossom bloom of her nineteenth year. Young John
Comfort's eyes witnessed to her success, as well, or better, than her
looking-glass. And she was at no loss for a pillion on which to ride to
Monthly or Quarterly Meeting.

John Woolman did not impose his own objection to dyed cloth upon his wife and daughter. The mysteries of women's dress were beyond him. It was still considered sober and conservative to wear, as Sarah did, aprons dyed green and blue, and Mary's dainty white caps and aprons, innocent of dye to be sure, savoured not a little of the fashions of the world. Woolman left it to his womenfolk and paid the bills.

Beside cedar-wood from his swamp, stone from his quarry, hay from his meadow, Woolman of course sold apples from his orchard, and also apple-trees, often grafted. Brother Abram Woolman is charged for "8 grafted Trees, eight shillings, and 31 Natural Growth fifteen shillings." It looks as if Abram had six children at school with his brother John that season, for he is charged for "6 primers, total one shilling and three pence." If so, he was paying for some one else's children, for he had only been married four years. John Woolman makes him a dozen coat buttons and a pair of leather Breeches (they cost one pound ten if anyone wishes to know, and lasted almost a lifetime) ; and "makeing John's jacket and Some Trim^{gs}"—Woolman's namesake nephew, Abram's first-born, must have been about three years old—cost three shillings and sixpence. Abram also got "42 feet of 2 Inch Ceder Planck" for five and tenpence. And John is acting as his younger brother's banker and lawyer—as he did for most of them—and notes that Abram owes him for "Cash paid on Danl Antram's Bond, two pound two and threepence," but against all this is some "Credit on a Bond, nine pounds" which John Woolman has collected for Abram. Abram settled part of his brother's bill by cash and part "By 600 Ceder rails at Joseph Burr's" and "By Ceder logs at the Swamp" (of which he also owned one-seventh part) —"as many as made 1534 feet board measure." Presumably this completed the balance, and John had the Ceder logs sawn up at cousin Joseph Burr's at his own expense.

It was a good life. The scents of hay, cedar-wood, and apples blow across the years. And there is the warm interlocking, the mutual trust, of brother with brother, cousin with cousin, uncle and nephew and niece ; all the strong, stout fabric of a great family clan. In that clan John Woolman was regarded as the best business adviser, the clearest head and soundest judgment of them all.

Perhaps it was because many of his nephews and nieces had been his pupils in school, or perhaps it was because of his reputation among them as an exact man of business, that a tradition grew up about Woolman's super-accuracy which we know he did not deserve. One day John Comfort, walking with him in the orchard, exclaimed, "There's a tree full of caterpillars !" John Woolman, looking at it with the eye of an expert orchardist, answered, "Not quite full."[1]   No doubt he meant, in a technical sense, that the tree could yet be saved ; but Comfort—or those nephews of Woolman's to whom he passed it on—interpreted it as an instance of meticulous exactness of statement.   Two of his nephews, with this in mind, made a wicked plot to entrap their too truthful uncle into a lie.   They enlisted the services of John Comfort, who was living in the house as an orchard apprentice.   "When you see us coming," they said, "you are to go into the house.   One of us will get Uncle Johnny to come out.   As soon as he is outside you must leave by the back door—don't let him see you ; just stand there hidden on the back stoop.   Then we shall ask if you're in there, and he'll say you are ; but you won't be !   So we can prove him to have said something that is not true—we can call it a lie !—and tease him ever after."   John Comfort was amused, and they carried out the plot.   But when Woolman came out and one of the young men asked him, "Is John Comfort in the house ? " perhaps Woolman smelled a rat.   After all, he had been about a little ; and his worst enemies had always found him too keen-witted for their comfort.   Why all this ceremony ?   Why didn't the youngsters go inside for themselves and see ?   So he answered, "Well, he was when I left ! " and looked kindly sardonic at their crestfallen laughter.   You just can't catch Uncle Johnny, they said.

His love of animals was so marked that it was mentioned in the Memorial which his meeting at Burlington wrote of him after his death. Yet he never mentions a horse by name or makes any sweet remarks about them, like Samuel Fothergill's "my good old faithful companion who carried me 2300 miles last winter."   True, Samuel Fothergill rode his horse to death (he was a heavy man, unaccustomed to the care of a mount on such long journeys through such wild country), and Woolman never did.   But Woolman relegates his horses to that part of his life occupied by his cows, and Mary's smaller pets, and his farm and his home affairs generally—that is to say, his private life.   John Comfort remembered a day when they were working together cutting down the harvest that Woolman discovered blood on his scythe and found he had

[1] Dillwyn Parish papers, Historical Society of Pennsylvania.   Recollection of John Cox, of Oxmead, Burlington, born 1757 at Moorestown.

killed or injured some animal concealed in the grain. "Such was his distress that he called off his labourers to assist him in making search for it. The circumstance affected him so deeply that he did not recover from the pain it occasioned for a considerable term afterwards."

When it became necessary to slaughter a calf he did not—like some squeamish people—relegate the horrid task to others, but did it himself in order to make sure that it was done painlessly. Binding the calf so that it could not struggle away, he laid it on a slab of smooth wood he had prepared for the purpose, and instead of slitting the jugular vein and letting it bleed to death—the accepted mode—he took a sharp axe and killed the creature with a single blow.

As to sheep, he only kept a few, perhaps borrowed from Asher's flock for the orchard's sake :

> Sheep are pleasant company on a plantation, their looks are modest, their voice is soft and agreeable ; their defenceless state exposeth them a prey to wild beasts and they appear to be intended by the great Creator to live under our protection and supply us with matter for warm and useful clothing. Sheep being rightly managed tend to enrich our land.[1]

There is some difficulty in deciding the exact size and the precise site of John Woolman's small farm. The eleven acres which he bought from Peter Andrews in 1747 for twenty-five pounds he sold back to Peter's son, Benajah, in 1760 for twenty-eight pounds. But Benajah already had a house—the substantial house on his father's farm ; and Woolman does not suggest, nor do any traditions concerning him, that he himself moved from his original home and bought another at any time after the move from Mill Street. He left house and lands to his wife and daughter when he died. And all the entries in his later Account Books suggest an estate of at least several acres. Perhaps Benajah's purchase was a straw sale for the sake of clearing a title, and Woolman both remained in actual possession of the eleven acres we know about, and later also in real final possession. Perhaps the sale was something to do with Woolman's being an executor for the wills of Peter Andrews and of Esther Andrews, both now deceased, and with the eleven acres being "part" of a larger tract inherited by Benajah.

Most estimates of Woolman's total farm place it at about thirty acres.

---

[1] *Conversations on the True Harmony of Mankind and How it may be Promoted* (Gummere, p. 461).

but   cut   hut   nut   rut
rex   fex   vex   fix   fix
box   fox   the   for   out
cry   dry   fly   thy   try

The Sun is up my Boy,
Get out of thy Bed,
Go thy way for the Cow,
Let her eat the Hay.
Now the Sun is fet,
And the Cow is put up,
The Boy may go to his Bed.
Go not in the Way of a bad Man;
Do not tell a Lie my Son.

blab   crab   ftab   fwab   ft   ffi
chub   club   grub   fnub   ff   ffl
bred   bled   fled   fhed   ff   ffl
brag   drag   flag   fnag   fi   fh
brim   grim   fwim   trim   fi   ct
crum   drum   plum   fcum ,   fl   &
bran   clan   plan ,   fpan   fl

No. 9 A Birkbeck

A
First Book for Children.

Much useful reading being fullied and torn,
by Children in Schools before they can read,
this Book is intended to save unneceffary expence.

By JOHN WOOLMAN.

The third Edition enlarged.

ABCDEFGHIJKLMN
OPQRSTVUWXYZ
a b c d e f g h i j k l m n
o p q r f s t u v w x y z

Note. When the above Alphabet is defaced, this Leaf
may be pasted upon the Cover, and the Alphabet on the
other Side made ufe of.

PHILADELPHIA:
Printed, and Sold by JOSEPH CRUKSHANK, in Second-
street; and by BENJAMIN FERRIS, Stationer and
Bookbinder, in Wilmington.

Two Pages from Woolman's *Primer or First Book for Children*

[See page 314]

strengthned with his Love and ßent
inwardly waiting for his Councill —

This afternoon saw Portland
of England calld the Lizard and
with a pleasant breeze of wind
Stood our course and So, So along
in plain sight of the green fields
before night

Some dunghill ford's yet
remained alive, of those which the
passengers took for eating on the
way. — I believe about 14
perished in the storm, at sea and
I believe near as many dyed with

Cag them under a necessary
Alass mans understanding to Seas to believe
would be more agreable to true wisdom
on me
4: 6: a pilot came of from
Dover and my beloved friends
Saml Emlin and Sarah Logan
Came here with a view to go in
a Stage Coach to London it being
about 78 miles

hasting with the Same at this
time was a tryal upon me, to
go on shore felt most agreable to
my own will, the yearly
meeting at London was now near,
and though the passage by water

There are two other entries in Woolman's accounts which cast some light in this direction. The first is dated September 1762.

> On the twenty-sixth day of the Eighth month in the Year of our Lord one thousand and Seven hundred and Sixty-two Then John Shinn Wheelwright agreed to take the Shop which I have built on in other lot and the north end of the lot as enclos'd and to pay to me as rent Three pounds and fifteen Shillings proclamation money p^r year to be made in one payment on the 26th da 8 mo in each year and it is agreed that I Shall not turn him out of the Shop without rendering a Sufficient Reason and that he shall not leave the Shop without rendering a Sufficient Reason Witness my hand JOHN WOOLMAN.

The other is dated "10 mo 1763," two months before the sudden move to Asher's house for the winter. It reads :

> Memorandum. Aquilla Shinn agrees to take the North End of my orchard next year and to put on what Dung his stable affords and hath now in his hands 18s as due for Rent for Said ground from James Dobins which is intended to purchase Dung as to Rent from Aquilla we defer any agreement till next fall.

Another later entry undated is a list Woolman made, naming some of the planting in his orchard, row by row, beginning "Sweeting behind and Smoakhouse from T. Haineses."

The favourite and likeliest site of the little farm is the traditional one in the Springfield Road beside the Buttonwood Run.[1]

[1] Now in possession of Louis J. Kaser, Burlington County Superintendent.

XXXV

THE WALKING JOURNEYS

I KNOW of no employ in life more innocent in its nature, more healthy and more acceptable in common to the minds of honest men than husbandry, followed no further than while action is agreeable to the body only as an agreeable employ," was Woolman's opinion ; and he speaks with intense enjoyment of "the sweetness thereof . . . so agreeable and inviting to us . . . carried on in the open air . . . a healthful honest employment." But dark visions flowed before his eyes from time to time, under the apple blossoms of the spring, under the reddened apples of the fall, dim shapes but haunting of "poor Captives, bound with thongs, heavy laden with Elephant's Teeth," that pass on their way to the sea. He saw "three or four hundred slaves put into the hold of a vessel in a hot climate" and a whiff of their tainted air came to him among the orchard scents. He saw the captives sold in America and made to labour, and what with grief, unfamiliar diet, and hard labour, he saw "some thousands of them die every year in what is called the Seasoning." He saw the survivors and their children "under the Command of Overseers in a painful Servitude." And he felt for the young "as with the affliction of my children" and for the old "their Misery hath felt to me like the Misery of my Parents." Their bitter lamentations day after day rang in his ears, and their mournful cries in the night hindered him from sleeping.[1]

<hr>

[1] Gummere, pp. 500, 502.

In all his hours of happiness the burden never left him.   There it was,
waiting his attention as he performed his delicate grafting of a Smoakhouse with a Sweeting, or hived the swarming queen bee, or swung
the scythe in the green hay.   And as its pressure weighed, and the
immediate season seemed "convenient," he must perforce leave this
sweet employ and bend again to his unpleasant task.   In 1766, 1767, and
1768, in addition to visiting families in Pennsylvania and New Jersey—
near home, or away on the sea-coast, from Cape May to Squan—
Woolman made three journeys south into Maryland : one down the
Eastern Shore of the Chesapeake, one down the Western Shore, and one
to the gathering of the Maryland Yearly Meeting at West River.

There was a marked difference between these Southern journeys and
any he had taken before.   He made them on foot.   It was uncomfortable, exhausting, and—what he sometimes minded most of all—
slow.   In the first journey, down the Eastern Shore, the weather was
hot, although it was the month of May ; and there had been a long
drought.   Plodding along, ankle-deep in dust, bundle on back, tormented by flies and thirst, stifled in the airless forest stretches, grilled in
the miles of cleared land among the parched tobacco-fields, when he
with his companion arrived at his destination he still had the hardest
part of his task before him—the personal dealing with the slave-holder.
Woolman finally fell ill and had to delay to rest.   He resigned himself,
like a good soldier.   After all, "we had gone forward much faster than
I expected before we came out," and "I saw that I had been in danger
of desiring to get quickly through the journey."[1]   So he thanked God
and took courage and calmed his mind.   The very exhaustion to which
he had to succumb was an argument in favour of the tedious walk.   He
had always found that "conduct is more convincing than language."[2]
Now when, haggard with fatigue and covered with dust, he presented
himself at a wealthy planter's house, and in return for hospitality urged
him to throw away his comforts and do without slave labour, his words
were supported by the silent witness of his own abandonment of comfort.   Again, the other side of his reason for walking was to stimulate
his own imagination.   The Indian visit had meant so much to him
partly because he had felt in his own body, with his five senses, what it
was to live like an Indian.   Now he felt in his body, as far as it was
possible for a free man to do so, what it was to live like a slave.   That is

---

[1] Whittier ed., pp. 193-194.   [2] *Ibid.*, p .86.

to say, to live at the very bottom of the social scale "that I might have a more lively feeling of the condition of the oppressed slaves." When he toiled along the road under the hot sun, his eyes dazzled with glare, his nose and throat parched with dust, his body soaked with sweat, his physical sensations were exactly similar to those of the slaves he passed, toiling among the rows of tobacco.

The difference came at the end of the day. He was cordially welcomed to a spacious, comfortable house, built for coolness ; he could bathe, and wash his socks, put on clean linen, and brush the dust from his coat and shoes. He would be given cooling drinks and good food, and would sleep between linen sheets in exquisitely clean surroundings. He could imagine then how it would be if his skin were black, if he had to go home to a hot and fly-ridden hut and eat a scanty supper of parched corn and potatoes, and hardly even achieve comfortable rest between the days of excessive labour ; and all without hope of respite. So as he sat at evening on a tree-shaded porch, talking to a courteous host and a sweet and gracious hostess, his aching limbs bore reminder of the sufferings of the slave, and he braced himself against his perennial temptation to merely enjoy good company. This was the nub of the unpleasant task laid before him. To break through the comfortable veneer, shatter the smooth surface of elegant behaviour, hurt the kind people who were trying to entertain him—seem to insult them, even—this was what he shrank from with every fibre of his being. It was not the public meetings, though they were sometimes a "hard exercise." It was the private remonstrance, the incisive criticism of those who had taken him in unaware, which seemed to go against the grain of his natural gentleness and of his sense of manners. He hated to see their faces turn from warm cordiality to shock, surprise, offence. It was not easy to submit to the Divine Commander and be "made content to appear weak or as a fool for his sake."[1]

"I have experienced," said Woolman, "that in the midst of kindness and smooth conduct to speak close and home to them who entertain us, on points that relate to outward interest, is hard labour. Sometimes when I have felt truth lead towards it I have found myself disqualified by a superficial friendship." And yet real friendship was made of sterner stuff. "To see the failings of our friends and think hard of them without opening that which we ought to open, and still carry

[1] Whittier ed., p. 150.

a face of friendship, tends to undermine the foundation of true unity."

On the Eastern Shore walk he was accompanied by "my beloved friend John Sleeper," a neighbour and landowner in Mount Holly. But the next year, April 1767, Woolman set off to the Western Shore alone, "rode to the ferry opposite Philadelphia," then left his horse and continued on foot. This "lonesome walk" was exceedingly depressing, and, like the medieval saints, Woolman—the fatigued body reacting on the spirit—tended to welcome this depression as taking him deeper into a feeling sense of the misery of those who were oppressed. The pleasure he experienced from the company of a fellow-traveller, as a set-off to sad thoughts, was this time absent. Whatever went wrong on the journey he had to deal with alone. And it is likely that he did not strike less hard on that account, whether in a private conference or a public meeting. At Gunpowder Quarterly Meeting, for instance, "in bowedness of spirit I had to express with much plainness my feelings respecting Friends living in fullness on the labours of the poor oppressed negroes." And the next day, too, laboured "honestly and fervently among them."[1]

With his light-coloured clothing and hat and brief, uncompromising language, he was like an embodied conscience and was sometimes regarded with dread. He hurt, and he knew that he hurt. But the times were urgent. Not the most far-seeing statesman of the period was more aware than John Woolman that some tremendous catastrophe was imminent. Choiseul, the French Minister of Louis XV, might see its form more exactly—or perhaps the wish was father to the thought—when he sent a secret agent to America to study signs of the insurrection against the Mother Country of England, which he expected as a result of the English colonists' no longer needing England's protection against the French. But Woolman knew, "in that which is immutable," that the cancer of slavery, though itself only a symptom of a larger disease, would go far to cure that disease if it were boldly cut out. He launched his heaviest attack on slavery, because that was concrete, removable, and intolerable ; but he attacked the whole system of selfish profit and the luxury which it supported and which in vicious circle made it necessary. It led to misery, it led to war, and it led, above all, to spiritual death. All luxury of any kind must go by the board. Only a deadened imagination, according to Woolman's thought, could be

[1] *Ibid.*, p. 199.

content to use or possess anything superfluous—giving that word a reasonably liberal interpretation—while any fellow-creatures were short of the necessities of comfortable living.   And he was not thinking only about slaves.

There was a move on foot among the colonies in those years to combine in a passive defence against the Navigation Acts by a complete boycott of goods imported from England.   Woolman made no direct comment on this political movement, or on the greed for profit on the part of individual importers which brought about its failure—leaving the united boycott on tea alone, as a symbolic act, a thumbing of the nose at authority, less injurious than insulting.   But he expressed himself several times on the advisability of curtailing the export and import trade, thinking that "were all the fruits of the country retained in it that are now sent abroad in return for strong drink, costly array, and other luxuries," and more inter-colonial trade promoted between more settled districts and less settled ones, there would be a more general level of prosperity.   In the Essay written in 1772 as a *Dialogue between a Labourer and a Rich Man* he makes the Labourer say :

> Now, my friend, I have beheld that fulness and delicacy in which thou and thy family live.   Those expensive articles brought from beyond the sea . . . serve chiefly to please the desire of the eye and to gratify the palate, which I often observe in thy family as in other rich families. . . . Our merchants, in paying for these delicacies, send a great deal of grain and flour abroad out of our country.   Hence grain is more scarce and dear, which operates against poor labouring men.

It is easy to see that it was not only the hot-blooded Southern planter, sensitive about slaves, who would be uneasy in Woolman's company, and who might publicly or privately indulge in a retaliatory harshness of speech which might even draw tears from his tender-hearted opponent. Woolman might be so far removed ; but less because his own feelings were hurt than because he realized how deep his words had gone in the heart of the other.   A man who would lose half a day's labour hunting for a wounded hare to put it out of its pain was made conscious that he had, with well-aimed and deliberate stroke, wounded the spirit of a friend.   But like the surgeon who uses the knife for health's sake, he would not pause, even if his own heart bled.   Not only the slave-holders, but Israel Pemberton, William Logan, John Smith, and John

Smith's sister Elizabeth, long ago hostess for her father, and now, un-married still, giving herself to good works, sharing Woolman's projects —even they would suddenly find themselves cut to the quick.

> I observe thou livest easy as to bodily labour, and perceive thou takest interest at seven per cent. . . . I am now thinking of that Christian exhortation Love as Brethren ! and propose to thee my neighbour, whether a way may not be opened for thee and thy family to live comfortably on a lower interest, which if once rightly attained would I believe work in favour of labouring people.

And Elizabeth in particular found herself dealt with—very gently indeed, as to a woman loved as a sister—because of her use of silver vessels on her table, which were not only "superfluous" and savoured of luxury but were a product of the silver mines.   And the conditions of slaves in the silver mines of South America were well reported to be past belief. Woolman was also an observer of "Landholders who paid interest for large sums of money, and being intent on paying their debts by raising grain have by too much tilling . . . robbed the earth of its natural fatness. . . . To impoverish the earth now to support outward greatness appears to be an injury to the succeeding age."   He had definite and vivid information to give as to what he meant by the hardships of ordinary poor people and is ready to describe the common problems of the day labourer who pays rent for a small house and raises up children. In his dramatic dialogue he makes the Poor Man say :

> Some keep a cow, and labour hard in the Summer to provide hay and grain for her against winter ; but in very cold winters hay is sometimes gone before spring, and grain is so scarce, thro' much sending it and flower abroad, that the grain intended for a Cow is found necessary to be eaten in the family.   I have known grain and hay so scarce that I could not get near so much as my family and creatures had need of ; being then sparing in feeding our Cow, she hath grown poor.   In her pineing condition she hath called aloud. I knew her voice and the sound thereof was the cry of hunger.   I have known Snowy, Stormy weather of long Continuance.   I have seen poor creatures in distress for want of good Shelter and plentiful feeding, when it did not appear in the power of their owners to do much better for them, being straitened in answering the demands of the wealthy.   I have seen small fires in long cold Storms, and known sufferings for want of firewood.   In wasting away under want, nature hath a voice that is very piercing.   To these things I have been a witness, and had a feeling sence of them ; nor may I easily forget what I have thus learned.

This sort of thing was uncomfortable hearing for the New Jersey or Pennsylvania Quaker who was thanking his stars that he was not as those tobacco-growing Southerners with all their slaves. And they would have liked to encourage John Woolman to behave in a more orthodox manner and deal in those safe Christian generalities which Benjamin Franklin found so unreal. But John Woolman was incurably interested in the hard facts of life ; disagreeable as they might be, you could get your teeth into them. To him the Kingdom of Heaven was as real as the City of Philadelphia, and the one ought to have been inclusive of the other. He could speak, certainly, in the language of heaven ; but it was no transition at all to him to begin to talk like an economist about real wealth and artificial wealth, about trade, and about gold.

If gold is brought into our country through means which renders the condition of the poor more difficult, it appears evident that of that gold the country had better be without. I believe the real use of gold amongst men bears a small proportion to the labour of getting it out of the earth and carrying it about from place to place. It doth not appear to have much use but that of a currency, and if trade extended no further than was consistent with pure wisdom I believe trade might be carried on without gold.

And as to creating artificial scarcity in order to raise prices and get more of this gold, Woolman knows about that too, and speaks of it so gently, so moderately, that it suggests he was touching some one very near.

This of making grain scarce in a plentiful country for the sake of getting a little fine mettal as a Currency amongst us which doth not appear to be worth its weight in Steel for instruments relating to the common business of getting a living in the world, appears to me to work against the general convenience of poor labouring people, and is often a snare to others respecting the inward state of their minds. The members in society appear to me like the members in a man's body, which only move regularly while the motion proceeds from the head. In fits, people sometimes have convulsive motions which, though strong, are only manifestations of disorder.

So he expressed his thoughts on the body politic, in conversation, in brief addresses—"very close and plain," as an appreciative hearer commented[1]—and in his writings ; and increasingly he sought after the exactness and comparative permanence of the written word. The least

[1] Benjamin Ferris, of Wilmington. See *Friends' Miscellany*, XII, 273. Also printed Gummere, p. 97.

self-conscious and egotistical of men, conditioned never to think of his work as an art, he yet worked as an artist, and could not avoid some of the artist's thoughts. A sentence flashes unexpectedly, incongruous in its context—"He who forms things out of nothing, who creates and having created doth possess, is more truly rich than he who possesseth by receiving gifts from another."

Most of his days were, after all, frames for slow creation, slow ripening. Between the years 1767 and 1772 Woolman's exact times away were : April of '67, the Western Shore walk, about a month ; September, a fortnight in Bucks and Philadelphia counties, on horseback ; in the winter some visits in families in Mount Holly ; in 1768 about a month in Maryland, without a horse ; and then no more trips away from home until the last ; a quiet interval of four years.

During these six years John Woolman was given tangible evidence that he had helped forward the cause of the slave in his own province. In 1767 the New Jersey Assembly passed an act imposing a duty on every slave imported for the next two years, and was able to enforce it ; and when the two years were up so well had it worked, so sufficient was the backing of the best public opinion, that a stronger act was passed, to be in force for ten years, imposing a duty of fifteen pounds on every imported slave. New Jersey's Charter, Penn's Concessions and Agreements, enabled her to do what Virginia strove to do in vain, "for it put the power in the people."

Still more deeply was the Society of Friends affected by Woolman's labour, especially throughout the Philadelphia Yearly Meeting. Quakers began to be uneasy at owning a slave—it was very hard to defend themselves to John when he came for a visit ; and he had been known to walk straight out of the house when he came to take a meal with a prominent elder and had a surprise and shock in finding a slave in attendance. As for buying a slave, that felt worse ; but selling a slave felt worst of all. The slave system in the Society of Friends in the two Quaker provinces was dying out fast. Anthony Benezet helped forward the reform equally by his writing and his wide correspondence with many outside the Society of Friends. Most valuable of all was the example of his evening school for Negroes, and his emphatic statements that the Negroes' intelligence was equal to that of white children. In 1770 Benezet's Negro school was taken over officially by the Philadelphia Monthly Meeting, and a building provided for it.

The change in mental attitude of the average well-meaning Quaker is exemplified by Henry and Elizabeth Drinker, whose diary shame-facedly confesses the sale of a slave girl in 1756, and the aftermath. In 1807, October 12, Elizabeth Drinker notes :

Our black Jude, whom we sold 51 years ago when she was a child, was here this afternoon. I thought she was dead, as we have not seen her for many years ; she is now not far from sixty years of age. When we sold her, there was nothing said against keeping or selling negroes ; but as we were going to board out we knew not what to do with her. Some time after, we were more settled in our minds, and were very sorry we had sold the child to be a slave for life, and knew not what would be her fate. We went to Springfield to repurchase her, but her mistress, a very plausible woman, refused to sell her, though we offered her forty pounds and had sold her two months before for twenty-five. Some time afterward her mistress sold her to Parson Marshall. It was several years after she had grown up, and when there was much talk of the iniquity of holding them in bondage ; my husband called upon her master, and had some talk with him, who did not see the matter in the same light as we did, but at his death he left her free.

The advantage of John Woolman's slow, thorough, individual way of working was that every one convinced became one to convince others in his turn.

Incidentally, when Woolman was making the walk down the Eastern Shore a man called Joseph Nichols—not a Quaker—attended several of his public meetings, and was deeply impressed by him. Nichols was himself a powerful speaker, had begun to hold meetings on his own account, and had a number of followers. Some ten years after Wool-man's death the Nicholites organized into a sect.[1] One of their tenets was an objection to the mixture of colours or materials in their dress, and they all wore headgear of natural wool—the men hats, the women caps. It would be far-fetched to suppose that this had any connexion with Woolman's undyed clothing. True, he was all much of one colour, but he "mixed materials" freely, wearing in the usual way woollen cloth, linen, leather, and fur all at one time. But a deeper principle of the Nicholites may well have derived from, or been strengthened by, their leader's contact with John Woolman. It was made in 1780 a disownable offence for any Nicholite to own a slave.

[1] They were localized in Maryland, chiefly on the Eastern Shore.

XXXVI

DIDO'S WEDDING; PLEURISY

WHEN Woolman was in his forty-seventh year, the year of the lonesome walk, Uncle Joseph Burr died. It was to Sarah, and to John Woolman through her, as if she had lost a father. Henry Burr Junior now became master of Peachfields, Joseph Junior getting some extra money, because he did not need the house; and Aunt Jane continued to live at Peachfields with her son and daughter-in-law. Hospitality was no less, contacts were frequent and affectionate, but, as wistful human beings say, clinging to the familiar and the known, "it was not the same." They were reminded painfully of the impermanence of this world.

As John Woolman sought to console his sorrow-stricken wife a panorama of memories of Peachfields passed through his mind. Memories first and dearest of the days of his own courtship of that sweet Sarah who now clung to him. But a memory of a later courtship, very different on the surface, brought a smile. Two black faces by the kitchen door or in the moonlit yard behind the house; slave-born Dido, servant of Aunt Jane, courted by the slave boy, William Bowen. Woolman had for a long time been interested in Bowen, an intelligent young slave owned by cousin Moses Haines at Springfield. When going over to Springfield on family visits Woolman had often taken time from social hours to give William Bowen lessons, finding him quick and responsive, and had taught him to read and write. Moses Haines had cordially approved, and seeing that this Negro, at any rate, had a soul, he used to have Bowen come into the meeting-house when he drove his master and mistress to meeting, and sit through the meeting on the back bench. Under this treatment William Bowen became in heart and mind a Quaker, but not all John Woolman's efforts on his behalf could persuade even Mount Holly Meeting to accept the Negro's humble application to join in membership. Woolman was more successful, however, in dealing with good Moses Haines on the subject of Bowen's freedom ; and Moses Haines entered into a written agreement that Bowen should be free when he attained the age of thirty. At twenty-eight, with only two more years to run, and a regular job promised him with his old master, William felt that his love for Dido need wait no longer. He consulted his friend John Woolman, and Woolman was warmly in favour of their marrying at once. William Bowen and Dido had been keeping company for years. Dido had been born a slave on the Haines plantation, and had been obtained by the Burrs in girlhood. It goes without saying that any uncle of John Woolman's would be very uncomfortable owning a slave, and Joseph Burr had given Dido her freedom several years before. She was living in the house now as a paid servant, saving up her wages against her wedding, and whenever Moses and Patience Haines drove over to visit at Peachfields with their Negro coachman the sound of liquid darky laughter was heard from the kitchen.

All the people concerned easily agreed that William and Dido should marry this year ; but the method of the marriage was another matter. There was no such thing as legally protected Negro marriage if either partner was a slave. Almost any routine would do. But William Bowen was at heart a Quaker, and he wished, he deeply longed for, a Quaker wedding. John Woolman was determined he should have one. The meeting-house could not be used, but every other essential of membership was made available to the young Negro by John Woolman's efforts. He organized the marriage, went through all the proper formalities, wrote out a wedding certificate in his own clear, beautiful handwriting, and obtained the full co-operation of Joseph Burr. Since the bride had long been a servant in Burr's house, it seemed a natural and fatherly gesture for him to consent to hold the wedding there. Anyhow, after he had talked to nephew John he felt it would hardly be possible to do otherwise. So on May the third, 1763, a dozen or more Quakers and fifteen Negroes assembled in the spacious square living-room at Peachfields and sat down in two companies, on either side of the room, divided by the barrier of race and custom but united in a common purpose and a common worship. The deep silence flowed about them like a river, and dissolved the barriers between heart and heart.

History was made there when, in complete spiritual equality with their masters, William and Dido, instructed in their part, rose and softly repeated the Quaker formula of marriage. And history was made again when, at the close of the long meeting hour of mingled silence and speaking, twelve white people and fifteen Negroes set their hands as witnesses to the same document, and that document a Negro wedding certificate.[1] Among the names of the signers appear those of Joseph Burr and John Woolman and Sarah ; and Patience Haines's signature also represented—"by her order"—the signature of the illiterate Negro Catherine, mother to Dido, and Josiah White's also stood for Negro London, Dido's father, which suggests that Catherine and London were respectively the servants of Patience and Josiah. Most of the Negroes, however, made shift to sign their own names, one way or another, and Primas, Woolman's Negro labourer, signed his good and clear, as became his master's servant. A day of extraordinary happiness, stolen from "the shape of things to come."

Blessings, then, on Uncle Joseph Burr. And the future history of William Bowen and Dido, who thus became symbols of their race, was all that their friends could wish. Forty-two years after John Woolman's death William Bowen was received into membership with Friends at Mount Holly Meeting—by that time an independent Monthly Meeting, able to accept members on its own without reference to Burlington. John Woolman's published writings had sunk deep into many hearts, and in his own neighbourhood they were anxious to live up to him. William Bowen was well known to be Woolman's protégé and pupil ; and, moreover, Bowen's constant devout attendance at meeting, as a free man, and the quality of his life gradually wore down prejudice. When Bowen died at the age of ninety, having been a Quaker in good standing for the last ten years, the meeting wrote a testimony about him. Once some one, referring patronizingly to Woolman's influence on Bowen, said to the old Negro, "I suppose you're trying to follow in the footsteps of John Woolman." To which Bowen replied, with that inborn simplicity and dignity of the African which survived the degradations of enslavement, "I am trying to follow in the footsteps of Jesus Christ."

[1] Appendix V.

Up to the year 1772, however, when William and Dido attended Mount Holly Meeting—now generally held in the Little Meeting-house in the lane off Mill Street—they saw John Woolman sitting in the ministers' gallery, and sometimes heard him speak.   And in the year '69 the Woolman clan in Mount Holly, already large, was increased by two weddings.   Uriah Woolman, eighth child and fourth son of Samuel, married Susanna, daughter of John Burr.   And later in the year Asher Woolman married Rachel Norcross.   How Uriah got away with marrying his first cousin is impossible to tell.   It was not allowed ; people were disowned for it.   When a later generation Eber, son of Abraham, fell in love with his cousin Rebecca, daughter of Asher, he had to elope with her in a canoe down the Rancocas on a Sunday morn when everybody was in meeting, and be married by a magistrate.   But it is ridiculous to suppose that Uriah, a prosperous merchant of forty-one, would elope with the thirty-three-year-old Susanna.   They must have been married without meeting permission, by a minister of some other church—a hireling priest, in fact—and no doubt they came under discipline for it.   Yet they were not enough in disgrace to prevent them from taking up their residence composedly in Mount Holly, in a beauti-ful country house on the Rancocas, built by Uriah and called by him Breezy Ridge ; and there they lived a happy and highly respected life. They had no children.

All this made life in Mount Holly more delightful to John Woolman and Sarah and Mary.   There was another home to visit ; another centre of sociability and affection.   And yet that year John Woolman's heart was restless.   The sense of those "toyling out of sight," upon whose toil perhaps his comfort in some way depended, weighed on him con-tinually.   He had done his best to clear his life of any dependence on them.   He had given up all use of sugar and molasses and rum and dye, products of the West Indies ; he had given up trade ; he earned his money as far as possible within an area which he could watch, and so keep clear of all connexion, however subtle, with the accursed things of oppression.   But his health was below par, and his conscience suffered sickness with his body.   He was dieting himself ; always a risk, but still more so in the eighteenth century.   His adviser was Josiah White rather than Dr Ross ; but perhaps that was no odds.   The location of the trouble was his nose, where he had some not easily diagnosed diffi-culty ; it sounds like sinus trouble, since it was not of a nature to show outwardly, and did not attract the attention of observers or of the doctor who attended him in his last illness. But headache, lack of energy, and a feeling of blockage in the nose—he called it a lump—made him conscious that he was unfit for road travel. He was, however, an excellent sailor, and perhaps he could travel by sea. Maybe this condition was an indication that something of a sea voyage was demanded of him. He was reading a horrifying pamphlet by Anthony Benezet about conditions in the West Indies. He loved and admired Benezet, and was deeply depressed by the pamphlet. He could think of nothing more to be dreaded, nothing more against the grain, than to go where those atrocities were perpetrated and see them for himself. Yet just because he shrank from it, he began to feel more and more that that was what his Inward Guide required.

It was at this time that he realized the wrong he had done years before to Negro James, and set to work to rectify it ; and while he was on the business of rectifying, what about those profits he had made aforetime on the sale of rum, molasses, and sugar ? Would it not seem an admirable piece of justice to use them for a voyage to Barbados on behalf of the tormented slaves from whose labours he had ignorantly profited ?

Common sense reasserted itself through his malaise and told him that these reasons were not good enough. They did not amount to the urgent need to go to a definite place which had driven him forth before. But after a period of indecision very unlike himself, he came to a most uncharacteristic compromise. He would get all ready to go, and then see.

So he obtained his certificate from the Monthly Meeting, and from the Quarterly Meeting and the Spring General Meeting, saying very little in support of it ; but he was by this time in such a position of influence and trust that there was no Friend living who would venture to question John Woolman's "concern." He put his affairs in order so that his wife and daughter might not be inconvenienced by his absence, released himself from engagements, and held himself in readiness.

The Pemberton brothers and John Smith, West Indian importers as they were, put themselves as usual at his service. John Woolman did not see life quite as they did ; indeed his practices, "avoiding the use of plate, costly furniture and feasting," had to their view sometimes "the appearance of great austerity," but they believed him peculiarly enlightened, and they could not help loving him. That word "avoid" shows that Woolman was not regarded by his rich friends as a poor man, and that when he wrote his dialogue between a labouring poor man and a rich one, even if he was in part repeating conversations he had really had, he was not speaking as a poor man in his own person.   The hungry cow and the fireless house were not his own.   One does not say of such a one that he avoids the use of plate.

In November Uriah, who had been into Philadelphia on business, rode out to Breezy Ridge and called at John's house in passing to leave a letter for his brother.   The careful Pembertons kept Woolman's answer :

11 da, 11 mo, 1769

BELOV'D FRD,

I rec'd last Evening a letter from my brother Uriah wrote at the request of James Pemberton informing me that James hath a Vessel in port which he expects may sail for Barbadoes the latter End of this month or beginning of next.

I know not but that I may look toward this Vessel for a passage, but am desirous to inform thee of this my information, as thou Exprest a brotherly care for me respecting a passage.

I remain thy

Loving frd, JOHN WOOLMAN

For John Pemberton, in Philad[a].

He then had a note from Israel Pemberton offering him the loan or gift of a bed for the voyage, but replies :

17-11-'69.   I yesterday saw a Mattress, and have this Morning agreed for some coarse wool, and expect to make one at home.   I feel gratefulness toward thee for thy kind offer, but believe to make one may be best for me.

thy loving frd

JOHN WOOLMAN[1]

Better not be obligated to an importer at such a moment, even if he had always been one of your dearest friends.   Woolman was also anxious not to take cheap passage, correctly estimating that the low rates were a result of the great trade.   On the contrary, as "a testimony in favour of less trading" he wanted to "pay more than is common for others to pay if I go at this time."[2]

---

[1] Pemberton Papers, XXI, 85, 87.
[2] Whittier ed., p. 209.

In the end, however, he did not go. The preparation to go had eased his mind and cleared his heart. It had silenced within him the false self-accusation that he shrank from the service because it was disagreeable. Two days spent in complete readiness and quiet meditation in Cousin Reuben's house in Philadelphia had given him a perception that to harrow himself by seeing the cruelties of which he had read would do nothing to make them stop, but to protest to his friends who were deep in the Barbados trade might set something going that would get results. So he prepared a written statement pleading against the "trading in or frequent use of any produce known to be raised by the labour of those who are under such lamentable oppression," especially confessed his own practice when in trade with restrained regret, and took the paper to his friend, John Smith, in Burlington. Then, accompanied by John Smith, he took it to James Pemberton, in Philadelphia. Both read the paper with deep attention and respect, and had some "weighty conversation" with their friend, which gave him hope of results. Woolman then left it with them and went back to Mount Holly.

Although for some days after John Woolman "felt like a sojourner with my family," he gradually sank back with relief into neighbourhood duties and the winter life of home. On December 13 there was Asher's wedding, and all who could possibly go must be there. John loyally went, though feeling unwell and weakened by dieting. The weather was damp and raw, and when he got back after a long meeting and a tiring family gathering at the old homestead afterwards he was seized with shivering chills. The long-drawn-out period of being below par had come to a violent climax. Sarah with warming-pan, and Mary with hot herb brews, could not make him 'throw off' this cold. He woke in the morning with a high fever and a bad attack of pleurisy.

In this illness John Woolman nearly died. But since he did not die, he came out of it cleared and strengthened. Many times his anxious nurses gave him up, and he had himself "no expectation of recovery." But before he lapsed into delirium he had told his wife not to send for a doctor, and Sarah, touchingly trustful of Johnny's judgment in this as in other things, did not do so. This precaution probably saved Woolman's life, because he was in no condition to stand the bleeding which his high fever would have made Dr Ross consider absolutely necessary. Instead, he had the hot poultices and mild natural drinks prescribed by his good friend, Josiah White, and the tender, constant nursing of his

Y

wife and daughter, aided by many friends. Sarah and Mary took their turns by day ; and at night John Woolman's men friends divided the hours between them. Some of the names flash into the record this one time only, yet they were loved and loving familiars in John Woolman's befriended life. Aaron Smith, and John Sleeper, and William Calvert ; and John Bispham, whose wife's grandfather was Sir Patrick Reynolds, Lord Mayor of Dublin ; and Henry Paxon ; and Caleb Carr, whose great-grandfather had been Governor of Rhode Island. And always, night and day, coming in at odd hours to oversee the patient's condition with his bright black eyes, was faithful, intelligent Josiah White. Burrs and Woolmans haunted the house, running errands, bringing dainties, doing what they could. If love could cure him he would be cured soon. But the sickness was of the heart as well as of the body, and could not be readily reached.

In lucid moments he would sometimes ask his watchers to take down sentences at his dictation, so they got into the way of having pen and ink handy. In their minds as they wrote was often a conviction that they were taking down the last words of their friend.

On January 4, 1770, about five o'clock in the morning, Caleb Carr so took at Woolman's dictation the following, writing it into a blank page in the Account Book :

I have seen in the Light of the Lord that the day is approaching when the man that is most wise in human policy shall be the greatest fool ; and the arm that is mighty to support injustice shall be broken to pieces ; the enemies of righteousness shall make a terrible rattle, and shall mightily torment one another ; for He that is omnipotent is rising up to judgment and will plead the cause of the oppressed.

And Mary wrote on another page a fragment of good sense uttered by her father in delirium, to the effect that

the holy Spirit that now works within me (in a weak and broken Constitution) may work in young lively Constitutions and may strengthen them to travel up and down the world in the feeling of pure Wisdom, that many may believe them and the purity of their lives, and learn instruction. . . .

On Sunday mornings a group of his friends and their wives would gather in Woolman's room for an hour of worship, a "meeting," and this passage was uttered on such an occasion. Half-conscious of his surroundings, perhaps, seeing Mary's beautiful strong young form outlined against the window, with John Comfort beside her and the sunshine making a nimbus of her hair, his suffering spirit was ready to lay down its burden and leave the next generation to carry on the work. Mary added the explanation, "Taken from the Mouth of my Father as he uttered it in my hearing on a first day meeting while dying." The last word is almost illegible, and was perhaps intentionally erased. John Woolman, after recovery, added the date "7:1:1770," and a confirmatory comment that he believed these words "proceeded from the Spirit of Truth operating on mine understanding, and I meddle not with the Fever."[1]

Woolman's watchers being trained in this way to write things down, Aaron Smith makes a record of his own.

One Saturday morning, in the dark small hours when the pulse of all life is low, and John Woolman's illness, with its ups and downs, was a fortnight old, a group of three or four were watching in his room. They did not expect him to survive the night. He was cold to the touch, and they could not warm him, though a fire was burning on the hearth and the window was tight closed against the January frost. The air in the room was not bad, because the large chimney acted as ventilator, but the odours of simmering herb tea and wood-smoke mingled with the odour of death. John lay in an apparent coma. On a sudden he roused and called for water, and there took place a painful scene which reveals some of the subconscious self-torment which lay below Woolman's controlled surface and steady common sense. It had recently been stirred up by the paper he had written for the Pembertons on the subject of the Barbados trade and his own regrettable share therein. His illness smudged the years together and made him feel that this sin against humanity had been committed by him yesterday.

On 7th day Morning about ye 3rd hour, ye 13th of ye 1st Mo. 1770, John Woolman having for some time lain like a man a Dying, did then call for Water to Wet his tongue for it was dry, and he wanted to Use it, and then told us then present that the forepart of the Same night he had very great horrours on his mind for Departing from the purity of his Testimony in relation to the West India traffick. Under this Anguish of Soul, Evident to all about him, he Stood up on his feet, tho' week, and with a lamentable Voice Cryed mightily to God that he would have Mercy upon him a Miserable Sinner for

[1] Gummere, p. 112.

that he had lately, under Extream weakness, given up the purity of his Testimony against the West India trade, In partaking freely of rum and Molasses ; After long Conflict with these Horrors he appeared more Easy, as believing God would be gracious to him. He now informed us he had found the mercys of God to be toward him, and that he had an Evidence of Inward Peace, and that God had Excepted of his great conflict with the power of darkness the fore part of this Night.

Uttered by John Woolman's lips and wrote by Aaron Smith.[1]

All this was part of the debt exacted by nature for a life strung to a pitch superhumanly high.   But perhaps no worse than the price exacted from genius in any form.   In Woolman's slow, brooding, polished, close-packed writing he had turned his thoughts in one direction too constantly for comfort or for health.   He had audaciously set his life against the torrent of the world's suffering.

This period of sickness was marked by hideous nightmares, the most macabre of which took place during Woolman's convalescence, a parting kick of the disease he had conquered. With his respect for dreams he recorded it, but with his usual good judgment he did not include it in his Journal.[2]   It is a kind of parable, in dream terms, of the overwhelming horror of the slave trade and the general indifference to it.   One dream, however, that Woolman had during his illness was to him as if he had been through the experience of death and come to life again ;   and though painful no doubt to endure, it became a beautiful symbol in the aftermath.   It was too sacred to tell at once.   Woolman probably wrote it down soon after his recovery in that secret notebook that we never see ;   but it dwelt with him for two years before he wrote it, under special circumstances, into the Journal itself.

He chose to conclude the account of his illness with the great resurgence of returning health, when, still too weak to write, the tides of his being were all flowing again strong and free, and the frightful overstrain which had almost broken him was for ever past.

Near a week after this, feeling my mind livingly opened, I sent for a neighbour, who at my request wrote as follows—

The place of prayer is a precious habitation. . . . I saw this habitation to be safe—to be inwardly quiet when there were great stirrings and commotions in the world.

Prayer at this day in pure resignation is a precious place ; the

[1] Gummere, p. 112.   [2] Ibid., pp. 115–116.

trumpet is sounded ; the call goes forth to the church that she gather to the place of pure inward prayer ; and her habitation is safe.[1]

Convalescence moved forward with the spring. His own blood began to quicken with the running of the sap in the maple-trees, his conviction that he had still more work to do began to cheer him with forward, not backward, looks as the grass flushed green. His progress to steady health was sure, if slow. He got on with his writing—the set of essays called *Considerations on the True Harmony of Mankind.* And presently he could move a little out of doors in the sunshine, and then make little riding excursions, two miles to Peachfields, one mile to Breezy Ridge. The first prolonged excursion from home was to Monthly Meeting at Burlington, where his welcome was royal indeed ; and he went to dine at the house of John Smith. But the happiness of that occasion was badly marred. John Smith had thoughtlessly got out the Logan silver, which had belonged to his dear Hannah, and "the drink was brought in silver vessels and not in any other." John Woolman was thirsty. He did not want to wound his friend. He had loved John Smith from boyhood, and was ready to allow for differences in their point of view. But the use of silver vessels seemed to Woolman worse than the use of rum or molasses. Silver was stained with the suffering of slaves ; and the only reason for using it was a bad one—worldly glory, parade of riches, luxury. No one could say that glass and china, or even wood and pewter, would not serve its purposes just as well. Yet Woolman did not like his first party with John Smith to be clouded with remonstrance or even with indirect rebuke, hated to chill the affectionate honour with which he was being treated ; but he would almost as soon drink poison as take his beer or cider from a silver cup. In his weak state the struggle to express this with all tenderness to his friend and host brought tears to his eyes. "Wanting something to drink, I told him my case with weeping, and he ordered some drink for me in another vessel."

John Smith never forgot it. As usual, conduct was more powerful than language. From this time onward, through the short remainder of his life, Woolman always consistently refused the use of silver table service in other people's houses as he had always refused to adopt it in his own ; and he was able to record that both at home and abroad, "none, I believe, have ever been offended at what I have said on that subject."[2]

---

[1] Whittier ed., p. 213.   [2] *Ibid.*, p. 241.

In March he was able to ride to Philadelphia and call for the money he had left with Cousin Reuben Haines to pay for the Barbados voyage, had he gone. And with finis completely written on that episode, he turns with a whole heart to the sweet employ he loves best.

"*Four days after* [the above] . . . *29:3:1770.* Grafted near the South-west corner of my Nursery, about 4 joynts of fence North of the corner, about 30 Molasses Sweetings." And in April, with the blossoms dormant in their buds :

grafted 2 short rows of Newark sweeting (a winter apple) the north row the longest. Stands about 15 foot from the west side of the Nursery (and extends Eastward) near the Middle of the Board fence on the ditch bank. . . . Grafted Sundry short rows in divers parts of my Nursery with a good Winter Sweeting.

His rest from public activity was complete. He did not speak at any meetings all that year.[1]

[1] Whittier ed., p. 241.

XXXVII

MARY'S HOUSE

WHEN spring came round again, and April painted the countryside with delicate colours, John Woolman was preparing for the wedding of his only daughter with John Comfort.

On April 3 the company gathered in the meeting-house at Mount Holly, and Woolman and Sarah, with the strange ache that comes to parents' hearts at such a time, watched the well-grown pair standing up amid the silence in the modest strength of their youth to take their lasting vows. Grandmother Elizabeth Woolman was also present, and signed the certificate in a clear though infirm hand. She was seventy-five years old.

For a year or two past John Comfort had been living with John Woolman to learn orcharding, and now he did not propose to take Mary away, but, in the old patriarchal fashion, to move into married quarters with her in her parents' house. In literal truth John Woolman had gained a son rather than lost a daughter. But Woolman's views on simplicity did not involve putting up with inconvenient and overcrowded living. A small house had allowed ample room for himself, Sarah, and Mary, with a house servant and often a resident orchard apprentice. But there was no room for an expanding family. So in the summer of '71 the Account Book carries the itemized statement of the "Expence of Building a Brick House." "Cash paid to Hancock in full for 8800 Bricks, 8 pounds 18 shillings ; Cash paid to Zachariah Rossel in full for 9800 Bricks, 12 pounds 5 shillings" ; nearly two thousand more bricks were got from two other places, and six hundred special ones, at three shillings and sixpence a hundred, were brought from Philadelphia. Stone and lime and timber and glass are mentioned ; and hooks and hinges "for ye doors."   Matthew West is paid four pounds for "makeing Door cases winder cases and Sash," and another four pounds ten for "Expence of boards and timber used" by him. Negro Primas and John Wright, Joseph Mullen, Joseph Wever, and other "labourers" get their pay ; William Norton gets four pounds for the use of his wagon and team in "hawling 17 loads of Stone," and another four pounds ten for "Expence of hawling 18,600 Bricks Supposed to be." The expense of "Diging the Celler supposed to be" is three pounds ten.   John Bispham sells quantities of "Scantlen laths and Boards" ; and Woolman gets pounds and pounds of nails from William Calvert at his old shop. Adam Forker does the "Glaising" and painting. Brother Jonah helps supervise.   The fascinating scene of busy activity confirms the tradition that this house was built for Mary and her husband, and was given to them as soon as it was ready.   Circumstantial evidence is all in favour of it.   Woolman was not a builder by trade, and there is no record of the sale of this house which he took such detailed interest in just after his daughter's wedding, and paid for from the cellar up.   John Comfort had eight brothers and sisters, whereas Woolman had only Mary to provide for.   Why should he not give her a house ?   And if this house is not for Mary, why all this fuss about digging and "hawling" and sawing and painting and "glaising," all this adding up of the price of bricks and lime and labour, to fill up the days of the last summer John Woolman was to spend at home ?   Mary's house, then, was duly built and finished.   But the exact location of the house is lost.[1]   It was

[1] The Woolman Memorial, at 99 Branch Street, Mount Holly, was for a long time supposed to be this house.   Recent research, principally by George de Cou, has established that the "Memorial" house was built in 1786 by Jabez Woolston.   But the lot on which it stands was bought from John and Mary Comfort, and—since Mary's name is included as joint owner in the deed of purchase—it was almost without doubt part of the land she inherited from her father.   A deed of sale dated 1/25/1776, "John, and Mary Comfort and Sarah Woolman to John Shields," for a lot containing a little more and an acre park of John Woolman's farm shows that as long as Mrs John Woolman lived her name also had to appear as a grantor in the transfer of land in which she has an inherited interest.   And another deed of sale, dated 10/28/1791, from "John Comfort and Mary, his wife, to Samuel Stockton for 156 acres including the John Woolman farm," although it also includes some tracts purchased independently by John Comfort, is additional evidence that Mary was required to appear as a grantor in any deed involving sale of her inherited land.   On this evidence—since none of the other Woolman houses are standing except the Burr House, now privately owned and rather remote—it seems not unsuitable to retain the Branch Street house as a Woolman Memorial.

somewhere on John Woolman's land ; and its site is mistily suggested
when, in laying out Garden Street in Mount Holly in 1775, the old road
book states that Garden Street was opened from "the Burlington Road
to the bars of John Comfort's apple orchard." John Woolman had then
been dead only three years, and his brother Jonah was the commissioner
who laid out the road. Error as to the boundary line of the apple
orchard recently inherited by John Comfort, through Mary, from John
Woolman would be out of the question.

Woolman's decision to end his period of retirement with a major
journey was unknown yet to any beyond his family. But one indication
that it was already determined on and being carefully prepared for is
shown in the fact that he paid for all the materials and labour in the
building of Mary's house with cash. The settlement was immediate.
There was no carrying on the books of alternative long-term services
of teaching or surveying or legal work to balance part of the account.
Another piece of evidence of the same kind is in relation to a nursery
of apple-trees he was preparing for Asher. The first plan written down
was that Asher was "to have the ground the trees grow on for 4 years
from the 25 of 4 mo. 1771, to pay me for them six Pounds ten shillings
in two years from the above date. The trees to stand at owner's risque."
But later a change was made in the margin—"Asher agreed to buy trees
out of my nursery, and give up this distant bargain."

Something had happened then between April, when Asher's nursery
was staked out, and August, when the house was begun, something that
had clinched John Woolman's intention to travel far. And that was
the visit of Samuel Neale. He was a prominent Friend from Dublin,
Ireland. Like Jane Crosfield before him he probably stayed with Asher
—who now had a wife to carry the duties of hostess. Mrs Samuel
Woolman, though not bedridden, was enfeebled, and content to let her
half of the kitchen fall under another's sway. John Woolman and
Sarah, and John and Mary, took two horses and two pillions and rode
over to the old home meeting on the Rancocas to hear—or at any rate
see—the interesting stranger. It is Samuel Neale who gives us the
account, and it is obvious from it that he had heard of Woolman and
looked forward with a good deal of eagerness and curiosity to meeting
him.

    7th mo, 23rd, 1771. I was at Rancocas meeting. . . . Here I saw
John Woolman for the first time. I take him to be a sweet, clean-

spirited Friend ; his unity with the true Seed may be felt by his savoury conversation and . . . selfdenying life.

24th. Went to Mountholly meeting, where very many Friends assembled from different meetings. . . . I was much afraid of this Meeting, as they have had great privileges . . . here lived Abram Farrington, and to this Meeting belongs that worthy exemplary Friend John Woolman, whose life and conversation shines in Christian purity. . . . Pomp and splendour he avoids, does not choose to use silver or useless vessels . . . his house is very plain, his living so also ; and yet he enjoys plenty of the good things that are necessary for Christian accomodation. We dined with him, and were kindly entertained.[1]

The Little Meeting-house in Wood Lane was not large enough for occasions like these. The old large meeting-house in Woodpecker Lane was opened and used.

As Neale himself remarks, "It happens when a stranger travels the intelligence becomes so universal that the public assembles, and those who seldom attend any place of worship then come."

Neale was a friendly and vital man, whose early experience had been somewhat similiar to Woolman's own. Now he was happy to be under that much-discussed Friend's roof, and to experience at first hand Woolman's unexpected charm. They had plenty to talk about. The worst heat of the July day was past when they gathered round the board. John Woolman at the head, a little lean still, had yet recovered, by his wise regime, a serene health. His eye was bright and clear, his face tanned by outdoor life. He was fifty-one years old, and his hair, tied tightly back at the neck without a bow, was touched with grey. Since his illness he had allowed his beard to grow, keeping it clipped with scissors, and there too silver hairs were intermingled. His light suit was cool and pleasant-looking in the summertime, and Neale did not at any time comment on it. The evening sun through the vine-shaded window flashed on the incongruous gold button sleeve-links which Woolman wore in his cuffs for sister Elizabeth's sake. Mrs John Woolman at the foot shed her shy, sweet smile on the company, and her delicately gracious manners gave ceremony to the meal. The young married pair were absorbed in each other, but not to the exclusion of interest in the guest from the old country. Their happy faces, ruddy with health, their splendid bodies, were examples of the young America that was growing up everywhere, better fed, less exposed to hardship, ready to carry

---

[1] Barclay, *Lives of Samuel and Mary Neale*, p. 167.

unthought-of burdens under a flag that was not yet made. The servant
Betsy, almost one of the family, served the meal hot from the brick oven,
with beer chilled from the spring. And perhaps a guest or two were
present, close friends who would not break the intimacy of the hour ;
Josiah White and his wife, maybe, or John and Hannah Sleeper, or the
Bisphams. Brother Uriah Woolman, or Cousin Henry Burr, dear
as they were, and always welcome, would perhaps not be quite the
right mixture for this specially valuable time. And the talk, round
the table or out under the trees afterwards—whatever it was about, it
made the necessary difference. Ever since the visit of Jane Crosfield
Woolman had had a stirring in his heart which said "perhaps." The
visit of another Englishwoman, Rachel Wilson, in the year of Woolman's
illness, had intensified the question, had made him feel still more of a
drawing towards England and towards that part of England—the North
Country—of which they wistfully told. And now he was thoroughly
well again and as strong as he would ever be, his daughter was safely
married, his wife had an excellent protector in her new son-in-law ;
there was nothing to prevent him from going if he felt he had to go.
The conversation with Samuel Neale made Woolman feel without
any doubt that he had to go.

One thing that might have influenced Woolman's decision, and that
was almost sure to have arisen in their talk, was the attitude of the
English Government on the slave trade, and the indifference of the
English public. In December the King in Council had issued an order
under his own hand to Virginia, commanding the Governor "Upon
pain of the highest displeasure to assent to no law by which the importation of slaves should be in any respect prohibited or obstructed."

Such orders could not be issued if the inhabitants of England were
alive to their duty ; more, thought Woolman, even if the Quaker inhabitants were alive to their duty. Quakers in England were shut out of
political life, but they tended to be articulate, they were generally well-
to-do people who were influential in their neighbourhoods, and they
were powerful in the world of finance. The banking business of England
was largely in Quaker hands.

From the time of Neale's visit Woolman began to prepare, with his
usual efficiency, for crossing the seas in order to visit Friends in England
and do his part to rouse them up ; particularly Friends in the northern
parts of England and specifically Yorkshire. He made up his mind in

July. He built Mary's house and paid the bills ; called in and settled most of his outstanding accounts ; put all his affairs in order, concluded and arranged for the publication of his current set of essays, the dialogue called *Conversations on the True Harmony of Mankind* ; wrote a long farewell epistle ; arranged for the publication of his Journal ; obtained the necessary Quaker certificates—from Burlington Monthly and Quarterly Meetings, and from the Spring General Meeting, in March— and embarked on the first of May, 1772.

It was plenty to do in the time, but not too much. Normally Woolman disliked dawdling, but he equally disliked hurry. He got through business with dispatch, because he combined a clear, direct mind with a will that did not permit of that slack thief of time and efficiency, procrastination. He did not bind himself to a sailing date. It made for a feeling of calmness and peace simply to say that he would go when he was ready. But he worked towards being in England for the London Yearly Meeting, which met in June.

Calmness and thoroughness were never more necessary. Thoroughness, because he was going away for an undetermined length of time and would be beyond easy reach by letters. Calmness, because he might never return, and these last days would be precious memories.

One tie with his youth was already broken. John Smith was dead. The month before Mary's wedding John Woolman had stood by his old friend's grave. Only forty-nine years old, John Smith was resigned to go to where he believed he would meet again his beloved Hannah. His elder brother, Samuel, and his elder sister, Elizabeth, survived him, the latter not for long. Samuel, busy with his *History of New Jersey*, wrote a panegyric for his brother in which affection and admiration mingle with shrewd touches of character. John's warmth of temper, his love of writing, his gift for friendship and for compromise, are all there ; and two sentences in particular show how it was that these Smiths and Pembertons, who had developed so differently, yet appreciated Woolman. John Smith, like Woolman, "thought that the imputation of Faults without the Friendship of at least helping to mend them, was like finding a Traveller wrong and ungenerously refusing the little Assistance he wanted and had in it something cruel." And "Actions he thought the best interpreter of a man's religion to others."

Samuel Smith concludes on a note of unguarded grief, forsaking the pious phrases intended to propitiate a touchy Deity, and candidly harking back, forlorn and sad, to the early days of the bright Burlington circle. "He was in every conjugal relation affectionately tender :—a fond Father—an indulgent Master ;—He was more, but I must stop.—He was —my Brother—my most intimate Friend and Companion. I loved him sincerely."[1]

Elizabeth Smith decided to obtain a woman companion, and go to England with John Woolman. But when the time came she was dying.

On October 19, '71, Woolman closes his agreement with his current orchard apprentice, William Lee, and releases him. In April '72 he notes that he has paid his poor tax. And his last entry in the Account Book is a power of attorney to his son-in-law, "All due to me from people on Accompt I commit to the care of John Comfort to him to collect the same in a neighbourly way and apply it to the use of my Wife and his Wife and the rest of our Family as he may find Occasion. JOHN WOOLMAN."

This informal little note did not involve large sums. John Woolman had decided, however, that for an absence of the length and uncertainty of this one it was necessary formally to appoint a trustee for his estate, with power to act. His young son-in-law he thought too inexperienced for such a responsibility. Yet Woolman was sensitive about hurting John Comfort's dignity. Whoever was appointed must be some one whose authority would not be irksome to the young man, besides being some one whose first thought would be the welfare of John and Mary. Woolman's brothers Uriah, Asher, and Jonah, all in the neighbourhood, would not quite fill the bill. Even gentle Sarah might not like being in the hands of a younger brother-in-law, however competent. What Woolman was looking for was a father for the family. And he could think of no one more natural for the place than the other father, Stephen Comfort, to whom Mary was now a daughter. Stephen Comfort lived at the Falls, above Trenton, but that was a not too distant ride. And Stephen Comfort willingly consented to undertake the care of John Woolman's family's estate during his absence. On April 27 then John Woolman drew up in legal form a Deed of Trust which could also, in case of his death, operate as a will. And it was duly signed, sealed, and delivered in the presence of two witnesses, Aaron Barton and Bathsheba Barton.

[1] R. Morriss Smith, *The Burlington Smiths*, p. 277.

I John Woolman of Mountholly in Burlington County, West jersey having bought in time past Some Lands And John Comfort Son of Stephen Comfort having married our Daughter Mary And I the said John Woolman having it in my heart to prepare for a Voige to Great Britain on a Religious Visit do not see any way in which I may dispose of the Lands and buildings which I possess more to my own peace than to Commit them to the said Stephen Comfort In Trust for my Use and for the Use of my beloved Wife Sarah during the time that we and the Survivor of us may live in this world And that the Said Stephen Comfort may convey or devise all the Lands which I now possess to his Son John or to our Daughter Mary or to either of them and to their heirs and Assigns for ever as he in the fear of the Lord may believe right.

Now for the Uses aforesaid I John Woolman do fully clearly and heartily Grant Convey and Confirm all the Lands buildings and Improvements which I hold in fee simple To the Said Stephen Comfort his heirs and Assigns To the only proper Use and behoof of the Said Stephen Comfort his heirs and Assigns for ever.   Only Reserving to mee and my beloved wife and to the Survivor of us the whole benefit of all the Said Lands buildings and Improvements During the time of our living in this world.   In confirmation whereof I Set my hand and Seal the twentyseventh day of the fourth month in the year of our Lord one thousand Seven hundred and seventytwo.   JOHN WOOLMAN.[1]

This is the only will John Woolman made.   Stephen Comfort's will, made October 20 the same year, "Being Sick and weak in body yet sound mind and Memory," included the following clause—"I give and bequeath unto my son John Comfort and Mary his wife to them their Heirs and assigns for ever all that Estate of John Woolman Lying in the Jerseys or anywhere else that I have any Right to by will or otherwise." By that time the young Comfort couple had an heir.   Mary's first baby was born on the twentieth of June, and she very naturally named him John.

About the time of his grandson's birth John Woolman, far away amid an older civilization, where the miseries of the poor and the indifferent luxury of the rich were differently presented but no less striking than at home, was wrestling with himself again over the ever-recurring problem about laying up treasure.   It had been hard to leave Mary on the eve of her first confinement ; but he knew her to be surrounded with

---

[1] MS. copy by John Woolman, Historical Society of Pennsylvania.   Original in the office of the Secretary of State, Trenton, New Jersey.

tenderest care of many friends and relatives. His consolation was that she would want for nothing. And when his thoughts turned hourly to his wife he knew the same of her. When William Penn was abroad he had had to write to his wife, "I beseech thee to live low and sparingly till my debts are paid." But John Woolman's charge to his could always be "Spare no cost to make thy life comfortable as may be." This year and next and as far ahead as he could see that would be safe advice. Even after his death, as long as New Jersey real estate could give security his wife and daughter were secure. And New Jersey real estate, the basis of the province's stable currency, was inferior to no other investment in the New World. And what was all this but to lay up treasure for oneself ?

John Woolman grapples with this, not begging the question, even if he does not solve it.

There is an inclination in the minds of most people to prepare at least so much treasure for their children that they with care and moderate industry may live free from these hardships which the poor pass through. Now this subject requireth our serious consideration : to labour that our children may be put in a way to live comfortably appears in itself to be a duty so long as these our labours are consistent with universal righteousness ; but if in striving to shun poverty we do not walk in that state where Christ is our life then we wander.[1]

He forbids not laying up in the summer against the wants of winter ; nor doth he teach us to be slothful in that which properly relates to our being in this world ; but in this prohibition he puts in *yourselves*. Lay not up for *yourselves* treasures here on earth.

The poet Whittier, reading this passage, jumped to the conclusion, and went into print with it, that John Woolman said that it was all right to lay up treasure for your children. This would enlarge the needle's eye to let through almost every rich man's camel. Woolman is by no means so simple.

If we gather treasures in worldly wisdom we lay up *treasures for ourselves* ; and great treasures managed in any other spirit than the spirit of truth, disordereth the affairs of society. . . . They who hold plentiful estates have power over those who have only their hands to labour, and if they misapply this power the joints and bands of society are disordered. . . . A man may intend to lay up wealth for his children but may not intend to oppress ; yet in his fixed intention to

[1] Last essays, Gummere, p. 494.

increase his estate, the working of his designs may cause the bread of the needy to fail, and at the same time their hardships may remain unnoticed by him. . . . There is often a growing exaltation of mind, and imaginary superiority over such who have a small portion of the things of this life, and thus may become estranged from the tender feelings of true brotherly love and charity. . . . So far as power is put forth separate from pure love so far the government of the Prince of Peace is interrupted. . . .[1]

And he draws his conclusion, no easier to cut to pattern than the Sermon on the Mount itself. "While we love God with all our hearts and love not ourselves in a love different from that which we feel towards mankind universally, so long the way remains open for that *Life* which is the *Light* of men to operate in us."

A man selfishly engaged in the pursuit of riches for himself or his children was like a man lost in the dark ; like a man stumbling upon the dark mountains (memories these surely of the Indian journey). Worse, like a man falling, who has lost control of his actions, and will land he knows not where.

"To keep to right means in labouring to attain a right end is necessary."

Before John Woolman left for England he placed in the hands of his friend John Pemberton the manuscript of his Journal, his last essays, and an Epistle to be circulated among Friends. Neither the Epistle nor the Journal was to be published except in case of his death. The Journal ended with the close of his illness in 1769.

In March 1772, preparing to fold up—perhaps for ever—the short but full years in his own country, he sat writing his last American essay at his familiar table by the window. It was the *Conversations*, but it had bored him to keep the form, and he had abandoned it long before the end. Quill in hand, he looked out, brooding on his closing passage. The apple-branches, their buds hidden, stretched bare against the pale blue sky. A couple of woolly sheep, so pleasant in the plantation, were sober and matronly beside their leggy, prancing lambs. Over there, above the bank that dipped down to the Run, John Comfort had a bon-fire, burning up the winter twigs and brush, and Mary had gone out to speak to him. Their voices and laughter came faintly on the wind, mingled with the mild bleating of the sheep. How safe, how quiet it was, how protected from the cruel world's evil. What cause had these

[1] Last essays, Gummere, pp. 491, 470, 471.

dear ones to promote, what axe to grind, what uneasy ambition to drive them on ? This orchard was like a corner of Eden. John Woolman put his pen in the ink and wrote in his flawless hand :

> In the love of money and outward greatness the mind is perplexed with selfish devices ; how to keep ! how to defend from the crafty designs of the proud and envious ! and from the desperate attempts of the oppressed. Now in the bottom of these devices there is unquietness. . . . The mind in this state is left naked.[1]

So. What then was his last word to these children, to his grandchildren unborn, to his fellow-citizens, yes, and to his fellow-men, if this should in very deed and truth be the last thing he should say ?

He wrote it with care, and closed the book. Perhaps those who read it after could not bear it ; felt that that saying and all the essay beside was "the high that proved too high, the heroic for earth too hard." At all events, that essay and its conclusion did not come to print for sixty-five years, until the year that Queen Victoria came to the English throne. Until that time few read the line that carried that March day the quintessence of John Woolman's social and political theory—"we have no cause to promote but the cause of pure universal love."

[1] Gummere, p. 473.

XXXVIII

PREPARATION TO SAIL

THE choosing of a ship was a knotty problem to the eighteenth-century Quaker. Not only date of sailing and destination had to be considered, but it was necessary to go on board and sit about in the ship and "feel" whether this was the right ship or not. Sometimes a ship which had been rejected because it did not feel right was caught in a dangerous storm and delayed or sent to the bottom, and then the Quaker felt that he had received subtle advance information. If, on the contrary, the rejected ship did well and got in first it aroused no comment. If one's own ship was caught in a storm one had been "sent" there to take advantage of an opportunity of cheering and helping the rest of the company. So the test of "feeling out" the ship could not fail. It was absolutely watertight. Samuel Neale tells how when he was ready to sail home—a month later than Woolman—he "went on board a vessel bound for Cork to feel if I could go in her, but found a stop." That was June 6. Three days later "I went on board a good vessel bound for Cork, but could not see my way in her, though in appearance much better and more complete than another bound for Waterford and not likely to sail so soon." However, the inferior Waterford vessel "felt" right, so was chosen ; and Neale triumphantly records that the Cork vessel, in

354

spite of its brash looks and its sailing ten days sooner, "put into Waterford about 3 hours after us," while Neale had been able to get some
important meetings into the extra ten days on shore.

So Woolman went into Philadelphia, to Cousin Reuben's, prepared
for a lengthy process of choosing a ship. But there was a ship in harbour
called the *Mary and Elizabeth*, bound for London. The double name—
his dearest sister and his daughter—was like a call. Surely that combination could not fail. He went to "feel" her, and found that his
particular friend, Samuel Emlen, was booking passage in her. He
urged Woolman to join him. They went together to the cabin, a
commodious but too much ornamented room, and that did not feel
right. Then they went into the sailors' quarters, called the steerage,
where "we sat down on a chest, the sailors being busy about us. The
owner of the ship also came and sat down with us."

John Head, the Philadelphia owner, was himself a Quaker, and had
transported many Quaker passengers. He knew about the test of
feeling out ; but he was anxious to have it go right, and here on this
chest, among the bustle of the sailors stowing cargo and what not, did not
seem the right place for such a delicate process. So he presently suggested that they should "go and sit in the cabin as a place more retired."
Woolman's deep reverie was broken, and he rose, not to go to the cabin,
but to make his polite farewell. Mr Head was disconcerted to hear him
say that if he did take passage on the *Mary and Elizabeth* he "believed it
would be in the steerage."

Woolman went back to his room to think it over, but the news of
his bizarre intention flew about among his friends—spread by Head and
Emlen—and there was a tremendous fuss. Israel Pemberton, the "King
of the Quakers," who was known to have influence with Woolman, and
who knew ships, came down in all his might and majesty to call on
Woolman and persuade him out of this unreasonableness. He "laid
before me the great inconvenience attending a passage in the steerage"
and for a time it did appear very discouraging. In the morning two
friends—probably the Pemberton brothers—called for Woolman and
went on board the vessel again, and they considered the cabin and the
steerage, and no doubt emphasized their points on the spot.

But Woolman was in no Barbados mood. In vain the Pembertons
reasoned with him, and Cousin Reuben Haines and other friends and
relatives entreated ; in vain captain and fellow-passengers remonstrated.

John Woolman was only so far influenced as to think it necessary to explain himself fully to the owner, and took Samuel Emlen with him to the interview to hear what he had to say. But that settled, and John Head's consent obtained to his travelling in the steerage, Woolman merely turned on the others his usual charming and impervious front, with no intention of changing his mind and little inclination to talk about it. They might only get their feelings hurt if he did. Samuel Emlen, indeed, was hurt, even to tears.

The reason Woolman gave to John Head was that he had noticed a lot of superfluous trimmings and carvings about the cabin, both inside and out, and that he supposed "the moneys received from the passengers are calculated to defray the cost of these superfluities, as well as the other expenses of their passage. I therefore felt a scruple with regard to paying my money to be applied to such purposes."

If Woolman had been short of money he could have been helped out by Quaker funds. During the few days that remained before he sailed he had a large number of invitations from friends who wished to see him again before he went, and everywhere they "expressed their desire that I might have a more convenient place than the steerage" or were "concerned for me on account of the unpleasant situation of that part of the vessel in which I was likely to lodge." Woolman had only to lift a finger to have travelling funds placed at his disposal. But he had enough of his own. Economy had nothing to do with his choice, except in so far as he grudged spending his money for extras which he did not even admire, when so many were suffering direst distress for want of sheer necessities.

So Woolman travelled at his own expense. But Samuel Emlen, who was a wealthy man, has an item against him in the records of the London Meeting for Sufferings, November 20, 1772—"A Bill was brought in for the Passage and Accomodation of Our Friends, Samuel Emlen and Thos. Thornborough to New York, amounting to 63 pounds."

The last days dragged out as usual, waiting for wind, weather, and cargo. Twice during that time Woolman got home again to Mount Holly, once for two days. The second morning was his final farewell, and he went. But, unexpectedly, he returned again, coming in at the door as they sat at their evening meal, like one restored from another world. They could hardly believe their eyes, and sat staring. He leaned his hand on the doorpost, looking in at them, the April dusk behind his grey-clad form. And if to them he was almost an apparition they also to him seemed like a picture of the past. This was just as he had imagined them, with the candlelight upon their faces, only their eyes were larger with surprise. The china and pewter gleamed on the dark walnut table, and the spinning-wheel cast a shadow on the white wall. He took it all in deeply with his brooding glance to stamp it upon his memory to keep. Three places at the table now. His place was empty. Then the momentary spell was broken, eager voices spoke, chairs were pushed back over the smooth boards, John was answering their questions even as he got to his wife and held her trembling figure to his heart. Whatever chance it was that brought him—whether he had driven out with John Smith, or with Uriah, or had come out on the stage, or what —sure it is he came. They had that precious extra evening after all was over ; a day more life, beyond the final sentence. How quickly they set his place at the table, and Betsy hurried in with more food. . . . And listen, there are the frogs. . . .

"Last things" had all been said before. The talk, no doubt, was cheerful and quiet ; of friends, of Asher's nursery, of the ship. The chief thing was that his hand was fast in Sarah's and she felt his beating pulse. He stayed that night ; and in the first grey dawn he got up softly and dressed without a sound. Shoes in hand, he looked long at his wife, sleeping so quietly on the pillow, her long childish braids lying out on the sheet. In the dim light she looked to him like the young bride whom he had lifted from her horse on that autumn evening twenty-three years ago. But he would not wake her even with a kiss to the mutual anguish of another parting. In silence he surrendered her to the care "of Him who is Omnipotent" ; and so he went away for ever.

Sarah presently awoke and anxiously put out her hand. But the place beside her was empty. The dread hidden in her dreams had come true. She sat up. No one was stirring in the house. Johnny's clothes were not there on the chair. She flung on quickly a skirt, shoes, a cloak over her night-dress, and hurried out. The birds were beginning to twitter in the budding trees. A brisk wind scurried the clouds across the grey sky. Sarah stood in the King's Highway and strained her eyes in the direction of Philadelphia. The road was empty.

He had come like a spirit, and he had gone like a spirit. Her limbs turned to water ; she could hardly get back to the house. But though her heart was wrung, she understood him. She felt in her spirit his silent farewell.   Back in the room where he had been last night as one given back to her from the sea, she sat down in the chair where his coat had lain and got out from a private drawer a much-read letter in his clear handwriting.   "My dear and Tender Wife . . . To Him I recommend thee, my dear Companion. . . ."

Ah, Johnny . . . thy people shall be my people and thy God my God. . . . The Lord do so to me and more also if even death part thee and me.

THE wind whistled in the cordage, the sails bellied out in the sun with a curve like a bird's wing. The little ship slipped lightly over the waves like a nutshell, with a skimming, easy motion. The Capes of the Delaware were left behind, and she was out in the great expanse of sea. Woolman had never before been out on the open ocean, with nothing to be seen on either hand but the round horizon, the circle of the sky. The frightful pangs of parting were over, the farewells said. And with the forward look of a decisive character which has entered on an intended task he gave himself up to the interest of the new life. The *Mary and Elizabeth* was a ship of 180 tons, James Sparks master, owners Head, Mildred, and Roberts. Mildred and Roberts were Londoners. Incidentally, Woolman's Negro servant, Primas, married John Head's Negro Polly in the Philadelphia Lutheran Church six years later.

The ship's company numbered thirty, and there were six passengers. The passengers had their sleeping-quarters in, or opening off, the single central cabin, a pleasant, commodious room   Mr Whitefield mentions at the start of his voyage to America in 1740 that "I lay with my friend H. upon the Floor in a Matress in the great Cabbin." All passengers brought their own mattresses, and Woolman had got his in the steerage —the very same mattress that he had made for himself, or at any rate stuffed, for the Barbados voyage, and had left stored at Cousin Reuben Haines's ever since. But, steerage or cabin, privacy was at a premium.

The captain was the only person who had private quarters. If a sea-going passenger was of a temperament which really needed a little daily peace and quiet that was just unlucky. Mr Whitefield had been up against the same difficulty ; but he believed in miracles. He prayed about it, and then he innocently told the captain about his prayer. The expected miracle occurred. "To-day obtained what I prayed for, viz a Place to retire into ; for Captain W. on my bare mentioning my Want of such a Thing, offered me the free Use of his own Cabbin, a Place very Commodious for that Purpose."

John Woolman instead gave himself up to the vivid realization of the lifelong lack of privacy, the overcrowded discomfort, and the barriers in the way of mental life of those who pursue their business on great waters. "I was now desirous to embrace every opportunity of being inwardly acquainted with the hardships and difficulties of my fellow-creatures." This and his objection to helping to pay for wastefulness of decoration and furnishing in the cabin are the two sides of the same coin. "My lodging in the steerage," he says, "now near a week, hath afforded me sundry opportunities of seeing, hearing, and feeling with respect to the life and spirit of many poor sailors." The cabin passengers, all of them friends or acquaintances of Woolman, had begged him to give them as much as possible of his company. But for the first week the passengers could not enjoy anybody's company, even their own. The weather set in rough and squally, and the little boat slid up and down the hills of water with a terrible motion that almost twisted their souls out of their bodies, and abandoned them to the miseries of seasickness.

Woolman was a good sailor, though he expressed himself more modestly about it than the equally seaworthy Mr Whitefield on a similar occasion. "Brisk gale of Wind," noted Mr Whitefield exuberantly. "Some of the Passengers, amongst whom was Mr H., began now to be sick . . . on the contrary God enabled me to rejoice with exceeding great joy." But Israel Pemberton had not exaggerated the inconveniences of the steerage. Worst of all was the foul air. After three weeks of it Woolman admitted that he :

had been weakened through much rainy weather and high winds and being shut up in a close unhealthy air. Several nights of late I have felt my breathing difficult ; and a little after the rising of the second watch, which is about midnight, I have got up and stood near an hour with my face near the hatchway, to get the fresh air at the small vacancy under the hatch door, which is commonly shut down, partly to keep out rain and sometimes to keep the breaking waves from dashing into the steerage.

Townspeople were beginning to think that night air was dangerous, and to shut their windows against it ; but John Woolman had slept out under the sky too many times for that. He was as dependent as an Indian on clear clean air, just as he was beyond his time in cleanliness of dress and person. He does not mention the difficulties of the steerage in regard to cleanliness ; but the lack of air half stifled him. He was glad to have felt it, however—remembering the slave ships ; he took it "as a kindness from the great Father of mankind who in this my floating pilgrimage is in some degree bringing me to feel what many thousands of my fellow-creatures often suffer in a greater degree."

Many of the sailors had been on slavers, and

Opportunities were frequent of hearing conversation among the sailors respecting the voyages to Africa and the manner of bringing the deeply oppressed slaves into our islands. They are frequently brought on board the vessels in chains and fetters, with hearts loaded with grief under the apprehension of miserable slavery.

But though this was intensely interesting and moving, and confirmed what Woolman had heard or read before, another and new phase of what was wrong with the world was opening out before him in the life that these men, his companions, were living. And with ink-horn and quill, in some blank leaves stitched together into a little book for a sea journal, Woolman wrote daily, in the rocking boat, his impressions of the life of seamen.

A ship at sea commonly sails all night, and the seamen take their watches four hours at a time. Rising to work in the night, it is not commonly pleasant in any case, but in dark rainy nights it is very disagreeable, even though each man were furnished with all conveniences. If after having been on deck several hours in the night they come down into the steerage soaking wet and are so closely stowed that proper convenience for change of garments is not easily come at, but for want of proper room their wet garments are thrown in heaps, and sometimes, through much crowding, are trodden under foot in going to their lodgings and getting out of them, and it is difficult at times for each to find his own. Here are trials for the poor sailors.

Now as I have been with them in my lodge, my heart hath often yearned for them, and tender desires have been raised in me that all owners and masters of vessels may dwell in the love of God and therein act uprightly, and by seeking less for gain and looking carefully to their ways they may earnestly labour to remove all causes of provocation from the poor seamen, so that they may neither fret nor use excess of strong drink ; for indeed the poor creatures, in the wet and cold, seem to apply at times to strong drink to supply the want of other convenience. Great reformation is wanting in the world, and the necessity of it among those who do business on great waters hath at this time been abundantly opened before me.

These perceptions, hidden from the cabin passengers, unique among the travelling Quakers of the period who went so freely to and fro with their minutes and their inward looks, were bought cheap by a passage in the steerage. If one had the guts to stand it, it was worth doing. Woolman soon had the sailors in the hollow of his hand. They swapped yarns with him, told him bits about their families—those that had them —told him more about their troubles, in their crude way, than they knew. Few could read or write. Their vocabulary was scanty and foul. But if Woolman was shocked by their language, their cursing at each other or the weather, their drinking and rough ways, he took care that they should not know it. They felt infallibly that he was not looking down on them, but that he *liked* them. His warm humanity expressed itself in unostentatious kindness. He helped them find their boots, and divide wet clothes from dry. And from time to time he exercised his skill in personal intimacy. "I have, from a motion of love, taken sundry opportunities with one of them at a time, and have in free conversation laboured to turn their minds towards the fear of the Lord."[1] He did not preach at them. He only shared his faith that there was kindness at the heart of the Universe ; God is Love ; and that as we get near that heart we become kind. As long as they were with Woolman they believed it, because they could feel it. There were no exciting meetings. ("Ere I had prayed long Mr Bull dropped down as tho' shot with a gun. . . . The Power soon spread abroad. . . . Tears trickled down apace."[2]) Merely a curiously all-pervading feeling in their dim minds that goodness was present. "At times I expressed a few words in his love to my shipmates in regard to the all-sufficiency of Him who formed the great

---

[1] Whittier ed., p. 218.
[2] Whitefield's *Journals*, August 9, 1739.

deep, and whose eare is so extensive that a sparrow falls not without his notice."[1]

Yet at the same time Woolman did not lose sight of his clear knowledge that their troubles were many of them preventable. Not the will of heaven but the selfish fault of the shipowners, indifferent and unimaginative. And the owners of that particular ship were Quakers.

Even worse was the condition of the young apprentices, the ship boys, roughly treated and untaught. On the *Mary and Elizabeth* there were three Quaker boys.

> Five lads training up for the seas were on board this ship. Two of them were brought up in our Society, and the other, by name James Naylor, is a member.[2] . . . How great is the danger to which poor lads are exposed when placed on shipboard to learn the art of sailing. . . . The general state of the sea-faring life in general appears so opposite to that of a pious education, so full of corruption and extreme alienation from God, so full of the most dangerous examples to young people, that in looking towards a young generation I feel a care for them that they may have an education different from the present one of lads at sea.

Woolman thought if parents knew what their children were exposed to they would hesitate to place them "out to an employment among a people whose common course of life is corrupt and profane." And he "felt a tenderness of heart towards these poor lads . . . as though they were my children according to the flesh."[3]

All these new friendships and responsibilities caused him rather to neglect his friends in the cabin. But on the eighth of May the dirty weather blew up to a violent storm, and Woolman went to the cabin to get out of the way.

> This morning the clouds gathered, the wind blew strong from the south-east, and before noon so increased that sailing appeared dangerous. The seamen then bound up some of their sails and took down others, and the storm increasing they put the dead-lights, so called, into the cabin windows, and lighted a lamp as at night. The wind now blew vehemently, and the sea wrought to that degree that an awful seriousness prevailed in the cabin, in which I spent I believe about seventeen hours, for the cabin passengers had given me frequent invitations, and I thought the poor wet toiling seamen had need of all

[1] Whittier ed., p. 221.
[2] His great-uncle was the James Nayler who was a friend and contemporary of George Fox.
[3] Whittier ed., pp. 222 and 219.

the room in the crowded steerage. They now ceased from sailing and put the vessel in the posture called lying-to.

The passengers who eagerly welcomed John Woolman's company—although some of them were too seasick to be more than aware of him as a consoling presence—were four men and a woman. Or rather two women, for young Mrs William Logan was travelling with her maid. Sarah Portsmouth, a doctor's daughter, had made a runaway match with William Logan, junior—son of William and Hannah Emlen Logan, and grandson of James—when he had been in the British Isles studying medicine at London and Edinburgh. They had returned to Pennsylvania naturally somewhat under a cloud. Even as to young Dr Logan's medical work, Dr John Fothergill had written to warn his father that William "was too presumptious ; thought himself equal to any difficulty." This disappointing son of a great house had recently died, and his widow of three months was returning home to her own people. Her weakly baby son was left with the Logan grandparents until he should be old enough to cross the Atlantic and rejoin her. Perhaps there was some thought at first of bringing him up to be heir of Stenton, but the law of primogeniture never held in America, and the little heir being manifestly unsuitable, Stenton went to another grandson, also called William, and William Portsmouth Logan died in England in his twenties. Seasick and unhappy, Mrs Logan was attended by her seasick maid, and by her escort. Her stately in-laws had seen to it that their son's wife was well attended on her journey. They had put her in care of two gentlemen, one her husband's uncle, Samuel Emlen, and the other a young Dr John Till Adams, who was returning to his home in Bristol. Samuel Emlen and Dr Adams were old acquaintances, and had a number of common friends. On a former visit to England with Abraham Farrington—the same who had taken Woolman on his first journey on the eastern side of New Jersey—Samuel Emlen had stayed in England two years, had married an English wife, and had two sons born on English soil ; and Bristol had been the place of his habitation.

The other two passengers were Woolman's friend and neighbour, John Bispham, and his brother-in-law, James Reynolds. John Bispham's mother had been a Backhouse, one of the great Lancashire Quaker clan. James Reynold's grandfather had been Lord Mayor of Dublin. Like all the Reynolds family, James was not a Quaker. He was later one of the wardens of Christ Church, Philadelphia.

Woolman found them all congenial. Even poor Mrs Logan, so luxurious and selfish, who could not speak half a syllable of his language, he found touching, like an afflicted child ; and during the storm particularly he was tender with her terror. But it was Samuel Emlen who was nearest his heart. Emlen was ten years younger than Woolman, a gentle and winning character with a finely cultivated mind. He was an only son, born to wealth. Although when he was a youth he had worked for a short time in James Pemberton's counting-house with some idea of going into the Pemberton importing business, he had found it irksome, and since he had no incentive to continue had given it up. Riches had come to him unsought, and as far as he knew he practised no oppression to retain them, but he always had an uneasy glance cocked towards that needle's eye. John Woolman often cut him to the quick, as now, when he despised the curlicues and luxuries of the cabin and went to take his quarters in the steerage. There was not a syllable of criticism, it is true, not even of argument, on Woolman's part, but a sensitive rich man who valued comfort could not help feeling put subtly in the wrong. Samuel Emlen loved Woolman, and earnestly desired his good opinion. But he was a frail man,[1] delicately bred ; he really could not face the steerage. It was he who had booked his passage first, and it was on his account that Woolman had chosen this ship. He had hoped for the constant pleasure of his company. Still, there he was. And now in the storm they had really delightful hours of closest comradeship, and if this was—as it well might be—the start of the last journey of all each would find the road more easy in the company of the other.

Woolman, the only one on his feet, soothed and comforted the rest. This was certainly the place where he could at the moment be of most use. And Captain Sparks was glad to see him there. But after many hours in the lamplit cabin, hardly knowing whether it was night or day, and feeling the motion of the ship, wallowing and tossed, even more extravagant than before, curiosity drove Woolman up on deck to see how the storm looked. He was well rewarded. It was a sight to be seen.

About eleven at night I went out on the deck. The sea wrought exceedingly, and the high foaming waves round about had in some sort the appearance of fire, but did not give much, if any, light. The sailor at the helm said he lately saw a corposant at the head of the mast.

[1] Dr John Fothergill said of Emlen, "He was a man little of stature, frail and singular" (Fox's *Dr Fothergill and his Friends*, p. 245).

I observed that the master of the ship ordered the carpenter to keep on the deck, and though he said little I apprehended his care was that the carpenter with his axe might be in readiness in case of any extremity. Soon after this the violence of the wind abated, and before morning they again put the ship under sail.

That was a Friday ; and on Sunday they had a Quaker meeting in the cabin to which the seamen were invited, and most of them came. Woolman had returned to his lodge in the steerage, though for the rest of the voyage he shared some of his time during the day with his cabin friends, both on deck and in the cabin. The prevailing wet and cold weather kept the steerage at a maximum of discomfort, and Woolman's appetite failed, added to the loss of sleep in the close, stuffy nights. But whenever there was a clear pleasant morning, and he got out on deck to sit in the sea breezes, he felt a ready "reviving in my nature." And in the worst discomforts, and in his keenest blame of the love of money responsible for some of them, and in the backward-looking moments when he "felt a tender sympathy of soul for my poor wife and family left behind," his inmost soul was kept "how safe, how quiet."

So at last, after thirty-three days of sail, they made landfall. "The seamen found bottom at about seventy fathoms . . . we saw that part of England called the Lizard," and the cocks crew. Rebecca Jones remarked of her later voyage with Samuel Emlen and others that they mostly sat on deck upon a chicken coop, "which is ordinarily fitted for a seat." And on that voyage there were also sheep on deck, taken along for fresh food, one of which fell through the skylight of the cabin and narrowly missed Samuel Emlen. Woolman, sitting above the chickens, regarded them with pity, mewed up in dirty straw and without exercise, very different from the chickens which ran zestfully about his own farm.

Some fowls yet remained of those the passengers took for their sea-store. I believe about fourteen perished in the storms at sea by the waves breaking over the quarter-deck, and a considerable number with sickness at different times. I observed the cocks crew as we came down the Delaware, and while we were near the land, but afterwards I think I did not hear one of them crow till we came near the English coast, when they again crowed a few times. In observing their dull appearance at sea, and the pining sickness of some of them, I often remembered the Fountain of goodness who gave being to all creatures. . . . I believe where the love of God is verily perfected . . . a tenderness towards all creatures made subject to us will be experienced, and a care felt in us that we do not lessen that sweetness of life in the animal creation which the great Creator intends for them under our government.

The "ordinary provision" of the ships, and almost all that the sailors got, consisted of salt beef and pork and ship's biscuits, and, to wash them down, rum and water.

The emotion of seeing land for the first time after weeks at sea is something in itself, but when the glimpse of cloudlike haze across the water shapes itself, in the sun gleam, into the white cliffs of England those to whom it is the land of their ancestors feel a peculiar knocking at the heart. All the members of the English colonies in America who travelled at all looked forward some day to the major effort, the great adventure of travelling to England, the mother country of their culture, their religious faith, and their own blood. In the case of the Quakers, the constant intervisitation involved by the theory and the organization of their Society kept the ties peculiarly close and vibrant.

For many years such a visit had been in the back of John Woolman's mind as being bound to happen in the future. When Peter Andrews bade him farewell and set sail the intention took a great leap forward. But affairs at home were too exacting ; the time had not yet come. Then Andrews left his body in English soil, and the drawing tie with England tightened. Now the years had rolled through "some time" and "presently" and "soon," to that throbbing immediacy called "to-day." And this view before his eyes, appearing and disappearing in the mist like unsubstantial fairy earth, was England, where his grandfather was born.

On June the fourth—the wet weather, high winds, and occasional fog having continued to make life as uncomfortable as possible for both fowls and humans—they were well up the English Channel, and "about noon a pilot came off from Dover, where my beloved friend Samuel Emlen went on shore and thence to London, about seventy-two miles by land ; but I felt easy in staying with the ship."

By staying on the ship instead of accompanying Samuel Emlen on the London coach John Woolman made himself late for Yearly Meeting. The *Mary and Elizabeth* had to lie at anchor for the tide ; then they had a head wind up the Thames, and more lying at anchor from time to time. It was very tedious, working up that narrow, twisted, tidal channel. However, John Woolman displayed no impatience ; "saw many ships passing and some at anchor near ; and I had large opportunities of feeling the spirit in which the poor bewildered sailors too generally live."

Above all he had the fascination of the gradual approach by water to the great city of London. Passing the flats, the marshes, the fields, the willows that gave gentle introduction to the English countryside, they came at last to that then unequalled, unsurpassed city. Daniel Defoe came up that way a while before and described it.

Drawing near to London we come to Ham and Petersham, little Villages, the first famous for a most pleasant Palace close by the River . . . a House King Charles II used to be frequently at, and be exceedingly pleased with. First beginning from Ham House,[1] as above, Richmond Palace salutes the Eye. . . . From Richmond to London the River Sides are full of Villages, and those Villages are so full of beautiful Buildings, charming Gardens, and rich Habitations of Gentlemen of Quality, that nothing in the World can equal it, no, not the Country for Twenty Miles round Paris, though that indeed is a kind of Prodigy. . . . I find none has spoken of the what I call the distant Glory of all these Buildings. There is a Beauty in these Things at a Distance, which few People value and fewer understand. The whole Country here shines with a Lustre not to be described.[2]

The Thames was small beside the Delaware, and the natural approach to London was modest compared with the approach to Philadelphia, but how ordered, how settled, how smoothed and calmed and tamed was this old country, where Saxon and Dane and Roman and Norman had struggled with Nature and subdued it, and made it live the friendly companion of man. Young Mrs Logan was weeping with joy. But Woolman, seeing the anchor cleave the silver waters of the river for the last time, could have wished that it was sinking not into the Thames but into the Delaware. There was something less exhilarating and less free in this air. He called himself an Englishman, but he looked at this impressive city, the home of his king, the seat of his law, with the interested, appraising eyes of a foreigner. And he stepped on shore with the testing foot of an American Friend.

Thirty-nine days after leaving Philadelphia the *Mary and Elizabeth* came to her final wharf. "On the 8th of sixth month, 1772, we landed at London, and I went straightway to the Yearly Meeting of Ministers and Elders which had been gathered, I suppose, half an hour."

---

[1] The "palace," Ham House, was owned fifty years later by the Quaker Samuel Gurney, said to be the richest man of his time, brother of Elizabeth Fry.
[2] Defoe's *Tour of the Whole Island of Great Britain.*

XL

LONDON

THE London Yearly Meeting of Ministers and Elders was the most august body in Quakerdom. Its deliberations often coloured those of the general London Yearly Meeting which immediately followed. The Friends who were most likely to have "messages" for the Yearly Meeting, those most likely to present "concerns," to bring forward matters of new business for discussion, were largely among this group. It was the cream, the "weight" of the Yearly Meeting. John Woolman of course was a member of the equivalent body in Philadelphia, and a very important member. It was only in the year of his illness, three years before, that he had laid down the office of being Presiding Clerk of the Burlington Quarterly Meeting of Ministers and Elders. He was, in his own home, a Friend of great "weight." And diffidence had never been one of his failings. By now both he and his friends had got so accustomed to his dress that he seldom gave it a thought. He did not think about it now. No doubt he had saved up clean linen to land in, and he made the best toilet he could in the steerage, and walked through the dazing hurly-burly of the London streets to the great meeting-house in Gracechurch Street where the Yearly Meeting assembled. Any passer-by could direct him, and it was not far from the river.

The ministers and elders had been in session about half an hour. There they sat, in the large, dim room with its high windows, rank after rank of respectable men. The handsome Samuel Fothergill was not present ; but Dr John Fothergill was there, neat in cravat and curled white wig ; and John Townsend, Pewterer, London ; and Elihu Robinson, who had ridden down from the north, four days' journey, and "Putt up his Mare at ye White Boar in Bassinghall Street." Gurneys had come from Norfolk, and Backhouses from Lancashire ; Lloyds from Birmingham ; and Hoares and Frys and Barclays from round about. Most of the great private banks of England, already established —like Gurneys, Lloyds, and Barclays—or in their infancy—like Backhouses—were there represented. Ten years before, David Barclay and his wife had entertained King George III and his Queen at their London house, to see the Lord Mayor's Show, and Dr Fothergill had presented the King with a copy of Barclay's *Apology*.[1] The Barclay sons were dressed in plain cloth, the daughters in "plain Silkes with dress'd black hoods," and—though suitably Quakerly—made a genteel appearance, their mother thought, and acted their part very well. These were the kind of men who sat there, in sober, silent rows, shut out from Parliament and shut out from the Universities—therefore somewhat discouraged from the learned professions—but conscious that their influence in public affairs was anything but negligible. Parliament itself perhaps could hardly offer a more solidly well-to-do group. In neat plain suits of excellent material and cut—buff or brown or black or grey—with knee breeches and buckled shoes, and spotless linen at neck and wrist, they conformed sufficiently to the fashion to avoid being conspicuous, and would pass in any company. Most of them wore hats of black beaver, some drawn up with cords into three-cornered shape, and some left to flop in a less shapely but more protective manner, broad-brimmed over the ears.

Into this dim and dignified assembly there suddenly entered a most extraordinary apparition.

His dress was as follows—a white hat, a coarse raw linen shirt, without anything about the neck, his coat, waistcoat and breeches of white coarse woollen cloth with wool buttons on, his coat without cuffs, white yarn stockings, and shoes of uncured leather with bands instead of buckles, so that he was all white.[2]

A slight stir of horror went over the meeting as this figure advanced confidently to the Clerk's table and laid down his certificate. He then

---

[1] The standard and earliest exposition of Quakerism, written by Robert Barclay, of Ury, grandfather of David here mentioned.

[2] Contemporary English manuscript loaned by Herbert Pickles, Jordans, England.

quietly looked round for a vacant place, and took his seat. After a moment's pause the Clerk, William Fry, rose and read the travelling minute to the meeting, presenting our friend John Woolman "as one in good esteem among us, and recommending him to your Christian care."

Well, one never did quite know what was coming from America. But this was the worst ever seen yet. This was worse than the Wesley and Whitefield people and their extravagant revivals. The much-dreaded symptoms of "enthusiasm"—of which Fox, by the way, had been quite an exponent, but his followers had forgotten that—could go no farther. Not only did they feel the very reverse of welcome for this Friend, but they dreaded to have him go about the country with a minute and have him pointed at by other people as a "Quaker." Quakers were not like that. He would bring the whole Society into disrepute. So after another brief, hostile pause Dr John Fothergill rose and certainly expressed in his cold and careful phrases the feeling of the meeting. He suggested that perhaps the stranger Friend might feel that his dedication of himself to this apprehended service was accepted, without further labour, and that he might now feel free to return to his home.[1]

The stunning humiliation of that blow sank home in a silence that could be felt. Such a sharp public rejection of any visitor, unheard, was without precedent. The man in white started as if unable to believe his ears, and then sat with his face covered. Those near him were aware that tears were wrung from him in the agony of that discomfiture. It was like a dagger in the heart.

Practised in silence, the meeting waited. Most of the London Friends expected one of two things—either an unseemly outburst from this wild man or slinking departure. The latter seemed the more likely, for the assembly of the London Ministers and Elders was daunting to strangers at the best. The silence prolonged, while Woolman sought deep within himself, first for control, then for wisdom.

At last he rose, and removed his hat. Then, speaking in those resonant, harmonious tones which were noted in his own country, he expressed himself with pain but with assured dignity. The battery of eyes did not trouble him. As a practised speaker, often on unpopular subjects, he was well used to that. He said without comment and with the utmost brevity that he could not feel himself released from his prospect of labour in England, but he could not travel in the ministry without the

[1] Whittier's footnote, Journal, p. 233, quoting Wm. J. Allinson for authority.

unity of Friends.   While that unity was withheld he did not feel easy
to accept hospitality or be of any cost to them.   He had the good fortune to be acquainted with a mechanical trade, and while the impediment
to his services continued he hoped Friends would be kindly willing to
employ him in such business as he was capable of, that he might not be
chargeable to any.

He sat down, and in spite of themselves they were impressed.   He
held their attention.   They were unable to proceed with business.   No
doubt Samuel Emlen was tempted to speak for his friend, but either his
courage failed or he would not presume to.   The silence continued
unbroken, and the quality of it was different.   It was no longer gathered
away from him, repelling him ;   it was surging towards him with a
question and a doubt.   Was it possible that anyone could dress like that
and not be "queer" ?   Yet his tongue, his courage, his control of the
situation, were equal to any of their finest.   That greatest enemy of
love, scorn, was no longer present.   And as they sat in the quiet, in the
shadowy house, Woolman was subtly aware of the difference.   All of
them there believed that Light is never denied to the seeker.   They all
together sought for Light.

That long silence, in a gathering which held the readiest, most fluent
speakers in the Society of Friends, shaped itself into an invitation.   Had
it been a secular meeting they might have said, "The floor is yours.   If
you have a message on your mind we are ready to hear it."   The Quaker
gathering believed that the call to speak must come from elsewhere ; but
they markedly yielded opportunity.   The Clerk left his Minute Book
untouched.   No one stirred.

A smaller man might have refused that opportunity out of pique and
wounded feelings.   A weaker man might have refused it from a self-
conscious feeling that to speak now would seem to give a demonstration
in support of his credentials.   But Woolman had lived in the world for
fifty-two years, and such feelings, if he had ever had them, he had long
outgrown.   Although his reception had shocked him profoundly, he
was now bowing his heart to accept it as a discipline of some sort—a
lesson in humility or what not—from a higher Hand than theirs.   And a
blow from God loses its smart ; carries at least no scar to a man's pride.
At last the silent wish of the meeting was fulfilled.   The stranger again
rose to his feet, removed his hat, and with his brow serene and lifted,
his eye dark with thought, he threw away the personal difficulty that

had been between himself and them ; he ignored it, and spoke to them as to Burlington or New Haven or Philadelphia, in the love of God and the "pure life of truth."

When his resonant tones had ceased they sat still a while more ; and then Dr Fothergill rose and begged John Woolman's pardon in a voice that was husky, and urged the meeting's endorsement of his minute, which was unanimously accorded.

The diary of Elihu Robinson reads :

> 5th day. Our Frd Jno Woolman from Jersey made some pertinent remarks in this Meeting as in many others, and tho ye Singularity of his Appearance might in some Mee^tngs Draw ye Attention of ye Youth and soon cause a change of Countenance in some, Yet ye Simplicity, Solidity and Clearness of many of his remarks made all these vanish as Mists at ye Sun's rising—he made sev^l beautifull rem^ks in this Meetng with resp^t to ye benifit of true Silence and how Incense ascended on ye oppening of ye Seal and there was Silence in heaven for ye space of half an hour. . . .

John Fothergill wrote to his brother Samuel, "The affairs of the Meeting go on well. The Americans help us much. John Woolman is solid and weighty in his remarks. I wish he could be cured of some singularitys. But his real worth outweighs all the trash."

Then, reading his letter over, his respect for Woolman made him reject that word "trash." Who, after all, was he to judge for so manifestly clear a spirit ? So he crossed out the word "trash" and substituted "husk." Certainly a husk is sometimes trash ; we throw it away, but it has served a necessary purpose. It has protected a kernel. This is the final evidence of Woolman's complete, unconscious conquest of the most polished and brilliant Quaker of his time.

John Woolman's friends, the Pembertons, had not been unaware of the unfortunate first impression that Woolman might make upon conservative Englishmen. And James Pemberton, writing to David Barclay—the same that had been the King's host—would have spared him all the pain of that first insult if he could. But Woolman got there before the letter. It is dated May 16.

> . . . Our friend Jno Woolman embarked with Capt. Sparks on a religious visit to some parts of your Island. He is a Friend in good Esteem among us, of blameless Life, a good understanding, and deep in Spiritual Experience, tho Singular in his Dress & deportment. Is not a

Censorious Mind, & I believe apprehends it his real Duty to appear as he does.

Samy Emlen also Embarkt in the same Vessel on the like business ; he is well known among you.[1]

According to his reserved habit in personal matters, Woolman makes no reference to that first experience, in his Journal or letters. James Pemberton was reassured—if, as is likely, he heard of the affair from David Barclay or another—by a letter from the London shipowners of the *Mary and Elizabeth*, dated July 1, and enclosing a copy of the London Yearly Meeting Epistle. The letter read :

We were favoured with the company of several valuable Friends from your parts—William Hunt, Sarah and Deborah Morris, Samuel Emlen, and John Woolman. The last two just reached it in time. . . . John Woolman is gone northward. His peculiar Habit may render him disagreeable to some few, but there is that, I think, which attends his Words, both in Testimony and Private Converse, which will make his way, wherever he goes.

[*signed*] MILDRED AND ROBERTS[2]

The enclosed epistle bears the mark of Woolman's influence in the following paragraph :

It likewise appears that the Practice of holding Negroes in oppressive and unnatural Bondage hath been so successfully discouraged by Friends in some of the Colonies as to be considerably lessened. We cannot but approve of these salutary Endeavours and earnestly intreat they may be continued, that thro' the Favour of Divine Providence a Traffick so unmerciful and unjust in its Nature to a Part of our own Species, made equally with ourselves for Immortality, may come to be considered by all in its proper Light, and be utterly abolished, as a Reproach to the Christian Profession.

This was the first public utterance of the London Yearly Meeting on slavery.

John Woolman's host in London—for all was now cordiality and warmth, and invitations poured upon him—was John Townsend, a wealthy merchant who made his money out of pewter ware. His pewter business was on such a scale that John Townsend, Pewterer, London, was sufficient address for his mail. And it is lucky that Woolman did not know at the time that Townsend's chief output was pewter

---

[1] Pemberton Papers, XXIII, 164.
[2] *Ibid.*, p. 174.

cups and plates for the Army and Navy, and "Guinea basons." The last were pewter basins used on the slavers for the captives' rations.

Long after Woolman's death John Townsend, who was quite a man for travelling in the ministry, visited America, and took pains to go to the slave-owning Friends in Virginia. He recommended "the poor blacks" to "sobriety and chastity, to avoid bad company and to be faithful to God and their employers." And he adds, "We were led closely to advise their master and mistress to faithfulness to their God and to do strict justice to these poor oppressed people." Evidently a much easier guest to a slave-owner than John Woolman. Townsend was a short, thick man, very lively and energetic. The sailors on board his vessel said of him and his larger companion, "The little 'un would thrash the big 'un with his hands tied behind him."

He was well thought of by Friends because he was generous with money, and a forceful speaker ; "all that he said he evidently felt strongly." But a more peculiar host for Woolman could hardly have been found. However, in his comfortable and hospitable house Woolman found time and opportunity, as soon as the five crowded days of the Yearly Meeting were over, to get off some letters ; first, of course, one to his wife—a brief account of his voyage and landing, and his present whereabouts and plans, and then that intimate touch in which she felt him close.

13 da, 5th mo.

DEAR WIFE
. . . The tender concern which I have many times felt for thee and for Mary, and for John, and even for Betsy, I may not easily express. I have often remembered you with tears ; and my desires have been that the Lord, who hath been my helper through many Adversities may be a Father to you, and that in his love you may be guided safely along.
. . . Several friends remembr kind love to thee. My love is to my dear friends.

JOHN WOOLMAN

The next day he wrote to his hospitable and good-natured Haines cousins, and here again homesickness is irrepressible.

COUSINS REUBEN AND MARGARET,[1]
I am middling well, in London, and believe I may go northward in a few days. Your care for me toward parting hath felt inwardly

[1] *Née* Margaret Wistar, an heiress in her own right. She had inherited the Wyck House, at Germantown.

gathering toward the true union in which I hope we may at last unite.   My heart hath been often contrite since I saw you ; and I now remember you with tears.

JOHN WOOLMAN

My friend Suse and my little cousins, I remember you all.

Woolman refused a good many invitations in London, because the smallpox was in town, and he was anxious to avoid it unless unmistakable duty led him into the infection.

Yearly Meeting ended on June 13, and on the fifteenth Woolman left London, but not alone.   Among the Americans present mentioned in Woolman's letter to his wife was William Hunt.   William Hunt was John Woolman's first cousin, son of that Aunt Mary who had lived in the homestead on the Rancocas with her brother Samuel until the year John Woolman was born.   She got married that year and soon after was taken south by her husband to North Carolina.   William, thirteen years younger than John Woolman, was now living at Guilford, North Carolina, much beloved by and loving the elder cousin whom he so seldom met.   He had been travelling in England for a year.   Between the morning and afternoon sessions of Yearly Meeting those Friends whose houses were within reach of Gracechurch Street entertained lavishly with enormous dinners, and all the American visitors were able to get together by going in twos or threes to one or other of the hosts who were keeping "open house."   William Fry, the Presiding Clerk of the Yearly Meeting, was one of the principal hosts, in his large, wealthy, and conveniently situated house at St Mildred's Court.   Woolman and his cousin met and discussed mutual plans at one or other of these times, and Hunt succeeded in persuading Woolman to give him his company on the first lap of the journey.   Hunt had a travelling companion, his nephew Thomas Thornborough, and they were making for the East Coast to take ship for Holland from Colchester.   Woolman's intention was generally for the North of England, but he had some invitations to various Quarterly Meetings which would prevent him from taking a route too directly north.   So the cousins arranged the mutual pleasure of travelling together as far as Hertford, some twenty miles north of London, where there was to be a Quarterly Meeting on the sixteenth.   It is quite certain they did not walk there—on the fourteenth Woolman was still writing letters in London.   The probabilities are that some Friend returning to that neighbourhood drove them all down in his private chaise.   Certainly they were all there, duly noted on the minutes :

> At a Quarterly Meeting held at Hertford, 6thmo, 16th, 1772. Our Friends John Woolman William Hunt and Thomas Thornborough from America being likewise Present in the course of their religious visits to this Island, their company and Labour of Love was likewise greatly to our comfort and satisfaction.

John Woolman mentions being at this Quarterly Meeting in his rapidly sketched itinerary, but with his chariness at mentioning names does not say anything about his companions.   He does, however, risk a rare date, and with his usual endearing inaccuracy in such details, he is wrong. He says it was the seventeenth.   But the Minute Book cannot err.

On June 21 William Hunt writes from Colchester to Uriah Woolman :

> We parted from dear cousin John Woolman two days since.   He was then well as usual.   He has great and acceptable service here. The singularity of his appearance is not only strange but very exercising to many valuable Friends, who have had several opportunities of conference with him.   Some are still dissatisfied ; others are willing to leave it.   The purity of his ministry gains universal approbation. I hope he stands on that Foundation which will bear him through it all. He is now gone toward Yorkshire.

XLI

THE ENGLISH SCENE

THROUGH the pleasant English summer John Woolman walked north-westward at a leisurely pace. Around him spread the leafy landscape, as green as an American spring, refreshed with frequent rain. Where the presence of cattle in a meadow made a fence necessary it was often a quickset hedge, blooming with the wild rose.[1] The ditches at the side of the road were deep with flowers. Above his head, in the pale blue sky, white puffs of cloud drifted unhurried or bowled friskily before the wind, and the different melodies of the birds were enchanting to the ear. The skylark, the blackbird, the thrush, the chaffinch, the linnet—he had heard of them all ; the three first, with his country ear, he no doubt learned to distinguish. And in the dusk, passing solitary woods, he heard the nightingale. It was peaceful, walking along without horse or companion. He felt in the English countryside almost the same sensations of being an explorer as Daniel Boone had felt two years before when he broke into the vast grassy savannahs of Kentucky. But Kentucky, "the Dark and bloody Ground" between the Indians, was the undisputed home of the buffalo, and Boone had written down in his simple diary the blissful magic of the empty wilderness—"all things were still." There were quiet miles for Woolman, too, unbroken by any but the sounds of nature ; but then a stage-coach would come roaring past at the gallop in a cloud of choking dust ; or a peal of church bells would announce a village hidden round the bend. He would meet a loaded

---

[1] The 'hedged' look of all England did not come until the turn of the century.

wagon or a train of pack-horses, twenty strong. And then again, populated towns would lie across his march, and he would seek the Quakers living there, and stay the night, and hold a meeting, and enter into intimate human intercourses. His endorsed certificate was his passport among Friends, and ensured him respect and hospitality. But always there was the preliminary shock of his clothes.

By the end of June he was in the heart of Oxfordshire, the middle of the Midlands. Here those animals the sheep, of which he was so fond, abounded. Their pleasant bleating filled the meadows, and on either edge of the road was a wide border of turf, so that the sheep might travel soft, and pasture as they travelled, when being driven in from the outlying villages to Oxford or Banbury market. On June 30 the Banbury Meeting records contain a minute of "being favoured with the Company of our Friend John Woolman from America," and how he also "went into the Women's Meeting and preached them a moving sermon . . . to the Youth in particular." Here he saw grey castles, such as he had read of, plain to view, near the road, complete with moat and battlements and turreted towers ; embodied story. And, walking on up to Coventry and Birmingham, he passed through the ineffable poetry of Shakespeare's country—Stratford-on-Avon and Warwick. This was the air breathed by the greatest master of English speech, and carried with it, in the knowledge, an exhilaration not to be found in forests or savannahs. Here was the region of a Burning Bush, which no sensitive spirit could fail to feel.

On July 17 he was at Birmingham, a city grimy and odorous from the iron- and coal-fields, roaring with smelting furnaces, ringing with smithies. Here were Uncle John Burr's ironworks repeated on every side, unameliorated by a surrounding rural beauty. Birmingham was the centre of the metal trade of England and of Europe. Iron pots and pans, pitchforks, ploughshares, sickles, hinges, nails, and the like ; and chains for slaves. Metal buttons, gilded and lacquered, and large metal buckles for shoes, were a large part of its output when Woolman was there ; luxury trades, superfluities. But all was done by hand or water-power. The day of steam was not yet, though it was coming fast. A man named James Watt had already taken out patents for his experimental inventions, and two years after Woolman's visit Boulton brought James Watt to Birmingham to manufacture his steam machines.

There were many Quakers in Birmingham, and Woolman was

engaged in public and private speaking on his theme of the great human brotherhood, and each one's responsibility for the distress of others. He made friends with them, he touched them deeply, but it was with relief that he left the narrow, ill-smelling streets behind him, and went forward north into the beautiful hills of Derbyshire, and the high pure air.

> Having of late often travelled in wet weather through narrow streets in towns and villages where dirtiness under foot and the scent arising from that filth which more or less infects the air of all thickly settled towns were disagreeable, and being but weakly, I have felt distress both in body and mind with that which is impure.[1]

On July 26 he was at Nottingham, the centre of the lace industry, and saw the manufactories where the women came to spin the thread and to work over their lace pillows in concert, at fixed hours and wages ; and he saw the far larger number who were working over their pillows and bobbins inside their cottage room, with one foot on the cradle, or cheerfully sitting, two or three together, at a cottage door in the sun, getting on with their lace at their own time and in their own way, between their household tasks. He stayed at Nottingham a day or two. "The forenoon meeting was especially . . . a heart-tendering season" ; and he dealt with a wealthy Friend in his family the next day, "a time to be thankfully remembered." So on up through the wild heart of England, and now many sheep were pasturing on the hills and dales, different and more wiry sheep from those on the rich southlands, but good woolbearers. He was back among the industry that he knew best, and that was more widespread through England than any other, the sheepfarming and woollen industry. And here were the cottage woolspinners and the banging of the cottage looms, and he was over the border into Yorkshire.

John Woolman had now come a hundred and sixty miles in six weeks through the best walking country in the world. There were no mountains to negotiate, no fallen trees and rocks to block the road, no rivers to ford. The country had been lived in so long, and been so much used by restless mankind, that there were bridges over all the streams but the very smallest, and one could get through the hill ranges on the turnpike road. Compared with the walking journeys Woolman had taken in America, this was easy. Even when it rained it was not a rain which beat upon you like the beginning of a new Flood ; it was in general a

[1] Whittier ed., p. 243.

gentle rain that fell softly and steadily in a friendly fashion, and sometimes had gleams of sunshine through it. Inns were frequent along the way, where the traveller could get rest and refreshment. The bread and meat and cheese were good ; the beer and ale were of the best. He could even get water, if his constitution would stand it. As Dr Fothergill advised his patients, "If water does not disagree value the privilege and continue it."

But Woolman had never had his full strength back since the pleurisy. He was easily fatigued. The hardships of the voyage had not been salutary. So why tax a not robust health by going on foot ? In his own country Woolman had made his walking protest—so far as it could be so regarded—only among the large slave-holders ; he had used a horse when travelling in New Jersey. As we know, he would often ride to the ferry, and then continue on foot. The inhabitants of England were not slave-holders. The ownership of an occasional little black page by a few fashionable ladies in London does not make this less true ; nor the curiosity of a Negro footman now and then behind a fashionable London chariot. Legally, these Negro people were no more slaves than their white fellow-servants. The final test case had already been fought and won[1] that no slave, of any colour, could be in England, or be brought to England, without at once obtaining freedom by the mere act of stepping on to British soil. Being in attendance on a master who was just passing through the country made no difference. The slave was at once free, and would be protected. So, under this pleasing condition of affairs, could not Woolman feel free to ride ?

Woolman's answer to such kindly arguments was disconcerting, because it had relation to immediate facts which his friendly interlocutors had chosen to ignore. His going on foot in England had nothing to do with the Negro slave trade, except in that remote sense in which all evil is interrelated. Nor was it a personal asceticism ; nor owing to those good Quaker reasons, so soothing to hear, about a "stop in his mind" or "a leading." No, it was plainly and simply because he would not by one penny support the stage-coaches. Woolman's innate originality of outlook was aided by the fact that he had never before seen a stage-coach. Stage-wagons, primarily for the transport of goods, had appeared in England about two years before they appeared in New Jersey, and were gradually replacing the pack-horses. But the stage-coaches,

[1] May 1772.

concentrating on transport of passengers, were only about ten years old.
In order to compete with the wagons, which carried both goods and
passengers at first, the coaches had to aim at speed.   With six horses—
a riding postilion for the two leaders, the rest driven four-in-hand by the
coachman—they went full tear, as far as possible, up hill and down.
Their promoters called them Flying Machines.   Riding on the top of
the lurching coach, holding on precariously by a little handle, was nerve-
racking ; riding inside was bone-shaking and almost as hard on a weak
stomach as sea travel.   Fresh-harnessed horses were ready at each stage,
and trained ostlers whisked the old ones out and the new ones in with
such celerity that it hardly took more than sixty seconds.   With all this,
the Flying Machines achieved an average speed of eight miles an hour ;
but such an average means much faster travel on good stretches to make
up for pauses and long hills and patches of heavy mud.   Woolman, an
expert in horses, observed these vehicles on the road.   He saw them
reharnessed at the inns.   He saw the postilion boys—young, so as to
be light—lifted stiff from the leader, staggering into the inn, white-
faced and sick, for poor food and insufficient rest.   And his heart burned
again for the world's cruelty.   He watched the horses, too, foaming
at the mouth, red in the eyes, breathing hard, being led to their stalls
for just the minimum of food and rest that would enable them to keep
up the killing pace, under the whip, when their turn came round again.
And this was summer weather ; conditions were at their best.   How
would things be in the winter, when snow drifted in the hollows, and ice
made roads slippery, and the bitter night wind met that unprotected boy
upon the leader ?   There were plenty of people to tell him.   Perhaps
the woman who served him at the bar was herself the mother of a post-
boy.   The men who sat outside on the settle at evening, taking the mug
of bitters, were the cousins and uncles of postboys.   Many a tale came to
the ear of this casual stranger whose unaffected manners made him so
easy to talk to, and who—since he was walking up the country with his
little bundle on his back—seemed to interpose no barriers of class.

But when the coach came clattering up to the inn and the steps were
lowered and the passengers got out, nice, good-natured people, Christians
with high standards—Christians at any rate, because it was a Christian
country and only Christians could hold any office or practise any profession—they were tired and sick themselves to a milder degree, and
saw only the cheerful room and the table spread.   They did not see,

with conscious eyes, the postboys or the horses. All the other Quakers travelling in England at that time used the stage-coaches. Most of them, before and after, kept journals. None comment on what to Woolman was so glaring. Of course many of the wealthy English residents, with whom Woolman stayed, used their own private chaise when they travelled, and were very free to discuss with Woolman the abuses of the coaching system, and to agree that really something ought to be done about it.

"As my journey hath been without a horse," says Woolman,

I have had several offers of being assisted on my way in these stage-coaches, but have not been in them, nor have I had freedom to send letters by these posts in the present way of their riding, the stages being so fixed and one boy so dependent on another as to time, and going at great speed, that in long cold winter nights the poor boys suffer much. I heard in America of the way of these posts, and cautioned Friends in the General Meeting of Ministers and Elders at Philadelphia, and in the Yearly Meeting of Ministers and Elders in London, not to send letters to me on any common occasion by post. And though on this account I may be likely not to hear so often from my family left behind . . . yet for righteousness sake I am content. . . . Stage-coaches frequently go upwards of one hundred miles in twenty-four hours ; and I have heard Friends say in several places that it is common for horses to be killed with hard driving, and that many others are driven till they grow blind. Post-boys pursue their business, each one to his stage, all night through the winter. Some boys who ride long stages suffer greatly in winter nights, and at several places I have heard of their being frozen to death. So great is the hurry in the spirit of this world that in aiming to do business quickly and to gain wealth the creation at this day doth loudly groan.

Here again that ounce of action which Woolman supplied spoke more loudly and was longer remembered than any of his words.

It is not really surprising that Elihu Robinson's fears proved ground-less—that Woolman's unconventional dress would provoke young men to ribald mirth. It was the young men who listened to him the most eagerly. John Woolman's visit in many places was noted as " a fresh visitation to many, in particular to the youth."

Not only the postboys roused that clear, first-hand attention which even those who knew him best never quite got used to. He saw, in his leisurely progress, deep below the smiling surface of England. William Hunt had been travelling in England for a year. Samuel Emlen had

lived in England for more than two years at a stretch.   John Churchman
kept a careful journal of his four years' travel in England.   None of them
knew a fraction of what Woolman found out in a few weeks.   After
all, there is no better way of seeing a country than walking through it.
If the Flying Machine averaged eight miles an hour Woolman averaged
three and a half miles a day.   He looked at the fields with the eye of a
farmer, at the houses with the eye of a landlord.   He was a trained
appraiser and surveyor ; values and equivalents leapt to his mind.   And
above all he was skilled in human intercourse.   That native gift of
friendship which had often got him into trouble had become developed
by the long practice of a life into a marvellous instrument of love.   He
had used it in the constant performance of some of the most difficult
feats of human relationships.   His clearer insight and his higher standards
were always putting people in the wrong ; yet the most critical of his
wealthy friends in America could say of him eagerly that he was "not
censorious."

So how easily—when he paused here and there to rest in a hayfield
or beside a cottage spinner, or under a farm wagon in a shower, or when
he joined company for a mile with a fellow-traveller of a poorer class—
he got people to talk to him.

On enquiry in many places I find the price of rye about five shillings ;
wheat eight shillings per bushel ; oatmeal, twelve shillings for a
hundred and twenty pounds ; mutton, from threepence to five pence
per pound ; bacon from sevenpence to ninepence ; cheese from
fourpence to sixpence ; butter from eightpence to tenpence ; house-
rent for a poor man from twenty-five shillings to forty shillings per
year, to be paid weekly ; wood for fire very scarce and dear ; coal in
some places two shillings and sixpence per hundredweight ; but near
the pits not a quarter so much.   Oh, may the wealthy consider the
poor.

The wages of labouring men in several counties towards London
at tenpence per day in common business, the employer finds small
beer and the labourer finds his own food ; but in harvest and hay time
wages are about one shilling per day and the labourer hath all his
diet.   In some parts of the north of England poor labouring men
have their food where they work and appear in common to do rather
better than nearer London.   Industrious women who spin in the
factories got some fourpence, some fivepence, and so on to six, seven,
eight, nine, or ten pence per day, and find their own house-room and
diet.   Great numbers of poor people live chiefly on bread and water

in the southern parts of England as well as in the northern parts ; and there are many poor children not even taught to read. May those who have abundance lay these things to heart.

The enclosure of the common lands was proceeding at a steady pace, subject entirely to the caprice or greed of the local landowner. Any squire who felt inclined to thus obtained, by a statement to the Parliament Committee through his attorney, and at the expense of a fence, acres of land which he had neither bought nor paid for. Small farmers were crowded out, and reduced to becoming hired labourers to earn their bread ; labourers, by the loss of the old free pasturage for cow or pig, of fuel rights, and of gleaning rights, were reduced to the bitter edge of want, with no possible hope of bettering themselves by thrift. Perhaps the use of the common lands in a haphazard way by the poor was wasteful in the long run. But it had made for comfortable and thrifty and self-respecting living. The English peasantry might not have education, but they had milk and eggs. An energetic woman following the reapers could glean enough to last her family for half a year ; an active man could cut in his spare time enough fuel to keep his family warm all winter. The enclosers argued that extra work and extra wages provided by their improved farming of the enclosed commons would more than make up the difference. Woolman's figures speak for themselves.

As usual he did not go into complicated economic argument. The basis of the harm was moral. "Love thy neighbour as thyself." Indifferent selfishness was the root of all. "To labour for a perfect redemption from this spirit of oppression is the great business of the whole family of Christ Jesus in this world."

In the depth of his feeling, and a consciousness that his time was short —for he did not want to stay in England long—the natural eloquence that he had always regarded as a snare sometimes overcame him in spite of himself. "My heart was like a vessel that wanted vent. For several weeks after my arrival when my mouth was opened in meeting it was like the raising of a gate in a water-course when a weight of water lay upon it." Even so had he often seen the released torrent of the water at the raised sluice-gates at Mount Holly by the sawmill. And his homesickness breathes in the metaphor.

Deeply did he long for his wife, and the sweetness of his home, and the great warmth and spontaneity of American life. Below the beautiful

2 B

polished surface of eighteenth-century England he felt its essential hardness of heart.

This was the year that Boswell came up to London from Scotland to plead before the House of Lords the appeal of a Scottish schoolmaster against a lower court which had thrown him out of his job for cruelty to his scholars—"cruel and unreasonable chastisement." With the help of his friend Dr Johnson, who provided him with cogent arguments, Boswell won the appeal. Johnson argued that one could not decide what was unreasonable chastisement until one knew what amount of obstinacy and sullenness it was designed to correct ; that a schoolmaster was within his rights in producing, by any means he wished, any amount of present pain, short of maiming or death. Thus London, in 1772 Philadelphia, under the inspiration of a distinguished educator, Anthony Benezet, was already escaping from this outworn barbarity.

Again, no Negro slave could come to England without being set free. But chains for slaves were made in Birmingham ; and bowls for slaves were made in London ; and textile goods—made even by good Quaker firms—were taken by slave ships from Liverpool to Africa, exchanged there for a cargo of slaves, the slaves taken to the West Indies or Virginia or Carolina, exchanged there for a cargo of sugar, spice, or tobacco—and the innocent-looking cargo brought back to be retailed in England. It is not to be wondered at that Woolman wanted to be freed from any contact with the sugar trade. Yet the Clerk of the London Yearly Meeting himself was an importer of tea, coffee, sugar, and spices. The Wilsons of Kendal—shearman weavers, fullers, and dyers—chiefly dealing in woollen cloth, exported "Kendal cottons" for some mysterious foreign trade via Liverpool. Beyond Liverpool they lost sight of them ; they were used somewhere in foreign parts for "natives." Where ? For what ?

"I have felt great distress of mind," said Woolman,

since I came on this island on account of the members of our society being mixed with the world in various sorts of traffic carried on in impure channels. Great is the trade to Africa for slaves ; and for the loading of these ships a great number of people are employed in the factories, among whom are many of our Society.

The first public pronouncement of the Society of Friends in England against slavery was that made by the London Yearly Meeting during Woolman's visit and under his influence. How far they were ahead of

the common public opinion of their time is shown by Boswell's argument with Johnson on the subject of slaves even five years later.   Johnson
was against slavery, and argued that "no man is by nature the property
of another."   Boswell thought his friend influenced by prejudice and
false information.   Said he :

> To abolish a *status*, which in all ages God has sanctioned, and man has
> continued, would not only be *robbery* to an innumerable class of our
> fellow-subjects ; but it would be extreme cruelty to the African Savages,
> a portion of whom it saves from massacre or intolerable bondage in
> their own country, and introduces into a much happier state of life,
> especially now when their passage to the West Indies and the treatment
> there is humanely regulated.   To abolish that trade would be to
> "shut the gates of mercy on mankind."[1]

Woolman did not stay long enough to discover what other forms of
slavery there were existing surreptitiously in England, known, yet not
known ;   a matter of very common knowledge, yet "unknown" to the
law—such as the sale of English children to sweeps, or for "slavery" in
the coal-mines.   The word "apprenticeship" disguised these sales, and
if the children lived to grow up they acquired freedom by simply ceasing
to be useful for their job, which required immature smallness.   Then
they perhaps became master sweeps or real miners themselves.   But their
condition while in servitude was no better than that of any Negro slave
on the worst plantation in Barbados.   And this again was one of the
fruits of excessive poverty, allowed to exist by the unimaginative selfishness of the well-to-do.

Although stealing carried a death penalty, thieves and highwaymen
abounded.   Against these the governing classes invoked the protection
of religion.   Burke, who could put things so well at times, was the
excellent mouthpiece of their point of view.   The poor, said he, "must
respect that property of which they cannot partake.   They must labour
to obtain what by labour can be obtained ;   and when they find, as they
commonly do, the success disproportioned to the endeavour, they must
be taught their consolation in the final proportions of eternal justice."
That was not John Woolman's view of religion or of eternal justice ;
nor his view of society's responsibility towards the making of thieves.
Ten years before the district around Mount Holly had been profoundly

[1] Boswell's *Johnson*, Modern Library edition (John Lane), p. 749.

shocked by the execution of three men at Burlington for theft. John Woolman had written to a friend,

> In regard to thieves, I have had many serious thought, and often been jealous over myself, lest by witholding from a poor man what our heavenly Father may intend for him through me, I should lay a temptation in his way to steal, and have often felt a care that no desire for riches or outward greatness may prompt me to get that in our house which may create envy, and increase this difficulty.[1]

So he moved up England, entertained more often than not at the houses of the wealthy ; and he presented these thoughts as occasion arose, especially if he saw such things about—silver ornaments and plate and what not—as indicated a beginning of that indifference to the needy which might end in the worst of human fates—hardness of heart.

At John Haslam's house, on the edge of Yorkshire, he stayed for several days' rest, and had that best kind of holiday for a foreign traveller, a reunion with some of his own compatriots. Sarah Morris, from Philadelphia, with her niece and travelling companion Deborah, was there too. Sarah Morris was an intimate friend of Joyce Benezet, very able and lovable wife of Anthony, so the pleasant free-and-easy conversation of "Do you remember—", "Were you there when—" could provide the best of cheer.

Their poor old host, John Haslam, was eighty-five and afflicted with palsy, which impaired his memory. But he caught fragments of clues in their talk now and then, and brightened to hear them. For he knew many of the people of whom they spoke. He had spent a whole winter in '42 with Elizabeth Estaugh at Haddonfield, cut off from further travelling by ill-health, only well enough to fulfil his concern by making short trips around the neighbourhood. That was the winter John Estaugh had gone away on a Quaker journey to Tortola, and had died on the island.

In this homelike atmosphere John Woolman, when the Morrises had left to continue their journey, settled down to write letters. One to his wife, one to his kind host in London, and one to his Haines cousins.

There must always some time be a last letter. It is no more important intrinsically than any other. Yet once, on the Indian journey, John Woolman had thought to himself, "This may be the last"—and he had

---

[1] Folio MS. Journal, p. 279.

weighed his words with care. This time he had no such thought. Since his letters were not going by the post, but being carried in the private care of friends, he wrote them on as small pieces of paper as possible, to take up small room in a pocket. This letter to Sarah measures four inches by six. It was sent enclosed in a note to John Townsend, directing him to keep it until he had convenient opportunity to send it to Philadelphia. Fatigue and homesickness and suppressed longing vibrate in the lines.

MY DEAR WIFE,

Though I feel in a good degree resigned in being absent from you, my heart is often tenderly Affected toward you, and even to weeping this morning while I am about to write.

The numerous difficulties attending us in this life are often before me, and I often remember thee with tender desires that the Holy Spirit may be thy leader and my leader through life, and that at last we may enter into rest. . . . I see but a little way at a time. . . .

Thy loving Husband

JOHN WOOLMAN

About 160 miles northward from London.

31 da. 7 mo. 1772. For Sarah Woolman.

It came to her at last. And his tears had smudged the writing. She knew, at least, that even as she had wept for him, Johnny had wept for her.

XLII

THE NORTH

IN August, while the first partition of Poland was quietly taking place in Europe, at the initiative of Frederick the Great, John Woolman moved north through Yorkshire on a westward slant. On the second at Sheffield, the seventeenth at Settle, the twenty-third at Preston Patrick; up over the wide high dales, the loose stone walls, the moors with yellow gorse and purple heather, the half-wild sheep, and the wise dogs. There were whole areas here which the Enclosure Acts had not touched, and a hardy independent peasantry lived in a way which gave Woolman heart again. So he passed the border into Westmorland, and came among the loveliest scenery in England. And on foot is the way to cross it. Around him were the bold, bare fells, travelled by the cloud shadows, and around their feet the soft lakes; a dreamy country opalescent in mist and sunshine, all afloat and a-shimmer. But the people were anything but dreamy—a clear-eyed, practical, energetic, kindly race. Woolman pressed towards Low Park, the comfortable farmhouse outside Preston Patrick where his friend, Jane Crosfield, lived; and what a delightful reunion was that, and how rejoiced was the vigorous North Countrywoman to show her American friend what North County hospitality was like; while her husband, George Crosfield—to whom she had written when away that she "would freely give away Gould for one day or our of thy company"[1]—vied with her to welcome one who had been kind to his dear.

From their house Woolman was driven over one day to the town of Kendal to visit his other friend, Rachel Wilson. She was unfortunately from home on a religious visit to other parts of England, but her husband and children received him cordially. Like Deborah Morris, he could have said, "I remember with sweetness a Pretty Circle round thy parlour in which I sat, and hope for their present and future well being, for I love them." The house, however, was unexpectedly rich and fine, and John Woolman wrote tenderly to Rachel, when he got back to Low Park, to remonstrate about the use of superfluities. "I feel that pure love towards thee in which there is freedom."

Isaac Wilson was a shearman weaver, dyer, and fuller, somewhat after the fashion of Josiah White but on a larger scale. Hundreds of cottage spinners and hand-loom weavers brought their products in to him from all the country round. The wives spun and carded the wool, the husbands wove, and the children were employed also in many a family. It was limiting to liberty and to education, but in the tenderness and semi-freedom of the family group, in wholesome air and surroundings, it was infinitely better than what was ahead, when the steam factories would sweep up all the home industries ; but that was fortunately hidden. Isaac Wilson had his dyed webs pegged out on the hills in a very decorative way, but Woolman, taken so kindly around to see everything,[2] was sickened by the smell of the dyes and the dirt of them underfoot. He was glad to get back to the fresh air of the farm, and the simpler living of the Crosfield home.

It was during the peace and rest that he had there that he felt moved to write down in his Journal the account of the dream which had made a lasting impression on him in his illness, and which seemed to express a profound experience of the spirit.

In time of sickness a little more than two years and a half ago . . . I was brought so near the gates of death that I forgot my name. Being then desirous to know who I was, I saw a mass of matter of a dull, gloomy colour between the south and the east, and was informed that this mass was human beings in as great misery as they could be and live, and that I was mixed with them, and that henceforth I might not consider myself as a distinct or separate being. In this state I remained

[1] MS. letter of Jane Crosfield, loaned by Bertram Crosfield. *Our*=hour.
[2] Especially by young John Wilson, to whom he wrote a tender letter afterwards.

several hours. I then heard a soft melodious voice . . . the words were "John Woolman is dead." I soon remembered that I was once John Woolman, and being assured that I was alive in the body, I greatly wondered what that heavenly voice could mean.

I was then carried in spirit to the mines where poor oppressed people were digging rich treasures for those called Christians, and heard them blaspheme the name of Christ, at which I was grieved, for his name to me was precious. I was then informed that these heathens were told that those who oppressed them were the followers of Christ, and they said among themselves ; "If Christ directed them to use us in this sort then Christ is a cruel tyrant." . . . In the morning my dear wife and some others coming to my bedside I asked them if they knew who I was, and they telling me "John Woolman," thought I was light-headed . . . nor was I disposed to talk much to anyone, but was very desirous to get so deep that I might understand this mystery. . . . Then I perceived that the language "John Woolman is dead" meant no more than the death of my own will.

The telling of the dream reminded John Woolman of his illness, and he adds an unexpectedly intimate and very important piece of auto-biography. After his illness, he says, he did not speak in any public meetings for a whole year, but "my mind was very often in company with the oppressed slaves as I sat in meetings." His emotion, unstable through physical weakness, and denied the normal outlet of speech, found vent in tears, and he confesses during this period "abundance of weeping, in feeling the oppression of this people." Half ashamed of confessing so much—or at least of including so personal a touch in a work intended for public reading—he explains apologetically, "It being so long since I passed through this dispensation, and the matter remaining fresh and lively in my mind, I believe it safest for me to commit it to writing."

A little boy sitting in Mount Holly Meeting at that time and seeing Woolman weep, without any background of previous knowledge of him to set against it, and having him disappear from the scene about two years after, got an impression from it of Woolman's tearfulness, and passed it on as a tradition seldom contradicted. In point of fact Wool-man, in spite of extreme sensitiveness, wept no more often than any other man, and less than many—the emotional Mr Whitefield, for instance. Though Mr Whitefield's exuberance would cover any number of tears.

As a public speaker he was too little emotional for the taste of the time, which liked to see a man carried away by religious fervour beyond the reaches of the intellect. Woolman's brief, succinct, ordered speaking, with a very definite point to make, and sometimes an uncomfortable relation to current facts, bore unmistakable traces of "the intellectual deep." Only his charm, his gentleness, and his extraordinary awareness of the Divine presence and direction saved him from being condemned as unorthodox. As long as he was present no one could doubt him, nor even resist his influence, as we see by his effect on the London Yearly Meeting. But after his death the Journal and such writings as were published were submitted to severe revision before they were given to the public.

Twenty-three years after Woolman's death Elizabeth Drinker notes in her diary, "*April 9th, '95*. I read this evening a little book entitled— A word of remembrance and caution to the Rich, by John Woolman. I believe there are few, if any, who live up to J.W.'s plan or rule, yet I think there are some who go a great way towards it." This was Woolman's *Plea for the Poor*.

One who heard John Woolman speak said, "He was a man of few words, and his public communications were generally short, but there was a savour attending his ministry and there was a peculiar melody in his voice."[1]

Woolman left the Crosfield home with regret, but he must on with his journey, though at an ever-diminished pace. Somehow, not even the Yorkshire air could blow away an increasing feeling of lassitude. On September the sixth he was at Counterside, in Yorkshire, where he addressed a large meeting. On the thirteenth he was at Leyburn, where the townspeople crowded into the Quaker Meeting and overflowed it ; and again Woolman spoke with power. But at this place he received a blow on the heart in the unexpected and shocking news of the death of his cousin, William Hunt. Returning from Amsterdam, the ship had been blown out of her course, and had put in near New-castle. Hunt, evidently ill, had been taken to Friends at Newcastle, and had died there. What, then, was his sickness ? It was not with full composure that Woolman learned the answer. Smallpox.

The messenger who brought the news—taking pains to bring it soon and direct to Hunt's nearest relative in England—had perhaps come from Hunt's bedside. Certainly a short time afterwards Woolman could

[1] John Cox in the Dillwyn Parish Papers, Historical Society of Pennsylvania.

quote Hunt's last words in a letter to his Haines cousins. It might even have been young Thornborough himself. It would be natural for him, in his grief and loneliness, to seek out his uncle's cousin, who, himself, was almost like an uncle to him. And Woolman in Yorkshire was easily reached from Newcastle. Woolman and Thornborough had already been together in the South without Woolman's mentioning it, so the omission of the messenger's name cannot be accepted as evidence. And a fortnight later Thornborough was carrying letters for John Woolman and others from York to London, irrefutable evidence that at least he was in Yorkshire near the time.[1]

From Leyburn Woolman walked on, making three days' travel, to Thirsk, where he wrote a letter to "the Children of Stephen Comfort," to whom his love suddenly overflowed as he thought of his daughter and son-in-law. "I am now, this 16th, 9th, 1772, at Robert Proud's in Yorkshire, so well as to continue travelling, though but slowly. Yesterday as I was walking over a plain on my way to this place . . . my mind was opened to behold the happiness, the safety and beauty of a life devoted to follow the heavenly Shepherd." Such thoughts might readily come, with their customary serenity, as he walked on that pleasant upland among the grazing sheep, and saw the protecting shepherd collect the flock at evening into the fold.

At Thirsk he was again in most congenial company. Robert Proud was a cultivated man, with interests broad enough to include those educational incompatibles, classics and science. In the latter he had been a pupil of Dr Fothergill, to whom he was related ; and in the former he had qualified himself sufficiently to become teacher of "the Public Latin School of Friends in Philadelphia," the Penn Charter School. He had only resigned that position two years before Woolman's visit, to go into a business partnership with his brother John, which had brought him back to Yorkshire. Proud's eagerness was great at entertaining Woolman, not only a friend of former days, but one who could give recent news of hosts of others dear to him—Anthony and Joyce Benezet, the Pembertons, the Logans, the Drinkers, Rebecca Jones, and many more. Robert Proud was beginning to write his *History of Pennsylvania*, and perhaps to read to Woolman, as a fellow-writer, some

[1] As soon as Hunt knew that he had the smallpox he had sent his beloved nephew away from him into another house. But the first few days Tom had tenderly nursed him.

of the preliminary passages ; certainly they created for each other an American air, and one more really akin to Woolman's own interests, more his natural mental atmosphere, than the other breath of his native heath which he had got at Haslam's house. Woolman never had time to write any but the fewest and shortest of letters, because wherever he paused long enough to obtain a sensation of leisure—at Proud's house, at Haslam's, at Low Hall—he was working at his Journal and also at a set of new essays. During his four months in England—constantly on the move, frequently in demand to address large meetings, and between them engaging in that most exhausting form of intercourse, rapid intimacy with strange hosts—Woolman somehow completed five essays : *On Loving Our Neighbour as Ourselves, On the Slave Trade, On Trading in Superfluities, On a Sailor's Life,* and a very short one *On Silent Worship.* Perhaps he reciprocated by reading to Proud some passages from these and from his sea journal, as they sat together in the sheltered English garden with the heavy scent of the brown-and-gold wallflowers and the busy bumble-bees, or under the tall candles in the book-lined study, smelling so pleasantly of dust and leather. Proud's fine hooked nose leaned to attention like the beak of an eager bird.

It would have been nice to stay longer, but Woolman felt an urgency to be on. Plans had been made. He was expected at York. "Where after York ?" said Proud. Woolman looked at him with unexpected dreaminess. "I don't know. York looks like home to me."

Perhaps he meant that after York he would feel free to return to America, his mission accomplished as far as he was able.

The last passage that he wrote in his Journal was a warning to himself against the temptation to eloquence.

So he bade farewell to Robert Proud and the Philadelphia scene which they had revisited together, and started by easy stages on the twenty miles to York.

XLIII

YORK

YORK is a walled city. The Romans had a town there—Eboracum—during the long centuries of the Pax Romana, when Britain was a Roman colony. The arts of civilization had time to flourish, and the Romans made beautiful villas and baths, with central heating against the long, damp winter, and sanitation far superior to that which the Christian eighteenth century put up with. But although Roman 'remains' in the way of coins and nails and pottery shards were turned up every time a man went to plough, or dug foundations for a new building, it was the Middle Ages which had set their lovely mark upon the present town. And those relics of the Middle Ages permanent enough to remain solid and dominating features of the landscape in any place are chiefly those related to the two contrary activities of the human spirit—religion and war. Ruins of bygone abbeys lay around York. The Minster rose up gloriously in her midst, holding the awe of the forest aisles turned into stone, the splendour of the sunset crystallized in the great rose window.

But all around the city were the walls, built to keep out the enemy and built to last. Towers here and there afforded shelter for archers or for pourers of lead. Solid ramparts of earth, covered for hundreds of years with green grass, cosily enclosed the city streets, and on top of them ran the white walls. People could walk on the top of the walls three abreast, with a bulwark of crenelated stone on one side of them, more than waist-high. And one entered the town through the deep shadowed

396

archways of the medieval gates, defended by protective towers and battlements—Micklegate Bar,[1] Walmgate, Monkgate, and Bootham Bar.

John Woolman, coming down from the north through the Plain of
York, saw those white walls lifted up and gleaming in the afternoon
sunshine like stories of the heavenly Jerusalem. But the traffic on the
road was brisk and human—horses and carriages, wagons and sheep ;
and presently he was accosted courteously by a youth, who introduced
himself as Henry Tuke and announced that he had come out to meet
him and guide him in. Woolman always found the society of young
men delightful, and his oppressive lassitude, which had now become a
definite feeling of not being well, was thrown off in the pleasure of this
greeting. They completed the mile of dusty road together in cheerful
talk. When Henry Tuke, then eighteen years old, was asked to tell in
after years about this walk he never once mentioned the peculiarities of
Woolman's dress. The undyed cloth and beaver, useful as distinguish-
ing marks when one was sent to meet a stranger, became invisible, or at
least negligible, ever after. Who is so carefully, correctly conventional
in dress and behaviour as a youth of eighteen ? But all Henry Tuke
would mention was the spell of fascination that Woolman cast upon him
—"the indescribable sweetness of his company."

So they entered the city of York by Bootham Bar, and came to the
house of Henry's father, William Tuke, a comfortable house in Castle-
gate, in a bustling, narrow medieval street. The smells of the city—
sanitation unimproved since the Middle Ages—rose about them. The
Tukes were used to it, but Woolman was not, and a surprising sensation
of nausea seized him even as he entered the house and was surrounded
by the welcoming family. But when he had bathed and rested he felt
better, and was able to appreciate that his hosts were a most attractive
couple. William Tuke, with a handsome, strong, alive face, was a
prosperous tea merchant, forty years of age. His wife, Esther, was that
rare human object, a beautiful woman. William Tuke had five children
by his first wife, of whom Henry was the second son ; and three little
ones had since been added to the family. Esther Tuke, having cut her
teeth on five stepchildren, was immensely interested in education, and
had theories of the importance of starting children right which were
closely akin to Woolman's own. Woolman had the experience of his

---

[1] 'Bar' really means gate. In the course of time the repetition has arisen, through
custom and forgetfulness.

school-teaching to support his theories, and could point as well to that
of Benezet and Rebecca Jones.   William Tuke was filled with zeal to
apply the same kind of basic theory—the rule of love and reason—to the
care and cure of the insane, whose barbarous treatment in the York
Asylum had struck him with the same kind of horror as that of slaves
had struck Woolman.   These were subjects which provoked the best
kind of conversation, and this should have been one of Woolman's
happiest hours ; but eagerly as his heart entered in, there was something
wrong with him.   He could not concentrate, and the noises of the street
outside broke in distractingly, though the others seemed not to notice
them.   Henry and his older brother, William, joined in the talk, and their
sister, a serious and sweet girl named Sarah, aged sixteen, made one of
the group.   Esther was very much on the *qui vive* to see that her step-
daughters—and when they were old enough, her daughters—should be
in on all that was going, and not be relegated to merely domestic interests.
Indeed, as she told Woolman in her lively way, one of the great needs
of the world was educated women.   Even their friend Thomas Priestman—whom he would meet—who held that women should stay at
home and not gad about at this and that, even *he* was forced to admit
that a home was all the better for having an educated woman at its
centre !   She felt that Quakers needed educated women members more
than any other church, since in the Society of Friends women were
equally responsible with men for the ministry, and yet they were not
doing enough about it.

Woolman told of Anthony Benezet's school for girls in Philadelphia,
and how they even learned French and a little Latin ; and how there
were no punishments of any kind, and a regular period allotted for
exercise every day during school hours—outdoors if fine, indoors if wet.
But his head throbbed and swam ; and when they asked him respectfully
if he would explain to them his reason for his adoption of a peculiar
style of dress he told them freely, but could hardly be sure that his remarks
were making sense.   He must be excessively fatigued ; and he excused
himself early after supper for bed.   But the town noises kept him long
awake.

Next day[1] was the York Quarterly Meeting, and John Woolman
pulled himself together and attended it, and spoke at it on the subject
of the slave trade.   But when the long, crowded day was ended he

[1] 23rd day of Ninth Month.

appealed candidly to his kind hostess. For some reason he did not feel well, and, much as he valued their company—and she knew he did value it—the street noises in their house overwhelmed him. He begged he might be given a country lodging and have a few days' quiet in which to recuperate. Esther Tuke arranged it at once. The Priestmans had a roomy house outside the city walls, right in the middle of quiet meadows. If Woolman did not mind the odour of a tanyard—— Woolman thought he did not ; it was always said to be a wholesome smell. So the remove was promptly made.

The house which the Tukes now brought Woolman to was called Almery Garth, and was formerly part of the ground of St Mary's Abbey. At the back the garden of lawns and flowers ran down to a meadow, which then ran down to the bank of the river Ouse. All was open and calm and quiet. The tanyard was alongside the house. Sometimes the wind blew the smells over the garden, and sometimes blew them the other way. Thomas Priestman, a man of thirty-five, had bought the place five years before. His wife also was named Sarah, and they had several young children, the oldest of whom was seven. Incidentally, that child—Rachel—grew up to marry Henry's elder brother, William Tuke, Junior.

The Priestmans were hospitably pleased to welcome the American Friend, and had got ready their best guest-room for him. But after he had seen it he asked, gently but restlessly, if he might not have a smaller, simpler room. Thomas Priestman had a reputation for roughness—"he had little of the polish which education gives"[1]—but like others, he felt that singular sweetness which pervaded Woolman's manner ; and he took no offence, but asked the guest to look over the house and pick whichever room he took a fancy to. Woolman accepted the offer very simply and chose a small room, pleasantly but simply furnished, with one window looking out into the lane at the side of the house. It took the morning sun, aslant. The room measured twelve feet by seventeen, and nine feet high. The bed-hangings were of natural linen.

Here Woolman felt at home—nothing superfluous but everything needful. As at last he relaxed, in the country silence, between the cool sheets he felt that he was feverish. And he philosophically resigned himself to a few days' rest in bed. Before he went to sleep he wrote a

[1] The Robson MS., care of Friends' House, London.

short note to Reuben and Margaret Haines, telling them of William Hunt's death and last words, "Truth is over all," and of his own whereabouts.

> BELOVED COUSINS. . . . I am now at york at a quarterly meeting 23 da: 9 mo : 72. So, well in health as to continue travelling. . . . I feel quiet in my mind believing it is the Lord's will that I should for a time be in this part of the world. I often remember you, and friends in your parts, as I pass along in this journey. . . . I left my bed and Some things on board the Ship I came in, directing the people to convey them to you if they arive safe at Philadᵃ.
>
> JOHN WOOLMAN[1]

A bed was an unhandy thing to carry about on a journey, even if going on horseback or by stage-coach. Rachel Wilson and Jane Crosfield, given mattresses and bedding to take back on their return to England from America, had evidently each left those they came with to go back on the ship which brought them. Woolman's letter is quite clear in its expectation of his being able to continue travelling after a short time.

On Sunday the twenty-seventh of September, as the Tukes were joyfully getting ready to go to meeting, hoping John Woolman would be well enough to be present and would speak, Thomas Priestman appeared on horseback, knocking at their door. William Tuke went out to him, and they spoke earnestly together. He returned with a grave face and at once told his wife. John Woolman had that morning come out with the smallpox. Esther Tuke did not hesitate a moment. It was by her initiative—her fault—that this contagious and dreaded disease had broken out in the Priestmans' house instead of hers. John Woolman had been her guest. She consulted with her husband for a few moments behind closed doors. They faced together the grim possibilities without much talk. And, though white of face, he saw the honourable thing to do, as she did. So, her colour high, her beauty like a flag, she came out presently and was lifted by her husband to sit pillion behind Priestman, and rode to Almery Garth to nurse her guest.

The Priestmans had not asked or expected this, but they welcomed it gratefully. Thomas was ready to take his share, but Sarah Priestman must not be allowed to run such a risk, for the sake of her nursing child. John Woolman lay alone in his little room, feeling the rapid onset

[1] Appendix VI. This letter was carried up to London by Thomas Thornborough, who left York on the following Monday, September 28, carrying also the news of John Woolman's illness.

Almery Garth, in York, where John Woolman died

Reproduced from a painting by kind permission of the owner, William Worsdell

of the disease, remembering his sister ; far from his country and his home and his wife, caught by that evil thing which he had taken as much pains to avoid as a courageous man may. And now he felt for that hidden reserve of strength, and it did not fail him. Steadily he faced the possibility of death in the form he most dreaded. A sensitive and imaginative man cannot belittle the fear of death. John Woolman said to himself (and later to his nurse) that the pains of death must be hard to bear ; but if he escaped them now he must some time pass through them, and he did not know that he could be better prepared. After all, he had settled his outward affairs to his mind, had taken leave of his wife and family as never to return. "Though I feel them near to me at this time, yet I have freely given them up." So he braced himself to endure alone, and by serenity of soul to find a heart of good even in this disaster. But the God in whom he believed had something more for him. There was a jewel hidden in this dung-heap, which could only have been found in that place. The door of his room opened softly, and there entered in a woman, Esther Tuke. "Dear friend, I've come to nurse thee."

John Woolman saw her as a messenger from heaven. Not necessarily to bring him life, for as to that he had little hope, but as a reassurance of that heart of love which he believed was behind the bewildering appearance of things temporal. For this woman was of regal loveliness, abounding health, the centre of a family circle, and full of interesting plans for the betterment of mankind ; and she laid it all aside for him, a stranger. Coming in to him easily and with a smile, at the call of a loving duty, not personal but human, she offered him, as a suffering human being, her life and her beauty. And without compunction he accepted it, as the gift of God. One does not argue with the angels.

Her nursing was so skilful, her presence so soothing, that he could not bear to think she was out of call. When the night came he frankly begged her not to go home ; and she took up her quarters in the house. When Woolman woke uneasily in the night there was William Tuke's handsome face casting a bold profile of shadow on the wall ; then again Thomas Priestman was there, anxious and bluff-looking in the candle-light. And the next night, or the next—for time grew dim—Woolman was carried back to his illness in Mount Holly, and thought himself in his room at home, for John Bispham was by his bedside, with careful tendance learned before.

He could not bear more than one person in the room at a time, as they soon found, and they crept about on stockinged feet, and lifted the latch with utmost care, for the least noise "beat on his head like hammers." But Woolman became aware of a young girl who had joined the band of his ministrants. Sarah Tuke was taking turns to relieve her adored stepmother. Her soft young voice murmured in his ear like his daughter Mary's.

"Could thou now take a little nourishment? See, I have some for thee."

At last he answered from a long way off, "My child, I cannot tell what to say to it. I seem nearly arrived where my soul shall have rest from all its troubles."

Another night his fluctuating consciousness perceived that it was Sarah who was on duty with him, and had just given him a drink which he could hardly swallow. Her anxious little face touched him with pity. He dragged his voice to the surface to say, "My child, thou seemest very kind to me, a poor creature. The Lord will reward thee for it."

Once, when some treatment had failed to be alleviating, and he lay apparently unconscious, lost in suffering, his distracted nurse, Esther Tuke, said aloud, "What shall I do now?" The dark eyes opened, and the weak voice unexpectedly said, "Rejoice evermore, and in everything give thanks." Then with a flash of his old sardonic humour he added drily, "This is sometimes hard to come at!"

His last lengthy connected speech, in the height of his illness, summed up his lifelong struggle with the unnecessary unhappiness of man. "O Lord my God! the amazing horrors of darkness were gathered around me and covered me all over, and I saw no way to go forth. I felt the depth and extent of the misery of my fellow-creatures separated from the divine harmony, and it was heavier than I could bear, and I was crushed down under it. . . . In the depths of misery, O Lord, I remembered that thou art omnipotent; that I had called thee Father; and I felt that I loved thee, and I was quiet in my will. . . ."

About two o'clock in the morning on the day he died he asked for that best-loved of his various tools, his pen, and "at several times, with much difficulty wrote thus: 'I believe my being here is in the wisdom of Christ; I know not as to life or death.'"

The last act, the act of death, is often more terrible to anticipate than to endure. On the tenth day his devoted nurses, at his request for a little change that might give relief, got him up in a chair, and :

> towards morning had on some of his cloaths and with leaning on two, walked over the room ; but wearied out, was laid down again upon the bed, and after some time, fell asleep ; waked about the sixth hour, and breathed a few times, and departed without struggle, sigh, or groan.[1]

The voyage, not long but not easy, was over. The anchor was safely cast ; not in the dark waters of the Rancocas, or majestic Delaware, or silver Thames, but in that river of crystal which flows beneath the trees whose leaves are for the healing of the nations.

[1] Letter of Esther Tuke, Appendix VIII.

XLIV

EPILOGUE

Two days after John Woolman's death York Friends and others gathered in the large meeting-house at York to do honour to his memory. Three of his friends "from about home" were present—John Bispham, John Pemberton, and Thomas Ross. The apothecary who had attended him longed to bear witness to his remarkable character, but not being a Quaker was afraid of giving offence ; but the Methodist minister, who had become acquainted with Woolman—no one knows how, unless at the Quarterly Meeting—could not restrain himself ; and it would have pleased Woolman to know that one of another Church spoke acceptably along with the Quakers at his grave—"with which divers of us were well satisfied, tho' not prudent to tell him so," said Esther Tuke.[1]

Woolman's body was buried in the Bishophill Quaker burying-ground at York, just outside the wall of St Mary's Church. At that time Quaker graves were not marked, but later a stone was placed to mark the spot. "Near this stone rest the remains of John Woolman of Mount Holly, New Jersey, North America, who died at York 7th of 10th month 1772 aged 51 years." October was Woolman's birthday month, and he was twelve days short of completing his fifty-second year. Inside the wall of the near-by church is a tablet marking the vault of Sarah Woolman's ancestor, James Mauleverer, 1664.

[1] Appendix VII.

Esther Tuke wrote a long letter to Samuel Emlen, giving a full and tender account of John Woolman's last days, which Emlen could both treasure himself and take home with him for John Woolman's wife.

> . . . Though to us he appeared in some things singular, and the path he trod straiter than the liberty some of us thought the truth gives, yet I may say to thee that I cannot help thinking it was the way truth led him, and tho tis not for us to endeavour to step into the same strait way except from the like call, yet we may be thankful that we are allowed more liberty, and can in a more comfortable manner enjoy the temporal blessings afforded us; and looking at this it . . . brought an enquiry what returns I made and whether I walk'd answerable to what I enjoyed, far beyond merit, and I sometimes thought his singular and abstemious way, so conspicuous and striking, may be a means to draw others to the like examination.[1]

It is uncertain where John Woolman caught smallpox. But the incubation period of the disease is fourteen days, and it was exactly fourteen days between Woolman's hearing the news at Leyburn of William Hunt's death of smallpox, and his manifesting the disease himself. Esther Tuke said :

> I have sometimes thought there might be a providential hand in his taking and dying of the small-pox ; for if he had gone off in almost any other disorder, we might have feared his manner of living and the hardships he was exposed to had caused it ; but in this disorder his manner of living might be a fit preparative ; and the apothecary (so skilful in it) said, before we saw him, that no person living as he understood he had could be much afflicted by . . . small-pox ; but he found his mistake, and diligently attended him, expressing an anxious solicitude for his recovery ; and divers times with tears in his eyes, expressed his astonishment to see as he said, such a perfect and upright man upon the earth.[2]

None of Woolman's nurses took the smallpox, such is the caprice of that disease. Young Sarah grew up and married and became Sarah Grubb. William Tuke lived to found the Retreat at York, the first humane and scientific hospital for the care of the insane. And Esther Tuke carried her beauty untarnished into later life. Fourteen years later she started a unique boarding-school for girls, which she both superintended free of charge and had several volunteer teachers for,

[1] MS. loaned by my aunt, Rachel B. Braithwaite. For complete text see Appendix VII.
[2] *Ibid.*

so as to keep it cheap enough to persuade people to spend that money on their daughters.[1] Rebecca Jones came to England just as she was about to open it, and they became tremendous friends. The captain of Rebecca Jones's ship, much impressed by her conversation on the voyage, spread abroad among the taverns that he had brought over an American Quaker lady who had more sense than both Houses of Parliament. But Rebecca said of Esther, "She is a kind of Princess."

That same year, 1784, Esther Tuke headed up a movement among the Women Friends of England to have a Women's Yearly Meeting established. Up to then the women had met at the same time as the men, but had not had the right to transact official business. She was delegated to take the request into the Men's Meeting, and when she walked up the meeting with her stately step the Clerk, rising to receive her, confessed afterwards that he had said to himself, "What wilt thou, Queen Esther, and what is thy request ? for it shall be given thee even to the half of the kingdom."

With his usual care in business details, John Woolman had arranged to defray all the expenses of his death and funeral, even to the digging of the grave. Such effects as he left, including his short English journal, were taken back to America by Samuel Emlen, at the same time as Thomas Thornborough took back the effects of William Hunt. Most of Woolman's things were at John Townsend's, and that good-hearted man—in spite of his "Guinea basons"—sent a loving letter[2] to John Woolman's widow. Some years later, when he went to America— shocking Friends with his "red-spotted handkerchief"—he took pains to find her out and visit her, and exchange with her memories of her husband.

Many loved John Woolman, and some few partly recognized his greatness. York Friends were aware that "he was a man endued with a large natural capacity." Yet none can point to his achievement and say he brought about this or that. He greatly accelerated the freeing of America from the slave trade ; but the coming in of cotton-growing in the South set things back another century. What we most thank him for is the demonstration of a clearness of spirit seldom equalled in any age or any country, lived out in the common terms of human life. The saint American.

---

[1] The fee per pupil was £14 a year, board and tuition. And the year was twelve months. See *History of the Mount School, York*, by H. Winifred Sturge.
[2] Appendix IX.

His dust is in English soil, but he belongs to the valley of the Delaware. It is that spot on earth which has witnessed the great burgeoning forward of the human race in the slow growth of evolution which he represents. It is there we would wish to think of him last.

One day he sat alone in the Burlington Meeting-house, writing out the minutes of the Meeting of Ministers and Elders of which he was Clerk, and bringing up to date the list of the present members. Then, ruffling over the leaves, he read some back pages in the minutes made by some of his predecessors in that office, now dead. One of them— the last—was his friend the Honourable Richard Smith. The sight of that ink upon the pages, traced by hands now gone for ever, moved him to reverie ; and he wrote these words :

As looking over the minutes made by persons who have put off this body hath sometimes revived in me a thought how ages pass away, so this list may probably revive a like thought in some when I and the rest of the persons above named are centred in another state of being. The Lord who was the guide of my youth hath in tender mercies helped me hitherto ; he hath healed my wounds, he hath helped me out of grievous entanglements ; he remains to be the strength of my life ; to whom I desire to devote myself in time and in eternity. JOHN WOOLMAN.

APPENDICES

I. Marriage Certificate of John Woolman I and Elizabeth Borton[1]

Whereas, there hath been an intention of Marriage duly published at two several Monthly Meetings of ye people called Quakers in Burlington upon ye river Delaware in ye Province of West New Jersey in America. Between John Woolman of Northampton River, Husbandman, and Elizabeth Bourton near ye same place also in Province aforesaid, inquiry being made no obstruction appearing, also ye consent of Parents being had ye meeting gave their consent unto ye same.

Now these may certifie ye truth unto all conserne yt on ye day of ye datte hereoff in our sight and hearing and in an assembly of ye Lord's People ye said John Woolman did take and declare ye said Elizabeth Bourton to be his Wife, and ye said Elizabeth Bourton did take and declare the said John Woolman to be her husband according to ye example of ye Lord's People Recorded in ye Scriptures of truth each of them consenting or Promising to be loving, faithful and true in ye capacity as Husband and Wife ye tenure of their naturall lives together.

In Witness whereoff ye Parties themselves have first of all subscribed their names and wee also as Witnesses this eighth day of ye eighth Month 1684.

JOHN WOOLMAN

ELIZABETH WOOLLMAN

John Bourton	Freedom Lippincott	Mary Wills
Thomas Bourton	J. Hollinshead	Bridget Guy
Tho. French	Jo. Haines	Grace Hollinshead
Tho. Olive	Ann Bourton	Mary Hudson
Wm. Evans	Jane Bourton	Mary Cooke
Robt. Dimsdale	Ester Bourton	Mary Harding
Daniel Wills	Jane Bourton	Ben. Moore
Wm. Peechee	Ann Jennings	Henry Ballinger
Thos. Harding		

[1] Book I (Marriages), Burlington Monthly Meeting Records.

II. Children of Samuel and Elizabeth Woolman

Samuel Woolman married Elizabeth Burr, October 21, 1714

	Born	Married	Died
Elizabeth	Nov. 1715	(unwed)	winter, 1747
Sarah	March 1717	Robert Elton, April 8, 1737	
Patience	Dec. 1718	Joseph Moore, 1738	
JOHN	Oct. 19, 1720	Sarah Ellis, Oct. 18, 1749	Oct. 7, 1772
Asher	Aug. 27, 1722	Rachel Norcross, Dec. 13, 1769	April 1796
Abner	July 1724	Mary Aaronson, 1752	Nov. 1771
Hannah	June 1726	Samuel Gauntt, Oct. 1749	
Uriah	June 1728	Susanna Burr, March 1769	1804
Esther	June 1730	Zebulun Gauntt, 1752	
Jonah	April 1733	Martha Mullen, Nov. 1764	1799
Rachel	Nov. 1735	(unwed)	1798
Abraham	Dec. 1737	Elizabeth Newton, Nov. 1765	1784
Eber	Feb. 1739	Rebecca Stokes	

III. Indenture of a Bound Servant

THIS INDENTURE made the 24th Day of February in the Year of Our Lord God One Thousand Seven Hundred and forty Between John Moan of Ireland of the one part and William Willen of ye same of the other Party Witnesseth that the said D. Morgan of his own free will and Consent doth hereby Covenant, Promise and Grant to & with the said John Mone, his Executors, Administrators and Assigns, from the Day of the Date hereof until the first and next Arrival at Philadelphia in America and after, for and during the Term of four Years, to serve in such Service and Employment as the said John Mone or his Assigns shall there employ him in according to the Custom of the Country in the like Kind. In Consideration whereof the said John Moon doth hereby Covenant and Grant to and with the said D. Morgan to pay for his passage and to find and allow Meat, Drink, Apparel and Lodging, with other Necessaries during the said Term, and at the End of the said Term to pay unto ye said Dalett Morgan the usual Allowance, according to the Custom of the Country in the like Kind. In Witness whereof the Parties above mentioned to these Indentures have interchangeably set their Hands and Seals the Day & Year first above written.

IV. Negro Maria, her Estate

1760

15da. 11mo.	To Cash paid to pay the man who came up to bring account of her deceace	5^s
	To Cash paid Zach Rossel for the two Children's passage up in Mountholly Stage	4^s
	To Sundry Expenses in making the division twixt Toney's Estate & Maria's & making an Inventory of Maria's	6^s
	To Cash paid Weldon for digging the grave	5^s
	To Self & horse 2 days in the above affairs	10^s
	Delivered Seven pounds in Cash to Asher Woolman he being a Co trustee	
7da. 12mo.	To Cash pd Benjamin Lippincott for Lard and flower had by Maria in her life-time	19^s.9^d
	To my time one day going to Mother's when Henry Burr took Isabella	4^s

V. Marriage Certificate of William Boin (Bowen) and Dido
5mo. 3d. 1763

Whereas, William Boin a Negro man now Employed in the Affairs of Moses Haines of Springfield who by an Agreement with the said Moses Haines Set forth in Wrighting and Signed Expects to Enjoy the full benefit of his Labour on the first day of the fourth month in the year of our Lord one thousand seven hundred and sixty five And Dido a negro Woman of late servant to Joseph Burr who now enjoys the whole benefit of her labour Having for Some time manifested an Enclination to joyn in Marriage with each other, and On Enquiry no Difficulty appearing in respects to marriage Engagements with any others, They, the said William Boin and Dido on the third day of the fifth month in the year of our Lord one thousand seven hundred and Sixty three At a little meeting held in a Dwelling-house on that Ocasion did publicly inform us the Witnesses to this Instrument that they took each other as Husband and Wife and mutually promised to use their best Endeavours through Divine Assistance to be Faithfull and true to Each Other until Death Should Separate them. And in Confirmation thereof have hereto Set their hands

WILLIAM BOIN

DIDO BOIN

Witnesses present—

Joseph Burr	
Patience Haines (by her order)	for Negro Catherine, mother to Dido
Josiah White	for Negro London, her Father
Thomas Antrim	Hager
David Ridgway	Daphne
Amey Stratton	George Subeter
Ann Brooks	Cesar Morry
Sarah Fenimore	Simon Bustill
Sarah Woolman	Elizabeth Morton
Daniel [Illegible]	Primos
Amey Antrim	hager gewant
John Woolman	[illegible—Gauntt ?]
	Susannah Fenimore
	Catren Fenimore
	Jeams hage

VI. LAST LETTER WRITTEN BY WOOLMAN

(To Reuben and Margaret Haines)

BELOVED COUSINS :—I am now at york at a quarterly meeting 23da: 9mo: 72 So well in health as to continue travelling I appoint a few meetings, but not so fast as I did some time ago. I feel quiet in my mind, believing it is the Lord's will that I should for a time be in this part of the world. I often remember you, and friends in your parts, as I pass along in this journey, and the Truth as it is Separate from all mixture. The Truth as it is in Jesus was never more precious to me than I feel it in this my Sojourning ; in which my mind is often deeply affected with that which is not of the Father but of the world. I hear that dear W. Hunt departed this life with the Small pox 9: 9: 72 and that some of his last words were The Truth Is Over All. The rest of the America friends on the visit were lately living, and mostly midling well so far as I hear.

I left my bed and Some things on board the Ship I came in, directing the people to convey them to you if they arive safe at philad^a.

JOHN WOOLMAN

VII. LETTER FROM ESTHER TUKE TO SAMUEL EMLEN, ON THE ILLNESS AND DEATH OF JOHN WOOLMAN

YORK, *14th of 10th mo., 1772*

DEAR FRIEND,—Under the humbling dispensation we have lately passed through, my mind hath many times been drawn near to thee ; and after the departure of our dear friend, John Woolman, there seemed a strong inclination to salute thee with a few lines, to let thee know a little how he was in the course of his painful affliction ; and though it may seem rather a repetition, as several accounts have been sent to London, yet, as no one was more with him, nor had greater opportunities to observe the state of his mind, a few hints concerning him, with a copy of some expressions dropped at sundry times, I believe will not be unacceptable. He was exceedingly afraid from the first of giving needless trouble to any, but his disorder increasing so much that constant attendance was necessary, he desired I would stay with him, and not sleep out of the house till I saw an alteration, which I very willingly complied with ; and though it was exceedingly trying to see him labour under unspeakable affliction and could render so little relief, yet I have many times been thankful, in being favoured to attend him ; for as I never saw one bear so much before, so I never beheld the like fortitude, patience, and resignation—his hope and confidence was so strong and firmly fixed, that the greatest storms of affliction were not able to move him, or even cause him to utter an impatient word—indicating, [that] he thought anything too hard ; and though he was not free to take much medicines, yet, he attended so much [to] the progress of the disorder, and his own feelings, as to what was suited for healing or cause nourishment, that our apothecary (a man we think of singular judgment in that complaint, not a Friend) said, he did not know he could be better ordered than he ordered himself ; except toward the last he seemed to need something more cordial, which he was not unwilling to take ; but his throat was then so closed, that he could not swallow but with the greatest difficulty ; and often strove, when it was distressing to see him under his great weakness, and the pain it occasioned ; and at times he quietly said, "I believe I must in a little time give it over and try no more" ; and it seemed twice wholly closed up.   But as a further detail and exceedingly afflicting to me to relate, I shall leave them and say, though he appeared to us in some things singular, and the path he trod, straiter than the liberty some of us have thought the truth gives, yet I may say to thee, that I cannot help thinking it was the way truth led him ; and though it is not for us to endeavour to step into the same strait way, except from the like call, yet we may be thankful that we are allowed more liberty, and can in a more comfortable manner enjoy the temporal blessings afforded us ; and, at looking at this, and at the little comfort he had, it was cause of humbling to my mind and brought to an enquiry, what returns I made, and whether I walked answerable to what I enjoyed far beyond merit ; and I sometimes thought his singular and abstemious way so striking and conspicuous, may be a means to draw divers others to the like examination ; and I know nothing in this luxurious and licentious age, more likely to begin a reformation, than a solid consideration of this sort ; for do not we see how pride, superfluities in meats, drinks, and apparel, abound amongst us, and like a torrent, seems to carry all before them, and I think cry aloud for a stop ; for my part, the prospect is often so distressing, on account of training up our own children, and the like difficulties other religious parents lay under, that my life is frequently a life of mourning and lamentation, for it seems scarce possible to bring them up in the way we would have them walk ; and if we could, there seems little probability, without something extraordinary, that they would be kept in it, such is the example—such the giving way in general ; and with sorrow it may be said so, of many that should be leaders.   And if this good man's example in life and in death, should have a tendency (as I hope it may) to draw some to consider and inspect a little closer than they have hitherto done, we should be careful how we take off the weight, by blaming a singularity, which, if compared with our holy pattern, we shall find I think not far out of the way. And now I hope, though we are pretty much strangers to each other, as to the outward, thou wilt be sensible, that my thus communicating my private thoughts is in that love in which there is freedom, and with a hope thou wilt treat me in like manner, and am far from supposing thou hast judged hardly of John Woolman ; but I believe some here-a-way, will, and would be glad, perhaps, to find flaws in his singularity, to cover themselves and stave off a narrower scrutiny and retrospection into their own conduct and example. I am far from mourning that he is gone, believing his day's work is finished and his measure of suffering filled up. And I scarce ever expected his recovery during his sickness, though there were many favourable symptoms ; for looking at the path, the unspeakable difficulties that would have attended his travelling, etc., it seemed often clear to me that he would either be delivered from it by death, or have more liberty in his mind respecting the use of some things. I have sometimes thought there might be a providential hand in his taking and dying of the small-pox; for if he had gone off in almost any other disorder, we might have feared his manner of living, and the hardships he was exposed to had occasioned it ; but in this disorder, his manner of living might be a fit preparative ; and the apothecary (so skilful in it) said, before he saw him that no person, living as he understood he had, could be much afflicted by having a great load of small-pox ; but he found his mistake, and diligently attended him, expressing an anxious solicitude for his recovery, and divers times, with tears in his eyes, expressed his astonishment to see, as he said, such a perfect and upright man upon earth. John Woolman frequently conversed with him, with great openness, and when he differed in his judgment from the doctor, he gave him such reasons as were to him satisfactory. He attended his funeral, and said afterwards, he could scarce forbear giving testimony concerning him to the audience ; but forbore, knowing it would be an intrusion upon us. Indeed a Methodist preacher did, in a few words at the grave side, with which divers of us were well satisfied, tho' not prudent to tell him so. I think now to conclude being afraid of being tedious ; after saying we were truly sorry to be disappointed of seeing thee here; but as thou intended it, I would hope we may yet see thee before thy return, which would be a little reviving in these drooping days to thy sincere friend, and poor little fellow-traveller, in the hope and fellowship of the gospel.

ESTHER TUKE

VIII

ESTHER TUKE TO ANOTHER FRIEND

(Manuscript preserved in England)

The state of his mind throughout the whole of his unspeakable affliction was one continued calm ; a firm trust in the Lord, with perfect resignation to his disposal, appeared throughout the whole ; patient beyond description ; his hope and confidence so firmly fixed, that no outward distress seemed to be able to discompose or ruffle him.

I think it a favour we had the privilege of attending him. He could bear but a low voice, nor seldom more than one or two in the room at a time, and mostly without shoes ; his head at times being violently bad, he said the lifting up of a door latch, or stepping hard on the floor, was as if we had beat him with hammers ; and yet throughout, his understanding was perfect ; could bear to speak but little, but when he did, about his nursing or anything needful, it was so expressive, that every word seemed a sentence, and carried frequently deep instruction with it.

The day before he died, his throat was closed up, that he could scarce speak intelligibly, which distressed me much, but he in great measure removed this difficulty by asking for pen and ink, which we got and held the paper, and he wrote the words very legibly, though he was quite blind, and had been so for some days ; twice his throat was quite closed, that he could not swallow one drop of anything, and we had the most distressing prospect that he might continue some days in that situation. The Doctor syring'd his throat, but at last gave it up the night before he died, and said nothing could be done ; but my husband, who will never give up using means as long as there is the least relief, set on to foment, with his consent ; and continued it for two hours. He had the great satisfaction to find it open again, and he swallowed better than he had done for some days before, and we were ready to flatter ourselves with hope ; but it was of short duration. For though he got a little ease in that respect, yet he was for several hours exceeding bad, and could not lie in bed. Was got up in a chair, and towards morning had on some of his cloaths, and with leaning on two, walked over the room ; but wearied out, was laid down again upon the bed, and after some time, fell asleep ; waked about the sixth hour, and breathed a few times, and departed without struggle, sigh, or groan.

LETTER ON WOOLMAN'S DEATH FROM NANCY YOUNG TO POLLY FARMER [1]

Desire of letting my Polly know as soon as possible that she is often the Subject of my Thoughts induced me to send this shameful scribble.

Thine my Dear Friend of the 9th ult. I with joy received, such tokens of remembrance are always pleasing, & never more so than when ones so Distantly

---

[1] Later married to Charles Lloyd.

seperated from some of those we Love. How much Do we owe to the first
Inventors of this silent Converse by which we can make known our Hopes,
Fears & inmost Thoughts as soon, and with greater Ease than transport our Bodies
from place to place.

> What joyful Balm by Letters is convey'd
> Or o'er our Pleasures how they cast a Shade.

Several I've received of late have had this Effect they have brought me repeated
Accounts of my Dear Brothers Indisposition this often much affects me, too much
to be Described, but I strive to be as chearful as I can, and think to trust in that
Kind Providence who has wonderfully supported and is as Able as Ever to
restore. The numerous Blessings I enjoy call loudly for Gratitude. May my
Breast more ardently glow with this Flame It can't Blaze too High.

.   .   .   .   .

The Death of the American Friend is very affecting How Distressing must it
be to W. Hearst's Companion. I this morning am informed by Letter of His
Decease. O what an afflicting Circumstance these Sincere Labours to be cut off
so far from their nearest earthly connections. My intelligence of this last particular is so Brief that I rather hope its a mistake by understanding W. H.'s companion
for J. Woolman.

My journey down here was on the whole very agreable . . . some parts of
Wales we came through was very pleasant, the Delightful Season shew'd the
Landskips to advantage wch were many of them inexpressibly Beautiful ; the
Majistick Height of the Cloudcapt Hills pleasingly awfully affected me ; and the
frequent ruins of Castles etc. added to the charming romanticness of some of the
prospects. Were at Swansea a week. . . . Provisions are very plenty there
especially Fish, a great advantage to the Poor, who make as squalid an Appearance
as most I've seen, particularly the Women, nor can this be much wondered at
when we know what Intolerable Slaves they are, and while those poor Females
are prompted by Necessity for their maintenance & perhaps the support of
helpless Infants, to great Hardships viz loaden Coal Ships etc. those who ought
to Exert their utmost abilities to exempt their Partners from such Toils are Sunk
in Indolence. O the Despicable Wretches ! Excuse me my Dear I can't avoid
thinking it perverting the Design of Providence in the Creation for the reputed
Lords of it supinely lazily to sculk about or be employ'd in Trifles while those who
seem form'd for Gentle Cares and with Naturally Soft Humane dispositions are
by such Menial Service that leads into the roughest Company contracting ferocious Manners. . . .

IX. JOHN TOWNSEND'S LETTER TO JOHN WOOLMAN'S WIFE

DEAR FRIEND WOOLMAN

Feeling my mind drawn towards thee in near love and tender sympathy for
thy great loss of so near a bosom friend thy dear husband. The church's loss is
great for which the hearts of many are deeply affected and mourn. But thine
and children's loss is much greater I trust and believe that gracious hand which

called him forth into the harvest field will sanctify and sweeten this bitter cup of which thou hast to drink even to the fulfilling of that gracious promise that all shall work together for good to those who love and fear God.

He lodged at my house when in London. His company and self-denying example were truly profitable to me and family. I doubt not but he has gone to reap the reward of the faithful labourer who loved not the world but was made truly willing to lay down his life in his heavenly master's cause, in that he might be made helpful to any poor soul or souls. He divers times told me that he had not had the small pox, and desired I would tell Friends that was the reason why he did not go to their houses, but if he was spared to return again to this City, he believed he should have liberty to visit them. He frequently said he was resigned to the will of Providence. He was not afraid of the disorder, and if he catch'd it in going to meetings and in the way of his duty he should have no cause to reflect upon himself. He left a few things at my house which we have now forwarded by our dear friends Samuel Emlin and Thomas Thornborough who are able to give thee further information of the last days of thy dearly beloved Husband, to whom I refer thee, hoping that Divine providence will be with thee and thine and help you with that helping which maketh truly rich, and adds no sorrow with it. So wisheth and so prayeth thy sincere Friend,

JOHN TOWNSEND

P.S. I shall be truly glad to hear from thee. Please direct for me, pewterer, in London.

X. Marriage Certificate of John Woolman and Sarah Ellis

WHEREAS John Wollman of the Tounship of Northampton in the County of Burlington in the Province of New Jersey And Sarah Ellis of the town County and Province aforesaid having declared their intentions of mariage with Each other before Several Monthly Meetings of the People Called Quakers at Burlington aforesaid according to the Good order used amongst them and having consent of Parents Concerned their Said proposeall of Mariage was allowed by the Said Meeting Now those are to Certifie whome it may concern that for the full accomplishing Their Said intentions this Eighteenth Day of the Eight Month in the Year of our Lord One Thousand Seven hundred forty Nine 1749 The Said John Wollman and Sarah Ellis appeared in a publick Meeting of the Said People in their Meeting house at Mount Holly in Northampton aforesaid And the Said John Wollman takeing the Said Sarah Ellis by the hand and in Solom mannor Openly declare that he Took her the said Sarah Ellis to be his Wife promising through Divine assistance to be unto her a Loveing and faithful husband untill death Should Separate them And then and there in the Same Assembly the Said Sarah Ellis did in Like mannor declare that She Took the Said John Wollman to be her husband promising to be unto him a Loveing and faithful Wife untill death Should Separate them And Moreover they the said John Wollman and Sarah Ellis She according to the Custom of Mariage assuming the Name of her

husband as a further Confirmation thereof did then And there to those presents
Sett their hand and we whose Names are hereunder allso subscribed being present
at the Solemniseation of the said Mariage and Subscription have, as Witnesses
thereunto Set our hands the day and Year above Written

JOHN WOOLMAN

SARAH WOOLMAN

Josiah Foster	Solomon Ridgway	Joseph Burr
Amey Foster	Mary Ridgway	Jane Burr
Peter Fearon	Joseph Burr Junr	Samuel Gauntt
Josiah White	Henry Burr	Hannah Gauntt
Rebeca White	Sarah Haines	Sarah Elton
Esther Andrews	Joseph Lippincott	Patience Moore
Mary Sleeper	Elizabeth Lippincott	Abner Woolman
Uriah Woolman	Caleb Haine	Timothy Abbott
Esther Woolman	Abigail Burr	Restore Lippincott
Jonah Woolman	Samuel Woolman	John Abbott
Rachel Woolman	Elizabeth Woolman	Asher Woolman

XI. JOHN WOOLMAN'S JOURNEYS

1743 (5th of 9th mo.)	East Jersey (with Abraham Farrington). Out about 2 weeks
1746 (12th of 3rd–16th of 6th)	First journey South—Virginia, North Carolina, and Eastern shore of Maryland (with Isaac Andrews), 3 months
1746 (8th of 8th)	Jersey sea-coast (with Peter Andrews), 340 miles, 22 days
1747 (16th of 3rd–13th of 7th)	Long Island and New England (with Peter Andrews), 1500 miles' ride, 150 miles' sail, 4 months
1748 (7th of 8th)	Lower countries of New Jersey and Eastern Shore of Maryland (with John Sykes), 550 miles, 6 weeks
1751 (2nd of 9th)	Great Meadows, upper part of New Jersey (alone)
1753 (in 9th mo.)	Bucks County (with John Sykes), 2 weeks
1754 ("next winter")	Burlington Monthly Meeting families (with 2 Friends from Pennsylvania)
1754 (winter)	Chesterfield families (alone), Several weeks
1755 (winter)	Ditto around Shrewsbury (with John Sykes), several weeks
1756 (12th of 5th)	Long Island (part of the time with Matthew Franklin), 316 miles, 24 days
1757 (13th of 5th)	Burlington Monthly Meeting family visits (with Friends)
1757 (early 5th mo.–early 7th mo.)	Second journey to Southern provinces—Maryland and Virginia and North Carolina (with brother Uriah, travelling on business), 1150 miles, 2 months

1758 (in 8th mo.)	Chester County and County of Philadelphia (most of the time with Benjamin Jones), 200 miles, *2 weeks*
1758 (11th of 11th mo.–18th of 11th mo.)	Chester County Quarterly Meetings and family visits re slaves (with Daniel Stanton and John Scarborough), *1 week*
1758 (first of 12th)	Visits re slavery (with John Sykes and Daniel Stanton)
1759 (in 1st mo.)	Visits in Philadelphia re slaves (with John Churchman), *about a week*
1759 (24th of 3rd)	Visits in Philadelphia re slaves (with John Churchman)
1759 (14th of 6th)	Friends about Salem, and Quarterly Meeting (alone), *7 days*
1759 (in 7th mo.)	More personal visits re slaves (first alone, then with John Churchman)
1759 (11th of 12th)	Bucks County (Pa.) re slaves (with Samuel Eastburn)
1760 (17th of 4th–10th of 8th)	Long Island and New England (2nd), (with Samuel Eastburn) *4 months*
1761 (10th of 5th)	Haddonfield and Philadelphia to noted Friends re slaves (alone)
1761 (in 8th mo.)	Shrewsbury, Squan, etc.
1762 (in 11th mo.)	Families in Mansfield (with Benjamin Jones), *a few days*
1763 (in 2nd mo.)	Families at Ancocas (with Elizabeth Smith and Mary Noble)
1763 (in 4th mo.)	Families at Mount Holly (with "some Friends")
1763 (7th of 6th–26th of 6th)	Visit to Indians (with Benjamin Parvin), *19 days*
1764 (early winter)	Visits to Mount Holly families (with several Friends)
1764 (late winter)	Visits to Mansfield families (with William Jones)
1765 (24th of 10th)	New Jersey sea-coast from Cape May to Squan (with Benjamin Jones)
1765 ("soon after")	Burlington, 50 families (with Elizabeth Smith and John Sleeper)
1766 (6th of 5th)	Eastern Shore of Maryland on foot (with John Sleeper)
1766 (13th of 11th)	Upper part of New Jersey (with Benjamin Jones)
1767 (20th of 4th)	Western Shore of Maryland (rode to ferry, afterwards walked, came back through Western Q. M. and Concord, Middletown, Providence, and Haddonfield). "The lonesome walk."
1767 (2nd of 9th)	Upper part of Berks and Philadelphia Counties (alone), 11 meetings, *2 weeks*
1767 (winter)	Family visits around Mount Holly (with some Friends)
1768 (5th of 5th)	Maryland "without a horse" (Q. M. at Philadelphia and Concord, then Chester River, crossed the bay)
1769	Abortive preparations for West Indies (illness, and consequent year of silence)

1772 (1st of 5th)   Voyage to England : London Y. M. ; Hertford Q. M., Sherrington Q. M., Northampton Q. M., Banbury Q. M., Shipton Q. M. ; Birmingham, Coventry, Warwick, Nottingham, Sheffield, Rushworth, Settle, Preston Patrick, George Crosfield's Westmorland ; Jane Crosfield ; Kendal, Greyrig, Counterside, Leyburn, York.

XII. John Woolman's Writings and Publications

1753 or 1754   *Essay on Some Considerations on the Treatment of Negroes. Part I

1758   Considerations on Pure Wisdom and Human Policy :
> On Labour
> On Schools
> On the Right Use of the Lord's Outward Gifts
> On Trade (postponed, said Woolman in 1769 in a note in the folio MS. at the back)   (Historical Society of Pennsylvania)

1760   *Essay on Considerations on Keeping Negroes. Part II (published 1762 by Franklin and Hall).

1763   *A Plea for the Poor (not published until 1793)

1770   Considerations on the True Harmony of Mankind (published in 1770)

1772   *Conversations on the True Harmony of Mankind and How It May be Promoted (published 1837)

1772   An Epistle to the Quarterly and Monthly Meetings of Friends (written just before leaving for England)

1772   The Journal (begun in 1765)

1772   The small journal of the Voyage and Travel in England

1772   Five essays written at Sea and in England :
> On Loving our Neighbours as Ourselves
> On the Slave Trade
> On Trading in Superfluities
> On a Sailor's Life
> On Silent Worship

(These last essays were bound up with the essays "Serious Considerations on Various Subjects of Importance," "On the True Harmony of Mankind," and the farewell "Epistle" and published in London in 1773 by the Quaker publisher, Mary Hinde.)

* Originals written by Woolman into the Folio manuscript.

XIII. ALLEGED PORTRAIT OF JOHN WOOLMAN

The evidence for believing that the profile frontispiece of Mrs Gummere's book is a portrait of John Woolman will not stand the test of even slight examination.

First, this drawing was originally neither signed nor named. It is stated by Mrs Gummere to be "almost certainly" the work of Robert Smith III, of Burlington, New Jersey, son of Daniel Smith (who died 1781) and grandson of Judge Robert Smith, of the Court of Common Pleas, Burlington County. Mrs Gummere says that Robert Smith III, who was very much given to making amateur portraits of his friends, was a "friend and contemporary" of John Woolman.

But it was the elder Robert Smith, the lawyer and judge, who was Woolman's friend, and not the grandson. (See Account Book, "1754, 31 da, 5mo, To Going to Burling^n, by Appointment to meet Robt Smith, Joseph Scattergood and Thomas Earle, on an affair betwixt Sd Earle and J.S.")

The portrait itself, a sepia drawing, has as background a representation of the medal of the British and Foreign Anti-slavery Association, and perhaps that is why Governor Samuel Pennypacker, when it found its way unnamed into his collection, wrote on the back his guess, "John Woolman?" But the Association was not founded until 1787, so that would place the portrait as having been drawn at least fifteen years after John Woolman's death.

Mrs Gummere suggests that it is a memory sketch of Woolman, and Robert Smith III liked to draw from memory. But even if Robert had been his own grandfather and known Woolman intimately it is a rare artist who would rashly trust his memory for fifteen or twenty years.

To conclude, this portrait represents a man old enough to be toothless, whereas Woolman died in middle life. If, like Judge Pennypacker, I were to venture a guess as to the unnamed subject I would suggest that this is intended for Anthony Benezet, who had a better right to the Clarkson Medal background (having directly influenced Clarkson by his writings) and who was notoriously ugly. He died in 1784 at the age of seventy-one.

The drawings in the present book are based on the family type as represented by the authentic silhouette of Woolman's brother Uriah.

BIBLIOGRAPHY

Printed Material

ADAMS, JOHN : *The Works of John Adams*, vol. ii, edited by Charles Francis Adams (Charles C. Little and James Brown, Boston, 1850).

ALLINSON, WILLIAM J. : *Memorials of Rebecca Jones* (Charles Gilpin, London, 1849).

ARMISTEAD, WILSON : *Anthony Benezet* (A. W. Bennett, London, 1859).

BANCROFT, GEORGE : *History of the United States* (6 vols.) (Macmillan, London, 1876).

BARCLAY, JOHN (edited by) : *Lives of Samuel and Mary Neale, 1729-92* (Charles Gilpin, London, 1845).

BOSWELL, JAMES, ESQ. : *The Life of Samuel Johnson, LL.D.* (John Lane, London, 1935).

BOWDEN, JAMES : *History of the Society of Friends in America* (2 vols.) (Charles Gilpin, London, 1850-54).

BRAINERD, THOMAS : *Life of John Brainerd* (Presbyterian Publication Committee, Philadelphia, 1865).

British Friend for 1874—for account of John Townsend.

BROOKES, GEORGE S. : *Friend Anthony Benezet* (University of Pennsylvania Press, Philadelphia, 1937).

BROWNE, WILLIAM HAND : *American Commonwealth Scenes—Maryland : the History of a Palatinate*, edited by Horace E. Scudder (Houghton, Mifflin and Co., Boston, 1894).

Burlington in New-Jersey (printed and sold by James Parker. Sold also by David Hall in Philadelphia, 1765).

BYRD, WILLIAM : *Histories of the Dividing Line betwixt Virginia and North Carolina*, with introduction and notes by William K. Boyd, Ph.D., Professor of History, Duke University (the North Carolina Historical Commission, Raleigh, 1929).

CHURCHMAN, JOHN : *An Account of the Gospel Labours and Christian Experiences of John Churchman* (printed in Philadelphia and London, 1781).

CLARKSON, THOMAS, M.A. : *History of Rise, Progress, and Accomplishment of the Abolition of the African Slave Trade by the British Parliament* (2 vols.) (London, 1808).

COMLY, JOHN AND ISAAC (edited by) : *Friends' Miscellany*, vols. ii and vi (J. Richards, Philadelphia).

DE COU, GEORGE : *Historical Sketches of Mount Holly and Vicinity* (pamphlets No. 1 and No. 2 ; copyright 1936).

—— *Historical Sketches of Rancocas and Neighbourhood* (pamphlet, copyright 1937).

—— *Moorestown and Her Neighbours* (copyright 1929).

DONEHOO, GEORGE P. (edited by) : *Pennsylvania: A History* (Lewis Historical Publishing Co., Inc., 1926).

DRINKER, ELIZABETH : *Journal of Elizabeth Drinker, 1759–1807*, edited by H. D. Biddle (Philadelphia, 1889).

EARLE, ALICE MORSE : *Child Life in Colonial Days* (Macmillan Co., New York, 1899).

FISHER, H. A. L. (Warden of New College, Oxford) : *A History of Europe* (Eyre and Spottiswoode, London, 1935).

FISKE, JOHN : *Old Virginia and Her Neighbours* (2 vols.) (Macmillan and Co., London, 1897).

FITZPATRICK, JOHN C. (edited by) : *The Diaries of George Washington* (4 vols.) (Mount Vernon Ladies' Association, Boston and New York, 1925).

FOTHERGILL, SAMUEL : *Memoirs of the Life and Gospel Labours of Samuel Fothergill*, edited by George Crosfield (Liverpool, 1843).

FOX, GEORGE : *George Fox, An Autobiography*, edited with introduction and notes by Rufus M. Jones (Ferris and Leach, Philadelphia, 1904).

FOX, R. HINGSTON, M.D. : *Dr Fothergill and His Friends* (Macmillan, London, 1919).

FRANKLIN, BENJAMIN : *The Autobiography of Benjamin Franklin* (Hamish Hamilton, London, 1937).

The Friends' Meeting-House Fourth and Arch Streets Philadelphia ; A Centennial Celebration Sixth Month Fourth, 1904 (John C. Winston Co., Philadelphia).

GARBER, JOHN PALMER : *The Valley of the Delaware and Its Place in American History* (John C. Winston Co., Philadelphia, 1934).

GIBBON, EDWARD : *Autobiography of Edward Gibbon*, with introduction by J. B. Bury (Oxford University Press, London, 1911).

—— *Gibbon's Journal to January 28th, 1763*, with introductory essays by D. M. Low (Chatto and Windus, London, 1929).

GOODELL, WILLIAM : *Slavery and Antislavery* (published by himself, New York, 1855).

GRAHAM, JOHN W., M.A. : *William Penn, Founder of Pennsylvania* (Headley Bros., London, 1917).

Guilford College, North Carolina, pamphlet : *A Narrative of Some of the Proceedings of N. C. Yearly Meeting on the Subject of Slavery within its Limits*, published by order of the Meeting for Sufferings of North Carolina Yearly Meeting, Greensboro, North Carolina (printed by Swain and Sherwood, 1848).

GUMMERE, AMELIA MOTT, *The Journal of John Woolman*, edited from the original manuscripts with a Biographical Introduction (Rancocas Edition, Macmillan, London, 1922).

HAMMOND, J. L. AND BARBARA : *The Town Labourer, 1760–1832* (1925), and *The Village Labourer, 1760–1832* (Longmans, Green, and Co., London, 1927).

HART, ALBERT BUSHNELL (edited by) : *The American Nation History* (27 vols.). Vol. vi, *Provincial America, 1690–1740*, by E. B. Greene ; vol. vii, *France in America*, by Reuben Gold Thwaites (Harper and Bros., New York and London, 1904–8).

HAZARD, CAROLINE : *Thomas Hazard, Son of Rob't, call'd College Tom* (Houghton Mifflin Co., Boston and New York, 1893).

—— *The Narragansett Friends' Meeting in the XVIIIth century* (Houghton Mifflin Co., Boston and New York, 1899).

JEFFERSON, THOMAS : *Notes on the State of Virginia* (J. W. Randolph, Richmond, Virginia, 1853).

JOHNSON, R. G. : *An Historical Account of the First Settlement of Salem in West Jersey by John Fenwick Esq., Chief Proprietor of the Same* (Orrin Rogers, Philadelphia, 1839).

JONES, RUFUS M. : *The Quakers in the American Colonies* (Macmillan, London, 1911).

KALM, PETER : *Peter Kalm's Travels in North America* (2 vols.), edited by Adolph B. Benson (Wilson-Erickson, New York, 1937).

KIRK, REV. JOHN : *The Mother of the Wesleys* (Jarrold, London, 1876).

LEE, FRANCIS B. : *New Jersey as a Colony and as a State* (4 vols.), vols. i and ii (Publishing Society of New Jersey, New York, 1902).

MYERS, ALBERT COOK (edited by) : *Hannah Logan's Courtship—A True Narrative—1736–52* (Ferris and Leach, Philadelphia, 1904).

New Jersey Archives.

Pennsylvania Gazette.

ROGERS, HENRY : *The Works of Jonathan Edwards, A.M.* (2 vols.) ; also containing the Diary of David Brainerd (William Ball, London, 1839).

SHARPLESS, ISAAC, LL.D. : *A History of Quaker Government in Pennsylvania* (2 vols.) (T. S. Leach and Co., Philadelphia, 1900).

SMITH, R. MORRISS : *The Burlington Smiths* (E. Stanley Hart, Philadelphia, 1877).

SMITH, SAMUEL : *Samuel Smith's History of New Jersey* (Burlington in New Jersey, printed and sold by James Parker ; sold also by David Hall, in Philadelphia, 1765).

SOMERVELL, JOHN : *Isaac and Rachel Wilson, Quakers, of Kendal, 1714–85* (Swarthmore Press, London, 1924).

STURGE, JOSEPH : *A Visit to the United States in 1841* (Hamilton, Adams, and Co., London, 1842).

THOMAS, GABRIEL : *An Historical and Geographical Account of the Province and Country of Pennsylvania and West New Jersey, in America* (London, printed and sold by A. Baldwin at the Oxon Arms in Warwick Lane, 1698).

UPDIKE, WILKINS : *History of the Church in Narragansett* (Henry M. Onderdonk, New York, 1847).

WATSON, JOHN F. : *Annals of Philadelphia and Pennsylvania* (3 vols.) (Edwin S. Stuart, Philadelphia, 1900).

WHITEFIELD, GEORGE, A.B. (of Pembroke College, Oxford) : *Journals* (Philadelphia, printed and sold by B. Franklin in Market Street, 1740).

WOODFORDE, REV. JAMES : *The Diary of a Country Parson, 1758–81*, edited by John Beresford (Oxford University Press, London, 1924).

WOODWARD, MAJOR E. M., AND HAGEMAN, JOHN F. : *History of Burlington and Mercer Counties, New Jersey* (Everts and Peck, Philadelphia, 1883).

Manuscript Material

Abbott : Manuscripts and records of the Abbott and Mauleverer families (by kind permission of Richard Mauleverer Abbott, New Jersey).

Crosfield : Manuscript Journal of Jane Crosfield (by kind permission of Bertram Crosfield, England).

Fothergill : Manuscript letters of John Fothergill (Friends' House, London).

The Logan Papers (the Library Company of Philadelphia, Pennsylvania).

Minutes and Epistles of London Yearly Meeting (Friends' House, London).

Minutes of London Meeting for Sufferings (Friends' House, London).

Minutes of Maryland Yearly Meeting (in care of Park Avenue Friends' Meeting, Baltimore, Maryland).

Minutes of North Carolina Yearly Meeting (vol. i), 1704–93 (Guilford College Library, Guilford College, North Carolina).

Minutes of Philadelphia Yearly Meeting and its constituent Quarterly and Monthly Meetings, 1700–72, Fourth and Arch Streets, Philadelphia, Pennsylvania).

Minutes of various Monthly Meetings, Quarterly Meetings, and that Yearly Meeting in North Carolina (Guilford College Library, Guilford College, North Carolina).

Minutes of Virginia and Maryland (in care of Homewood Meeting House, Baltimore, Maryland).

Minutes of York Monthly and Quarterly Meeting and of Scarborough and Scalby Monthly Meeting (York).

The Parrish Papers (Historical Society of Pennsylvania, Philadelphia, Pennsylvania).

The Pemberton Papers (Historical Society of Pennsylvania, Philadelphia, Pennsylvania).

Proud, Robert : Manuscript History of Pennsylvania (Historical Society of Pennsylvania, Philadelphia, Pennsylvania).

Robinson : Manuscript Journal of Elihu Robinson—1768–72 (Friends' House, London).

The Robson Manuscript (Friends' House, London).

Smith : Family and other documents in the private collection of Mrs Edward Wanton Smith, Germantown, Philadelphia, Pennsylvania.

Smith : John Smith's Diary (the Library Company of Philadelphia, Pennsylvania).

Weston : Mary Weston's Journal (privately printed for family circulation) (Friends' House, London).

White : Manuscript records of the White family (loaned by Walter Rhoads White, Westtown, Pennsylvania).

Wilson : Manuscript Journal of Rachel Wilson (loaned by Anna B. Thomas, Baltimore, Maryland).

Woolman :

In care of Swarthmore College, Pennsylvania :

 Earliest manuscript of Journal, incomplete (largely quoted in present text).

 Second copy of manuscript of Journal, complete.

 Little Journal kept at sea and in England.

 Manuscript of Essays "Considerations on the True Harmony of Mankind" and "On Serving the Lord in Our Outward Employment," and of Woolman's farewell "Epistle to the Quarterly Meetings of Friends, 1772."

 Sundry letters and deeds.

In care of Historical Society of Pennsylvania :

 Folio manuscript of Journal prepared by Woolman for the printer, and including the Essays on Negroes, the Poor, and Conversations on Harmony.

 Account books kept by John Woolman :

  1. The early little one.

  2. The leather-bound large Account Book.

  3. The leather-bound Ledger.

 Sundry letters and deeds.

In care of Friends' House, London :

 A few letters.

In care of Rutgers University :

 Manuscript fragments written by John Woolman, including the Dream of visit to a dictator in war-time.

—— Manuscript Journals, letters, and other documents of John Woolman, in care of Swarthmore College, Pennsylvania, and Historical Society of Pennsylvania, Philadelphia, Pennsylvania.

Wormall's Diary (manuscript) (Friends' House, London).

INDEX